Alexander H. Grant

The Church seasons

Historically and poetically illustrated

Alexander H. Grant

The Church seasons
Historically and poetically illustrated

ISBN/EAN: 9783741192340

Manufactured in Europe, USA, Canada, Australia, Japa

Cover: Foto ©Lupo / pixelio.de

Manufactured and distributed by brebook publishing software (www.brebook.com)

Alexander H. Grant

The Church seasons

THE CHURCH SEASONS.

The Church Seasons

HISTORICALLY AND POETICALLY ILLUSTRATED.

BY

ALEXANDER H. GRANT, M.A.,

AUTHOR OF "HALF HOURS WITH OUR SACRED POETS."

"*Our festival year is a bulwark of orthodoxy as real as our confessions of faith.*"
PROFESSOR ARCHER BUTLER.

LONDON:
JAMES HOGG & SON, YORK STREET, COVENT GARDEN.

LONDON:
PRINTED BY GEORGE BERRIDGE AND CO.
EASTCHEAP WORKS, E.C.

PREFACE.

IN this volume the aim of the Author has been to trace the origin and history of the Festivals and Fasts of the Ecclesiastical Year, and to illustrate in poetry the circumstances under which they began and continue to be celebrated, and the principal ideas and doctrines which they severally incorporate.

Whatever authorities promised to throw light upon any question of historical interest have been consulted indifferently and at first hand; and in order to facilitate the reader's estimate of the comparative value of testimony or enactment, so far as that depends upon considerations of time or precedence, dates have been freely and almost uniformly introduced throughout the volume. With the same object in view, an Alphabetical Index of authorities has been prepared, by the consultation of which the chronology of the more important events and persons can at once be either precisely or approximately ascertained.

The selection of illustrative poetry has been made from a field as wide as the aggregate contributions of the Christian Muse, irrespective of age, nationality, or ecclesiastical order; and a few biographical particulars about the writers have been offered wherever it seemed possible to introduce them profitably and pertinently.

On the whole, the work seeks to combine the advantages of a manual of historical authority with those of an anthology of verse applicable to the Seasons which have been already systematically celebrated—to exclude the mention of any but departed names—by Wither, Ken, and Keble.

The obligations of the author to the labours and the kindness of others are numerous; and his acknowledgments are especially due to those who have, with such general frankness, granted him their permission to make use of poems in which, either as authors, or as holders of copyright, or as both, they were interested. His thanks are accordingly tendered to Mrs. Alexander, of the Palace, Derry; the Very Reverend Dean Alford; Reverend Edward Caswall; Reverend John Chandler Mrs. Charles, author of the "Voice of Christian Life in Song;" Venerable Archdeacon Churton; Reverend Robert Aston Coffin; Sir Archibald Edmonstone, Bart.; Reverend R. S. Hawker; J. T. Hayes, Esq. (Dr. J. M. Neale's "Hymns of the Eastern Church"); Messrs. Houlston and Wright (Reverend Robert H. Baynes's "Lyra Anglicana"); Reverend F. W. Kittermaster; Reverend Dr. Kynaston; Messrs. Longmans and Co. ("Lyra Germanica"); Messrs. Joseph Masters and Son (Dr. Neale's "Mediæval Hymns and Sequences"); Reverend Dr. Monsell; Reverend A. M. Morgan; Reverend Gerard Moultrie; John Murray, Esq. (Dean Milman's "Poetical Works"); Reverend Dr. Newman; Messrs. James Nisbet and Co. (Dr. Horatius Bonar's "Hymns of Faith and Hope"); Reverend Canon Oakeley; Reverend Phipps Onslow; James Parker, Esq. (Reverend John Keble's "Christian Year"); Editors of the "People's Hymnal"; S. B. M.; John Sheppard, Esq.; Reverend Orby Shipley; and Miss Catherine Winkworth.

December 1st, 1869.

ALPHABETICAL INDEX

OF THE PRINCIPAL

AUTHORITIES CITED IN THIS VOLUME.

[The dates which follow the names of *official* persons, as Popes or Sovereigns, are, for the most part, those between which they exercised authority. A Council, the publication of an edict, or of a volume, are each occasionally marked by a single date. No attempt has been made to affix dates to the names of living authors; and, in two or three instances, the same remark will apply to those who have very recently died. Names printed in italics are those of writers who have contributed the poetry of the volume. In the very few cases where verses are quoted anonymously, the source is given from which they are transcribed].

Acta Sanctorum
Adam of St. Victor . died A.D. 1177
Alcuin . . . abt. 735—804
Alexander I., Pope . . 109—119
Alexander II. ,, . . 1061—1074
Alexander III. ,, . . 1159—1181
Alexander, Mrs. (C. F. H.)
Alford, Dean
Ambrose, St. . . abt. 340—397
Ammianus Marcellinus. . . abt. 320—abt. 390
Andrew of Crete abt. 640—abt. 732
Andrewes, Bishop . . 1555—1626
Augustine, St. . . . 354—430

Bacon, Lord . . . 1561—1626
Baronius, Cardinal . . 1538—1607
Barreaux, Jacques Vallée des 1602—1673
Barrow, Dr. Isaac . . 1630—1677
Bäsaler, Ferdinand
Beaumont, Sir John . . 1582—1628
Bede, Venerable . abt. 673—735
Benedict XIV., Pope . . 1740—1758
Bernard, St., of Clairvaux 1091—1153
Berno, Augiensis . . d. 1045
Bethune, George W.
Bingham, Rev. Joseph . 1668—1723
Bonar, Dr. Horatius
Boniface III., Pope . . 606—606
Brady, John . . . 1813
Breton, Nicholas . . 1555—1624
Butler, Dr. Alban . . 1710—1773
Butler, Professor Archer . 1814—1848
Buxtorf, John . . . 1564—1629

Campbell, Thomas . . 1777—1844
Casaubon, Isaac . . 1559—1614

Cassian, John . . . d. 448
Caswall, Rev. Edward
Cave, Dr. . . . 1637—1713
Chandler, Rev. John
Charlemagne, Emperor . 800—814
Chronicle, Anglo-Saxon . 883
Churchman's Family Magazine
Churton, Archdeacon
Chrysostom, St. . . abt. 347—407
Clement of Alexandria . d. abt. 220
Coffin, Rev. Robert Aston
Constitutions of Egbright . 740
Cosmas of Jerusalem . d. abt. 760
Councils :—
   Agde . . . 506
   Basle . . . 1431 to 1443
   Carthage . . . 397
   Cognac . . . 1254
   Elvira . . . abt. 305
   Laodicea . . . abt. 364
   Macon . . . 585
   Mayence, or Mentz . 813
   Narbonne . . . 589
   Nicæa . . . 325 & 787
   Orleans . . . 511 & 541
   Oxford . . . 1222
   Toledo . . . 633 & 653
   Tours . . . 566 & 813
   Trent . . . 1545 to 1563
   Trullo, In . . . 692
Cowley, Abraham . . 1618—1667
Cowper, William . . 1731—1800
Crashaw, Richard abt. 1615—abt. 1650
Cyril of Jerusalem . abt. 315—abt. 386

Daniel, Hermann Adalbert
Diocletian, Emperor . . 284—305

ALPHABETICAL INDEX.

Diogenes, Laërtius	fl. 2nd Century
Doane, Bishop	
Doddridge, Dr. Philip	1702—1751
Domitian, Emperor	81—96
Donne, Dr. John	1573—1631
Drummond, Sir William	1585—1649
Dryden, John	1631—1700
Ducæus, Fronto	1558—1624
Durandus, Bishop	abt. 1232—1296
Earconbert, King of Kent	640—664
Edmonstone, Sir Archibald	
Ephraim, Syrus	d. abt. 378
Epiphanius	abt. 320—403
Eupolis	abt. 446—411, B.C.
Eusebius	abt. 265—abt. 340
Faber, Dr. F. W.	1813—1863
Fletcher, Giles	abt. 1588—abt. 1623
Franck, Solomon	1659—abt. 1720
Fuller, Dr. Thomas	1608—1661
Gelasius I., Pope	492—496
Gervase of Canterbury	fl. abt. 1200
Gongora, Luis de.	1562—1627
Gratian	fl. abt. 1130
Gregory Nazianzen	abt. 328—abt. 390
Gregory Nyssen	abt. 332—abt. 400
Gregory Thaumaturgus	abt. 212—abt. 270
Gregory the Great, Pope	590—604
Gregory II., Pope	717—731
Gregory IV., Pope	827—844
Guion, Madame de la Mothe	1648—1717
Habington, William	1605—1645
Hall, Bishop	1574—1656
Hampole de, or Rolle, Richard	d. 1348 or 1349
Harvey, Christopher	1597—1666
Hawker, Rev. R. S.	
Heber, Bishop	1783—1826
Hengstenberg, Dr. Ernest William	
Henry VIII., Convocation of	1536
Herbert, George	1593—1633
Herrick, Robert	1591—1674
Heywood, Thomas	abt. 1575—abt. 1658
Hildebert, Archbishop	1057—1134
Hildebrand, Joachim.	1623—1691
Hook, Dean	
Hooker, Richard	1554—1600
Hooper, Bishop	1640—1727
Hopkins, J.W.	
Hospinian, Rodolph	1547—1626
Ignatius, St.	d. abt. 115
Innocent III., Pope	1198—1216
Interiano de Ayala, Juan	1656—1730
Irenæus	abt. 130—abt. 200
Isidore of Seville	abt. 565—abt. 636
Ivo Carnotensis	1035—1115
Jahn, John	1750—1817
Jerome, St.	abt. 345—420
John of Damascus	700—754

John XXII., Pope	1316—1334
Joseph of the Studium	9th Century
Josephus	38—100
Julian, Emperor	361—363
Julius Africanus	d. abt. 232
Justinian II., Emperor	685—711
Kalendar of the English Church	1866
Keble, Rev. John	1792—1866
Kempis, Thomas à	abt. 1380—1471
Ken, Bishop	1637—1711
Kittermaster, Rev. F. W.	
Klopstock, F. G.	1724—1803
Knowles, Herbert	1798—1817
Kübler, Rev. Theodore	
Kynaston, Rev. Dr.	
Lactantius	d. abt. 325
Lapide, Cornelius à	d. 1657
Latimer, Bishop	abt. 1480—1555
Leo the Great, Pope	440—461
L'Estrange, Hamon	fl. 1660
Liguori, St. Alphonso Maria de	1696—1787
Logan, Rev. John	abt. 1748—1788
Lucian	4th Century
Luther, Dr. Martin	1483—1546
Mamercus, Bishop	fl. 5th Century
Mant, Bishop	1776—1848
Martene, Edmund	1654—1739
Martyrs of Vienne and Lyons	177
Mauburnus, Johannes	1460—1502
Maximus Taurinensis	fl. abt. 450
Menard, Hugo	1587—1664
Milman, Dean	1791—1868
Milton, John	1608—1674
Monsell, Dr. J. S. B.	
Montgomery, James	1771—1854
Montgomery, Rev. Robert	1807—1855
Morgan, Rev. A.M.	
Moultrie, Rev. Gerard	
Neale, Dr. J. M.	1818—1866
Neander, Dr. J. A. W.	1789—1850
Nelson, Robert	1656—1715
Newman, Dr. J. H.	
Newton, Rev. John	1725—1807
Oakeley, Rev. Canon	
Onslow, Rev. Phipps	
Origen	abt. 185—253-4
Palmer, Rev. William	
Paulinus, Bishop of Nola	409—431
Paulus Diaconus	abt. 740—abt. 799
Pelagius II., Pope	578—590
People's Hymnal	
Peter Chrysologus	d. 450
Philo Judæus	fl. abt. 40
Polycarp	abt. 80—abt. 168
Polydore Vergil	abt. 1470—1555
Pope, Alexander	1688—1744
Potho, Abbat of Prüm	fl. 1152
Prior, Matthew	1664—1721

Proclus of Constantinople . d. 447
Prudentius, Clemens Aurelius . . . . 348—abt. 413

Quarles, Francis . . 1592—1644

Riddle, Rev. J. E.
Rist, Johann . . . 1607—1667
Roscoe, Thomas
Rugby Hymn Book
Rupert, Abbat of Duits . d. 1135

Schenck, Henry Theobald . d. 1727
Sears, Edmund H.
Sergius I., Pope . . 687—701
Shirley, James . . 1594—1666
Sigebert of Glemboux . 1030—1112
Socrates . . abt. 380—abt. 440
Southwell, Robert . . 1562—1595
Sozomen . . . fl. 443
Sparrow, Bishop . abt. 1620—1685
Spenser, Edmund . abt. 1553—1599
Stephen, Bishop of Liege . d. 920

Taylor, Bishop Jeremy . 1613—1667
Telesphorus, Pope . . 127—140

Tertullian . . . . d. abt. 218
Theodore of the Studium . d. 826
Theodorus Lector . fl. 6th Century
Theodosius the Great, Emperor 379—395
Theodosius the Younger, Emperor . . . 409—450
Townsend, Dr. George
Trench, Archbishop

Vaughan, Henry . . 1621—1695
Venantius Fortunatus . 530—609
Verstegan, Richard . . fl. 1605

Walton, Izaak . . . 1593—1683
Waterland, Dr. . . . 1683—1740
Watts, Dr. Isaac . . 1674—1748
Wesley, Rev. Charles . 1708—1788
Wheatly, Rev. Charles . 1686—1742
Wilberforce, Bishop
Wilcox, Mr.
Williams, Dr. Isaac
Winkler, John Joseph . 1670—1722
Wither, George . . 1588—1667
Wordsworth, William ; 1770—1850

Zeno, Emperor . . . fl. 485

TABLE OF CONTENTS.

ADVENT.

Its Institution—Two capital Seasons of Advent—General longing for a Christ—Hymn of Eupolis—Subjects of Advent Poetry—The Ambrosian Hymn, *Veni Redemptor Gentium*—Poetry of the Second Advent—Theodore of the Studium—Ode on the Second Advent—George Wither's "Hymns and Songs of the Church"—Various Advents of Christ—Bishop Jeremy Taylor—His "Hymn for Advent"—Bishop Doane's "Two Advents." . . . 1

CHRISTMAS DAY.

Antiquity of Celebration—Various derivations of the Festival—Its relation to Judaism—And to Heathenism—The exact Time of the Nativity not ascertained—The three-fold Cycle of Sacred Seasons—Christmas Topics—Course of Prophecy—The Incarnation the great Fact in the History of the World—Defines and Limits the Fall of Man—Rationale of Christ's Poverty—Manhood the highest Offering of Earth to Heaven—Ephraim Syrus—His Hymn on the Nativity—Cosmas of Jerusalem—Ode from his Canon for Christmas Day—Mauburnus—*Heu quid jaces stabulo*—Luis de Gongora—"Sonnet on the Nativity"—Archdeacon Churton's Translation—George Herbert's Lines on "Christmas"—Herrick's "Ode of the Birth of our Saviour"—Wither's Christmas Hymn—Bishop Jeremy Taylor—His Lines on "Christ's Birth in an Inn"—Poetic Literature of America—Edmund H. Sears—His "Angels' Song." 13

b

ST. STEPHEN'S DAY—December 26.

Early Commemorations of the Martyrs—Probably of Apostolic injunction—Singular glory of St. Stephen—The Proto-Martyr the greatest of the Martyrs—Manner of Commemoration—Epistles of the Churches of Smyrna and Antioch—*Nativity* of the Martyrs—Meaning and acceptation of the word Martyr—Letters of the Churches of Vienna and Lugdunum of Gaul—Privileges of the Martyrs—Effect of the Novelty of the Hopes of Christianity—Volunteer Martyrdom—Definition of the expression "Christian Martyr"—The Ideal Martyr—Caswall's Translation of *Sanctorum meritis inclyta gaudia*—Martyrdom not one of the Evidences of Christianity—Various Victors over the fear of Death—Lord Bacon on "Death"—Dr. Donne's "Holy Sonnet"—Desire to anticipate Heaven—The Summons to die to be waited for—Death easier than Holy Living—Martyrs on calculation—The true Glory of the Martyr—Institution of the Festival of St. Stephen—Gregory Nyssen—St. Augustine—Juxtaposition of Christmas and St. Stephen's Day—Adam of St. Victor—His Sequence on St. Stephen—Discovery of the Relics of St. Stephen—Honours of St. Stephen—St. Augustine—St. Chrysostom—Cornelius à Lapide—Date of St. Stephen's Martyrdom—Peculiar Distinctions of St. Stephen—Dr. Monsell's "Gentle Witness"—The Three Aureoles—Martyrdom a proof of Convictions merely—Bishop Latimer . . **31**

ST. JOHN THE EVANGELIST'S DAY—December 27.

A Martyr in Will but not in Deed—Reason for the Order of St. John's Festival—Propriety of such a Festival—Its History—Call of St. John—His character and elevation of Mind—Venerable Bede—St. Jerome—Reasons for the production of St. John's Gospel—Five Reasons for Christ's peculiar Affection for St. John—All-Sufficiency of Love—Bishop Ken—Distinctions of St. John—St. Ambrose—Christ's Legacies—St. John at Jerusalem—On his Travels—Churches founded by St. John—At Ephesus—At Rome—The Caldron of Boiling Oil—Miraculous Preservation—Banishment to Patmos—Mrs. Alexander—St. John at Patmos—Again at Ephesus—Dying Blessing, and Death of St. John—Matthew Prior's poem on "Charity." **49**

THE INNOCENTS' DAY—December 28.

Various Orders of Martyrs—Martyrs in Deed but not in Will—Antiquity of the Day—Innocence—Crashaw's Poem—Number of the Innocents—Character of Herod, by Neander—Fulfilment of Prophecy—Sorrow of the Church—Daniel's *Thesaurus*—Hymn of Prudentius—*Salvete Flores Martyrum*—Keble's Translation—The Gospel of Childhood—Affinity of Infancy and Heaven—Practical Philosophy of Christianity—Wordsworth's *Ode*. . . . 60

THE CIRCUMCISION OF CHRIST—January 1.

History of the Day—Extravagances of the Heathen—The Devil's Festival—New Year Revellings—Sermon of Faustinus the Bishop—Legislation of Various Councils—"Octave of the Nativity"—Divers opinions on the Origin of the Circumcision—Maximus Taurinensis—Sacramentary of Popes Leo I. and Gelasius I., and of Gregory the Great—Decree of Reciswindus—Venerable Bede—Casaubon's Opinion—Council of Oxford—History of the Rite of Circumcision—Its Obligation on the Jews, and their Observance of it—Manner and circumstances of Circumcision—Prevalence of Circumcision—Philo Judæus—Pride of the Jews in Circumcision—The Circumcision of Christ a Fulfilling of the Law—A Proof of His veritable Humanity—Baseless Hypothesis of Cardinal Baronius—Poetical Treatment of the Festival—Jeremy Taylor—George Wither's Verses—Richard Crashaw—His Poem on the Circumcision—Robert Southwell—His *Mæoniæ*—Sorrows of the Virgin in the Circumcision—Christopher Harvey—Lines on the "Circumcision of the Heart," from "Schola Cordis"—Extract from Bishop Ken's Hymn—Jeremy Taylor on the Uses of Circumcision—Festival of the Name of Jesus—The Hymn *Gloriosi Salvatoris*—Dr. Neale's Translation—Peculiar Offices for the Day—Collect. . 72

THE EPIPHANY; OR, THE MANIFESTATION OF CHRIST TO THE GENTILES.—January 6.

The Epiphany anciently Associated with the Nativity—Common Idea of Manifestation—Mr. Riddle—*Epiphania prima et secunda*—

xvi CONTENTS.

Page.

Dr. Hook—St. Augustine's Account of Events Commemorated in the Epiphany—Sanctity of the Season—Bingham's "Antiquities"—Legislation of the Emperors—Epiphany Declaration of the Moveable Feasts—Cassian—*Epistolæ Heortasticæ*—Epiphany in the Greek Church—One of the Great Baptismal Seasons—The Day of the Holy Lights—Various Ceremonies—Designations of Epiphany — Wheatly—Offices for the Day—Epiphany in the Western Church—Dramatic representation—Royal Bounty in England—Dr. Trench's "Star of the Wise Men"—Nature of the Star—Mystical or Real—Opinions of St. Chrysostom, Mar Eusebius, and Neander—Divine Guidance of the Heathen—Poetry of the Star—Bishop Heber's Epiphany Hymn—Anonymous American Poem—Rev. F. W. Kittermaster's "Epiphany"—Star of Balaam—Keble's Picture of Balaam—Country of the Wise Men—Alban Butler—Neander—The *Natural* Development of the Heathen Mind—Tacitus—Suetonius—Character of the Magi—Gradual Degradation of Position—Quality, Number, and Names of the Wise Men—Rev. R. S. Hawker's "Armenian Myth"—Dr. Faber's "Three Kings"—Subsequent History of the Wise Men—Their Relics at Constantinople, and Cologne—Dean Alford's Epiphany Salutation—John Rist—His Poem—Milton's Ode on the Nativity—Discomfiture of the Heathen Deities . 93

LENT.

Philo Judæus—"Every Day a Festival"—Practical Solution of this Rule—Rationale of Humiliation—Observance of Fasts—Diogenes Laërtius — Abstinence of the Cynics—Of Epicurus, and Pythagoras—Legislation of Moses—One Fast of Obligation amongst the Jews—Superinduced Fasts—Significance of the Quadragesimal Period — Moses, Elias, Christ; the Law, the Prophets, and the Gospel—Fasts of our Lord and His Apostles—Rebuke of Pharisaic Fasting—When Fasting is commendable—Individual and Corporate Fasts—George Herbert's Poem on "Lent"—Institution of Lent—Diversities of Opinion and Practice—Tertullian—Irenæus—Sozomen—Socrates—Designations of Lent—Original Duration of Lent—St. Chrysostom—Epiphanius—Abstraction of Sundays, or of Saturdays and Sundays, from the Fast — Tithe of the Year — Institution of Ash-Wednesday — Legislation of the Councils of Orleans, Toledo, and Trent—King Earconbert, of Kent—George Wither's Verses on "Lent"—

CONTENTS. xvii

Rationale of the Fast—St. Chrysostom—Cassian—Lenten Charity of the Emperors—Robert Herrick—"To keep a True Lent"—James Montgomery—"The Poor Wayfarer"—Sundays in Lent—Andrew of Crete—"Stichera for the Second Week of the Great Fast"—True Use of Lent—Its Wholesome Effects . . . 122

ASH-WEDNESDAY.

Origin of Ash-Wednesday—*Caput Jejunii*—Radical Idea of Lent—Bishop Hooper—Purposes of Lent—Penitence and Contrition—Sir Archibald Edmonstone's Poem on Ash-Wednesday—Dr. Donne's "Hymn to God the Father"—A French Penitential Sonnet—Charles Wesley—His Poem on "Wrestling Jacob"—Ecclesiastical History of Ash-Wednesday—Bellarmine—Bingham—Gratian—Convocation of 1536—Commination Office—Spirit of the Church—Commination Sonnets of Bishop Mant, and Wordsworth 145

HOLY WEEK; OR, PASSION WEEK.

In Lent, but more than Lent—Antiquity of Holy Week—St. Chrysostom—Various Pious Observances—Testimony of Epiphanius—Wheatly—Offices for Holy Week—Public Reading of the History of the Passion—Hymn from Dean Milman's "Martyr of Antioch"—Vernacular Names of Holy Week—Disintegration . 161

MAUNDY THURSDAY—Vernacular Names—Ancient Names—Incidents of the Thursday before Easter—Sequence, *De Superna Hierarchia*—Rev. A. M. Morgan's Translation—George W. Bethune—His Poem on "Christ Washing the Disciples' Feet"—Southwell—"Christ's Bloody Sweat"—Jeremy Taylor's Lines "On Good Friday"—Council of Carthage—St. Augustine—Double Celebration of the Eucharist — Royal Almsgiving—*Redditio Symboli*—Reception of the Penitents—Manner of their Reconciliation 169

GOOD FRIDAY.—Vernacular Names—Grief and Prostration of the Church—Herrick's "Rex Tragicus"—Dr. Bonar's "'Twas I that did it"—Liguori's Lines "To the Instruments of the Passion of Jesus"—Giles Fletcher—"Christ's Triumph over Death"—"Juxta Crucem"—Dean Milman's "Crucifixion" . . . 179

EASTER EVE; OR, HOLY SATURDAY.—George Herbert on the "Sepulchre"—Solomon Franck's "Easter Even"—Lactantius—St. Jerome—The Paschal Vigil—Baptism of Catechumens . . 188

EASTER DAY.

The Perpetuation of a Hebrew Anniversary—Apostolic Authority of its Celebration—Disputes as to Time—Dean Stanley—The Easter Controversy—Council of Nicæa—Gradual Achievement of Uniformity—The two Paschs—Vernacular Equivalents—Conjectural Etymologies of "Easter"—Gregory Nazianzen—St. Chrysostom—George Herbert—Solemn Celebration of the Eucharist—Imperial Legislation—Gregory Nyssen—Immunities of Easter—Duration of Easter Rejoicings—Council of Macon—Constitutions of Egbright—St. Ambrose—Tertullian—St. Chrysostom—Council of Tours—Easter Greeting and Response—Rev. Phipps Onslow—"Christ is Risen"—Prime Idea of Easter—Poem by John of Damascus — Luther's Hymn on "Easter-Day"—Rev. Gerard Moultrie—"The Lord is Risen"—Light from Darkness—Historical Accessories of the Resurrection—Easter Aspects of Nature—Poem by Venantius Fortunatus—Easter Phenomena — Dean Alford's "Easter Ode" — Canon Oakeley's "Evening Benediction"—St. Paul's Exposition of Paschal Doctrine—Klopstock on the "Resurrection"—Certification of the Soul's Immortality—Crashaw's "Easter-Day"—Dr. Isaac Williams's Easter Sonnet—Professor Archer Butler—Easter Lessons . . 193

THE ASCENSION-DAY.

Antiquity of the Festival—Councils of Agde, and Orleans—Proclus—Tertullian—St. Chrysostom—Modern Designations—A *Great Feast* in the Eastern Church—Honours paid to the Day—Degradation — Bingham — Foreshadowings of the Ascension — Singular Glory of the Ascension of Christ—Gregory the Great—Benedict XIV. — Elias and Christ — Perfection of Christ's Activity—St. Bernard—Resurrection Greater than Ascension—The Psalms of David the Motive of Ascension Poetry—The Mount of Olives—Ode from the "Canon for Ascension" of St. Joseph of the Studium—Hymn, *Æterne Rex Altissime*—Rev. E. Caswall's

CONTENTS. xix

Page.
Translation—Charles Wesley's Ascension Hymn—Giles Fletcher—"Christ's Victory and Triumph"—Reception in Heaven—Dr. Monsell's "Link with Heaven"—Human Participation in Christ's Ascension—Verses by Rev. John Logan—Disputed Authorship—Celestial Law of Primogeniture—Dr. Donne's "Sonnet"—Dr. Watts—"Ascending to Christ in Heaven"—St. Augustine—Dr. Williams's "Sonnet." 223

PENTECOST, OR WHITSUNDAY.

The Gospel in the Law—Coincidences—St. Augustine—Pope Leo the Great—Twofold Significance of Pentecost—Tertullian—Council of Elvira—Duration and Privileges of the Season—Tertullian—Epiphanius—St. Augustine—Cassian—St. Ambrose—Mamercus, Bishop of Vienne—Institution of Litany, or Rogation Days—Councils of Orleans and Mayence—George Herbert—Richard Hooker—"Hallelujah"—Acts of the Apostles—Why read during Pentecost—St. Chrysostom's Reasons—Council of Toledo—Imperial Legislation—One of the Solemn Times of Baptism—Honours of the Season narrowed to a particular Day—Popes Leo the Great and Gelasius the First—Obligatory Communion—Council of Agde—Jewish Pentecostal Customs—Durandus—Dramatic Representations of Pentecostal Phenomena—Naogeorgus—Conjectures as to the Institution of Pentecost—Did St. Paul keep the Feast as a Jew, or a Christian?—Whitsunday—Paulinus, Bishop of Nola—Divers Etymologies—L'Estrange—Wheatly—Verstegan—Richard de Hampole—John Mirkus—*Liber Festivalis*—Dr. Neale's Theory—Vernacular Names—*Jam Christus astra ascenderat*—Translation by Rev. E. Caswall—Jeremy Taylor's Verses—Sinai and Sion—Keble's Whitsunday—*Minor Memorabilia*—Number of the Inspired—Nature of the Tongues—The "Day of the Holy Ghost"—His Attributes and Activities—*Veni Sancte Spiritus*—Disputed Authorship—Dryden's Translation of *Veni Creator Spiritus*—Ecclesiastical Retrospection—George Herbert on "Whitsunday"—Herrick's "Litany to the Holy Spirit"—Perpetuation of this Poem at Dean Prior—Doctrine of Whitsunday—Dr. Williams—"Let there be Light!"—"On the Descent of the Holy Ghost"—*Fiat Lux*—Tardy Fulfilment of the Command—Second Whitsunday Sonnet, by Dr. Williams—Mr. J. W. Hopkins—His "Rushing Mighty Wind." 245

TRINITY SUNDAY.

Bishop Heber's Hymn—Late Institution of the Festival—Pope John XXII.—The Baptismal Formula—Councils of Nicæa and Narbonne—Popes Alexander II. and Pelagius II.—Micrologus—Durandus—Rupert, Abbat of Duitz—*Decretal* of Alexander II.—Its Sense, according to Micrologus and Benedict XIV.—Carturfius—Charlemagne—Synod of the Franks—Stephen, Bishop of Liege—Dr. Waterland's Note on Wheatly—Octave of Pentecost—Protest of the Festival against Arianism—Rationale of the Festival, by George Wither, Bishop Sparrow, Durandus, and Joachim Hildebrand—Reasons for the tardy Institution of Trinity Sunday—The Festival not of an Event, but of a Creed—Creeds the Result of Heresies—Dr. Barrow's Sermon—The Divine Nature has no Symbol or Analogue—For ever Incomprehensible—St. Augustine and the Child—George Wither's Hymn—Man, the Image of God—Thomas Heywood—His "Hierarchie," and "Search after God"—The True Attitude of the Soul in Contemplating the Trinity—Sir John Beaumont—His "Ode of the Blessed Trinity"—Archbishop Hildebert's "Prayer to the Trinity"—Dr. Kynaston's Version—Canon Oakeley's Hymn, "The Most Holy Trinity"—Practical Connection of Prayer and Praise—The Universe a Temple—Man not the only Worshipper—Charles Wesley's Hymn—Doxology 276

ST. ANDREW'S DAY—November 30.

Birth-place and Family of St. Andrew—The first to propagate the Gospel—Vocation to the Apostolate—Dr. Monsell's Poem for St. Andrew's Day—"Domestic Care"—Antiquity of the Festival—Apostolic Province of St. Andrew—His Travels, Labours, and Martyrdom—His Address to the Cross—Paraphrased by Venerable Bede—Dr. Kynaston's Version—Uncertainty of the Date of St. Andrew's Death—His Relics removed to Constantinople—His stupendous Fortitude and Confidence—Campbell's "Last Man" 301

ST. THOMAS THE APOSTLE—December 21.

Hymn from the *Rugby Hymn-Book*—Names of St. Thomas—Phases of Discipleship—Magnanimity of St. Thomas—Challenged by St. Chrysostom—Death made easy by Fellowship—Bishop Ken's Poem "On St. Thomas"—Unbelief of St. Thomas—Was he really more Incredulous than the rest of the Apostles?—His gravest Fault—Value of Scepticism, and of his Scepticism—St. Augustine—Gregory the Great—Willingness to die—Promptness to Adore—Abraham Cowley—"Reason: the Use of it in Divine Matters"—Apostolic Province of St. Thomas—Travels and Labours in India—Death at Calamina—"Christians of St. Thomas"—Institution of the Festival—Extent of the Travels of St. Thomas—Madame Guion's Hymn—Version by Cowper—God, Father and Fatherland 310

THE CONVERSION OF ST. PAUL. JANUARY 25.

Roscoe's Sonnet—Durandus—Reasons for the exceptional Commemoration of the *Conversion* of St. Paul—George Wither's Hymn—Institution of the Festival—Innocent III.—His *Epistle* to the Bishop of Worms—Baronius—Councils of Cognac and Oxford—History of the Day in our own Calendar—Note from Wheatly—St. Paul commissioned to the Gentiles—Activity in the West—Nelson's Argument for his Visit to Britain—At Rome—Anger of Nero—Decapitation—Burial—Did St. Peter and St. Paul suffer at the same time?—Dr. Cave's Opinion—Dr. Monsell's Poem on the "Conversion of St. Paul." 322

PRESENTATION OF CHRIST IN THE TEMPLE, COMMONLY CALLED THE PURIFICATION OF ST. MARY THE VIRGIN—FEBRUARY 2.

Various Feasts of the Virgin—Conception—Nativity—Visitation—Assumption—Annunciation—Purification—The last two adopted by the English Church—The Purification a "Double Feast"—Bishop Sparrow—Disputed Antiquity of the Festival—St. Chrysostom—Pope Gelasius—Not of Universal Celebration till the time of the Emperor Justinian—Testimony of Sigebert of Gembloux—And of Paulus Diaconus—*Hypapants*—From what Adopted or Developed?—Joachim Hildebrand—L'Estrange—Dean Stanley—Various Derivations not Contradictory—Consecration of Tapers—Pope Sergius the First—Durandus—Symbolism and Lessons of the Tapers—St. Bernard's Sermon on

the Purification—Phenomena and Rationale of Processions—
Primary Idea of the "Double Feast"—Bingham's Argument from
the name *Hypapante*—Names, ancient and vernacular—Humility,
the special Virtue of the Virgin—Law of Purification—Benedict
XIV.—Neander's Apology for the Purification—Bishop Jeremy
Taylor's Hymn—*Schola Cordis*—"Humiliation of the Heart"—
Complement of the Epiphany and the Angelic Message—"The
Light to lighten the Gentiles"—Dr. Newman's "Lead kindly
Light!"—Poem of Ephraim Syrus, "*In Epiphania et Præsentatione Domini*"—Dr. Monsell's "Daily Prayer"—Artistic and
Poetic Affinities—Lessons of the "Double Feast." . . . 331

ST. MATTHIAS.—FEBRUARY 24.

Institution of the Festival—Irregularity of Observance—St.
Matthias probably one of the Seventy—The Election of St.
Matthias, a Warning—Multiformity of Betrayal—Treason of Self-Indulgence—George Herbert's "Self-Condemnation"—"Who is
the Traitor?"—Apostolic Province of St. Matthias—Julius
Africanus—Nicephorus—Different Accounts of the Death of St.
Matthias—And of the Disposal of his Remains—Poem from the
"Christian Year"—"Who is God's chosen Priest?" . . 351

THE ANNUNCIATION OF THE BLESSED VIRGIN MARY.—MARCH 25.

Origin of the Commemoration—Various Theories—Benedict
XIV.—Baronius—L'Estrange—Bingham—Primary character of
the Feast—Council of Laodicea—Council *in Trullo*—Mr. Riddle's
account of the Festival—Gelasius I.—Sergius I.—Council of Toledo
—Names and Titles of the Day—St. Bernard—Ivo Carnotensis—
Artistic Treatment—The Lily, the peculiar Emblem of the Annunciation—Purity of the Virgin—Wordsworth's Sonnet on "The
Virgin"—Occurrence of the Annunciation—At what time of the
Day?—At what age of the Virgin?—Baronius—Cajetan—Catharinus—Doctrine and Distinctions of the Day—Alban Butler—
Circumstances and Contents of the Annunciation—Vision of the
fulfilment of Messianic Prophecies—Pope's "Messiah"—Honours
of the Day—Mother and Son—Mary's Exemplification of the

"Mind of Christ"—Submission of the Will—John Joseph Winkler
—His Poem on "The Annunciation"—Happiness of the Soul that
has no Will but God's 360

ST. MARK'S DAY—April 25.

The Three Marks—Slight New Testament mention of the
Evangelist—Antiquity of the Festival—Dr. Waterland's Account
—Council of Cognac—Universality—Reasons of the Celebration
on 25th April—Origin of St. Mark's Gospel—Clement of Alexandria—Eusebius—Tertullian—St. Athanasius—Qualities and
Language of the Gospel—Diversity of Gifts—Dr. Doddridge's
Hymn—Labours and Martyrdom of St. Mark—Translation of
Relics to Venice—*Evangelium secundum Hunc*—Dr. Williams's
Translation of the Hymn *Vos Succensa Deo Splendida Lumina*—
Symbolical History of the Evangelists 373

ST. PHILIP AND ST. JAMES'S DAY—May 1.

The earliest Commemoration of the Apostles, an aggregate one
—Gradual Allocation of Special Days—The Feast of All Apostles
set apart for St. Philip and St. James—Origin of their Association
—Institution of their Festival—The Greek Church commemorates
them severally 382

St. Philip—His History—His anxiety to communicate—
Mr. Wilcox—His Verses on "Christian Activity"—Question of
Thomas and Philip—"I am the Way"—Bishop Hall's "Anthem
for the Cathedral of Exeter"—Labours and Death of St. Philip—
Was he Strangled, Crucified, or Stoned?—Buried at Hierapolis . 383

St. James—Brother of the Lord—"He was seen of James"—
Circumstances of the Apparition, according to the *Gospel of the
Hebrews*—Bishop of Jerusalem—Asceticism of St. James—Constant in Prayer—George Herbert's Lines on "Prayer"—St. James
taken to a Pinnacle of the Temple—Bears witness for Christ—The
Popular "Hosanna"—The Scribes and Pharisees cast St. James
headlong from the Temple—The mangled Apostle prays for his
Murderers—His Brains at length beaten out—Epistle of St.
James—"James the Just"—James Shirley—"The Memory of
the Just is Blessed." 387

ST. BARNABAS THE APOSTLE—June 11.

Cælestis Aulæ Principes—Parentage of St. Barnabas—Born in Cyprus—Educated at Jerusalem—Disciple of Gamaliel, and Fellow-disciple of St. Paul—Probably one of the Seventy—"Son of Consolation"—Introduces St. Paul to the Disciples at Jerusalem—Labours with him at Antioch—Their Co-operation during Fourteen Years—Separation—Uncertain History of St. Barnabas—Traditionary Labours in Cyprus—Martyrdom—Burial in a Cave near Salamis—Transference of his Relics to Constantinople by the Emperor Zeno—Catholic Epistle of St. Barnabas—Institution of his Festival—Imperfect Information—Keble's Poem—"The Son of Consolation, a Levite" 392

ST. JOHN BAPTIST'S DAY—June 24.

Position of St. John the Baptist with reference to the Mosaic and Christian Dispensations—In the Desert—Robert Montgomery's description from the "Messiah"—An Exceptional Celebration—*Festum Decollationis*—Nativity of John the Baptist—Of Early Celebration in the Church—Councils of Agde and Oxford—Career of John—His Baptizing of Christ—Dr. Newman's Verses on "Pusillanimity"—Collection and Distribution of the Relics of John the Baptist—Their Miraculous Virtues—Verses for the Day from the "People's Hymnal" 400

ST. PETER'S DAY—June 29.

St. Peter at Rome—Unnecessarily debated—Precedence of the Church of Jerusalem—Hospinian's Account of the Introduction of the Festival—Early Observance—Request of Festus to the Empress Ariadne—Splendour of Celebration—Family, Name, and Character of St. Peter—Stability by Falling—Poem from Quarles's "Emblems"—George Wither's Verses on "St. Peter's Day"—Later Character of St. Peter—Travels and Labours of the Apostle—At Rome—At Jerusalem—In Britain?—Again at Rome—Simon Magus Deified—Shamed and Discomfited—Proposes to fly to Heaven—Falls headlong to the Ground, fatally bruised and mangled—St. Peter blamed by Nero for this Catastrophe—Imprisonment—Escape—*Domine quo Vadis?*—Crucifixion of St. Peter—His Tomb in the Vatican—St. Peter's at Rome—Nelson on the Personal Prerogative of St. Peter—John Newton—"Lovest thou Me?" 407

ST. JAMES THE APOSTLE—July 25.

Surnamed the Great—His Parentage and Family—A Son of Thunder—Salome's Ambition—Bishop Mant's Sonnets—"The Ambitious Disciples"—"Christian Ambition"—Various Phenomena of Ambition—Series of "Sonnets"—On the Mount of Transfiguration—Herbert Knowles—"The Three Tabernacles"—Hermogenes the Magus—Baffled and Converted—St. James slain by order of Herod Agrippa—Miracle on a Paralytic—Conversion of Josias, the chief Accuser of the Apostle—Association in Martyrdom—Peace, a dweller in a far Country—Verses by Henry Vaughan—Proto-Martyr of the Apostles—Death of Herod—Probable Burial of St. James at Jerusalem—Boasted Possession of his Relics at Compostella—Patron Saint of Spain—Early Local Celebration of the Festival—Later achievement of Universality 418

ST. BARTHOLOMEW THE APOSTLE—August 24.

Institution of the Commemoration—Bartholomew a Patronymic—Conjectural Etymologies—Identity of Bartholomew and Nathanael—Vocation of Nathanael—Neander—Gospel for the Day—George Herbert's "Elixir"—Travels of St. Bartholomew—Remarkable escape of Bartholomew from the fate of Philip at Hierapolis—Further Labours—In Armenia—Martyred and buried at Albanopolis—Various translations of his Relics—Finally they rest at Rome—William Habington—His poem, "*Cupio Dissolvi.*" . 427

ST. MATTHEW THE APOSTLE—September 21.

Presumed identity of Matthew and Levi—Office and Repute of the Publican—Renunciation of Fortune—Sonnet by Nicholas Breton—Austerity of the later Life of St. Matthew—Quarles's

xxvi   CONTENTS.
                                                              Page.
"Emblems"—"Delight in God only"—Gospel of St. Matthew—
His Travels and Labours—Various Accounts of his Martyrdom—
Commemoration—Its first Institution—George Herbert's lines,
entitled "The Quip." 435

ST. MICHAEL AND ALL ANGELS—September 29.

Antiquity of Local Celebration—Sect of the "Angelites"—
Council of Laodicea—Apparitions of St. Michael—At Chonæ, in
Phrygia—At Mount Garganus, in Apulia—On Mount Tumba—
Mont St. Michel, in Normandy—St. Michael's Mount in Cornwall—Varieties of Celebration—Council of Mentz—Michael
Comnenus—St. Michael, the Angel of the Resurrection—His
special Offices—Drummond of Hawthornden—"On the Feast
of St. Michael the Archangel"—Michael as Champion and
Combatant—Gabriel, the Angel of the Annunciation—Raphael,
and his Mission to the family of Tobit—Uriel, the Enlightener
of Esdras — Spenser's "Ministration of Angels" — Angelic
Duties, Employments, and Manifestations—Bishop Ken's Doctrine about Angels—Enforced in "Hymnotheo: or the Penitent"—Opinion of St. Ambrose—Ken's Verses "On St. Michael"—
Number, Quality, and Nature of the Angels—Dr. Townsend—
Relative Dignity of Men and Angels—Dionysius the Areopagite on
the *Celestial Hierarchy*—Thomas Heywood—Angelic Precedence
undecided—Richard Hooker on the Nature of Angels—Spirit
becoming to this Festival—Its Suggestiveness and Sublimity—St.
Joseph of the Studium—"Stars of the Morning"—Dr. Neale's
Version—Joahann Rist—His lines on "St. Michael and All
Angels"—Dr. Newman's Sonnet on "Angelic Guidance"—Mr.
Keble's "Carved Angels"—Heaven, the Starting-point and Goal—
Three Eras of the Universe—Thomas à Kempis—"On the Joys
of Heaven." 442

ST. LUKE THE EVANGELIST—October 18.

No Certain Account of the Origin of the Festival—Mr. Riddle—
Dr. Waterland—Mr. Brady—Was Luke one of the Seventy?—
Assertion and Counter-Assertion—A Middle Theory—Was Luke
a Painter?—Denied by Hospinian—A Physician of Bodies and of

Souls—Rev. Gerard Moultrie's Hymn for St. Luke's Day—The All-Healer—On the way to Emmaus—Lines from Cowper's "Conversation"—Gospel of St. Luke—Approved and favoured by St. Paul—Dr. Watts—"Christ the Substance of the Levitical Priesthood"—Dr. Kynaston—"Only Luke is with me"—"Acts of the Apostles"—Labours of St. Luke—Various accounts of his Death—His Relics translated to Constantinople. 465

ST. SIMON AND ST. JUDE, APOSTLES—October 28.

Reason of Joint Commemoration 473

St. Simon—Styled the Canaanite, and Zelotes—Sect of the Zealots—Call of St. Simon to the Apostolate—His Labours—Traditionary joint Martyrdom with St. Jude—"Schola Cordis" —"The Inflaming of the Heart." 473

St. Jude—Of our Lord's Kindred—Called Labbæus and Thaddæus—His Apostolic Province—Meets his brother Simon in Mesopotamia—They engage in contests with two famous Magi—Power of the Apostles over the Demons—Their Fellowship in Death—Eusebius—Interview of the Emperor Domitian with the grandsons of St. Jude—Christ's Kingdom not of this World—Gnosticism the Apostolic *Antichrist*—Tenets and tendencies of that System—Its Ethics—Encouragement of Sensuality—Indifference of External Actions—Antagonism to distinctive Christian Doctrines—Poem for the Day from the "Christian Year." 476

ALL SAINTS' DAY.

The Pantheon—M. Agrippa—Dedication of the Pantheon—Christian Treatment of Pagan Temples—Emperors Theodosius and Honorius—Gregory the Great—The Emperor Phocas makes a Grant of the Pantheon to Boniface IV.—Bede's Account of the Conversion of the Pantheon—Santa Maria ad Martyres—Consecration of a Chapel to All Saints by Pope Gregory III.—Institution of the Festival—Gradual attainment of Universality—Exaggerated Respect for the Departed—Images of the Saints—Dean Milman's Statement of the Doctrine of Saints in the Ancient Latin Church—Dion Chrysostom—Frequency of Canonization—

Multiplication of Shrines—Assumption by Pope Alexander III. of the Prerogative of Canonization—Local Saints—Tutelary Saints—Superstition works upward from below—Luther's "Table Talk"—Wordsworth's Sonnet on "Saints"—St. Augustine's Doctrine—Richard Hooker—Chivalrous *clinamen* to a Worship of the Virgin—George Herbert's Poem, "To all Angels and Saints" —Sainthood of Reality, and of External Canonization—Church Militant and Church Triumphant—The Great Multitude—Topics of the All Saints' Muse—Saints of All Conditions—Antagonism of Flesh and Spirit—John Newton's Poem—"Inward Warfare" —Saints without the Limits of Christianity—Hidden Saints—Dr. Newman's Poem on "Heathenism"—Ideal Sanctity of Men, Angels, and Infants—Bishop of Winchester's Poem on "All Saints"—Sir Archibald Edmonstone—Sonnets on "The Church Militant," and "The Church Triumphant"—Present State of Departed Saints—"Book of Wisdom"—Incomplete Beatitude—The Resurrection Gathering of the Saints—Communion of Saints— Hooker—The Sword and the Palm—The Pro-Epistle—Sealing of the Elect of the Twelve Tribes—Schenck's Poem on "All Saints' Day"—Teaching of the Festival—Collect for the Day—John of Damascus—"Idiomela for All Saints"—The Future Glory. . 482

THE CHURCH SEASONS.

Advent.

ORIGINALLY, and with stricter verbal propriety than now, the word Advent was taken to mean the time of the birth of Christ—His arrival, or having come, rather than His coming. But the Church has always loved dutifully to cultivate the idea of preparation for seasons of uncommon sanctity; and one effect of this disposition has been to throw back Advent over a season of three or four weeks, intended to be spent as a long Christmas-eve in the contemplation of the incidents of which the approaching festival is commemorative, and in devout and self-questioning anticipation of the Day of Judgment. It is with Advent, therefore, which begins on the Sunday nearest—before or after—to St. Andrew's Day, that the ecclesiastical year commences. The exact date at which the celebration of this season first came into use is uncertain; but it is proved to have been practised before A.D. 450, by the fact of Maximus Taurinensis having, in that year, written a homily upon the subject. The Eastern Church, with the exception of the Nestorians, who observe a fast of twenty-five days at this season, has, strictly speaking, no Advent; a circumstance which has the effect of considerably limiting our ground when we seek, as now, for poetical illustrations of individual or ecclesiastical piety in this kind.

The history of the world, from the time of its first defection from being a loyal colony of heaven, to the time of its final resumption into the more direct and visible government of God, has little or nothing of significance that is not related to the redemption and to the judgment of mankind. All the interests of the descendants of a fallen ancestor culminate in the chances of recovery and final safety. The first Advent of Christ is the general pledge of the one; the second Advent will be the particular assurance of the other. The history of the world after Paradise, resolves itself, we say, into two capital seasons of Advent. The interval between the fall of Adam and the birth of Christ, was the first of these seasons; the interval between the first and the second coming of the Lord, is the second. The first interval was remarkable for the longing expectation of His coming as a Saviour; the second is characterised by the trembling hope with which is awaited His coming as a Judge.

Advent poetry, therefore, parts at the outset into two grand divisions—that which is prophetic or anticipative of one or both Advents; and that which, being commemorative of the first, is anticipative only with regard to the second. The first of these two grand divisions parts again as naturally and almost as palpably into two sub-divisions; the first sub-division being that which is characterised by the aspirations of a race amongst whom the line of successive revelations had been kept unbroken; and the second, that which is marked by the vague, darkling, and sometimes even despairing yearnings of nations amongst whom whatever of divine inspiration they had took rather the form of artistic, philosophical, and scientific culture than that of religious enlightenment. We would first speak a few words about the nations last mentioned, and forthwith dismiss them. Our gleanings in this field must be very scanty.

It would be idle to attempt to follow the efforts of the best thought of Heathendom after a just apprehension of the Divine, and its relations to the human. It is sufficient to say that the felt want of the most earnest minds, whether of Greece or of the further and more ancient India, was that of a Christ, a Redeemer. Whatever might be the case with the more extreme and more rigidly logical of Pantheists in the one country, or with the more *insouciant* of Epicurean speculators in the other, the average heart expressed itself in the invention of *avataras* and theophanies. Guided or not guided by the broken reflected lights of a revelation which their ancestors had forfeited, because they had not held it in honour, the masses wrote down a future incarnation as if past, and found their salvation in progressive manifestations of Vishnu, the Preserver, or in the benevolence of self-sacrificing or self-immolating heroes.

But such fables had not pith enough to be received as dogmas by more subtle intellects. The Greek mind especially wearied itself in restless speculations. A moral despair walked abroad, to which the dying words of Aristotle may persuade us to believe that even he succumbed. But despair was not perfect till it became indifference. Above the din of the funeral games celebrated at the sepulchre in which the Sophists had entombed all noble aims, there rises the refreshing and the startling strain of Eupolis, a poet of the Socratic way of thinking, who outvied his fellows in the expression of a hope, common to his school, of the coming of a celestial instructor. It is a genuine Advent hymn; and it may be quoted not only as the single heathen contribution to our anthology, but also as exhibiting one of the very highest sentiments in the sphere of morals and religion, which the unbaptised Muse has " wedded to immortal verse." We use Charles Wesley's translation.

Author of being, source of light,
With unfading beauties bright;
Fulness, goodness, rolling round
Thy own fair orb without a bound;
Whether thee thy suppliants call
Truth, or Good, or One, or All,

Ei, or *Jao*, Thee we hail,
Essence that can never fail;
Grecian or barbaric name,
Thy stedfast being still the same.

Thee, when the morning greets the skies
With rosy cheeks and humid eyes:
Thee, when sweet declining day
Sinks in purple waves away;
Thee will I sing, O parent Jove!
And teach the world to praise and love.

* * * * *

And yet a greater hero far
(Unless great Socrates could err),
Shall rise to bless some future day,
And teach to live and teach to pray.
Come, UNKNOWN INSTRUCTOR, come!
Our leaping hearts shall make Thee room:
Thou with Jove our hearts shalt share,
Of Jove and Thee we are the care.

O Father, King, whose heavenly face
Shines serene on all thy race,
We thy magnificence adore,
And thy well-known aid implore;
Nor vainly for thy help we call;
Nor can we want, for Thou art all!

The Advent of the Messiah was a glowing theme for the numbers of prophets and poets, and for the piety of saints of the Jewish dispensation; and not the less glowing or sublime on account of the indeterminateness attaching to many of the predictions and expectations of its nature. The paradoxes, which doubtless served at once to attract and to baffle inquiry in some directions, are to us so fully cleared up by events, that it is not necessary to dwell upon them longer than may suffice to indicate what a mysterious wealth of picturesque and pathetic metaphor the hopes of the Hebrew bards and people have stored up for the poetical commemoration of an Advent which has now to so many Christian generations been a glorious and accomplished fact. The theme is one from the associations of which is wanting no single element of grandeur, sublimity, majesty, tenderness, love, pity, and pathos. All the circumstances recorded, with an ever-increasing particularity of detail, as about to happen, and which were to authenticate and identify the Messiah, comprise the materials for Advent literature which Christian poets inherit, and which up to the present moment they combine and recombine with an exhaustless variety. And to these the evangelical narratives have contributed other materials—the graphic circumstances of the life and death of Christ, and the hopes and fears which gather about His second coming to judge the quick and the dead.

The King of Glory was to walk wearily along the highways of the world; the everlasting Son of the Father was to be born of a Virgin; the Infinite was to be brought visibly down to the conditions of space; the Eternal was to be subject to seasons and successions; the Word, the Wisdom of God, was to be incarnate in the form of man, and in that form to become the slighted of His own people, and the foolishness of the Greek. Poverty and hardship were to dog His footsteps through His short and sorrowful life; scorn, and dejection, and affliction were to be His beyond the wont of the sons of men; the sceptre of His everlasting kingdom was to be a reed; His crown was to be of thorns; in the place of receiving the anointing oil, He was to be spit upon by ruffianly soldiers; His throne was to be the base exaltation of a cross; and His last moments were to be eclipsed with the felt darkness of His Father's withdrawal. Over against these things were to be placed the visible, audible recognitions from heaven, and especially the glory of His ascension, which faintly imaged the manner of that second coming, in which He is to revisit earth with all the mercy and terror of a Judge. In such a picture the lights of heaven fall athwart the stolid blackness of the pit. Such a poem would out-tax the powers of collective angelic genius. Yet it is about such events that Advent poetry has to be conversant. They are gravely, simply, and therefore grandly epitomised in a few sentences of the *Te Deum*.

The hymns of Ambrose, to whom with St. Augustine, the authorship of the *Te Deum* has been referred by a well-known legend, like most of the earlier hymns of the Church, were chiefly objective, and had to do with the seasons of the Christian year, and the horary or the more capital divisions of the day. One of the most celebrated is that on the Advent, beginning "Veni, Redemptor gentium." We pass this by to offer another which appertains to the group of hymns called Ambrosian. In his admirable repertory, the "Thesaurus Hymnologicus," Daniel, whilst entering a caveat against its reception as an Advent hymn, records the fact that it is generally and even authoritatively appropriated to that season as "Hymnus in Adventu Domini ad Vesperas," under which heading it is inserted by Bässler in his "Auswahl Altchristlicher Lieder." Daniel gives two versions, the older one being identical with that offered by Bässler, and the newer one being that which is found in the Roman breviary. A translation—which we subjoin—of this later and rather shorter version, occurs in Mr. Orby Shipley's "Lyra Messianica," to which it is contributed by a certain or uncertain W. J. C. The original hymn commences "Conditor alme siderum," and is rendered by W. J. C. into the vernacular, as follows :—

> Creator of the starry height,
> Of hearts believing endless Light,
> Jesu, Redeemer, bow Thine Ear,
> Thy suppliants' vows in pity hear;

Who, lest the earth, through evil eye
Of treacherous Fiend, should waste and die,
With mighty Love instinct, were made
Th' expiring world's all-healing Aid:
Who to the Cross, that world to win
From common stain of common sin,
From Virgin Shrine, a Virgin Birth,
A spotless Victim issuest forth;
At vision of Whose Glory bright,
At mention of Whose Name of might,
Angels on high and Fiends below
In reverence or in trembling bow:
Almighty Judge, to Thee we pray,
Great Umpire of the last dread Day,
Protect us through th' unearthly fight
With Armour of Celestial Light.

The poetry of the Second Advent before the time of the Reformation seems to have been mainly devoted to the setting forth of the terrors of the Judge and of the Judgment. The minds of the writers seem to have been fascinated by those divine qualities which, taken alone, are the least favourable to the present comfort and the eternal happiness of a sinful creature. Wrath was anxiously deprecated. Hope seemed at times to be overshadowed by the gloom of a scarcely contingent personal interest in a general condemnation. Of course this tendency does not manifest itself uniformly; but it is to be detected, less or more, in the line of poems that, from Ephraim Syrus and Theodore of the Studium to Thomas de Celano and our own Richard de Hampole, treated exclusively or incidentally of the subject of the Second Coming to Judgment. This class of hymns of the Second Advent we find it convenient to represent by an ode of St. Theodore of the Studium, rather than by such better known ones as the "Dies Iræ" of Thomas de Celano. Theodore was Hegumen of the great Abbey of the Studium, at Constantinople; and suffered scourging, imprisonment, and exile during the Iconoclastic persecution under Leo the Armenian. He died in banishment, November 11, A.D. 826. "His hymns," says Dr. Neale, from whose work on the "Hymns of the Eastern Church," we make the quotation, "are, in my judgment, very far superior to those of S. Theophanes, and nearly, if not quite, equal to the works of S. Cosmas. . . . . The Canon that follows (of which the ode we are about to quote is a part) is unfortunate in provoking a comparison with the unapproachable majesty of the "Dies Iræ," yet during the four hundred years by which it anticipated that sequence, it was undoubtedly the grandest Judgment hymn of the Church."

> That fearful day, that day of speechless dread,
> When Thou shalt come to judge the quick and dead—
> > I shudder to foresee,
> > O God! what then shall be!
>
> When Thou shalt come, angelic legions round,
> With thousand thousands, and with trumpet sound;
> > CHRIST, grant me in the air,
> > With saints to meet Thee there!
>
> Weep, O my soul, ere that great hour and day,
> When God shall shine in manifest array,
> > Thy sin, that thou may'st be
> > In that strict judgment free!
>
> The terror!—hell-fire fierce and unsufficed:
> The bitter worm: the gnashing teeth:—O CHRIST,
> > Forgive, remit, protect;
> > And set me with the elect!
>
> That I may hear the blessed voice that calls
> The righteous to the joy of heavenly halls:
> > And, King of Heaven, may reach
> > The realm that passeth speech!
>
> Enter Thou not in judgment with each deed,
> Nor each intent and thought in strictness read;
> > Forgive, and save me then,
> > O Thou that lovest men!
>
> Thee, One in Three blest Persons! Lord o'er all!
> Essence of essence, Power of power, we call!
> > Save us, O FATHER, SON,
> > And SPIRIT, ever one!

From this point we would resolutely confine our quotations to the Advent poets of our own tongue, to whom alone, nay, to a list of whose names alone, the space at our command for this season would not suffice to do justice. But the loss on this account is the smaller because the reader is conversant, or can easily become so, with the Advent poems of Germany, from those of Luther and Paul Gerhardt to the present time, as well as with the more distinguished of other continental productions in this kind.

George Wither was a pioneer in this country in the way of projecting and producing a connected series of poems commemorative of the various Church Seasons. The poem on Advent, therefore, which occurs in his "Hymns and Songs of the Church," has a claim to consideration quite other than one founded on its poetic excellences. Indeed we fear that Wither's muse will be found an incorrigibly pedestrian one. His poem is little more than a rhymed statement of doctrine, a metrical body of Advent divinity. But that is, in itself, no inconsiderable merit. The reader will observe how faithfully in the preface which introduces the poem, as well as in the poem itself, Wither has sought to gather into one complex lesson all the more simple ones which the Church occupies four weeks, with appropriate lessons, collects, epistles, and gospels, in enforcing. "The Advent," says Wither, "is that for Christmas which John the Baptist was to Christ (even a forerunner for preparation); and it is called the Advent (which signifieth coming), because the Church did usually, from that time until the Nativity, commemorate the several comings of Christ, and instruct the people concerning them; which comings are these, and the like:—His Conception, by which He came into the Virgin's womb; His Nativity, by which He came (as it were) further into the world: His coming to preach in His own person: His coming by His ministers: His coming to Jerusalem: the coming of the Holy Ghost: His spiritual coming, which He vouchsafeth into the heart of every regenerate Christian: and, finally, that last coming of His, which shall be unto judgment, etc. All which comings are comprehended in these three, His coming to men, into men, and against men; to men, by His Incarnation; into men, by Grace; against men, to Judgment." Then he sings:—

> When Jesus Christ incarnate was,
>   To be our brother, then came He:
> When into us He comes by grace,
>   Then His belovēd spouse are we:
> When He from Heaven descends again,
> To be our Judge returns He then.
>
> And then despair will those confound,
>   That His first comings nought regard;
> And those, who till the trumpet sound,
>   Consumed their leisures unprepar'd:
> Curst be those pleasures, cry they may,
> Which drove the thought of this away.
>
> The Jews abjected yet remain,
>   That His first advent heeded not;
> And those five virgins knock'd in vain,
>   Who to provide them oil forgot:
> But safe and blessed those men are,
> Who for His comings so prepare.
>
> Oh, let us, therefore, watch and pray,
>   His time of visiting to know,
> And live so furnish'd that we may
>   With Him unto His wedding go;
> Yea, though at midnight He should call,
> Let us be ready, lamps and all.
>
> And so provide before that feast,
>   Which Christ His coming next doth mind,
> That He to come, and be a guest
>   Within our hearts, may pleasure find;
> And we bid welcome, with good cheer,
> That coming which so many fear.

BISHOP JEREMY TAYLOR'S ADVENT HYMN.

> Oh, come, Lord Jesus, come away
>   (Yea, though the world it shall deter);
> Oh, let Thy kingdom come, we pray,
>   Whose coming most too much defer;
> And grant us therefore such foresight,
> It come not like a thief by night.

We do not wish to lengthen out our remarks by the citation of popular favourites, whose verses will be in the hands and on the tongues of many of our readers in the season of Advent. It is our desire, generally, rather to introduce the unknown or to recall the forgotten, with a view to supplement that which is better known or more fondly cherished. The reputation of Bishop Jeremy Taylor is scarcely that of a poet—of a poet, at least, who submitted himself to the trammels of versification. Yet, as Heber says, in his life of Taylor, "at the end of the 'Golden Grove' are some hymns for different festivals, which, had they no other merit, would be interesting, as the only remaining specimens of that which a mind so intrinsically poetical as Taylor's was, could effect when he attempted to arrange his conceptions in a metrical form. They are, however, in themselves, and on their own account, very interesting compositions." It is from Bishop Taylor's Festival Hymns, that we transcribe the following "Hymn for Advent; or Christ's coming to Jerusalem in triumph."

> Lord, come away;
>   Why dost Thou stay?
> Thy road is ready, and Thy paths made straight,
>   With longing expectation wait
>   The consecration of Thy beauteous feet.
> Ride on triumphantly! Behold we lay
> Our lusts and proud wills in Thy way.
> Hosannah! welcome to our hearts! Lord, here
> Thou hast a temple too, and full as dear
> As that of Zion—and as full of sin;
> Nothing but thieves and robbers dwell therein.
> Enter and chase them forth, and cleanse the floor;
> Crucify them, that they may never more

Profane that holy place,
Where Thou hast chosen to set Thy face.
And then, if our stiff tongues shall be
Mute in the praises of Thy Deity,
The stones out of the temple wall
Shall cry aloud, and call
Hosannah! and Thy glorious footsteps greet. Amen.

The last poem which we shall lay before the reader is by Bishop Doane, of New Jersey, a name known favourably, if restrictedly, in this country, as the author of "Songs by the Way," and also as the American editor of Keble's "Christian Year." Bishop Doane celebrates at once the first and the second coming of Christ with considerable graphic piety in a poem entitled "The Two Advents."

He came not with his heavenly crown, His sceptre clad with power;
His coming was in feebleness, the infant of an hour;
An humble manger cradled, first, the Virgin's holy birth,
And lowing herds compassioned there the Lord of heaven and earth.

He came not in His robe of wrath, with arm outstretched to slay;
But on the darkling paths of earth to pour celestial day,
To guide in peace the wandering feet, the broken heart to bind,
And bear upon the painful cross the sins of human kind.

And Thou hast borne them, Saviour meek! and, therefore, unto Thee,
In humbleness and gratitude, our hearts shall offered be;
And greenly, as the festal bough that on Thy altar lies,
Our souls, our bodies, all be Thine, a living sacrifice!

Yet once again Thy sign shall be upon the heavens displayed,
And earth and its inhabitants be terribly afraid;
For not in weakness clad Thou com'st, our woes, our sins to bear,
But, girt with all Thy Father's might, His vengeance to declare.

The terrors of that awful day, oh! who shall understand?
Or who abide, when Thou in wrath shalt lift Thy holy hand?
The earth shall quake, the sea shall roar, the sun in heaven grow pale;
But Thou hast sworn, and wilt not change, Thy faithful wilt not fail.

Then grant us, Saviour, so to pass our time in trembling here,
That when, upon the clouds of heaven Thy glory shall appear,
Uplifting high our joyful heads, in triumph we may rise,
And enter, with Thine angel-train, Thy temple in the skies!

Christmas-Day.

THERE is nothing to fix the exact date at which the commemoration of the birth of Jesus Christ settled into an institution of the Church. By some it has been said that the observance of this feast began as early as about the year 68; and it would seem that Telesphorus, who flourished a century after this date, ordered divine service to be performed, with the singing of an angelic hymn, on the eve of the Nativity. The Emperor Diocletian, who publicly abdicated in the year 304, amongst the incidents of his inveterate persecution of the Christians, on one occasion caused a church to be fired in which a congregation had met in honour of the Nativity, and consumed them, together with the sacred building in which they were assembled.

Commemorations of the Nativity, if desultory ones, are thus shown to have taken place before the time of Constantine. But it was only about the period of his reign, and probably owing to his encouragement, that the natural tendency to the observation of this festival developed into a fixed celebration that promised to become at once Catholic and perpetual. The comparatively late date at which the honour of general recognition was paid to Christmas, was owing in part to the fact, that the early Church directed its attention to the public ministry of our Lord, rather than to the incidents of His birth, childhood, or even His manhood, so long as that was spent in retirement and preparation merely. Thus, St. Chrysostom observes, that "not the day of our Saviour's birth, but the day of His baptism, is to be regarded as His manifestation."

The institution of the festival of the Nativity in the fourth century has been variously, and, sometimes, rather capriciously accounted for. It has been derived by some persons from the Jewish feast of the Dedication, which Judas Maccabæus ordained after he had cleansed the sanctuary from the pollutions of the discomfited heathen, and had set up a new and purer altar for the service of the Lord. " Now, on the five-and-twentieth day of the ninth month (which is called the month Casleu), in the hundred forty and eighth year, they (Judas and his friends) rose up betimes in the morning, and offered sacrifice, according to the law, upon the new altar of burnt offerings, which they had made. Look at what time and what day the heathen had profaned it, even in that was it dedicated with songs, and citherns, and harps, and cymbals. Then all the people fell upon their faces, worshipping and praising the God of heaven who had given them good success. And so they kept the dedication of the altar eight days, and offered burnt-offerings with gladness, and sacrificed the sacrifice of deliverance and praise. They decked, also, the forefront of the temple with crowns of gold, and with shields; and the gates and the chambers they renewed, and hanged doors upon them. Thus was there very great gladness among the people, for that the reproach of the heathen was put away. Moreover, Judas and his brethren, with the whole congregation of Israel, ordained that the days of the dedication of the altar should be kept in their season from year to year, by the space of eight days, from the five and twentieth day of the month Casleu, with mirth and gladness" (1 Maccabees iv. 52-59). This narrative is substantially repeated in 2 Maccabees x. 1-8; and the Evangelist St. John has an allusion to this feast:—" And it was

ORIGIN OF THE FESTIVAL.

at Jerusalem, the feast of the dedication, *and it was winter*" (St. John x. 22). We have italicised the last few words, because it will be inferred from what is almost immediately to be mentioned as to the uncertainty of the day or the month in which the birth of Christ really took place, that a very colourable argument is found in them for identifying the feast of Christmas with that of the Dedication.

But there are other hypotheses. One of these is that the festival of the Nativity is a Christianized perpetuation of the heathen Saturnalia, during which an attempt was made to recall in practice the peaceful glory of the age of gold. Presents were interchanged amongst friends; feuds were forgotten; criminals were reprieved; war was postponed, and business suspended; and pleasure and license reigned supreme. The Saturnalia were celebrated on the sixteenth, the seventeenth, or the eighteenth of December; and it does not exclude the supposition of the Jewish origin of the observance of the Nativity, to imagine that some heathen practices were engrafted upon its celebration. Neither, if we may trust the reasoning of Hooker and of Bishop Andrewes,* would such a twofold derivation attaint the lustre of its sanctity. Mr. Riddle, who mentions the above amongst other more purely conjectural derivations of Christmas celebration, remarks that, after all, "the institution may, perhaps, be sufficiently explained by the circumstances, that it was the taste of that age (the fourth century) to multiply festivals, and that the analogy of the events in our Saviour's history, which had already been marked by a distinct celebration, may naturally have pointed out the propriety of marking His nativity with the same honourable distinction. It was celebrated with all the marks of respect usually bestowed upon high festivals; and distinguished also by the custom, derived, probably, from

* *A Learned Discourse of Ceremonies retained and used in Christian Churches.*

heathen antiquity, of interchanging presents and making entertainments.*

The precise day, or even the month, in which took place the birth of Christ has not been conclusively ascertained. Clement of Alexandria tells us that some persons referred this gladly-momentous event to the sixteenth of May. Others, again, reasoning from the time of year that would be convenient for a general taxation, such as took place at the Nativity of Christ, and also from the fact of shepherds keeping a nightly watch over their flocks at the time of its occurrence, have concluded it probable that it happened in one of the autumn months, say in September or October.

Be this as it may, the festival of the Nativity was at first celebrated in the East on the sixth of January. In the latter part of the fourth, and the beginning of the fifth century, that date was appropriated to the commemoration of the baptism of Jesus, whilst His birth was honoured, as now, on the twenty-fith of December. The Orientals only gradually adopted the latter date; and it was not until the sixth century that the whole Christian world became unanimous in observing the feast of the Nativity on the same day.

The consolidation of the festival in the fourth century, led to the adoption of a "three-fold cycle of sacred seasons, by which the personal history of our Saviour was represented in a kind of chronological order."† The first of these cycles is that of the Nativity, or Christmas, commencing with the first Sunday in Advent, and terminating with the Epiphany; the second is the cycle of Easter; and the third is the cycle of Whitsuntide.

It is proper at this stage of our progress to sketch lightly the topics about which the Christmas muse is religiously conversant. In treating of Advent we took the opportunity of showing how the metrical aspirations of Heathendom had furnished us with at least one genuine Advent

* *Manual of Christian Antiquities.* † *Ibid.*

hymn; and that the expectation of the coming of Christ was not limited to the line of direct revelation. But the hymns or songs of Christmas can have no such duplicity or twofoldness. The hopes both of the Hebrew and the Greek centre in fact, if unconsciously, in one and the same person. A Jew who recognised Jesus of Nazareth as bearing the *tessera* of his national predictions, and the Gentile who recognised Christ as bearing the *tessera* of his own vaguer hopes, respectively spiritualized his Judaism and vacated his heathendom by the very fact of such recognition. Every follower of Christ, from the mere circumstance of his hearty adherence, is a mystical child of Abraham, and an inheritor of Messianic promises and prophecies. We crave two sentences to indicate broadly the course of these.

A vague hope springs up to the dispossessed of Eden that a future victory over the Tempter will accrue to the seed of the woman; a hope which by successive limitations is found narrowing itself to the descendants of Shem, of Abraham, of Israel, of Judah, and finally of David. The seed of the woman is announced as Shiloh, Prince of Peace; as a Prophet like unto Moses; as the Lord no less than the Son of David; as a Priest no less than a Sacrifice; until prophecy does its utmost in the more precise evangelical predictions of such a seer as Isaiah.

An unfailing store of topics is thus opened up to the Christmas poet. There is a song in every promise; a lay in every fulfilment; an ode in every dovetailing and combination.

The great fact, not of Christmas alone, but of all time—and relatively to the natives of our planet, of all eternity—is the fact of the Incarnation, the fact that God "took upon Him the seed of Abraham," and was in human form, Immanuel, God with us. The minute metaphysical and physiological speculations which originated in the circumstances of this neighbourhood of natures in the person of Christ gave to a large extent a particular complexion to ancient heresies, and a particular character to ancient hymnology. The Incarnation is the settlement, so far as it can be understood or appreciated by mortal intellect, of the long-vexed question of the relation of the human to the Divine. It is the apotheosis of our race; which, before it, either humbly trusting in an announced, or else wearying itself in orphan-like speculations on a possible, Fatherhood, rose, in it, to apprehend the idea of a very *Brotherhood* of God. Doctrinally the Incarnation defined the quality and the limits of the Fall of man, and the depravity of his nature. The Fall was not utter in the strongest and ultimate sense of the word; for there was the hope of recovery. The depravity was not hopeless—not inveterate or ingrained enough to shut out the nature of man from affinity to the nature of God. These were still so much at one that at least they could co-exist in a joint occupation of the same tabernacle of flesh. Man had not exiled himself beyond recall. The earth—*his* earth—tearful wanderer and alien as she had long been from the harmonious sisterhood of the stars, found herself returning from the error of her orbit to be invested with the Imperial crown of space, to be a centre of the universe, the realm and throne of a present God. Christ was the Word and the Wisdom in which a renewed *systematic* trinity—God, Man, Nature—found expression. Universal harmony was, in the Logos, recovered or recoverable.

The series of contrasts arising from the juxtaposition of the Divine might with the weakness of infancy; of the Divine wealth with abject poverty; of the ALL with the least—these have ever been themes very dear to the heart of the Christmas poet, whether he has indulged himself in the popular, social, and half-secular carol, or confined himself, as we do now, to what are more strictly the utterances of the rejoicing soul. Apropos of this whole group of contrasts, many of which will be illustrated in our quotations, we are only careful at the moment to make one observation; and this shall be apologetic of the manifestation of the Creator and Ruler of all things in the guise of weakness and abasement. The midsummer sun needs not to borrow from a taper the light wherewith to eke out his day, nor would he care to be supplemented by a firefly. The moon does not crave the crawling lamp of the worm, does not borrow from the sea its atom stars, or pray to be enlightened by the flitting fires of the swamp. The monarch envies not the base palace of the snail; nor does the knight indued with plaited steel covet the mail of the wretched limpet. From less to greater—to all from nothing. How should God, upon the occasion of His Incarnation, stoop to dignify, by His adoption, the poor pomp of His creature-world? Earth hath no state equal to the demands of Divine magnificence. Manhood is the best that earth can offer to her Ruler; and manhood is greater than its modes or accidents.

> 'Tis thus all God-like voices sing,
>   And have sung since the world began,
>   That it is more to be a man,
> Than, being man, to be a king.
>
> For nought save us beneath the skies—
>   Save us, and peers of our estate—
>   Is worshipful; and nought is great
> Which it is greatness to despise.

Moreover, so far as we can see, it was only by the adoption of a life of poverty by Christ, that His religion could hope to be saved from becoming the honour and patent of a class, instead of being, as now, the glory and safety of a race. Had his kingdom been of this world—nay, had His fortunes been such as to have struck in any considerable degree upon the external senses, the heaven of another life would inevitably have seemed to be the purchase of the wealth of this. Even as the facts at present stand, such a doctrine is not at all hard to discover amongst the phenomena of popular wrong-headedness. Such a doctrine is indeed a deplorable heresy, and one best to be confuted amongst the poor by the benevolent and sympathetic action of the rich.

Ephraim Syrus, a monk and deacon of the fourth century, who " was entitled," says Sozomen, " to the highest honours, and was the greatest ornament of the church," was born at Nisibis, or in its immediate neighbourhood, in the first year of the reign of the Emperor Constantine the Great. By force of natural talent and power of application, he attained an easy mastery over the most abstruse theorems of philosophy. " His style of writing," to quote Sozomen again, " was so replete with splendid oratory and sublimity of thought that he surpassed all the writers of Greece." To his singular honour it is asserted that his works carried, undiminished, into a Greek translation, all the elegance, and nerve, and vigour of the original Syriac. Basil, Bishop of the metropolis of Cappadocia, the most eloquent and learned man of his age, was accustomed to express his reverence and astonishment at the vastness of Ephraim's erudition. He is said to have written verses to the number of three hundred thousand. Some of the productions of his fecund genius were hymns on the Nativity. One of these is so grand in the simplicity of its character as a Divine idyll, that, although its length places it beyond our limits, we cannot pass it by without a short abstract. The author pictures all Nature assembling to pay homage to the infant Saviour; the shepherds bringing Him offerings from their flocks—"a lamb to the Paschal-lamb, to the first-born a first-born"—the lamb bleating its praises to Him whose coming as the Lamb of God proclaimed to lambs and oxen an immunity from sacrifice. The shepherds praise Him as the Chief Shepherd, who shall gather all into one fold; as the child older than Noah, and younger. As David once slew a lion to save a lamb, so, they say, the

Son of David is born to destroy that ravening wolf who, in the beginning, slew Adam, then pastured as a stainless lamb in Paradise. Old men and ancient women throng out of the city of David with greetings; young men, maidens, wives, and mothers, group around Him who has come to lend a sanction and sacredness to every relation of domestic and social life. Ephraim's treatment of his subject is nearly unique, and altogether idiosyncratic. On some other occasion we may hope to improve our acquaintance with him.

Cosmas, of Jerusalem, is probably the most learned of the Greek ecclesiastical poets; and "his fondness for types," says the late Dr. Neale, "his boldness in their application, and his love of aggregating them, make him the oriental Adam of St. Victor," "His compositions are tolerably numerous; and he seems to have taken pleasure in competing with St. John Damascenus (his foster-brother) as in the Nativity, the Epiphany, the Transfiguration, where the canons of both are given." Cosmas, or St. Cosmas—for he was canonised, and his day commemorated by the Eastern Church on the 14th of October—was Bishop of Maiuma, near Gaza; a dignity to which he suffered himself reluctantly to be consecrated by John, Patriarch of Jerusalem. He died in a good old age about the year 760.

Cosmas has left a canon for Christmas Day, εἰς τὴν θεογονίαν, a long poem, of which the original is given in Daniel's "Thesaurus Hymnologicus," and which is translated in the "Hymns of the Eastern Church." Of the several odes into which Dr. Neale has divided this poem, which he is inclined to think is, on the whole, the finest of all the Canons of Cosmas, the first is as follows, prefixed by the opening lines of the original:—

> Χριστὸς γεννᾶται, δοξάσατε
> Χριστὸς 'ἐξ οὐρανῶν, ἀπαντήσατε,
> Χριστὸς ἐπὶ γῆς 'ὑψώθητε.

> Christ is born! Tell forth His fame!
> Christ from Heaven! His love proclaim!
> Christ on earth! Exalt His name:
> Sing to the Lord, O world, with exultation!
> Break forth in glad thanksgiving, every nation!
>   For He hath triumphed gloriously!
>
> Man, in God's own image made,
> Man, by Satan's wiles betrayed,
> Man, on whom corruption preyed,
> Shut out from hope of life and of salvation,
> To-day CHRIST maketh him a new creation,
>   For He hath triumphed gloriously!
>
> For the Maker, when his foe
> Wrought the creature death and woe,
> Bowed the Heavens, and came below,*
> And, in the Virgin's womb, His dwelling making,
> Became true MAN, man's very nature taking;
>   For He hath triumphed gloriously!
>
> He, the Wisdom, WORD, and Might,
> GOD, and SON, and Light of light,
> Undiscovered by the sight
> Of earthly monarch, or infernal spirit,
> Incarnate was, that we might Heaven inherit:
>   For He hath triumphed gloriously!

Our next representative poem is taken from a hymn-writer of the Latin Church, and from a Latin original, which may be consulted in Bässler's "Auswahl Altchristlicher Lieder"; in Daniel's "Thesaurus," or, in a slightly varied form, in Archbishop Trench's "Sacred Latin Poetry." The author, Johannes Mauburnus, who was of the very latest of mediæval hymnographers, was born at Brussels in 1460, and, after fulfilling several dignities in the church, died Abbat of the Cloister of Livry, in the neighbourhood of Paris, in 1502. The hymn in question is derived from

---

* The reference is, of course, to Psalm xviii., 9: "He bowed the Heavens also and came down."

the "Rosetum Spirituale," and taken from a longer poem of thirteen stanzas, commencing :—

> Eja mea anima
> Bethlehem eamus.

The three stanzas translated below, have long formed a Christmas hymn, which was in favourite use in its original Latin in the early reformed churches. It is now, Bässler informs us, to be met with in various Protestant "Gesangbücher," in an old German version, beginning with the line—

> Warum liegt im Krippelein,

which represents the *Heu! quid jaces stabulo* of Mauburnus. English versions are not of the rarest occurrence. We take one of the latest, done by the Rev. Dr. Kynaston, and published in his "Occasional Hymns."

> Swathed, and feebly wailing,
>   Wherefore art Thou laid,
> All thy glory veiling
>   In the manger's shade?
> King, and yet no royal
>   Purple decks thy breast;
> Courtiers mute and loyal
>   Bend not o'er thy rest.
>
> Sinner, here I sought thee,
>   Here I made my home,
> All my worth I brought thee,
>   Vile am I become;
> All thy joys redressing
>   On my birthday morn,
> Give my GODHEAD'S Blessing,
>   In a stable born.
>
> Thousand, thousand praises,
>   JESUS, for Thy love,
> While my spirit gazes
>   With the Host above;

> Glory in the highest
> For Thy wondrous birth,
> Lowly where Thou liest,
> Praise and love on earth.

We quote a Sonnet—an explanation of a solemn thought from one of the Fathers — translated by Archdeacon Churton, in the "Lyra Messianica," from the Spanish of Luis de Gongora, born at Cordova, in 1562. He was of a very distinguished family; studied at Salamanca, and took holy orders; was made chaplain to the King, and prebendary of the church of Cordova, in which preferment he died in 1689. In his life-time he published nothing. His posthumous works consist of Sonnets, Reliques, Heroic Verses, a Comedy, a Tragedy, and Miscellanies; which have been often published with notes and commentaries equal to the pretensions of a bard whom the Spaniards partially reckon as the prince of all their poets:—

> To hang transfixed upon the bitter cross,
> To bear Thy bleeding brows all pierced with thorn,
> For frail man's glory to abide foul scorn,
> And for his gain to welcome deepest loss—
> This was a hero's deed. But to be born
> In such poor abject lodging, such scant room,
> A doorless shed in icy blasts forlorn,
> So low to stoop. Who from such height didst come—
> Oh, what a choice was this, my Sovereign LORD?
> What strength did GODHEAD to Thy cradle lend
> To bear that outrage of cold winter's breath?
> Not more Thy bloody sweat, or body gored:
> For greater far the distance to descend
> From GOD to man, than from poor man to Death.

As we turn to our own lyrists, we are proudly conscious of an inexhaustible wealth of Christmas verse; proudly, and yet at present, rather embarrassingly. We know how little room we have left for further quotations, and how countless a number of authors must be left without so much as mention or allusion; albeit some of these are amongst the chief glories of our literature. It is fortunate, however, that such poems as we have still to present, do not demand words of introduction at our hands. "Holy George Herbert," for instance, may safely be trusted without comment to contribute his flower to our anthology. He thus sings of "Christmas":—

> All after pleasures as I rid one day,
>   My horse and I, both tired, body and mind,
>   With full cry of affections, quite astray ;
> I took up in the next inn I could find.
>
> There when I came, whom found I but my dear,
>   My dearest Lord, expecting till the grief
>   Of pleasures brought me to Him, ready there
> To be all passengers' most sweet relief?
>
> O Thou, whose glorious, yet contracted light,
>   Wrapt in night's mantle, stole into a manger;
>   Since my dark soul and brutish is Thy right,
> To man of all beasts be not Thou a stranger:
>   Furnish and deck my soul, that Thou mayest have
>   A better lodging, than a rack, or grave.
>
> The shepherds sing ; and shall I silent be ?
>   My God, no hymn for Thee ?
> My soul's a shepherd too : a flock it feeds
>   Of thoughts, and words, and deeds.
> The pasture is Thy word ; the streams, Thy grace,
>   Enriching all the place.
> Shepherd and flock shall sing, and all my powers
>   Out-sing the daylight hours.
> Then we will chide the sun for letting night
>   Take up his place and right,
> We sing one common Lord ; wherefore He should
>   Himself the candle hold.
> I will go searching, till I find a sun
>   Shall stay, till we have done ;
> A willing shiner, that shall shine as gladly,
>   As frost-nipt suns look sadly.
> Then we will sing, and shine all our own day,
>   And one another pay :
> His beams shall cheer my breast, and both so twine,
> Till even his beams sing, and my music shine.

Robert Herrick, that jovial poet, and simple-hearted man, who, in his "Hesperides," sang

> Of brooks, of blossoms, birds, and bowers,
> Of April, May, of June, and July flowers,

tuned his lyre with a sometimes amazing freshness and piquancy of devotion, for the accompaniment of his "Noble Numbers." The very soul of Herrick seemed one flower-bed; although a flower-bed from the corners of which a flaunting weed was not uniformly excluded. The following dewy poem is in keeping with the naïve simplicity of his poetic genius, and the devoutness of his religious inspiration. It is entitled, "An Ode of the Birth of our Saviour:"—

> In numbers, and but those few,
> I sing Thy birth, oh, JESU!
> Thou prettie Babie, borne here,
> With superabundant scorn here;
> Who for Thy princely port here,
>   Hadst for Thy place
>   Of birth, a base
> Out-stable for Thy court here.
>
> Instead of neat inclosures
> Of interwoven osiers;
> Instead of fragrant posies
> Of daffadills and roses,
> Thy cradle, kingly stranger,
>   As Gospel tells,
>   Was nothing els,
> But, here, a homely manger.
>
> But we with silks, not cruells,
> With sundry precious jewells,
> And lilly-work will dress Thee;
> And as we dispossesse Thee
> Of clouts, wee'l make a chamber,
>   Sweet Babe, for Thee,
>   Of ivorie,
> And plaistered round with amber.

> The Jewes, they did disdaine Thee;
> But we will entertaine Thee
> With glories to await here,
> Upon thy princely state here,
> And more for love than pittie:
>   From yeere to yeere
>   Wee'l make thee, here,
> A free-born of our citie.

Our next specimen is taken from the "Hymns and Songs of the Church," of the more sedate Wither. The author has prefixed to it, in that work, a prose abstract of the great Christmas doctrine, and an exhortation to the hospitality and charity of Christmas practice. "This day," he says, "is worthily dedicated to be observed in remembrance of the blessed Nativity of our Redeemer Jesus Christ; at which time it pleased the Almighty Father to send his only-begotten Son into the world for our sakes; and by an unspeakable union to join in one person God and man, without confusion of natures, or possibility of separation. To express, therefore, our thankfulness and the joy we ought to have in this love of God, there hath been anciently, and is yet continued in England (above other countries), a neighbourly and plentiful hospitality in inviting, and (without invitation) receiving unto our well-furnished tables, our tenants, neighbours, friends, and strangers, to the honour of our nation, and increase of amity and free-hearted kindness among us. But, most of all, to the refreshing of the bowels of the poor, being the most Christian use of such festivals, which charitable and good English custom hath of late been seasonably re-advanced by his Majesty's gracious care, in commanding our nobility and gentry to repair (especially at such times) to their country mansions."

> As on the night before this blessed morn
> A troop of Angels unto shepherds told,
> Where in a stable He was poorly born,
> Whom nor the earth nor heavens can hold;

Through Bethlehem rung
  The news at their return;
Yea, Angels sung
  That God with us was born:
And they made mirth because we should not mourn.

Chorus.
Their Angels' carol sing we then,
To God on high all glory be;
For peace on earth bestoweth He,
And showeth favour unto men.

This favour Christ vouchsafeth for our sake;
To buy us thrones He in a manger lay;
Our weakness took, that we His strength might take,
And was disrobed, that He might us array:
  Our flesh He wore,
    Our sin to wear away:
  Our curse He bore,
    That we escape it may;
And wept for us, that we might sing for aye.

With Angels, therefore, sing again,
To God on high all glory be;
For peace on earth bestoweth He,
And showeth favour unto men.

We select the following specimen from the "seasonable" poems of Bishop Jeremy Taylor, called "Festival Hymns, celebrating the mysteries and chief festivals of the year, according to the manner of the ancient church, fitted to the fancy and devotion of the younger and pious persons, apt for memory and to be joined to their other prayers." It is the bishop's third hymn for Christmas, and has for its theme, "Christ's Birth in an Inn:"—

The blessed Virgin travailed without pain,
  And lodged in an inn,
  A glorious star the sign,
But of a greater guest than ever came that way;
  For there He lay,
  That is the God of night and day,
And over all the powers of Heaven doth reign.

It was the time of great Augustus' tax,
    And then He comes
    That pays all sums,
Even the whole price of lost humanity.
    And sets us free
    From the ungodly emperie
    Of sin, and Satan, and of death.
O make our hearts, blest God, Thy dwelling-place,
    And in our breast
    Be pleased to rest,
For Thou lov'st temples better than an inn,
    And cause that sin
    May not profane the Deity within,
And sully o'er the ornaments of grace. Amen.

The poetic literature of America, so far as it combines vigour and originality of conception with correctness and beauty of expression, is the almost exclusive product of times subsequent to the Declaration of Independence. But since that event, and especially during the last and the present generations, America has made good her claims to be considered a fruitful and tender nursing-mother of the Muses. We derive from one of her poets, Mr. Edmund H. Sears, the Christmas hymn with which we conclude this chapter. If we had arranged our poetic illustrations of the season according to the order of Christmas events, instead of according to the chronological order of their production, we should have commenced, instead of leaving off, with "The Angels' Song."

It came upon the midnight clear,
    That glorious song of old,
From angels bending near the earth,
    To touch their harps of gold.
"Peace to the earth, good-will to men,
    From Heaven's all-gracious King:"
The world in solemn stillness lay
    To hear the angels sing.

Still through the cloven skies they come,
  With peaceful wings unfurled ;
And still their heavenly music floats
  O'er all the weary world :
Above its sad and lonely plains
  They bend on hovering wing,
And ever o'er its Babel sounds
  The blessed angels sing.

Yet with the woes of sin and strife
  The world has suffered long ;
Beneath the angel-strain have rolled
  Two thousand years of wrong ;
And man at war with man hears not
  The love-song which they bring ;
Oh ! hush the noise, ye men of strife,
  And hear the angels sing !

And ye, beneath life's crushing load,
  Whose forms are bending low,
Who toil along the climbing way
  With painful steps, and slow ;
Look now ! for glad and golden hours
  Come swiftly on the wing :
Oh ! rest beside the weary road,
  And hear the angels sing !

For, lo ! the days are hastening on,
  By prophet-bards foretold,
When, with the ever-circling years,
  Comes round the age of gold :
When Peace shall over all the earth
  Its ancient splendours fling,
And the whole world send back the song
  Which now the angels sing.

St. Stephen's Day:

DECEMBER 26.

THE great Festival of Easter is the only Christian commemoration which rests upon absolute Scripture precept and Apostolic injunction :—" Christ our Passover is sacrificed for us, therefore let us keep the feast" (1 Cor. v. 7, 8). For no other specific day, whether an anniversary in honour of Christ or of one of His followers, can so venerable a sanction be brought forward. Nevertheless, the feasts of the Martyrs may, in the aggregate, claim something like the prestige of an Apostolic exhortation. "Remember them," says St. Paul, "which have the rule over you, who have spoken unto you the word of God; whose faith follow, considering the end of their conversation" (Heb. xiii. 7).*

"It is not without reason that St. Paul is thought hereby chiefly to hint at the martyrdom of St. James, the Bishop of Jerusalem, who not long before had laid down his life for the testimony of Jesus. Hence proceeded the great reverence people then had for those who suffered for the profession of Christianity, and laid down their lives for the

---

* The above passage is more conclusive in the Greek; our English version having the misfortune of ambiguity in two or three particulars. Μνημονεύετε τῶν ἡγουμένων ὑμῶν, οἵτινες ἐλάλησαν ὑμῖν τὸν λόγον τοῦ Θεοῦ· ὧν ἀναθεωροῦντες τὴν ἔκβασιν τῆς ἀναστροφῆς, μιμεῖσθε τὴν πίστιν.

confirmation of it."* The martyrs were affectionately revered as the disciples and followers of their Lord; and on account of their exceeding great devotion to Him it was thought becoming to do all possible honour to their memories, whether as a tribute to which they were justly entitled as the posthumous reward of their virtue, or for the purpose of encouraging others to like patience and fortitude.

If it be lawful to justify the commemoration of any instance of self-sacrifice by the Pauline admonition just quoted, *à fortiori* will such justification include the commemoration of the proto-martyr, who was emphatically the greatest *because* the first, and who in no respect whatever could be degraded to a rank lower than the highest. The moral features of his death were simply and literally unsurpassable; and if, in a merely physical aspect, it may have lacked the acute and protracted agonies of such a death as that, say, of St. Laurence, it is impossible to doubt that in St. Stephen was a reserve of heroism equal to any demands which the ingenuity of persecuting or demoniac ages has ever exacted from humanity. St. Stephen, we repeat, was the greatest of martyrs, because he was the first. If *robur et æs triplex* were necessary to the breast of the man who first tempted in a frail skiff the perils of the deep, with what supreme hardihood must not *his* heart have been fortified who first adventured the pains and the issues of martyrdom for a faith, the sustaining power of which—with one Divine exception, and practically speaking, without any exception at all—in such circumstances, was all untried!

The annual solemnities in honour of martyrs are ascertained to have been observed in a Christian antiquity so remote that it is impossible to say, not so much when the practice was first instituted, as when it was *not* already established. It is as lawful as it is picturesque to imagine the first of such commemorations as possibly being by only one year more modern than the first of such martyrdoms.

* Nelson's *Festivals and Fasts; Preliminary Instructions.*

Tertullian asserts that the Christians of the second century were wont to celebrate annually the birth-days of the martyrs, as a custom received by tradition from their ancestors.*

When we begin to know something of the manner in which these festivals were observed in the early Church, we find that the faithful were accustomed to meet once a year at the tombs of the martyrs, and "there solemnly to recite their sufferings and triumphs, to praise their virtues, to bless God for their pious examples, for their holy lives, and for their happy deaths. Besides, they celebrated these days with great expressions of love and charity to the poor, and mutual rejoicings with one another, which were very sober and temperate, and such as became the modesty and simplicity of Christians." †

"The feasts of saints," says Martene, "and especially of martyrs, were celebrated by an anniversary commemoration in the very beginning and birth-time of the Church, a circumstance which an Epistle of the Church of Smyrna concerning the martyrdom of Polycarp does not suffer us to doubt." ‡ The epistle thus referred to is preserved at full length by Eusebius. The following extract contains everything necessary for our present purpose:—" For Christ we worship as the Son of God; but the martyrs we deservedly love as the disciples and imitators of our Lord, on account of their exceeding affection to their King and Master, of whom may we only become true associates and fellow-disciples! [The execution of Polycarp being completed], we took up his bones—more valuable than precious stones, and more tried than gold—and deposited them in a place convenient. There, also, as far as we can, the Lord will grant us to assemble for the celebration of the natal day of his martyrdom in joy and gladness, both in commemo-

* *De Corona Militis*; c. 3.
† Nelson's *Festivals and Fasts*; *Preliminary Instructions*.
‡ *De Antiquis Ecclesiæ Ritibus*; lib. iv., c. 30., ¶ 2.

ration of those who have already finished their contest, and to exercise and prepare those who shall be called upon to suffer hereafter." *

The martyrdom of Polycarp took place A.D. 168, and the Church of Smyrna, in making known the particulars thereof, had only followed the example of the Church of Antioch with reference to the martyrdom of St. Ignatius (about A.D. 110), whose *Natal Day* was published in order that the Syrian Christians might on its anniversary meet together in honour of the memory of so valiant a champion and witness for their Lord.

The birthdays of the martyrs were, in fact, the days on which they suffered, as being the days on which they were born into the glories of the life eternal. "As the Nativity of Christ," are the words of Durandus, "was His entrance into this world, so their departure from this world is said to be the nativity of the martyrs."

So far we have used the word *martyr* in its modern and acquired sense of one who bears witness to his convictions at the expense of his life—one who is thus regarded as the witness *par excellence*, and beside whom there are no other witnesses at all. But the word "originally signified simply a witness. It is used in the New Testament for living witnesses. It was used in the time of the Viennese and Lyons martyrs (A.D. 177) for living witnesses; and it was used some years after by a bishop as a designation of himself at the commencement of a letter. It was not till a century later that the term 'martyr' was confined to him who had sealed his testimony by his death."†

In the year 177, "the servants of Christ who sojourn in Vienna and Lugdunum of Gaul," addressed *Letters* to several churches, and especially a *Letter*, most of which is preserved by Eusebius, "to the brethren throughout Asia

---

* Eusebius : *Ecclesiastical History*; lib. iv., c. 15.

† Donaldson's *Critical History of Christian Literature and Doctrine*; vol. iii., p. 285.

and Phrygia," giving an account of the sufferings—by death, torture, and imprisonment—of the Christians during the violent persecution which broke out in Gaul in the reign of Marcus Aurelius. This *Letter*, which seems to have been conceived with the same general purpose as that to which we have seen the *Letters* of the churches of Antioch and Smyrna were devoted, throws considerable light upon the rise of that tendency to exalt those who suffered capitally for Christ's sake, and to expect blessings from them, which to so great an extent developed itself in the succeeding century. The privileges, as so developed, which were assigned to the martyrs were, "that upon their death they were immediately admitted to the beatific vision, while other souls waited for the day of judgment to complete their happiness. That God would grant chiefly to their prayers the hastening of His kingdom, and the shortening the times of persecution. That they should have the greatest share in the resurrection of the just, which is called the first resurrection, which was the more considerable because the primitive Christians looked upon the end of the world as near at hand; and many believed that those who were partakers of the first resurrection should reign with Christ a thousand years upon earth. That the martyrs and some other perfect souls should receive no hurt or prejudice from the general conflagration of the world, when others less perfect should be purged by that universal fire from the dross they had contracted in life. That martyrdom supplied the grace conveyed both by baptism and the holy Eucharist, and entitled men to the benefits of those Sacraments—viz., remission of sins. The martyrs had, also, a considerable hand in absolving penitents, who, through fear of suffering, had lapsed into idolatry, and in restoring them to the communion of the Church."*

The faith of the more youthful ages of Christianity

* Nelson's *Festivals and Fasts of the Church of England.*

being either in direct contact with its object, or separated therefrom by only a few removes, offered as ordinary phenomena such displays of simplicity, intensity, and enthusiasm, as are now-a-days characteristic of a minority of its adherents. The offence of the Cross once being surmounted on the part of its converts, there was little to dread on this account from the chilling effects of a heartless criticism that denied its historical accessories. The Christians of the earliest times had been called to the assumption of new privileges. They found themselves suddenly promoted to "an honour unto which they were not born." The salvation of Jesus rose on them as life did on Adam. Noon, to them, sprang at once resplendent from the dusky arms of midnight. Love hath, in some sort, suffered loss of freshness in transmission to us, their descendants. We were born to the estate, and do not trace so readily what we owe. Sons of many Christian generations, and taught to lisp of our great inheritance, our ancestral beggary fades from before us, retiring almost too far off for contrast. Nearer to heathenism, from which they or their fathers had been only just redeemed, and surrounded by which they lived, it was natural, on the other hand, that the earlier Christians should have a less clear perception of many of the demands and of the scope of their religion than we who have well-nigh worn out the taint of Pagan blood.

One of the practical errors into which they were liable to fall, and into which many of them did historically fall, was the prodigality with which they lavished on a scenic martyrdom their unsought blood. Theirs was the boast of Addison—itself not in perfect taste—self-roused into defiance, and enlarged to spectacular proportions:—"See how we Christians can die!" Thus they rushed to martyrdom, forgetful that to provoke or to compel other men to acts of wrong, or even wantonly to give others the opportunity of sinning against us, is, in deepest truth, to sin against them; is to do our best to turn the streams of justice upwards to their sources, to bring back chaos, to place the world under the dominion of violence, and to enthrone the devil. There is no Christian grace which is not founded on justice *all round;* to ourselves, as from others, to others as from ourselves. Read in this light, the precept which enjoins the turning of the left cheek to the striker of the other, is applicable only where there are good grounds for believing that the left cheek, so turned, will *not* be smitten. Satan seldom puts on the appearance of an angel of light with more effect than when an unprincipled weakness masks itself as Christian humility, forbearance, and charity,

It is, of course, unnecessary to declare that we have no wish to dim a single gem on the brows of the martyrs, whose *Te Deum* is accompanied by every Christian lip, and "whose praise is in the gospel throughout all the Churches." The jewels in their crowns do not owe their lightning lustre to the "applausive thunder" of a world-ful of admirers, but to the sustaining grace of God—to the faith, love, and endurance, with which He gifted them.

Seeing that all were "not *martyrs* who were of *the martyrs*," it may be well to fix, if possible, what is the meaning of the expression *martyr*, to the etymological significance of which we have already in a few words adverted; or, to put it at once into the form in which we are at present called upon to define it—what is contained in the expression, *Christian martyr?* These two things— two which are, strictly speaking, one; for the latter is contained in the former—(1) that the martyr should suffer for Christ; and (2) that his martyrdom should be necessary. These two things, we say, are not really two; for if a martyrdom be not necessary—called for, that is, directly or indirectly, in order to prevent dishonour to the Christian name—it is the glory of self, and not of Christ, that is really sought and achieved in it. That man is as certainly a fool and a suicide who throws away his life without cause, as that man is a coward who withholds his life upon reasons shown for its surrender. The ideal martyr is he, who, neither painfully and ignobly avoiding death on the one hand, nor vaingloriously courting it on the other, simply does his duty without reference to it, and faces it only when it is brought before him, without the alternative of honourable escape, in the good providence of Him in whose hands are the times of all men (Psalm xxxi. 15).

The following *Hymnus de Martyribus*, the production of an unknown author, of the eighth or ninth century, is written in praise of those who were martyrs indeed. Its opening line will be recognised, *Sanctorum meritis inclyta gaudia*. The translation is from the Rev. Edward Caswall's "*Lyra Catholica;* containing all the Hymns of the Roman Breviary and Missal."

> Sing we the peerless deeds of martyred saints,
> Their glorious merits, and their portion blest;
> Of all the conquerors the world has seen,
>   The greatest and the best.
>
> Them in their day the insensate world abhorred,
> Because they did forsake it, Lord, for Thee;
> Finding it all a barren waste, devoid
>   Of fruit, or flower, or tree.
>
> They trod beneath them every threat of man,
> And came victorious all torments through;
> The iron hooks, which piecemeal tore their flesh,
>   Could not their souls subdue.
>
> Scourged, crucified, like sheep to slaughter led,
> Unmurmuring they met their cruel fate;
> For conscious innocence their souls upheld,
>   In patient virtue great.
>
> What tongue those joys, O Jesus, can disclose,
> Which for thy martyred saints Thou dost prepare?
> Happy who in Thy pains, thrice happy those
>   Who in Thy glory share!

Our faults, our sins, our miseries remove,
Great Deity supreme, immortal King!
Grant us Thy peace, grant us Thine endless love
   Through endless years to sing.

The most generous class of volunteer martyrs—of martyrs without a distinct and specific vocation—was made up of men who thought they were necessarily doing their Master's will and work, if they did but increase the number of witnesses to the death-sustaining power of His religion. But such a power is not one of the evidences of Christianity; if for no other reason than that it is not peculiar to Christianity. All religions have this power, in common with the negation of all religion; all noble and ignoble passions have it, as well as the negation of all passion. "There is no passion in the mind of man so weak, but it mates and masters the fear of death; and therefore, death is no such terrible enemy when a man hath so many attendants about him that can win the combat of him. Revenge triumphs over death; love slights it; honour aspires to it; grief flieth to it; fear pre-occupieth it; nay, we read after Otho the Emperor had slain himself, pity (which is the tenderest of affections), provoked many to die out of mere compassion to their sovereign, and as the truest sort of followers; nay, Seneca adds, niceness and satiety: *Cogita quamdiu eadem feceris; mori velle, non tantum fortis, aut miser, sed etiam fastidiosus potest.* A man would die, though he were neither valiant nor miserable, only upon a weariness to do the same thing so oft over and over."*

The thought of the foregoing extract from Lord Bacon is substantially presented in the following short poem, one of the "Holy Sonnets" of Dr. Donne; which may, indeed, have been indebted to the passage just quoted for its immediate suggestion. With the divine, as was becoming,

* Lord Bacon's *Essays: Of Death.*

the ultimate and most rational defiance of death has its best warrant in the prospect of a Resurrection.

> Death, be not proud; though some have called thee
> Mighty and dreadful, for thou art not so;
> For those whom thou think'st thou dost overthrow
> Die not, poor Death, nor yet canst thou kill me:
> From rest and sleep, which but thy pictures be,
> Much pleasure, then from thee much more, must flow,
> And soonest our best men with thee do go—
> Rest of their bones, and soul's delivery,
> Thou art slave to fate, chance, kings, and desperate men,
> And doth with poison, war, and sickness dwell;
> And poppy, or charms, can make us sleep as well,
> And better than thy stroke. Why swell'st thou then?
> Our short sleep past, we wake eternally,
> And Death shall be no more: Death, thou shalt die!

In another class of volunteer sufferers, only, but still really, less generous than the first, the tendency to an uncalled-for sacrifice arose from a desire to anticipate the joys of an assured and certain Heaven. With a pious perversity they seem to have persuaded themselves that that evil was good, of which they were the victims. Yet if amidst their bravely endured tortures they could but have analysed their fanaticism, they must have recognised a subtler form of self-love intruding on their devotion to Christ. The riddle of the existence of evil is too intricate to excuse its being rendered more involved by the importation of amateur suffering. The pain and affliction which God sends, are sent autocratically—it is HE who sends them; but it is absurd to suppose that He who has no pleasure in the death of the wicked, can have more in the death of the righteous. As it would be a much misplaced loyalty that should lead a subject to force himself upon a royal circle on a state occasion without a royal command; so it would be a very blind loyalty to the King of Heaven, to attempt the approaches of His court by deputy of the violence of other men. It is not because there are many mansions in the house of the Divine Father, that we are to endeavour to occupy our place unbidden; not because there is a marriage feast in progress, that we are to enter at any stage we please. Human charity prays that when the souls of those who honestly believed themselves to be martyrs, and were not, present themselves for judgment, the question will not be fatally pressed, " Who hath required this at your hands?"

Another type of *soi-disant* martyr was furnished by men from whom was withheld this crowning grace—that the conviction of the intellect, the enlightenment of the conscience, and the purity of the life should march *pari passu*, and should develop symmetrically. To such men it was an object to be able to compound by death for the surrender of a life to law and holiness; for to such men the taming of their passions would be scarcely less than the bending of a planet to the allegiance of an alien system. But to a spasmodic obedience, and especially to an external one, they were equal; it was little for them to dash their heads against the obvious wall of martyrdom.

Lastly, when the incentives to become martyrs were so many and so great, on account of the honours and privileges referred to them severally in earth and heaven, it is not wonderful that some should put forth unholy hands to grasp the martyr's crown, even at the expense of bearing the martyr's peculiar cross. The case of such men was simply one of ignoble barter; they were to become members of the aristocracy of heaven, in exchange for a temporary passion and the death-pang of a moment. They were as much followers of Empedocles as followers of Jesus; and they rushed upon martyrdom with no more spiritual perception than a Viking of later times entered upon his dying voyage into the infinite ocean, or an Arab propagandist amidst the throes of an embattled death gasped and foamed for his carnal Paradise.

Has therefore a true martyr for Christ no proper glory, no peculiar distinction? Certainly he has; and especially in this—that he is able to give an actual and sensible proof of the intensity and stability of those convictions which are potentially as strong in the mind of every honest believer. Martyrdom is the sign and symbol, so to speak, in a sacrament of faith, in which a life is freely yielded because a higher life had antecedently been freely given—a body offered up a sacrifice to death, because a sinless Body had been Self-broken into the Bread of Life.

From these general considerations of martyrdom, we turn more especially to the prince and leader of the martyrs. We said a few pages back, that it was not impossible, seeing how the commemorations of martyrs took hold upon an Apostolic admonition, that the first commemoration of a martyr might be only a year later than the nativity of the martyr commemorated. Such a commemoration would, of course, at first be local or provincial only; and would require time to win its way to universality. What is certain about St. Stephen's Day is that it was an established feast throughout the Eastern Church in the fourth century, and that it had, even then, been placed in the calendar on the day next after Christmas. "Behold!" exclaims Gregory Nyssen, "we receive a feast from a feast, and grace for grace. Yesterday the Lord of the Universe fed us; to-day a follower of the Lord. How is this done by one and the other? By the first, by putting on humanity for us; by the second, by laying aside humanity for our example." *
St. Augustine, who everywhere manifests an extraordinary reverence for the memory of St. Stephen, and who was constantly introducing him into his works, † commences several of the *Sermons* which bear the title *In Natali Sancti Stephani*, with the same sentiments :—" Yesterday we celebrated the Nativity of our Lord and Saviour; to-day,

---
* *Encomium in Sanctum Stephanum Protomartyrem.*
† See *De Civitate Dei*; lib. xxii., c. viii., ¶ 15, etc.

with the greatest veneration, we commemorate the passion of the holy martyr Stephen. Yesterday we were bought with a price; to-day we are provoked to the imitation of an example. Therefore, well is the festivity of the day conjoined with the solemnity of yesterday, seeing that believing in one carries us to life; and following the other, leads us to a crown." The two fathers, therefore, who severally establish the fact of the general observance of St. Stephen's day in the Eastern Church in the fourth century, and in the Western Church in the fifth, show conclusively that the day was the day next after Christmas, that is, the 26th of December; to which date the anniversary had been transferred from the month of August, to which it really belonged, on the ground that the Nativity of the first martyr deserved to occupy the nearest possible place to the Nativity of his Lord. To this subject we shall have occasion shortly to recur, when we come to treat of the Feasts of St. John the Evangelist, and the Holy Innocents.

The history of St. Stephen, as recorded by St. Luke in the Acts of the Apostles, is as well known as it is short, graphic, and comprehensive; so that we do nearly all that is necessary in the way of biography, when we transcribe Dr. Neale's version of a *Sequence* for St. Stephen's day,[*] which is full of allusions to the sacred narrative. Four stanzas are left untranslated of the original poem, which has been considered by some to be the masterpiece of its author, Adam of St. Victor; who was a canon regular of Saint-Victor-es-Paris, where he died in the year 1177. He was interred in the cloister of his Abbey, where, up to the time of the Revolution of 1789, might have be seen his epitaph, in fourteen verses, of which two are sufficiently remarkable:—

> Unde superbit homo? cujus conceptio culpa,
> Nasci pœna, labor vita, necesse mori.

[*] *Mediæval Hymns and Sequences;* translated by J. M. Neale, D.D.

ST. STEPHEN'S DAY.

Yesterday, with exultation
Joined the world in celebration
    Of her promised SAVIOUR's birth;
Yesterday, the angel nation
Poured the strains of jubilation
    O'er the Monarch born on earth.

But to-day, o'er death victorious,
By his faith and actions glorious,
    By his miracles renowned,
Dared the Deacon Protomartyr,
Earthly life for Heaven to barter,
    Faithful 'midst the faithless found.

Forward, champion, in thy quarrel!
Certain of a certain laurel,
    Holy Stephen, persevere!
Perjured witnesses confounding,
Satan's Synagogue astounding
    By thy doctrine true and clear.

Lo! in Heaven *thy* Witness liveth:
Bright and faithful proof He giveth
    Of His martyr's blamelessness:
Thou by name *a Crown* impliest;
Meekly then in pangs thou diest
    For the Crown of Righteousness!

For a crown that fadeth never,
Bear the torturer's brief endeavour;
    Victory waits to end the strife:
Death shall be thy birth's beginning,
And life's losing be the winning
    Of the true and better Life.

Whom the HOLY GHOST endueth,
Whom celestial sight imbueth,
    Stephen penetrates the skies;
There GOD's fullest glory viewing,
There his victor strength renewing,
    For his near reward he sighs.

See as Jewish foes invade thee,
See how Jesus *stands* to aid thee:

   Stands to guard His champion's death :*
   Cry that opened Heaven is shown thee :
   Cry that JESUS waits to own thee :
    Cry it with thy latest breath!

   As the dying Martyr kneeleth,
   For his murderers he appealeth,
   And his prayer their pardon sealeth,
    For their madness grieving sore;
   Then in CHRIST he sleepeth sweetly,
   Who his pattern kept completely,
   And with CHRIST he reigneth meetly,
    Martyr first-fruits, evermore! Amen.

  The relics of St. Stephen are said to have been discovered through a dream, nearly four hundred years after his death, and were then translated from Jerusalem to Rome, and deposited in the same tomb with those of St. Laurence.

  The fathers generally attribute to St. Stephen a kind of primacy over the other deacons. St. Augustine, in one of his many *Sermons* about St. Stephen, calls him *primicerius diaconorum*; Lucian, the priest to whom the revelation of his body was vouchsafed, entitles him *archidiaconus* ;† and St. Chrysostom, in a *Homily on Psalm* L., speaks of him as *chief of the deacons*. Cornelius à Lapide, the exhaustive commentator, writes that St. Stephen was *Primus et quasi Princeps Diaconorum;* and proceeds to quote approvingly another writer, who says "that not only was St. Stephen the chief of the deacons, but that he was *inter Apostolos Apostolus, Propheta inter Prophetas, Doctor inter Doctores.*"‡

  The martyrdom of St. Stephen is believed to have taken place in the year 34; and the several incidents and circumstances which give to his history a glory above that of the generality of saints and martyrs, have been formally grouped

---

* Our Lord's *standing* at the right hand of the FATHER, here and here only, as a Friend to sympathize, as a Champion to help, is continually dwelt on by mediæval writers. (See page 46).

† *Epistola de Revelatione Corporis Stephani.*

‡ *Commentaria in Acta Apostolorum.*

into six classes. (1). He was distinguished for the angelic radiance which shone before the Council, and which has been aptly paralleled by St. Chrysostom and others with the intolerable glory of Moses as he descended from Mount Sinai. This angelic radiance, which had a natural base in the extreme beauty of his youthful person, symbolized the purity of his life and heart, his faithfulness to his Master's cause, and the divine rays of grace with which his soul was penetrated. (2). St. Stephen, as we have more than once said already, was the protomartyr of Christianity. (3). The miraculous powers with which he had been invested in his life-time, attached to his memorials and monuments —if we may believe various circumstantial narratives avouched by so grave an authority as St. Augustine—after his death, and before the discovery of his remains by Lucian. (4). To St. Stephen it was given to see the heavens opened, and Jesus *standing* at the right hand of God—not sitting, as in the Creed, in his capacity of Judge, but standing as an advocate to plead his cause while still his victory was incomplete; and standing, moreover, to receive him as a respected guest after his triumphant warfare had been accomplished. (5). The moral phenomena of his martyrdom were in many respects conformable with the Passion of our Lord. Both the Saviour and His protomartyr were charged with the same form of blasphemy. As Jesus had commended His departing spirit to the hands of His Heavenly Father; so Stephen prayed that his might be received by the Lord Jesus. As Jesus had prayed for His executioners, so did Stephen intercede in behalf of his murderers:— "Lord, lay not this sin to their charge." The Venerable Bede points out what, so far as we know—but the observation is so natural, that it must have been in circulation at a very early period—St. Augustine was the first to remark, that Stephen, when praying for himself, prayed standing; when he wished to plead for his enemies, he sank upon his knees. Even in his death-pangs he begat the most illustrious propagator of the faith for which he suffered. "O burning love!" exclaims St. Augustine. "O love without example! * * * If Stephen had not prayed, the church had had no Paul;" a sentiment which the same father repeats:—"It was the prayer of Stephen which gave Paul to the Church."*

It is in this connection that we may introduce from Dr. Monsell's "Parish Musings" his hymn for St. Stephen's Day, entitled, "The Gentle Witness."

> First of the martyred throng
>   To join his Lord above;
> First to commence the endless song
>   Of His redeeming love;
> First to essay the spear and shield,
> The holy Stephen sought the field.
>
> First to obtain a crown—
>   First—by the mercy-seat—
> To lay the blood-bought trophy down
>   At its own Owner's feet;
> Through the grave-gates his Saviour burst—
> He homeward, heavenward, entered first.
>
> Men thought the sufferer dead,
>   And high exultings kept;
> But on his blood-stained, stony bed,
>   The saint serenely slept.
> Wrapped in the banner of the cross,
> His all the gain—theirs all the loss.
>
> Lord, grant Thy grace, that we,
>   Whate'er our lot may prove,
> May learn his high fidelity,
>   His deep forgiving love;
> The boldness that dare part with life,
> And yet be *gentle* in the strife.

(6). The sixth and last distinction of St. Stephen is, that by his death he attained to each of what the schoolmen call the three aureoles, which marked the spiritual degrees of

* *Sermo in Natali Apostolorum Petri et Pauli.*

martyrs, doctors, and virgins, in the glory of the blessed. The red aureole of martyrdom belongs to St. Stephen, for he was the protomartyr; the white aureole of virginity is due to his chastity; and the aureole of the doctors is his for that discourse (Acts vii.) which the impatient malice of his enemies compelled him to leave so magnificently incomplete.

It may be allowed, in conclusion, to repeat that martyrdom is not one of the evidences of Christianity. Proving only the force of internal and subjective convictions, it is of little value as a witness to the external and objective truth of those principles for which death is encountered.* Thrice happy they who, like St. Stephen, contend aright for the right! To them the church militant exultingly accords the honour of being enrolled among that "noble army" who swell the *Te Deum* of cherubim and seraphim.

* Bishop Latimer, himself a martyr, has, in his *Fourth Sermon before the King* (Edward VI.), made substantially the same assertion:— "This is no good argument, my friends: 'A man seemeth not to feare death, therefore hys cause is good.' This is a deceaveable argument: 'He went to his death boldly; *ergo*, he standeth in a just quarrel.'" —*Sermons. Ed.* 1575-7; *Fols.* 55 *and* 55b.

St. John the Evangelist's Day.

December 27.

BETWEEN the festival of St. Stephen, the martyr in will and deed, and that of the Holy Innocents, martyrs in fact, but not in intention, the festival of St. John the Evangelist occupies a place as representing the intermediate class of martyrs in will but not in deed. St. John is the only one of the Apostles who is ascertained to be eligible for this particular position; for of him alone is it safe to conclude that he was not called upon to exhibit martyrdom *in both kinds*. Mr. L'Estrange conjectures that as a co-efficient with the desire of the Church to group together the celebrations of the typical martyrs, and to place all in their desired place in the immediate neighbourhood of the Nativity, there was a feeling of inconvenience arising from the fact of the incidence of the festival of St. John the Evangelist upon the same day as that of St. John the Baptist; a circumstance—both saints being so eminent as to demand a separate day—which had the effect of unsettling the festival of the Evangelist, which then naturally gravitated as near as possible to the Nativity of the Master he had loved and served so long and so well.[*]

It is proper, on the broadest grounds, that in the calendar of a religion which recognises the heart as the central abode

[*] *Alliance of Divine Offices.*

of purity; which regards thought as the root, flower, and fruit of action, and will as the subtlest form of deed; which proclaims that we are chiefly that which we chiefly love or affect, and which more and more jealously than any other system that the world has seen, guards the awful marches that separate sin from crime—it is proper, we say, that in the calendar of such a religion, there should be a day set apart to the apotheosis of Motive.

There is no mention of the festival of St. John the Evangelist in the records of the early centuries. According to Mr. Riddle, our own Venerable Bede is the first writer in whose works any trace of it occurs. Perhaps the observance of it, which was at first only local, became universal in the thirteenth century.

St. John was a native of Galilee, the son of Zebedee and Salome, and the younger brother of St. James the Greater, with whom he followed the business of a fisherman until his call to attend the Saviour, which is supposed to have occurred while he was yet under thirty years of age, so that he was considerably the youngest of all the Apostles.

It is unnecessary to attempt to reproduce in precise narrative sequence such events as are recorded in the Holy Gospels concerning the history of St. John, who appears to have been profound and speculative beyond his breeding, and of greater natural cultivation than his compeers, so that he was renowned throughout the ancient Church for a wisdom in advance of all the Apostles. The proof of this is found in the fact that whereas the other Evangelists occupy themselves more or less minutely with the humanity of Christ, he at once plunges into the sea of His Divinity, and the opening of his Gospel has been reckoned so splendid as to be beyond not only the wont, but even beyond the exceptions, of Scriptural magnificence. "If in the beginning of his Gospel," are words referred to the Venerable Bede, "John had flown higher, all the world would not have been able to understand him."

The reasons which weighed with the Evangelist in the inditing of his Gospel were twofold. In the first place, he was anxious to supply those circumstances in the life of Christ which the other Evangelists had omitted;* and in the second, as St. Jerome tells us, he wished to maintain, against a pestilent heresy that denied it, the Divinity of the Logos. "St. John, last of all the Evangelists, wrote his Gospel at the request of the bishops in Asia, that he might refute Cerinthus, and especially Ebion, who taught that Christ first came into existence in the womb of His mother."† But even the Gospel of St. John is not the measure of its author's genius, as is testified by his *Epistles* and his *Apocalypse*, concerning which last, the same St. Jerome writes: "There are in it nearly as many mysteries (*sacramenta*) as words."‡

Of the love with which Christ pre-eminently regarded St. John, there have been many explanations, and the fathers have generally recognised five several reasons for so remarkable and special an affection. The first is that which is based on their kinship; for whether regard be had to the kinship of the spirit or the flesh, John was equally related to his Divine Master. The second is that which is founded on their common celibacy; and the third on the fact, that in manner and disposition, as well as in name, John was *Johannes*, or *gratiosus*, amiable and courteous. The fourth reason has reference to the age of John as compared with the other Apostles; and those who advance it, presume, without sufficient authority, that John was only eighteen years old at the time of his vocation to the discipleship. The fifth and last reason for the singular love of the Saviour for St. John, lay in the fact that the "disciple whom Jesus loved," returned that love with a unique

* Eusebius: *Ecclesiastical History*, lib. iii., c. 24.
† St. Jerome: *De Viris Illustribus*.
‡ St. Jerome: *Epistola* liii. *Ad Paulinum; De Studio Scripturarum*.

ardour and devotion. This zealous and eloquent affection it was which procured for John, jointly with his brother James, the title of Boanerges, the "sons of thunder" (Mark iii. 17). Indeed, it was love to Christ, uncorrected, as for the moment it was, by reason and discretion, that dictated such outbreaks as the Gospels or ecclesiastical historians preserve of his exceptional narrowness, jealousy, and bigotry. His love for his Master led to a love for the disciples of his Master; and his life was a continued inculcation of the duty of Christian affection. When at the point of death he is recorded to have diligently repeated that grand summary of all his teachings: "Little children, love one another;" giving as a reason for his enforcement of the maxim, that "if this precept stood, it was all-sufficient."

> Love is the first, the great command, the test,
> The sovereign law, including all the rest;
> The evangelic code on love depends,
> That syllable all duty comprehends;
> Love's the propensive Fontal of our wills,
> From that all passions are but various rills;
> Our love can never rise to an excess,
> Within no bounds can ever acquiesce;
> Love to perfection ever strives to soar,
> When it loves most, grieves it can love no more;
> Loves God with all the heart, soul, strength, and mind,
> Loves boundless Love, with a love unconfined.

The foregoing lines are from Bishop Ken's long and almost utterly unread poem of "Hymnotheo: or, the Penitent," which sets forth in almost every couplet the affection with which St. John regarded not only the aggregate, but also the individuals, and especially the youth, of his flock at Ephesus. The historical nucleus of the poem is to be found in Eusebius.[*]

[*] *Ecclesiastical History;* lib. iii., c. 23.

Within the narrowest circle of those who were admitted to the intimacy of Christ, St. John stood alone; whilst within a circle a little more extended, he was joined by James and Peter. It was John who leaned upon the breast of Jesus; and he was one of the three who were present at the raising of the daughter of Jairus, at the transfiguration on Mount Tabor, and at the agony and bloody sweat in the Garden of Gethsemane. It was to John that the Crucified commended the care of His mother; so that, in words which have been ascribed to St. Ambrose, " the Author of our religion left a most excellent will, by which He bequeathed His cross to His Apostles; Paradise to the penitent thief; His body to the Jews; His spirit to His heavenly Father; but John as a bridegroom to His virgin mother."

It was this most pathetic and endearing of legacies which prevented St. John from immediately entering upon his apostolic work in Asia, which, after Pentecost, had been assigned to him as his province. He is said to have dwelt in a house which he possessed at Jerusalem, at least until the death of the blessed Virgin (about A. D. 48). Some time afterwards, he set out on his travels through Asia, and industriously gave himself to the task of propagating Christianity, preaching the gospel where it had not yet been proclaimed, and confirming it where it was already planted. Many churches of note and eminence were of his foundation—Smyrna, Pergamus, Thyatira, Sardis, Philadelphia, Laodicea, and others; but his chief place of residence was at Ephesus, where St. Paul had many years before settled a church, in which he had placed St. Timothy as Bishop. His teaching is believed to have extended eastward beyond the limits of Asia Minor, and to have penetrated as far as Parthia and India.

In the year 95, St. John, a martyr in will, was called upon to "drink of the cup" of our blessed Lord. He was apprehended at Ephesus, and sent prisoner to Rome;

where, in spite of his venerable age, the Emperor Domitian ordered him to be cast into a caldron of boiling oil. From the death which seemed inevitable, the miraculous providence of his heavenly Father saw good to deliver him; and he came out of his terrible bath uninjured.*

This glorious triumph of St. John over the devices of his tormentors, took place near the *Porta Latina*, so called because it was on the road to Latium; and it is to this day commemorated on the site of its occurrence by a circular chapel which has its dedication to *San Giovanni in Oleo*. A festival was instituted in honour of the signal deliverance of the Evangelist, which falls on the 6th of May, and is known as the day of St. John *ante Portam Latinam*. It is objected by Hospinian that the circumstances of the caldron of boiling oil are "narrated by Tertullian, while St. Jerome makes no mention of them; and there are some persons who say that the whole matter is uncertain, to such an extent that there is even a disagreement as to the locality, whether it was Rome or Ephesus."†

The miracle of St. John's preservation took so little effect upon the insensate Domitian, that the Apostle was banished by the imperial command to a desolate island in the Ægean, called Patmos; where he remained for many months, instructing the inhabitants in the faith of Christ, and writing his majestic Apocalypse. His venerable age and his affinity with childhood, establish the propriety of poetically illustrating this and the antecedent times of St. John's life by a poem for his day from "Verses for Holy Seasons," by C. F. H., now Mrs. Alexander, wife of the Bishop of Derry, from whose pen more than one poem of graphic power and tenderness have startled and charmed her readers. The volume from which we quote was

* Tertullian: *Liber de Prescriptionibus adversos Hæreticos*; c. 36.
† *De Origine Festorum Christianorum*.

published in 1846; and Dr. Hook, then of Leeds, says of it in a preface which he penned for it, that it "may be regarded as a *Christian Year* for children." It is in fact "to the author of the *Christian Year*, that this attempt to adopt the great principle of his immortal work to the exigencies of the school room is inscribed with feelings of reverence and respect by one of the many thousands who have profited by his labours."

> There lies a little lonely isle
>   Where dark the salt waves run,
> And Grecian fishers dry their nets
>   Against the eastern sun;
>
> And, many a hundred years ago,
>   Within that island fair
> There dwelt an exiled Jewish man,
>   A man of reverend air;
>
> His eye was bright as setting suns,
>   His aged form unbent;
> The little children following,
>   He blest them as he went.
>
> That head, beloved, at supper time
>   Had leant on JESUS' breast;
> That honoured hand had taken home
>   His Mother for a guest;
>
> That eye had seen in glorious trance,
>   Mysterious things to be,
> Wild visions of impending doom
>   On heaven, and earth, and sea;
>
> His pen had writ of times to come,
>   Of dearer times bygone;
> He was the fisher's chosen son,
>   The LORD's beloved Saint John.
>
> And he had drunk his Master's cup
>   So long, so patiently,
> And now he lingered there, the last,
>   Till CHRIST should set him free.

> I wish I'd lived in those old times,
>   And been a Grecian child,
> To hear that old man's blessing kind,
>   To meet him when he smiled,
>
> To learn the words of holy love
>   That ever from his lips
> Fell, gentle as the evening dew
>   The thirsty blossom sips.
>
> But love endureth through all age;
>   Nor time, nor distance drear,
> Divide the living and the dead,
>   Of CHRIST's communion dear.
>
> For all His saints in Him are one;
>   The exile o'er the sea,
> The child within his English home,
>   The struggling, and the free.
>
> The good Saint John hath rest at last;
>   He wears the promised crown;
> And still by the dear church he watched,
>   His words are handed down;
>
> And we shall meet him, not as once
>   On that far island shore,
> But where apostles, martyrs, saints,
>   Have peace for evermore.

When the exiles of Domitian's brutal rule were recalled by his gentler successor, Nerva, St. John returned to Asia, his ancient charge, but chiefly fixed his abode at Ephesus,[*] where St. Timothy, the Bishop, had been lately martyred by the people, for urging upon them the abandonment of their pagan games and holidays. With the assistance of seven bishops, St. John administered the affairs of his important province, in which employment he continued till his death, A.D. 101, when he was about ninety-eight years of

---

[*] Eusebius: *Ecclesiastical History;* lib. iii. c. 20.

age. The end of St. John, the latest survivor of all the apostolic band, was so peaceful as to lead many of the ancients, down to the time of St. Augustine, to imagine that he did not actually resign his breath, but only fell into a sleep, from which he was not to awake till the consummation of all things. It was thus that they persisted in interpreting, in spite of the instant disclaimer of such a sense by the Speaker Himself, the answer of our Lord to Peter's question:—"If I will that he tarry till I come, what is that to thee?" (John xxi. 22.)

The accounts of St. John's death are not perfectly uniform in every particular. The one most favoured by the industrious Hildebrand is to the following effect:—"At the feast of the Passover, when St. John was engaged about the divine offices, and had preached a sermon before the congregation, he added prayers of burning devotion for the Church, especially of Ephesus, and partook of the Eucharist. This being done, he commanded a tomb to be made, entering into which, with hands outstretched to heaven, he blessed the Church with the formula, *Filioli, Pax vobiscum*. Having so said, he reclined in the tomb, like one sleeping, and was covered with earth, amidst the lamentations of the church at Ephesus."*

Such was the termination of the long life of one whose unique honour it was to be at once an Apostle, an Evangelist, a Prophet, and a Martyr in everything short of the actual and fatal consummation of self-sacrifice. Amidst the various distinctions of so great a name, the Church has ever delighted to think of him chiefly in connection with that heavenly grace of which he was an incarnate exposition—that grace of which, as he himself said that it alone was sufficient, so another apostle said that "charity never faileth," and that though there "abide faith, hope, charity, these three; the greatest of these is charity." The senti-

---

* Joachim Hildebrand: *De Diebus Festis Libellus*.

ments of St. John, and the words of St. Paul, are enforced in the following poem, by Matthew Prior, who forbore what Cowper fondly called his "easy jingle," and his easier morals, to do honour to "Charity" in a "Paraphrase on the thirteenth chapter of the First Epistle to the Corinthians."

Did sweeter sounds adorn my flowing tongue
Than ever man pronounced or angel sung ;
Had I all knowledge, human and divine,
That thought can reach, or science can define ;
And had I power to give that knowledge birth
In all the speeches of the babbling earth ;
Did Shadrach's zeal my glowing breast inspire,
To weary tortures, and rejoice in fire ;
Or had I faith like that which Israel saw,
When Moses gave them miracles and law ;
Yet gracious Charity ! indulgent guest !
Were not thy power exerted in my breast,
Those speeches would send up unheeded prayer,
That scorn of life would be but wild despair ;
A cymbal's sound were better than my voice ;
My faith were form, my eloquence were noise.
Charity ! decent, modest, easy, kind,
Softens the high, and rears the abject mind ;
Knows the just reins and gentle hand to guide
Betwixt vile shame and arbitrary pride.
Not soon provoked, she easily forgives,
And much she suffers, as she much believes ;
Soft peace she brings wherever she arrives ;
She builds our quiet, as she forms our lives ;
Lays the rough paths of peevish nature even,
And opens in each heart a little heaven.

Each other gift which God on man bestows,
Its proper bounds and due restriction knows ;
To one fixed purpose dedicates its power,
And, finishing its act, exists no more.
Thus in obedience to what heaven decrees,
Knowledge shall fail, and prophecy shall cease ;
But lasting Charity's more ample sway,
Nor bound by time, nor subject to decay,

In happy triumph shall for ever live,
And endless good diffuse, and endless praise receive.
 As through the artist's intervening glass,
Our eye observes the distant planets pass,
A little we discover, but allow
That more remains unseen than art can show;
So whilst our mind its knowledge would improve
(Its feeble ray intent on things above),
High as we may we lift our reason up,
By Faith directed, and confirmed by Hope;
Yet are we able only to survey
Dawnings of beams and promises of day.
Heaven's fuller effluence mocks our dazzled sight,
Too great its swiftness, and too strong its light.
 But soon the mediate clouds shall be dispelled,
The sun shall soon be face to face beheld,
In all his robes, with all his glory on,
Seated sublime on his meridian throne.
 Then constant Faith and holy Hope shall die,
One lost in certainty, and one in joy;
Whilst thou, more happy power, fair Charity,
Triumphant sister, greatest of the three,
Thy office and thy nature still the same,
Lasting thy lamp, and unconsumed thy flame,
Shalt still survive—
Shalt stand before the host of Heaven confest,
For ever blessing, and for ever blest!

The Innocents' Day.

December 28.

As rays around the source of light
Stream upward ere he glow in sight,
And watching by his future flight
    Set the clear heavens on fire;
So on the King of Martyrs wait
Three chosen bands, in royal state,
And all earth owns, of good and great,
    Is gathered in that choir.

One presses on, and welcomes death:
One calmly yields his willing breath,
Nor slow, nor hurrying, but in faith
    Content to die or live:
And some, the darlings of their Lord,
Play smiling with the flame and sword,
And, ere they speak, to his sure word
    Unconscious witness give.

        The Christian Year: St. Stephen's Day.

TO the early Church it seemed fit that the commemorations of the representatives of the various orders of martyrdom should follow as closely as possible upon the celebration of the Nativity of their Lord, the degree of nearness to which anniversary was determined by their rank in the "noble army." "For, according to ancient classification, martyrs are of three kinds. The first grade are martyrs both in will and deed, as St. Stephen, who was not only willing to suffer for Christ, but was, in fact, put to death for His sake. Others are martyrs in will, but not in deed; as St. John the Evangelist who was ready to die for Christ, but did not undergo actual martyrdom. And, lastly, others are martyrs in deed, although not in will, as the Innocents, who were slain for Christ before they had attained to the use of reason."*

The Festival of St. Stephen, as that of the most illustrious representative of the highest order of martyrdom, was, by way of a peculiar honour, transferred from the historical anniversary of his passion—or, to speak ecclesiastically, of his *nativity*—to the day next succeeding the anniversary of the birth of Jesus; and a transfer, for a similar purpose, of the true day of the death of St. John the Evangelist, the typical martyr of the second order, was made to the day following the feast of St. Stephen. To these, on the third day after Christmas, was at length added the solemnity of the representative martyrs of the third order, those "sweet flowers of martyrdom" the Jewish children who were put to death by order of Herod (Matthew ii. 16-18). "We have no means of determining, precisely," Mr Riddle observes, "at what time these three commemorations began to be connected with the festival of the Nativity. The dates of the several commemorations themselves are various; and some of them may have existed before the celebration of the Nativity as a distinct festival. † The first of the three which was placed in connection with the Nativity appears to be St. Stephen's day. ‡ The feast of the Innocents is connected with that of our Lord's birth by

---

* Durandus: *Rationale Divinorum Officiorum*.

† The Nativity and the Epiphany of Christ were at first conjoined in one celebration. See the Paper on Epiphany.

‡ See extracts from the *Homilies* by Gregory Nyssen and St. Augustine, in which the festival of St. Stephen alone is connected with the Nativity; pp. 42 and 43.

Augustine, Leo, and Fulgentius; but it is observable that it is mentioned in their Homilies for the Epiphany, not in homilies for Christmas. Bernard of Clairvaux is the earliest writer in whose works we find mention of the four feasts in conjunction." *

The tender age of the infant martyrs leaves no virtue to be expressly celebrated on their anniversary, except that after which they are named. Spotless and innocent lambs, they were fit to be folded in the fold of God; spotless and innocent flowers, they were fit to be planted on the terraces of Heaven. In his "Steps to the Temple," and in a very short poem "Upon the Infant Martyrs," Crashaw thus alludes to their typical virtue:—

> To see both blended in one flood,
> The mothers' milk, the infants' blood,
> Makes me doubt if heaven will gather
> Roses hence, or lilies rather.

There has been some amount of speculation as to the number of martyred Innocents; one computation, common to the Greek and Æthiopian churches, making it reach to fourteen thousand. So high a number is open to two obections—first, as being too large for the locality to furnish; and, second as being too large even for the insane cruelty of a monster so reckless and insatiable as Herod. They who care to argue for the credibility of so vast a number, emphasize and extend the fact that it was the children "from two years old and under," not of Bethlehem only, but of "all the coasts thereof" who were collected within a practicable area, possibly under pretence of taxation; whilst the second objection falls self-answered on a moment's consideration of the ascertained achievements of Herod in the way of arbitrary and senseless bloodshed. "It was that HEROD," Neander observes, "whose crimes, committed in violation of every natural feeling, ever urged

* *Manual of Christian Antiquities.*

him on to new deeds of cruelty, whose path to the throne, and whose throne itself, were stained with human blood; whose vengeance against conspirators, not satiated with their own destruction, demanded that of their whole families (Joseph. Archæol. xv. viii. § 4); whose rage was hot, up to the very hour of his death, against his nearest kindred: whose wife, Mariamne, and three sons, Alexander, Aristobulus, and Antipater, fell victims to his suspicions, the last just before his death; who, in a word, certainly deserved that the Emperor Augustus should have said of him, *Herodis mallem porcus esse, quam filius.* It was that HEROD, who, at the close of a blood-stained life of seventy years, goaded by the furies of an evil conscience, racked by a painful and incurable disease, waiting for death, but desiring life, raging against God and man, and maddened by the thought that the Jews, instead of bewailing his death, would rejoice over it as the greatest of blessings, commanded the worthies of the nation to be assembled in the Circus, and issued a secret order that, after his death, they should all be slain together, so that *their* kindred, at least, might have cause to weep for his death. Can we deem the crime of sacrificing a few children to his rage and blind suspicions too atrocious for such a monster?"*

Whether the number of the massacred infants were greater or less, it was such as to suggest to the Evangelist a fulfilment of "that which was spoken of by Jeremy the Prophet, saying, 'In Rama was there a voice heard, lamentation and weeping, and great mourning, Rachel weeping for her children, and would not be comforted, because they are not'" (Matthew ii. 17, 18). And the Church, who, as a spiritual mother, has adopted these infants, followed in her offices for the day the example of Rachel, the typical mother of the prophet. She has forgotten her accustomed joy and exultation at the triumphs

---

* Neander's *Life of Jesus Christ.*

of the martyrs, in the maternal grief that so many buds of promise should never have opened upon her lap. "The office throughout the day was one of sorrow; in many places *Gloria in Excelsis* was not sung; in some not even the *Gloria Patri*."*

It is mentioned by Daniel that "in the more ancient Breviaries that had come under his observation, the Feast of the Holy Innocents had no hymns peculiar to itself; but its hymns are those of the Nativity or of the Common of Martyrs. This custom, however, did not prevail in all the churches; for, in the books of Wimpfelingius, Bebelius, Clichtovæus, and Cassander, our most beautiful hymn, *Salvete Flores Martyrum,* is expressly referred to that feast. It was originally compiled from a longer hymn on the Epiphany—*Quicumque Christum quæritis*—and the verses selected are not in every case the same."† Its author was Prudentius, a distinguished Christian poet of the fourth century; and the following translation has the advantage of coming from the pen of the Rev. John Keble, by whom it was contributed to the *Salisbury Hymnal*. It has been lately republished in a volume of posthumous issue, entitled "Miscellaneous Poems."

> Hail, martyr-flowers, who gleaming forth,
>   Just on the edge of your brief day,
> By Christ's keen foe were swept from earth,
>   As rosebuds by the whirlwind's sway!
>
> The first-fruits unto Christ are ye,
>   His lambs new-slain, a tender sort,
> E'en by the shrine in childlike glee
>   Ye with your palms and garlands sport.
>
> Ah! what avails so dire a doom?
>   What boots the stain on Herod's soul?
> The One of many 'scapes the tomb,
>   The Christ is gone, unharmed and whole.

* *Kalendar of the English Church.*
† *Thesaurus Hymnologicus.*

> Far from their streaming blood who shared
>   His birth-hour, He at rest is laid:
> The Virgin-born that steel hath spared,
>   Which many a matron childless made.
>
> So did one child of yore elude
>   The wild laws of the wicked king,
> With likeness of the Christ endued,
>   Ordained His people home to bring.

If the claim of the Holy Innocents to the title of martyrs seem to be incomplete on account of their ignorance of the cause for which they involuntarily suffered, it may be fortified by the fitness of commemorating such members of a class who were always dear to the heart of Christ. Christianity is, indeed, a gospel of childhood; whose mission it is to recover to the man, hardened with the cares and the wisdom of the world, the tenderness and the guilelessness of infancy. "Wisdom," it has been said, and *à fortiori* the wisdom of God—

> "Wisdom is found with children at her knee."

The young take kindly to the kingdom of heaven. Life hangs loosely about the child; the *torture* of death—the twisting and wrenching asunder of an inveterate habit of living—comes upon the mature and the aged, for the love of life grows with its continuance. The unaccustomed soul, scarcely weaned from the milk of heaven, finds little to attract in the calculations of earth; whilst a long life, the youth of which is unrenewed by religion, becomes, day by day, more and more of a process by which it is unfitted for death—more and more of a burlesque procession from the infinite to bagatelle. "A certain Rabbin," writes Lord Bacon, "upon the text, 'Your young men shall see visions, and your old men shall dream dreams,' inferreth that young men are admitted nearer to God than old, because vision is a clearer revelation than a dream: and, certainly, the more a man drinketh of the world the more it intoxicateth: and age doth profit rather in the powers of understanding than in the virtues of the will and affections."* When the natural youth of heart, and the connatural sympathy, is in danger of leaving a man, then is seen the practical philosophy of Christianity to offer a perpetual renewal and *Jouvence;* to fix eternally that which was in peril of vanishing for ever.

With no more particular introduction than this, we here transcribe Wordsworth's *Ode*, in which the bane and the antidote are both brought before the reader. It has for its subject and its title, "Intimations of Immortality from Recollections of Early Childhood;" and it is, we take leave to say, one of the most superb productions of the spirit of Christian Platonism which the world has seen.

There was a time when meadow, grove, and stream,
The earth, and every common sight,
  To me did seem
 Apparelled in celestial light,
The glory and the freshness of a dream.
It is not now as it has been of yore;
  Turn wheresoe'er I may,
  By night or day,
The things which I have seen, I now can see no more.
  The rainbow comes and goes,
  And lovely is the rose;
 The moon doth with delight
Look round her when the heavens are bare;
  Waters on a starry night
  Are beautiful and fair;
 The sunshine is a glorious birth;
 But yet I know, where'er I go,
That there hath passed a glory from the earth.

Now while the birds thus sing a joyous song,
 And while the young lambs bound
  As to the tabor's sound,

---

* *Essays: Of Youth and Age.*

THE DEPARTED GLORY.

To me alone there came a thought of grief,
But timely utterance gave that thought relief,
   And I again am strong.
The cataracts blow their trumpets from the steep,
No more shall grief of mine the seasons wrong;
I hear the echoes through the mountains throng,
The winds come to me from the fields of sleep,
   And all the earth is gay,
    Land and sea
   Give themselves up to jollity,
   And with the heart of May
   Doth every beast keep holiday.
    Thou child of joy
Shout round me, let me hear thy shouts, thou happy shepherd boy!

   Ye blessed creatures, I have heard the call
    Ye to each other make; I see
   The heavens laugh with you in your jubilee,
    My heart is at your festival,
    My head hath its coronal,
The fulness of your bliss, I feel—I feel it all.
    Oh, evil day! if I were sullen
    While the earth herself is adorning,
     This sweet May morning,
   And the children are pulling
    On every side.
    In a thousand valleys, far and wide,
Fresh flowers; while the sun shines warm,
And the babe leaps up on his mother's arm:—
   I hear, I hear, with joy I hear!
   —But there's a tree, of many one,
A single field which I have looked upon,
Both of them speak of something that is gone.
    The pansy at my feet
    Doth the same tale repeat:
Whither is fled the visionary gleam?
Where is it now, the glory and the dream?

Our birth is but a sleep and a forgetting;
The soul that riseth with us, our life's star,
   Hath had elsewhere its setting,
   And cometh from afar:

THE INNOCENTS' DAY.

      Not in entire forgetfulness,
      And not in utter nakedness,
But trailing clouds of glory do we come
        From God, who is our home:
Heaven lies about us in our infancy!
Shades of the prison-house begin to close
      Upon the growing Boy;
But he beholds the light, and whence it flows,
      He sees it in his joy;
The youth, who daily farther from the East
    ' Must travel, still is Nature's priest,
      And by the vision splendid
      Is on his way attended;
At length the man perceives it die away,
And fade into the light of common day.
Earth fills her lap with pleasures of her own;
Yearnings she hath in her own natural kind,
And, even with something of a mother's mind,
      And no unworthy aim,
      The homely nurse doth all she can
To make her foster-child, her inmate man,
      Forget the glories he hath known,
And that imperial palace whence he came.

Behold the child among his new-born blisses,
A four years' darling of a pigmy size!
See where 'mid work of his own hand he lies,
Fretted by sallies of his mother's kisses,
With light upon him from his father's eyes!
See at his feet some little plan or chart,
Some fragment from his dream of human life,
Shaped by himself with newly-learned art;
      A wedding or a festival,
      A mourning or a funeral;
      And this hath now his heart,
      And unto this he frames his song:
      Then will he fit his tongue
To dialogues of business, love, or strife;
      But it will not be long
      Ere this be thrown aside,
      And with new joy and pride
The little actor cons another part,

THE CHILD A PHILOSOPHER.

Filling from time to time his "humorous stage"
With all the persons down to palsied age,
That life brings with her in her equipage;
    As if his whole vocation
    Were endless imitation.

Thou, whose exterior semblance doth belie
    Thy soul's immensity;
Thou best Philosopher, who yet dost keep
Thy heritage, thou Eye among the blind,
That, deep and silent, read'st the eternal deep,
Haunted for ever by the Eternal mind,—
    Mighty Prophet, Seer blest!
    On whom those truths do rest,
Which we are toiling all our lives to find:
Thou, over whom thy Immortality,
Broods like the day, a master o'er a slave,
A presence which is not to be put by;
    To whom the grave
Is but a lonely bed without the sense or sight
    Of day or the warm light,
A place of thought where we in waiting lie!
Thou little child, yet glorious in the might
Of untamed pleasures, on thy being's height,
Why with such earnest pains dost thou provoke
The years to bring the inevitable yoke,—
Thus blindly with thy blessedness at strife?
Full soon thy soul shall have her earthly freight,
And custom lie upon thee with a weight,
Heavy as frost, and deep almost as life!

    Oh joy! that in our embers
    Is something that doth live,
    That Nature yet remembers
    What was so fugitive!
The thought of our past years in me doth breed
Perpetual benedictions; not indeed
For that which is most worthy to be blest;
Delight and liberty, the simple creed
Of Childhood, whether fluttering or at rest,
With new-born hope for ever in his breast:
    Not for these I raise
    The song of thanks and praise;

But for those obstinate questionings
Of sense and outward things,
Fallings from us, vanishings;
Blank misgivings of a creature
Moving about in worlds not realised,
High instincts, before which our mortal nature
Did tremble like a guilty thing surprised:
But for those first affections,
Those shadowy recollections,
Which, be they what they may,
Are yet the fountain light of all our day,
Are yet a master light of all our seeing;
Uphold us, cherish us, and make
Our noisy years seem moments in the being
Of the eternal silence: truths that wake
To perish never:
Which neither listlessness, nor mad endeavour,
Nor Man nor Boy,
Nor all that is at enmity with joy
Can utterly abolish or destroy!
Hence in a season of calm weather,
Though inland far we be,
Our souls have sight of that immortal sea
Which brought us hither;
Can in a moment travel thither,
And see the children sport upon the shore,
And hear the mighty waters rolling evermore.

Then sing ye birds, sing, sing a joyous song!
And let the young lambs bound
As to the tabor's sound!
We in thought will join your throng,
Ye that pipe and ye that play,
Ye that through your hearts to-day
Feel the gladness of the May!
What though the radiance which was once so bright
Be now for ever taken from my sight;
Though nothing can bring back the hour
Of splendour in the grass, of glory in the flower;
We will grieve not, rather find
Strength in what remains behind;

CONSOLATION.

   In the primal sympathy
   Which having been must ever be;
   In the soothing thoughts that spring
   Out of human suffering;
   In the faith that looks through death;
In years that bring the philosophic mind.

And oh! ye fountains, meadows, hills, and groves,
Think not of any severing of our loves!
Yet in my heart of hearts I feel your might;
I only have relinquished one delight
To live beneath your more habitual sway.
I love the brooks which down their channels fret,
Even more than when I tripped, lightly as they;
The innocent brightness of a new-born day
   Is lovely yet;
The clouds that gather round the setting sun,
Do take a sober colouring from an eye
That hath kept watch o'er man's mortality;
Another race hath been and other palms are won.
Thanks to the human heart by which we live,
Thanks to its tenderness, its joys and fears,
To me the meanest flower that blows can give
Thoughts that do often lie too deep for tears.

The Circumcision of Christ.

January 1.

THE day on which we at present commemorate the Circumcision of our Lord has a singular, if not unique, history amongst the "observable times" of the Church. Although from its earliest celebration regarded as a festival, it exhibited for a considerable time the outward phenomena of a fast; its observances being of a severe and penitential, rather than of a jubilant character. And for this there was good reason. The riot and license which, by the heathen world, were carried over from the Saturnalia—commencing about the seventeenth of December—to the calends of January, were so scandalous and extravagant as to force on Christian policy, no less than on Christian duty, the necessity of an active or a passive opposition. In the earlier life of the Church, the abstinence of her members from the pagan abominations of the season was nearly all that was possible; but, as her strength and influence increased, her teachers rose with these to the indignant height of protest, rebuke, and denunciation. The writings of the Fathers abound in severe invectives against the indecent and superstitious revelry of the day; and some of them are the fiercer in their wrath against it, that its excesses were not always confined to the unbaptized. St. Augustine, Peter Chrysologus, Maximus Taurinensis, and Faustinus the Bishop, amongst others, reprobated the prevailing riot of the calends of January, which, many years before their times, St. Chrysostom had indignantly described as ἑορτὴν διαβολικὴν, the Devil's Festival.

On this day especially, as throughout the Saturnalia, under the pretence of temporarily reviving the glories and immunities of the golden age, the attempt was made to resolve the order of society back into the elements of primæval chaos. In order to do honour to Janus, or Dianus, the god of the sun, the heathen, as the Fathers scornfully pointed out, feigned him to have two faces, of which one seemed to look back upon the past, whilst the other looked forward to the opening year. It was thus that stupid devotees, in their abortive attempts to fashion a god, succeeded in achieving a monstrosity, to which, at this season, some of them paid in their own persons the tribute of imitation. Others degraded themselves to the adoption of lower forms of life than their own; and, clothing themselves in the skins of cattle or of wild beasts, and assuming the heads of these, "rejoiced and exulted that they could no longer be recognised as human beings." Such voluntary degradation, it was said, proved the nature of the revellers to be more debased than that of the animals whose form or appearance they adopted. Further, men, putting off the vigour and roughness of their sex, masqueraded in the robes of women; whilst women, divesting themselves of their proper modesty and shame, blushed not to disport themselves in the garments of men. On the calends of January the superstitious consultation of auguries was pursued with an uncommon ardour; and people indulged freely in the interchange of "diabolical" *strenæ*,* or new year's gifts.

It was the observance of the calends of January "by

* So called from Strena, or Strenua, a goddess who divided with Janus the doubtful honours of the day. Her name is still preserved in the *étrennes*, or gifts, which it is the custom in France to exchange on *le Jour de l'An*.

the greater portion of the human race with lust and luxury, debauch, and impiety," that induced "the holy fathers of old to appoint, that by all the Churches throughout the world the season should be proclaimed as a public fast, in order that miserable men might know that, on account of their sins, fasting was imperative upon the Churches." "Fast, therefore," is the exhortation of Bishop Faustinus, from whose *Sermo in Kalendis Januarii* we condense this account of the heathen revelry, in which it was his most bitter complaint that some Christian people were seduced to partake—"Fast, therefore, most dear brethren, in these days, and with a true and perfect charity bewail the folly of these wretched men, who, haply, seeing us fast on their account, may come to understand their evil plight, and may even be touched and visited by God through our word and example." And it is a fact recorded by Isidore of Seville, and by Alcuin, in his *Liber de Divinis Officiis*, that several churches formerly kept the first day of January as a fast.

But such reprobation and such advice as those of Faustinus were not left to be iterated by the unassisted zeal of isolated preachers. They were enforced by the collective authority of various councils. The second Council of Tours, for instance, which was convoked by order of King Charibert, and commenced its session November 17th, 566, set itself to oppose the pagan superstitions which were observed on the first of January, by proclaiming that day as a fast, and prescribing for it particular litanies and services.* In the spirit of this ordinance, as Bergier remarks, "the first of January was long observed in France as a day of penitence and fasting, for the expiation, not only of the superstitions, but also of the disorders to which the votaries of paganism abandoned themselves. It was in 1444 that for this fast was substituted, in France, the solemn festival of the Name of Jesus."

The Council of Constantinople, convoked in 692, by order

* Edmund Martene's *De Antiquis Ecclesiæ Ritibus.*

of the Emperor Justinian II., and called *Quinisextum*, or, more popularly, *in Trullo*,* also ordained the suppression of the various indecent sports; the public dances of women; the disguise of women as men, and of men as women, which obtained at the time of the calends of January.

It will be seen that there was much to retard the consolidation of the Circumcision into a universal festival of the Church; and the date of its introduction is uncertain and debateable. "After the introduction of the festival of the Nativity," observes Mr. Riddle, "which took place in the fourth century, the first of January received a certain distinction, in accordance with the custom of continuing the celebration of the higher festivals during several days, or the adoption of the system of octaves from the Jewish ritual. From that period until the seventh century the day was distinguished as *Octava Natalis Dominis*, the Octave of the Nativity." By this title it is that Isidore and the more early writers mention it. It is pretty well established that, in the course of the seventh century, a festival was of very general observance, under the titles of the Circumcision, the Octave of the Nativity, and the Name of Jesus, any one of which would from that time be used indifferently, or according to the idea to which it was intended for the moment to give prominence. Such a commemoration, as Mr. Riddle points out, "would naturally take place in the Church, in accordance with the course of the general narrative, when once it had become usual to celebrate the Nativity on the twenty-fifth of December, independently of the influence of other octaves."†

---

* From the circumstance of its having been held in the *Dome* chapel of the palace. This council, at which two hundred and eleven bishops assisted, was regarded by the Greeks—not by the Latins, for the Pope was not represented—as a general one, and was supplementary to the fifth and sixth Councils of Constantinople, at which no canons of discipline were promulgated.

† *Manual of Christian Antiquities.*

The date of the introduction of the feast of the Circumcision is, we said just now, uncertain and debateable; and considerable diversity of opinion has been exhibited in regard to it. The truth seems to be, that one author or another is inclined to fix on every single and several stage of development between the first dawning or germ and the noon-tide or full growth of universality, as that in which the introduction of the festival is to be recognised. There are writers who assign the first commemoration of the Circumcision to the fifth century; and in support of this era refer to a Homily of Maximus Taurinensis, "On the Circumcision of our Lord, or, on the calends of January." But from the fact that no mention of the festival of the Circumcision occurs throughout the Homily, it is fair to infer that, in this case, as in many others, the title is of later origin than the work itself; and thus its evidence is invalidated. An ancient *Sacramentary* of the fifth century, with which the name of Popes Leo I. and Gelasius I. have been associated, does, however, give colour to the more modest proposition that in that century there was already a kind of incidental or *sub*-presentation of the festival of the Circumcision along with that of the Octave of the Nativity. In this *Sacramentary*, although the latter of the two titles just mentioned has the dignity of being applied to the day of the Circumcision, yet the Circumcision itself has a *nominal* recognition in the private prayers of the offices.[*]

Those who refer the origin of the festival of the Circumcision to the seventh century, appeal to a collect in the *Sacramentary* of Gregory the Great, in which occur the words, "*per Dominum nostrum Jesum Christum, cujus hodie Circumcisionem et Nativitatis Octavam celebramas:* through our Lord Jesus Christ, whose Circumcision, together with the Octave of His Nativity, we this day celebrate." Doubts have been raised, however, as to the

[*] Moroni, *Dizionario Ecclesiastico*.

genuineness of the *Sacramentary*; and, until these are laid, its evidence cannot be admitted as decisive with regard to the festival in question. Moroni, *per contra*, draws attention to the fact that, "we have a decree of Reciswindus, who ascended the throne of Spain in the year 649, in which the celebration of the festival of the Circumcision was enjoined."*

Our own countryman, the Venerable Bede, has left a Homily, produced, probably, within the first quarter of the eighth century, which is not only entitled *In Die Festo Circumcisionis Domini*, but which really and directly treats of that event as its subject. Casaubon, nevertheless, with whom Wheatly appears to have coincided without an effort, presumes that the festival of the Circumcision was first established by Ivo Carnotensis,—Ivo, Bishop of Chartres—at the close of the eleventh century; and that it was first mentioned by St. Bernard of Clairvaux, in a sermon preached early in the twelfth century. Casaubon further says that the festival was universally and canonically established by the Synod of Oxford, A.D. 1222. This Synod, or Council, was held by Stephen Langton, Archbishop of Canterbury, for the reform of the English Church, especially in relation to its monastic discipline, and its eighth statute appointed the festivals— that of the Circumcision being one—which were to be observed by the faithful with all reverence (*sub omni veneratione*). In the course of centuries, the first of January became generally recognised in Europe as the first day of the civil year; and this circumstance, Mr. Riddle justly surmises, may have added to the celebrity of the festival of the Circumcision.

It may be proper in this place to trace in a few words the origin and the course of circumcision as a rite and custom. Commencing in the days of Abraham, in the year of the world 2178, and several centuries anterior to

* Moroni, *Dizionario Ecclesiastico*.

the promulgation of the law on Mount Sinai, it was the first legal ordinance enjoined by God upon the Jews, in the person of their patriarchal ancestor and representative. It was the seal of a covenant stipulated between God and Abraham—on God's part, to bless Abraham and his posterity; on theirs, to become and continue His faithful and obedient people. Abraham was ninety-nine years of age when, in obedience to the divine appointment, he circumcised himself, his son Ishmael, and all the males of his family. But for the future, the rite was to be administered on the eighth day after birth; so that, in the words of Josephus, "when Isaac was born, they circumcised him on the eighth day; and from that day the Jews continued the custom of circumcising their sons within that number of days. But as for the Arabians, they circumcised after the thirteenth year, because Ishmael, the father of their nation, who was born to Abraham of the concubine, was circumcised at that age."*

The precept first given to the patriarch Abraham was repeated to Moses upon the occasion of the institution of the Passover, to which feast, submission to the rite of circumcision was made a condition of acceptance. This condition was binding not on the Jews alone, but also on all strangers who wished to qualify themselves to be partakers of it.

The Jews have always been tenacious of a ceremony which was the symbol of a peculiar grace and privilege. Even in Egypt they did not neglect it. Moses, however, while he sojourned in Midian, with Jethro, his father-in-law, omitted to circumcise the sons who were born to him in that country; forbearing, it would seem, to press its necessity out of deference to the maternal tenderness of Zipporah. Again, during the journeyings of the Israelites in the wilderness, their children were suffered to remain uncircumcised; the necessity of the rite as a mode of

* *Antiquities of the Jews.*

distinction, as well as the convenience of its administration, being curtailed by their unsettled and vagabond mode of life. But a profounder reason for the nearly forty years' intermission of the ordinance may have been to mark the abeyance of the fulfilment of God's covenant promise, in virtue of which He was to lead His chosen people to the possession of the land of Canaan.

The law determined nothing with reference to the minister, the instrument, or the place of circumcision. These were left entirely to the discretion of the people; and it is on account of this latitude that Juan Interiano de Ayala, a Spanish priest of the Order of Mercy, exposes the vulgar error of those painters, otherwise excellent and eminent, who represent the Circumcision of Christ as being performed by a priest—sometimes by the high priest—and as taking place in the Temple.* The ceremony was for the most part accompanied with mirth and feasting, and the child generally received a name at the time of its celebration.

But the practice of circumcision was by no means confined to the children of Israel.† Over and above those nations who, as descendants of Ishmael or of Esau, inherited it by tradition from their fathers, the custom would seem to have been imitated by other peoples with whom the Jews had as little as possible of the bond of blood and brotherhood. It is to this fact, and especially to the fact of the adoption of circumcision by the Egyptians—whom he calls "the most populous of all nations, and the most abounding in all kinds of wisdom"—that Philo Judæus appeals when he would defend the practice against the ridicule of his flippant contemporaries. Apart from the argument derived from its vogue and prevalence, Philo's apology for circumcision is conducted, firstly, on

* *Pictor Christianus Eruditus*; Madrid, 1720.
† Herodotus, *Euterpe*, c. 104.

physiological, and secondly, on symbolical principles. * It is curious that the members of the Coptic Church, who are generally supposed to be the most authentic representatives, both in blood and language, of the Egyptians of the Pharaohs, should still preserve this practice; whilst by the Æthiopian or Abyssinian Christians, it was regarded as of equal necessity with baptism. †

We have seen that circumcision was the sign of a peculiar grace and privilege, the distinguishing mark of the most illustrious aristocracy the world ever saw—the one aristocracy whose members have held their patents directly and visibly from the hand of God Himself. There is little wonder that the Jews should tenaciously observe and habitually vaunt an institution which gave them rank, as being in closer *rapport* with heaven, over any and every other nation. They carried, indeed, their sense of its dignity and importance so far as to make "circumcision" inclusive of all that was patriotic, pure, just or honourable; and conversely to make the term "uncircumcision" inclusive of all that was alien, impure, worthless, or imperfect (Ex. vi. 12 and 30; Jer. vi. 10; Acts vii. 51). The idea of giving their sister to one that was uncircumcised chafed the proud hearts of the sons of Jacob (Gen. xxxiv. 14); as the contemplated marriage of Samson with a Philistine woman grieved the spirits of his parents (Judges xiv. 3); and the prospect of being thrust through by the uncircumcised victors at Gilboa was one of so much bitterness that the warlike Saul, unbent though broken, did not shrink from anticipating it by self-immolation (1 Sam. xxxi. 4). It is needless to multiply illustrations; for they are to be found not rarely along the whole course of Jewish history. Circumcision was, in short, the very life of a Jew, as a citizen and an individual, so far as that life was outward and

---

* *Treatise on Circumcision.*
† Dean Stanley's *Lectures on the History of the Eastern Church.*

phenomenal; as it was the symbol of his national and individual life, so far as that life was inner and spiritual.

There was no ordinance of the ceremonial law which Christ did not honour by fulfilment before His death accomplished its abrogation. Every condition of the old covenant was to be observed until the "better covenant" should be perfected. The ancient law could be superseded only by being satisfied. As it was not till the *death* of Christ that His obedience and sacrifice were consummated, it followed that all His life, from the manger to the cross, was obnoxious to the requirements of the Law under which He was born. And the first example He could give of His obedience was His submission to the rite of circumcision. As a matter of expediency, even, it was well that Christ, whose mission was to preach, if not rather to *be*, a Gospel of universal and indifferent acceptability, should have first complied with the conditions of national exclusiveness.

Being sinless and spotless, Christ had no personal need of circumscision; but in humbling Himself to the assumption of human nature, He humbled Himself to all its disabilities, and consented to bear the shame, though free from the reality, of sin. His circumcision was, again, one of a series of circumstances which marked, in a public and especial manner, the reality of His human body; as if in anticipation of the cavils of those heretics—in whom the "spirit of Antichrist" was at work so early as the identical age of the apostles—who, having learned from Oriental systems of philosophy, the doctrine of the innate and hopeless depravity of matter, gave up all efforts after the sanctity of the body, and denied that Christ had come ἐν σαρκί, in the flesh, on the ground that He could not have allied His nature to what was inherently and irreclaimably depraved (1 John iv. 3).

To the statement of the reasons why the circumcision of our Lord should have occurred at all, we may add an ingenious but futile speculation as to the reason why it should have taken place at the time of year in which it is commemorated. Baronius points out a coincidence which is so apposite and picturesque that it is a pity it cannot be sustained. The fact is that this coincidence is a nearly baseless hypothesis, and it is to be regarded chiefly as an interesting and beautiful fancy, so long as it cannot be proved—as we have seen, page 16, that it cannot—that the birth of Christ took place on the 25th of December. The observance of the Nativity and the Circumcision on the several days to which we refer them, is to be taken as one of commemoration rather than as one marking an ascertained and actual anniversary. "In order," Baronius observes, "that He might dissipate the works of the devil, Christ consecrated, by the shedding of His blood, the very calends of January, a day above all days of the year polluted by the superstitions of the Gentiles; and recovered to Himself, by the *primitiæ* of His blood, those very *primitiæ* of the year which had been seized and occupied by the tyranny of the devil—a mystery which in certain symbolical words Isaias had foreshadowed, when he said, '*Delectabitur infans ab ubere super foramine aspidis.*'" *

The great truth to which the poets of the Circumcision seem to be irresistibly and almost exclusively attracted, is that of the infant commencement of the shedding of the blood of expiation. With them, the body of the Babe begins to feel the pain and smart of His adopted brethren; and that blood to fall in drops, which shall one day stream as a torrent. The Circumcision is a foretaste of death; an earnest that the victim, when the due time shall have arrived, will be ready for the sacrifice. Christ, in the words of Jeremy Taylor, "exposed His tender body to the sharpness of the circumcising stone, and shed His blood in drops, giving an earnest of those rivers which He did

* *Annales Ecclesiastici.*

afterwards pour out for the cleansing all human nature, and extinguishing the wrath of God." Elsewhere in the same connection, Bishop Taylor likens the blood shed by the Saviour in His circumcision, to "the prelibation of a sacrifice."* In the verses on the "Circumcision" which occur in his "Hymns and Songs of the Church," George Wither supplies us with a material rendering of the same idea; with which he very pertinently combines a reference to that "milder sacrament" which, under the new dispensation, was to be substituted for circumcision as a token of admission into the family of God. Wither proceeds to deprecate a merely external circumcision or baptism, which, affecting only the flesh, should fall short of the spirit and the heart; and concludes his poem with a prayer for a renewal of life with the renewal of the year.

> This day Thy flesh, oh Christ, did bleed,
> Marked by the circumcision-knife;
> Because the law, for man's misdeed,
> Required the earnest of Thy life:
> Those drops divined that shower of blood,
> Which in Thine agony began:
> And that great shower foreshowed the flood,
> Which from Thy side the next day ran.
>
> Then, through that milder sacrament,
> Succeeding this, Thy grace inspire;
> Yea, let Thy smart make us repent,
> And circumcisèd hearts desire.
> For he that either is baptized,
> Or circumcised in flesh alone,
> Is but as an uncircumcised,
> Or as an unbaptizèd one.
>
> The year anew we now begin,
> And outward gifts received have we;
> Renew us also, Lord, within,
> And make us new year's gifts for Thee!

* *Life of Christ.*

> Yea, let us, with the passèd year,
> Our old affections cast away;
> That we new creatures may appear,
> And to redeem the time essay.

We owe another setting of the same thought to the God-saturated muse of Richard Crashaw, whom his friend Cowley apostrophized:—

> "Poet and Saint! to thee alone are given
> The two most sacred names of earth and heaven."

During his residence at Cambridge, (1633—1644), Crashaw largely employed himself in writing devotional and other poetry; and he is said to have lived for the greater part of several years in St. Mary's Church, "like a primitive saint, offering up more prayers by night than others usually offer in the day." Crashaw was a preacher of great power and poetic fervour; but soon after his ejection from his fellowship, April 8th, 1644, he carried over his gifts and graces to the communion of the Church of Rome. Having thus become what in the language of his day was called "a revolter"—equivalent to the "pervert" of the present century—Crashaw repaired to Italy, and was made Secretary to Cardinal Palotta; the jealousy of some of whose *Seguita*, or followers, he had the misfortune to provoke. He died, probably, in 1650, whilst holding "some small employ" at the church of our Lady of Loretto; not without suspicion, according to Dr. John Bargrave, who had been his friend and contemporary at Peterhouse, of having been poisoned.

Crashaw's poem, which is supposed to be addressed by "Our Lord in His Circumcision to His Father," is taken from the work entitled "Steps to the Temple."

> To Thee, these first-fruits of my growing death,
> (For what else is my life?) lo! I bequeath.
> Taste this, and as Thou lik'st this lesser flood
> Expect a sea, my heart shall make it good.

Thy wrath that wades here now, ere long shall swim
The flood-gate shall be set wide ope for him.
Then let him drink, and drink, and do his worst,
To drown the wantonness of his wild thirst.
Now's but the nonage of my pains, my fears
Are yet both in their hopes, not come to years.
The day of my dark woes is yet but morn,
My tears but tender, and my death new-born;
Yet may these unfledged griefs give fate some guess,
These cradle torments have their towardness.
These purple buds of blooming death may be,
Erst the full stature of a fatal tree;
And till my riper woes to age are come,
This knife may be the spear's *Præludium*.

The thought we trace in the prose of Taylor and in the verse of Wither and of Crashaw is found also to pervade Milton's short "Ode upon the Circumcision." To this last we content ourselves with referring the reader, for it is, by hypothesis, immediately and momentarily accessible; and proceed to exhibit a poem in which the pangs of the Virgin Mother are seen blended with the sufferings of her Child. It is taken from the "Mæoniæ"* of Robert Southwell, a Jesuit priest, but an accomplished and estimable man, who, in 1595, at the age of thirty-three, fell a victim to the sensitive and persecuting jealousy cherished by the government of Elizabeth towards the Roman Catholics, especially from the time of the intrigues for and against the Queen of Scots. In the course of a three years' close imprisonment, during which he was many times put to the torture, he produced his "St. Peter's Complaint" and "Mary Magdalen's Funeral Tears." Southwell endured the agonies to which he was repeatedly subjected with heroic fortitude and reticence, and his poems are remarkable for

---

* "Mæoniæ; or, certain excellent Poems and Spiritual Hymns omitted in the last impression of "Peter's Complaint," being needful thereunto to be annexed, as being both divine and wittie. All composed by R[obert] S[outhwell]. 1595."

exhibiting no trace of acrimony towards either the authors or the instruments of his sufferings. A spirit of plaintive resignation or of manly and Christian fortitude breathes through even the saddest of his productions. Although they have lately been comparatively neglected, Southwell's works enjoyed a popularity which, between the years 1593 and 1600, carried them through no fewer than eleven editions. It may be premised that the Circumcision of Christ has occasionally been represented in hieratic art as the first of the "Seven Sorrows of the Blessed Virgin."

> The Head is lanced to work the body's cure,
>   With angring salve it smarts to heal our wound;
> To faultless Son, from all offences pure,
>   The faulty vassal's scourges do redound;
> The Judge is cast the guilty to acquit,
> The Sun defaced, to lend the star His light.
>
> The Vein of Life distilleth drops of grace,
>   Our Rock gives issue to a heavenly spring;
> Tears from His eyes, blood streams from wounded place,
>   With showers to heaven of joy a harvest bring:
> This sacred dew let angels gather up,
> Such dainty drops best fit their nectared cup.
>
> With weeping eyes His mother rued His smart,
>   If blood from Him, tears came from her as fast;
> The knife that cut His flesh did pierce her heart,
>   The pain that Jesu felt did Mary taste;
> His life and her's hung by one fatal twist,
> No blow that hit the Son the mother missed.

The poem which follows is entitled, "The Circumcision, or New Year's Day," and occurs in "The Synagogue, or the Shadow of the Temple, and Private Ejaculations in imitation of Mr. George Herbert," by Christopher Harvey, first published, anonymously, in 1640. Izaak Walton praises Harvey, that he, as Herbert, had power to

> * * Raise sad souls above the earth,
>   And fix them there,
> Free from the world's anxieties and fear.

The same enthusiastic admirer further commends Harvey conjointly with Herbert:—

> * * * Every hour
> I read you kills a sin,
> Or lets a virtue in
> To fight against it; and the Holy Ghost
> Supports my frailties, lest the day be lost.

Christopher Harvey, as recorded by Anthony à Wood, was "a minister's son of Cheshire, was born in that county, became a battler of Brazen-Nose College, in 1613, aged sixteen years; took the degrees in Arts, that of Master being completed in 1620, holy orders, and at length was made vicar of Clifton, in Warwickshire." He held this preferment from 1639 to 1663, the year of his death.

> Sorrow betide my sins! Must smart so soon
> Seize on my Saviour's tender flesh, scarce grown
>   Unto an eighth day's age?
>   Can nothing else assuage
> The wrath of heaven, but His infant-blood?
> Innocent Infant, infinitely good!
>
> Is this Thy welcome to the world, great God?
> No sooner born, but subject to the rod
>   Of sin-incensed wrath?
>   Alas, what pleasure hath
> Thy Father's justice to begin Thy passion,
> Almost together with Thine incarnation?
>
> Is it to antedate Thy death? To indite
> Thy condemnation Himself, and write
>   The copy with Thy blood,
>   Since nothing is so good?
> Or is't by this experiment to try,
> Whether Thou beest born mortal, and can die?
>
> If man must needs draw blood of God, yet why
> Stays he not till Thy time be come to die?
>   Didst Thou thus early bleed
>   For us to show what need
> We have to hasten unto Thee as fast;
> And learn that all the time is lost that's pass'd?

'Tis true, we should do so: Yet in this blood
There's something else, that must be understood;
    It seals Thy covenant,
    That so we may not want
Witness enough against Thee, that Thou art
Made subject to the Law, to act our part.

The sacrament of Thy regeneration
It cannot be; it gives no intimation
    Of what Thou wert, but we:
    Native impurity;
Original corruption was not Thine,
But only as Thy righteousness is mine.

In holy Baptism this is brought to me,
As that in Circumcision was to Thee:
    So that Thy loss and pain
    Do prove my joy and gain.
Thy Circumcision writ Thy death in blood:
Baptism in water seals my livelihood.

O blessed change! Yet, rightly understood,
That blood was water, and this water's blood.
    What shall I give again
    To recompense Thy pain?
Lord, take revenge upon me for this smart:
To quit Thy foreskin, circumcise my heart.

Harvey produced several other works indicative of his loyalty to church and state; and the authorship of the "Schola Cordis; or the Heart of itself gone away from God, brought back to Him, and instructed by Him," is claimed, it would seem conclusively, for him, as against the pretensions of Francis Quarles, to whom the honour has long been popularly referred. From the "Schola Cordis" we transcribe an epigram on the "Circumcision of the Heart."

    Here, take thy Saviour's cross, the nails and spear,
    That for thy sake His holy flesh did tear:
    Use them as knives thine heart to circumcise,
    And dress thy God a pleasing sacrifice.

This circumcision of the heart is what the rite symbolized

and aimed at in all ages, although its spiritual significance was never so fully declared as after the death of Christ (Rom. ii. 25-29; Gal. v. 6; Col. iii. 11; and *passim* in the Pauline Epistles).

With the death of Christ, the obligation and necessity of circumcision determined; and if, in exceptional cases, it was either administered or withheld, its observance and non-observance alike were dictated by considerations of expediency (Acts xvi. 3; Gal. ii. 3-5).

Bishop Ken has a characteristic poem " On the Circumcision " in his " Hymns for all the Festivals in the Year." We offer the first five stanzas out of twenty, of which the whole poem is composed.

> Upon the octave of Thy birth,
> Since Thou, God-Man, didst shine on earth,
> Thou, as the blissful light,
> Immaculately bright,
> Would'st a severity endure,
> Contrived to teach lapsed men they were impure.
>
> Thy heavenly Father it ordained,
> Love to obedience Thee constrained,
> Our spirits to incline
> To zeal for law divine;
> From infancy Thy Father's will,
> It was Thy care devoutly to fulfil.
>
> Thou, our affections to excite,
> Would'st stoop to an afflictive rite;
> Thou early did'st foreshow
> What Thou would'st undergo,
> Thy cross and agonizing pains,
> Which made Thy blood gush out at all Thy veins.
>
> But, Lord, from sin all pain arose,
> Sin is the cause of penal woes;
> A Babe Thou did'st begin
> To bear the weight of sin,
> And by the circumcising steel,
> Teach that Thy flesh our punishment should feel.

All heaven and earth which saw Thee bleed,
Saw Thee true Man and Abraham's seed:
He first received the sign
Of covenant divine,
And 'twas by Thee from him derived,
All dead in sin, to bliss should be revived.

"So mysterious were all the actions of Jesus, that this one [of the circumcision] served many ends: for, first, it gave demonstration of the verity of His human nature; secondly, so He began to fulfil the law; thirdly, and took from Himself the scandal of uncircumcision, which would have eternally prejudiced the Jews against His entertainment and communion; fourthly, and then He took upon Him that name which declared him to be the Saviour of the world; which, as it was consummate in the blood of the cross, so was it inaugurated in the blood of circumcision: for 'when the eight days were accomplished for circumcising the child, His name was called Jesus.'"* We are anxious to give a moment's prominence to the fourth and last of these purposes of the circumcision. It is to this name-giving incident, which sometimes is itself titular of the festival of the circumcision, that Ken devotes the other fifteen stanzas of the poem from which we have just extracted. The piety of the venerated bishop expands into a diffuse and affectionate rhapsody on the glories of the name of Jesus; as a "Hymn to the Name above every name—the Name of Jesus" is one of the most remarkable, the most rapt and saintly, of the productions of Crashaw. Crashaw's "Hymn" is, amongst other things, a sort of *Benedicite, omnia opera Domini*, adapted to the peculiar object of its inspiration. Its length makes it as unmanageable for purposes of reproduction here as its perfervid and passionate devotion makes it admirable. Yet it is with regret that we forbear to transcribe it, and content ourselves, as being more

* Bishop Jeremy Taylor's *Life of Christ*.

THE NAME OF JESUS.

amenable to our laws of space, with a poem from the late Dr. J. M. Neale's "Mediæval Hymns and Sequences." The translator, preserving the initial words—"Gloriosi Salvatoris"—by way of title, introduces it with a short paragraph, to the effect that it is "a German hymn on the festival of the holy Name of Jesus. All that can be said of its date is, that it is clearly posterior to the *Pange Lingua* of St. Thomas, which it imitated. This hymn has been adopted in several hymnals."

> To the Name that brings salvation,
>   Honour, worship, laud we pay;
> That for many a generation
>   Hid in God's foreknowledge lay;
> But to every tongue and nation
>   Holy Church proclaims to-day.
>
> Name of gladness, Name of pleasure,
>   By the tongue ineffable,
> Name of sweetness passing measure,
>   To the ear delectable;
> 'Tis our safeguard and our treasure,
>   'Tis our help 'gainst sin and hell.
>
> 'Tis the Name for adoration,
>   'Tis the Name of victory,
> 'Tis the Name for meditation
>   In the vale of misery;
> 'Tis the Name for veneration
>   By the citizens on high.
>
> 'Tis the Name that whoso preaches
>   Finds it music in his ear:
> 'Tis the Name that whoso teaches
>   Finds more sweet than honey's cheer:
> Who its perfect wisdom reaches,
>   Makes his ghostly vision clear.
>
> 'Tis the Name by right exalted
>   Over every other name:

That when we are sore assaulted
　Puts our enemies to shame :
Strength to them that else had halted,
　Eyes to blind, and feet to lame.

JESUS, we Thy Name adoring
　Long to see Thee as Thou art :
Of Thy clemency imploring
　So to write it in our heart,
That, hereafter upward soaring,
　We with angels may have part.　Amen.

　　The peculiar offices which the Church has assigned to the day are admirably adapted to explain the history, to expound the doctrine, and to enforce the lessons of the circumcision of Christ. "The First Lesson for the morning gives an account of the institution of circumcision; and the Gospel of the circumcision of Christ: the First Lesson at evening, and the Second Lessons and Epistle all tend to the same end, viz.: that since the circumcision of the flesh is abrogated, God hath no respect of persons, nor requires any more of us than the circumcision of the heart. The Collect, Epistle, and Gospel for the day were all first inserted in 1549."*

　We know not how better to conclude this paper than by placing the Collect directly under the reader's eye, which, in its pregnant comprehensiveness, turns into one short prayer the converging precepts of the festival :—

　"Almighty God, who madest Thy blessed Son to be circumcised, and obedient to the law for man; grant us the true circumcision of the spirit, that our hearts and all our members being mortified from all worldly and carnal lusts, we may in all things obey Thy blessed will, through the same Thy Son Jesus Christ our Lord.　Amen."

---

* Wheatly's *Rational Illustration of the Book of Common Prayer.*

The Epiphany;

OR, THE MANIFESTATION OF CHRIST TO THE GENTILES.

JANUARY 6.

IT is not uncommon for fasts and festivals to emerge first into view in the ecclesiastical firmament in the form of nebulæ, and gradually to shape themselves into distinctness and identity as proper and individual stars. Thus the feast of Epiphany was not originally a distinct festival, but formed a part of that of the Nativity; and the word Epiphany was originally applied to Christmas-day as well as to the day to which it is now peculiar. The idea common to both these seasons was that of manifestation—the Nativity commemorated the manifestation of Christ in the flesh, and, what we now call the Epiphany, His manifestation by a star to the Gentiles. Wheatly, however, maintains that the feasts of Christmas and Epiphany were always separate, and imputes it to the identity of the word used to designate them that they were ever regarded as having been one and the same; whilst Bingham contends for their primitive conjunction. It is not, however, beyond the limits of possibility to conciliate the statement of identity with the statement of difference. "The term 'Επιφάνια was used at first," says Mr. Riddle, "as equivalent to Γενέθλια, Nativity; but afterwards a distinction was made between *Epiphania prima et secunda*, the first and second Epiphany; the former denoting Christmas-day, the latter Epiphany so called."* But a paragraph of Dr. Hook's is more significant as a passage of accommodation:—The feast of the Nativity "being celebrated twelve days, the first and last of which, according to the custom of the Jews in their feasts, were high or chief days of solemnity, either of these might fitly be called Epiphany, as that word signifies the appearance of Christ in the world."† When it became convenient to mark the distinctive honour and purpose of either day with greater precision, it happened naturally enough that the first was adopted for the commemoration of the Nativity, whilst the last, or Twelfth-day, was associated with the Epiphany. The chief reasons for the celebration of this feast apart from the Nativity, are stated in one of the Sermons referred to St. Augustine. "On this day," he says, "we celebrate the mystery of God's manifesting Himself by His miracles in human nature; either because on this day the star in heaven gave notice of His birth; or because He turned water into wine at the marriage feast at Cana in Galilee: or because He consecrated water for the reparation of mankind by His baptism in the river Jordan; or because with the five loaves He fed five thousand men. For each of these contains the mysteries and joys of our salvation."

It was in the latter part of the fourth century that the celebration of the Epiphany was severed from that of the Nativity; and the former festival, or the joint festival under the name of the former, is shown by the *Homilies* of the two Gregories, and by other authors, to have been of common observance in the earlier part of the same century. Ammianus Marcellinus indicates pretty plainly the degree of reverence that was paid to the Epiphany, when he tells us that the Emperor Julian, before his open and declared apostasy, found it convenient to cover his latent infidelity by taking part with the other Christians in the special rites

* *Manual of Christian Antiquities.*
† Article "*Epiphany,*" in Hook's *Church Dictionary.*

of this high festival. And Gregory Nazianzen relates that the Emperor Valens, an Arian, followed the example of Julian. For he would have seemed an exile and alien from the Christian faith who should have neglected to associate himself with the observance of so high a solemnity,

The sanctity of the day developed more and more in the estimation of the faithful; and successive Christian emperors dignified it by the introduction of ever-increasing signs of external reverence. "Though at first this day," says Bingham, "was not exempt from juridical acts and prosecutions at law; nor were the public games and shows forbidden for some time to be exhibited thereon; yet, at length, Theodosius Junior (Cod. Theod. 1, 15, tit. 5, de Spectaculis, leg. 5) gave it an honourable place among those days on which the public games should not be allowed, forasmuch as men ought to put a distinction between days of supplication and days of pleasure. And Justinian (Cod. l. 3, tit. 12, de Feriis, leg. 7), reciting one of the laws of Theodosius the Great, makes both the Nativity and Epiphany days of vacation from all pleadings at law, as well as from popular pleasures. And so it is in the laws of the Visigoths, published out of the body of the Roman laws by Reciswindus and other Gothic kings, and the old Gothic interpreter of the laws in the Theodosian Code. From whence we may conclude that this was become the standing rule and custom throughout the Roman and the Visigoth dominions, to keep the festival of Epiphany with great veneration; neither allowing the courts to be open on this day for law, nor the theatre for pleasure."*

On the vigil of the Epiphany it was customary for homilies to be preached, for the Lord's Supper to be celebrated, and for slaves to enjoy a holiday. On the day itself it was ordered in the Roman Pontifical that, after the chanting of the Gospel, a priest should give notice to the congregation of the days on which Lent, Easter, and all the moveable

* *Antiquities of the Christian Church.*

solemnities were to be kept for the ensuing year. For this service a particular form was prescribed. The custom, in its essential features, was of pretty general observance by those to whom was committed the care of the Paschal cycle; or the rule for finding Easter. Cassian says that it was " an ancient practice in Egypt for the Bishop of Alexandria as soon as Epiphany was past, to send his circular letters to all the churches and monasteries of Egypt, to signify to them the beginning of Lent, and Easter day." The bishops of France, too, were enjoined to give notice on the day of Epiphany of the times when the festivals were to be kept in their churches. If any doubt arose about these seasons, the Metropolitan was to be consulted; and he again, if unable to resolve the difficulty, was to refer it to the arbitrament of the Roman See. The letters which issued on such occasions from the Metropolitans to their provincial bishops were commonly called Epistolæ Paschales and Heortasticæ, Paschal and Festival Epistles,—which, before giving the intimation of the times of incidence of the moveable fasts and festivals, discussed shortly some topic of usefulness and importance.

The Greek Church accorded an honour to Epiphany which the earlier Latin Church withheld. In the former communion it was the baptism of Jesus, over and above all the other phenomena or associations of the day, as enumerated already by St. Augustine, that was most strongly dwelt on in the commemoration of the Epiphany. It was at our Lord's baptism that His divinity was proclaimed to the world by the voice that came from heaven,—*Thou art My beloved Son, in whom I am well pleased.* "Why," asks St. Chrysostom, "is not the day on which Christ was born called Epiphany, but the day on which He was baptized? Because He was not manifested to all when He was born, but when He was baptized. For to the day of His baptism he was generally unknown, as appears from the words of John the Baptist, *There standeth one among you, whom ye know not.* And what wonder that others should not know Him, when the Baptist himself knew Him not before that day ? *For I know Him not,* says he ; *but He that sent me to baptize with water, the same said unto me, Upon whom thou shalt see the Spirit descending and remaining on Him, the same is He that baptizeth with the Holy Ghost.*" Regarding it as commemorative in a special manner of the manifestation of the Trinity at the baptism of Christ,* it was natural that the Greek Church should promote the Epiphany to be one of the three solemn times of baptism, of which the other two were Easter and Pentecost.† Of these three solemn times for baptism, from which even so high a feast as the Nativity was excluded, Easter, and after it Pentecost, was regarded with most favour and reverence. The reason for those solemn seasons, at which catechumens were accustomed to be baptized in the mass, is to be found in the necessity there was for the trial and probation of candidates. Baptism, in ordinary cases, was deferred till one of these seasons, lest hypocrisy, or ignorance, or mere impulsiveness, should bring a scandal upon the religion which was professed in that sacrament. Yet the anticipation of these times, in exceptional cases of accident or disease, or of uncommon graces and attainments, was left to the liberty and discretion of the ministers of the church.

Baptism was generally called φῶς or φώτισμα, light or illumination ; and the Epiphany, in so far as it commemo-

---

* St. Chrysostom tells us that this manifestation, together with the earlier one by the star of the wise men, and the later one by the miracle at Cana, in Galilee, all occurred on the same day, although of course not in the same year. But this assertion has not passed without challenge.

† "In the Latin Church it wanted this privilege—the Roman, French, and Spanish Churches for many ages not allowing of any other solemn times of baptism, but only Easter and Pentecost, except in case of sickness and extremity."—Bingham's *"Antiquities of the Christian Church."*

rated the baptism of Christ, "who from that time became a Light to them that sat in darkness," was known as the Day of Lights, or of the Holy Lights. That the practice of the Greeks might keep pace with their verbal symbolism, it was their custom to adorn their churches with a great number of lights and tapers when they came to perform the service of the day. On the vigil of the feast of Epiphany it was usual to consecrate the water to be used at baptisms throughout the year, as, in one of his "Homilies on the Baptism of Christ," we are informed by St. Chrysostom; who in another of them declares further that "in the solemnity [of Epiphany] in memory of our Lord's baptism, by which He sanctified the nature of water, they were used at midnight to carry home water from the church, and lay it up, where it would remain as fresh and uncorrupt for one, two, or three years, as if it were immediately drawn out of any fountain." "The like custom," Bingham tells us, "was observed by Fronto Ducæus to appear in the Syrian calendar."

The designations of the Epiphany vary as it is contemplated from different points of view. In addition to the simple idea of *manifestation*, when it is regarded as the day of the appearance of the star to the wise men, there is the idea of *Theophany*, or *Manifestation of God*, with reference more particularly to the events attending our Lord's baptism. It is, again, known as the *Festum Trium Regum*— the Festival of the Three Kings; as *Bethphania*, a name derived from the circumstances of the first miracle at Cana in Galilee; and, once more, as *Phagiphania*, a name derived from appending, as we have seen St. Augustine did, the commemoration of the feeding of the five thousand to that of the miraculous turning of water into wine. Not all apologists for the observance of the festival of Epiphany have put forward all the four reasons of St. Augustine. "Peter Chrysologus and Eucherius Lugdunensis confine themselves to the first three of these reasons; and Pope

Leo, who wrote eight sermons on the Epiphany, insists upon no other reason than that of the manifestation of Christ's birth to the wise men by means of a star." * In the service for the day in our own Church, the Collect and the Gospel point to the star; the Second Lesson at Morning Prayer to the manifestation of the Trinity at our Lord's Baptism; and the Second Lesson at Evening Prayer to the miracle at Cana. "The First Lesson," as Wheatly says, "contains prophecies of the increase of the Church by the abundant access of the Gentiles, of which the Epistle contains the completion, giving an account of the mystery of the Gospel's being revealed to them. The Collect and Gospel are the same as those which were used in the ancient offices; but the Epistle was inserted at the first compiling of our Liturgy, instead of part of the sixtieth of Isaiah, which is now read for the First Lesson in the morning."

It was only by degrees that the Latin Church accorded to the Epiphany the full honours which that season received from the Eastern communion, one of the earliest instances of its disposition to do this being that afforded by the fact that at Milan, according to the Ambrosian rite, "the morning service of the day was celebrated at night, very many lights being burned *after the Greek manner*." †

But, after all, it remained that the Latin Church directed its Epiphany ceremonials chiefly to the commemoration of the visit and adoration of the Magi; which were symbolized not less in popular customs than in religious rites and splendours. During the Middle Ages a kind of dramatic representation of the oblations of the wise men at Bethlehem was incorporated into the services of the Church; and the custom of offering,

* Bingham's *Antiquities of the Christian Church*.
† *Acta Sanctorum*.

on the day of the Epiphany, gold, frankincense and myrrh, on the altar of the Chapel Royal, in St. James's, by the Sovereign in person or by proxy, is still preserved in England. "What a witness have we for the hold of the Epiphany on the popular affections and imagination in the vast body of legendary lore which has clustered round it; in the innumerable mediæval mysteries which turn on the flight into Egypt, the massacre of the Innocents, or the coming of the Three Kings, and in all else of poetry and painting which has found its suggestion here!"*

There has been a general tendency to associate with the primary events commemorated by the Epiphany a consideration of those secondary ones which may be looked upon as occurring *in continuation* of the manifestation of the person and divinity of Christ. The tendency was to make the Epiphany to include every exhibition of infinite power—to embrace, that is, the whole series of miracles which illustrated the three years' public ministry of our Lord. The goal has never quite been reached; but the movement, we say, has been in this direction. Now, for poetical purposes, to widen is to weaken. Diffusion and concentration are contradictories. The graphic unity so precious to the Muse is in danger of vanishing entirely when it is distributed over a region which cannot be reproduced in, so to say, the cabinet picture of a lyric. It will be well if, in seeking for poetical illustrations of the season, we abstain from widening the area of commemoration beyond the limits which the usage of our own Church has indicated in her offices. And even within these limits we incline to fix our attention more especially upon the wise men, severally in their individual and their representative capacity; and upon the star which was the instrument of their illumination and attraction to the manger in Bethlehem.

* Trench's *Star of the Wise Men.*

NATURE OF THE STAR.

It is natural that the mention of a star as the guide of the wise men to the cradle of the Saviour, occurring without any expression to define the nature of that star, should have engaged the investigations of science and the activity of Biblical criticism, no less than the fancy of the poet and the genius and cunning of the painter. It is no purpose of ours to open the gates of controversy; it is nearly enough if we offer, without comment, and for the purpose of showing how the reason may disport itself when it becomes conversant about such matters, the process by which St. Chrysostom arrives at the conclusion that it was not so much a literal and veritable star as an angel that assumed the form of one. "This star," he says, in his Homily on Matt. ii. 1, 2, "was not of the common sort, or rather, not a star at all, as it seems at least to me, but some invisible power transformed into this appearance." This he infers from the course of the star being from north to south, and so far contrary to that of the other heavenly bodies, whose motion is from east to west; to the circumstances of its shining at mid-day, of its appearing and vanishing again, and of its being able to indicate—contrary again to the idea of a true star's remoteness—so small a spot as the stable at Bethlehem.

The popular mind would find more to interest it in an extravagant gloss upon the historical narrative, which was probably made from a fragment of one of the recensions of the Hebrew Gospel (Ignat., "Epist. ad Ephes.," sec. 19):— "The star sparkled brilliantly beyond all other stars; it was a strange and wonderful sight. The other stars, with the sun and moon, formed a choir around it, but its blaze outshone them all."* There is here an assumption of literalness—of literalness glorified and made more marvel-

* "The Star overpowered by its aspect all the stars that were in the heavens, as it inclined to the depth, to teach that its Lord had come down to the depth, and ascended again to the height of its nature, to show that its Lord was God in its nature."—*Discourse on the Star;* by Mar Eusebius, of Cæsarea (about A.D. 400).

lous—antagonistic to the mystical exposition of St. Chrysostom. Neander also accepts the literalness of the star; and to those who, whilst resting in this theory, may be troubled at the idea of a revelation of the Saviour being made through the instrumentality of astrological pursuits, a few words of his may have value and interest. "A few sages in Arabia (or in some part of the Parthian kingdom), who inquired for the course of human events in that of the stars, became convinced that a certain constellation or star which they beheld was a token of the birth of the great King who was expected to arise in the East. It is not necessary to suppose that an actual miracle was wrought in this case; the course of natural events, under divine guidance, was made to lead to Christ, just as the general moral culture of the heathen, though under natural forms, was made to lead to the knowledge of the Saviour.

"The Magi studied astrology, and in their study found a sign of Christ. If it offends us to find that God has used the errors of man to lead him to a knowledge of the great truths of salvation, as if thereby He had lent Himself to sustain the false, then must we break in pieces the chain of human events, in which the true and the false, the good and the evil, are so inseparably linked, that the latter often serves for the point of transition to the former. Especially do we see this in the history of the spread of Christianity, where superstition often paves the way for faith. God condescends to the platforms of men in training them for belief in the Redeemer, and meets the aspirations of the truth-seeking soul even in its error! In the case of the wise men a real truth, perhaps, lay at the bottom of the error; the truth, namely, that the greatest of all events, which was to produce the greatest revolution in humanity, is actually connected with epochs of the material universe, although the links of the chain may be hidden from our view."* In something like a

* Neander's *Life of Christ.*

pursuance and development of the same idea, we may here quote the thought with which Dr. Trench concludes the last of the Hulsean Lectures, delivered by him in 1846: "That star in the natural heavens which guided those Eastern sages from their distant home was but the symbol of many a star which twinkled in the world's mystical night, but which yet, being faithfully followed, availed to lead humble and devout hearts from afar off regions of superstition and error, till they stood beside the cradle of the Babe of Bethlehem, and saw all their weary wanderings repaid in a moment, and all their desires finding a perfect fulfilment in Him."*

Bishop Heber has spiritualized the circumstance from which Neander and Trench have drawn a moral. The general principle by which we are guided in the selection of flowers for our anthology is that of gathering our specimens from exotic or less available sources. But in the case of Heber's hymn on the "Epiphany" we find a different principle almost compelling us to its insertion here. It is so well known—to say nothing of its graphic beauty and pertinence—that its omission would be felt as a violation of completeness:— .

> Brightest and best of the sons of the morning!
>   Dawn on our darkness, and lend us thine aid;
> Star of the East, the horizon adorning,
>   Guide where our Infant Redeemer is laid!
>
> Cold on His cradle the dew-drops are shining,
>   Low lies His bed with the beasts of the stall;
> Angels adore Him in slumber reclining,
>   Maker, and Monarch, and Saviour of all.
>
> Say, shall we yield Him, in costly devotion,
>   Odours of Edom and offerings divine,

* *Christ the Desire of all Nations; or, the Unconscious Prophecies of Heathendom.*

> Gems of the mountain and pearls of the ocean,
>   Myrrh from the forest, or gold from the mine?
>
> Vainly we offer each ample oblation,
>   Vainly with gold would His favour secure;
> Richer by far is the heart's adoration;
>   Dearer to God are the prayers of the poor.
>
> Brightest and best of the sons of the morning!
>   Dawn on our darkness, and lend us thine aid;
> Star of the East, the horizon adorning,
>   Guide where our Infant Redeemer is laid!

The same thought has inspired the following verses on "The Epiphany," as given in "Lyra Americana," from the pen of an anonymous poet on the other side of the Atlantic:—

> We come not with a costly store,
>   O Lord! like them of old,
> The masters of the starry lore,
>   From Ophir's shores of gold;
>
> No weepings of the incense-tree
>   Are with the gifts we bring,
> No odorous myrrh of Araby
>   Blends with our offering.
>
> But still our love would bring its best,—
>   A spirit keenly tried
> By fierce affliction's fiery test,
>   And seven times purified.
>
> The fragrant graces of the mind,
>   The virtues that delight
> To give their perfume out, will find
>   Acceptance in Thy sight.

The relations of the star to the wise men are of course too intimate to allow of any exclusive treatment; yet it happens that in some poems appertaining to the season of

Epiphany the principal theme is the star, and, in others, the wise men. The poetry of the star—that, we mean, which gives prominence to the idea of the illumination coming from above, rather than to the persons enlightened below—may be completed by a poem which occurs in the Rev. Orby Shipley's "Lyra Mystica." Its author is the Rev. Frederick W. Kittermaster, who entitles it "The Epiphany."

> Beyond the barren mountain range,
>   Where Hor lifts up its sacred head,
> And buried lies in mystery strange,
> As years work out their silent change,
>   The City of the dead.
>
> Where proud Euphrates day by day
>   Winds through the plain, or sleeping lies,
> The watching Magi nightly pray,
> And seek the future's hidden way
>   From planet-lighted skies.
>
> Through the unclouded midnight air,
>   On vast Infinity's dark page,
> With deepest skill and constant care,
> They read the golden letters there
>   That wax not old with age.
>
> Lo! as they gaze with deep intent,
>   A Star more brilliant than the rest,
> The Herald of some great event,
> Moves through the gilded firmament
>   Onward towards the West.
>
> Then came the sound tradition brought
>   From Peor's top in days of old,
> What time the Seer entrancèd caught
> Prophetic power, and spirit-taught,
>   The future did unfold.

A Sceptre shall from Israel rise,
  A Star from Jacob doubly blest,
And now, before their wondering eyes,
The brilliant Meteor walks the skies,
  Still onward towards the West.

Where'er it leads, that fiery Light,
  Unhidden by the blaze of day,
And marking with intenser might
The darkness of the deeper night,
  They follow on the way.

With morning's blush, when sunsets fade,
  On over rock and steep and wild,
By palm and cedar tree and shade,
Till in the homely Manger laid
  They find the Royal Child.

Intruding doubts away they fling,
  Unheeding the unwonted stir,
They from their costly treasures bring
Free offerings for the Infant King,—
  Gold, frankincense, and myrrh.

Gold shadows forth His royalty,
  While frankincense His priesthood shows,
And myrrh that He shall buried be,—
And so the wondrous mystery
  With deeper meaning grows.

Oh for some heavenly light enshrined
  In God's dark ways or holy word,
To break upon each erring mind
With spirit-power, that all might find
  The Saviour, Christ the Lord!

Till, walking in a living way,
  To holier purpose we arise,
And on His altar, day by day,
Our thoughts and best affections lay,
  A willing sacrifice.

It will be observed that two or three stanzas of the foregoing poem glance at the relation of the star of Balaam to the star of the Magi, the appearance of which latter is to be regarded as indicating the highest and ultimate fulfilment of the parable of the wayward prophet of Pethor:—
"I shall see him, but not now: I shall behold him, but not nigh: there shall come a Star out of Jacob, and a Sceptre shall rise out of Israel, and shall smite the corners of Moab, and destroy all the children of Sheth. And Edom shall be a possession, Seir also shall be a possession for his enemies; and Israel shall do valiantly. Out of Jacob shall come He that shall have dominion, and shall destroy him that remaineth of the city" (Num. xxiv. 17—19). "The Messianic character of this prophecy being established, it will be impossible to misunderstand the internal relation between the star of Balaam and the star of the wise men from the East. The star of Balaam is the emblem of the kingdom which will rise in Israel. The star of the Magi is the symbol of the Ruler in whom the kingly power appears concentrated. The appearance of the star embodying the image of the prophet, indicates that the last and highest fulfilment of his prophecies is now to take place."[*]

There is scarcely anything in the "Christian Year" more grand and graphic than the poem in which Keble, in a few bold words, first calls up the vision of the weird prophet, and then proceeds to point the likeness and the differences of Balaam's position and our own. The poem is that for the second Sunday after Easter, and has for its motto two out of the three verses we have just quoted from the 24th chapter of the Book of Numbers, part of the First Lesson for that day.

<blockquote>
O for a sculptor's hand,
That thou might'st take thy stand,
Thy wild hair floating on the Eastern breeze,
</blockquote>

[*] Hengstenberg's *Christology of the Old Testament*.

>   Thy tranced, yet open gaze
>   Fixed on the desert haze,
> As one who deep in heaven some airy pageant sees!
>   *   *   *   *   *
>
>   Lo! from yon argent field,
>   To him and us revealed,
> One gentle Star glides down on earth to dwell.
>   Chained as they are below,
>   Our eyes may see it glow,
> And as it mounts again, may trace its brightness well.
>
>   To him it glared afar,
>   A token of wild war,
> The banner of his Lord's victorious wrath:
>   But close to us it gleams,
>   Its soothing lustre streams
> Around our home's green walls, and on our churchway path.
>   *   *   *   *   *
>
>   Sceptre and Star divine,
>   Who in Thine inmost shrine
> Hast made us worshippers, O claim Thine own;
>   More than Thy seers we know—
>   O teach our love to grow
> Up to Thy heavenly light, and reap what Thou hast sown.

If we turn from the contemplation of the star to the consideration of the wise men to whom it served as a guide, we shall find conjecture and opinion even more busy than about the star itself. And for this reason,—that there are more possible objects of doubt and difference. The country, the character and position, the persons, the number, and the names of the wise men, as being undecided by authority, have severally been open to discussion.

As to their country, claims have been put forward for Persia, as being the native land and home of the Magian religion; for Arabia, because the offered gifts were eminently—and one of them, frankincense to wit, as was hastily supposed, exclusively—the products of that land; and because the word of prophecy had expressly designated the "kings of Sheba and Seba" as amongst those that should bring their gifts of gold and incense. Other regions, whose claims have been supported, are Chaldæa and Mesopotamia. Something, of course, may be advanced in favour of each of these; for in each there was reason for such an anticipation of the advent of some extraordinary king, as would account for pious and observant people, skilled in the signs of the times, and willing to be led, surrendering themselves to the guidance of so remarkable a phenomenon as the star they followed. Alban Butler points out that Persia and Chaldæa would be prepared for some such great expectation and appearance by the Jewish captivity and dispersion, and the prophecies of Daniel; Arabia, by its proximity to Judæa, and the frequent intercourse between the two countries; Mesopotamia by the same, quickened by its traditions of the prophecy of Balaam, who was a native of that country. And Neander remarks that "the *natural* development of the heathen mind worked in the same direction as the movement of *revealed* religion among the Jews to prepare the way for Christ's appearance, which was the aim and end of all previous human history. There is something analogous to the law and the prophets (which, under revealed religion, led directly, and by an organically arranged connection, to Christ) in the sporadic and detached revelations which, here and there among the heathen, arose from the divine consciousness implanted in humanity. As, under the Law, man's sense of its insufficiency to work out his justification was accompanied by the promise of One who should accomplish what the Law could never do; so, in the progress of the pagan mind under the law of nature, there arose a sense of the necessity of a new revelation from heaven, and a longing desire for a higher order of things. The notion of a Messiah, carried about by the Jews in their intercourse with different nations, everywhere found a point of contact with the religious sense of men; and thus natural and revealed religion worked into each other, as well as separately, in preparing the way for the appearance of Christ." "We do not insist," Neander adds in a note, "upon *Tacitus,* 'Hist.' v. 13, and *Suetonius,* 'Vespasian' iv., who speak of a rumour spread over the whole East, of the approaching appearance of the great King, as it is yet doubtful whether these passages are not imitated from Josephus." *

The indefiniteness of the term *Magi* leaves much in controversy as to the character of the wise men. The Magi, as described by Herodotus, were " a tribe of the Medes, uniting, as the Levites among the Jews, and the Chaldæans among the Assyrians, a common family descent, and the exclusive possession of all sacerdotal and ecclesiastical functions—a priest-caste. As such they were the sole possessors of all science and knowledge, and not merely exercised most decisive influence in all private matters as prophets, as interpreters of dreams, but in political affairs as well. The education of the king was in their hands; they filled his court, composed his council; and although they had not the government so directly in their hands as the Egyptian hierarchy, yet they exercised the strongest influence thereon. In all liturgic matters they were supreme; they interpreted the holy books, and, what brings them into more immediate relation with the matter in hand, they observed the stars, and read in them the future destinies of men. The name Magian, then, in this its first sense, was a name of the highest dignity and honour."†

But in its progress westward the name lost its specific meaning, and was applied to those who affected the studies of the Magi proper. Thus the word suffered degradation; so that some of the Fathers, understanding it as equivalent to Magician, have actually regarded these celebrated and

* Neander's *Life of Jesus Christ.*
† Trench's *Star of the Wise Men.*

canonized pilgrims to Bethlehem as so many "impostors and instruments of Satan." It need hardly be said that there is no reason for thus regarding them; and there is much greater colour for concluding, with Dr. Trench, that "they belonged to the original and nobler stock of the Magi, rather than to the later and degenerate offsets." "To me, at least," are St. Chrysostom's words, "they seem to have been at home teachers of their countrymen."*

But it was not enough to rescue them from the imputation of being professors of an evil magic; other honours must be invented and accorded to them. Thus, by some of the Fathers, the word *Magi* has been translated Principes or Dynastæ; and it has become almost an article of faith with the Church of Rome to regard them as kings. "Royalty was early attributed to them, in accordance with Isa. lx. 3; Psa. lxxii. 10, 11. Tertullian twice quotes this last passage as having its perfect fulfilment in the adoration of Christ by these wise men of the East; while Hilary also calls them princes, and quotes this last passage without apparently any doubt that it, as so many more, found now its fulfilment. It needs not to observe how universally this belief prevailed in the Middle Ages, so that it gave to Epiphany one of the titles by which it was most commonly designated, namely, the Feast of the Three Kings—nor how Christian art, poetry and painting alike, were, and in part are still, penetrated with it—nor yet how innumerable are the legends which turn on the kingly dignity of these august visitors."† It is probable that if they had any claim to the honour of rulers, it was rather as *reguli* than *reges*—as sheikhs or emirs, rather than as wielders of empire.

The number of the wise men is as little determined by the Evangelist as their quality. In the Eastern Church,

* Homily vi.; Matt. ii. 1, 2.
† Trench's *Star of the Wise Men*.

though chiefly among the Nestorians, they were believed to have been twelve; but the favourite number fixed upon is three. Such a number agrees very well with the pictorial proclivities of popular piety; for, on this theory, each of the wise men has his several gift to offer, and each typifies one of the three great families into which all post-diluvian humanity may be distributed. To give names to the wise men was the next not very difficult step; and our own Bede is said to have been the first, in this part of Christendom, at least, to have given them a *nominal* introduction to the applause of the faithful, as Melchoir, Gaspar, (or Jasper), and Balthasar.

Traditions vary with localities and times as to which of the several presents is offered by each of these, and which of the groups of mankind it is that each represents. It would be idle to particularize varieties which are often accidental or capricious; but generally in Christian art, Melchior is depicted as an aged man with a long beard, as the bearer of the offering of gold, and as typical of the family of Shem. Gaspar, a beardless youth, of a Moorish or Ethiopian complexion, offers the frankincense, and represents Ham; and Balthasar, with a large and spreading beard, presents the myrrh, and is typical of Japheth.

The following short but startling "Carol of the Kings" is described by its author, the Rev. R. S. Hawker, as "An Armenian Myth." It partakes somewhat of the marvellous, but a great truth underlies its hyperbole and exaggeration. It is not only that the whole Gentile world is figured by the wise men, but these wise men are identified with the patriarchs themselves, upon whom, after the flood of Noah, the re-peopling of the world devolved. The slight grotesquerie of the thought of the legend cannot detract from the grandeur of the event, and is indeed a consequence of a conviction of that grandeur struggling into adequate ideal representation, and adequate verbal expression:—

Three ancient men in Bethlehem's cave
  With awful wonder stand;
A voice that called them from their grave
  In some far Eastern land.

They lived, they trod the former earth
  When the old waters swelled;
The Ark, that womb of second birth,
  Their house and lineage held.

Pale Japhet bows the knee with gold,
  Bright Sem sweet incense brings,
And Cham, the myrrh his fingers hold—
  Lo the three Orient kings!

Types of the total earth, they hailed
  The signal's starry frame;
Shuddering with second life, they quailed
  At the Child Jesu's Name.

Then slow the Patriarchs turned and trod;
  And this their parting sigh,—
Our eyes have seen the Living God;
  And now—once more to die.

The late Dr. Faber treats the subject of the wise men with a nearer approach to realism. There is enough, however, of graphic movement and expression; and too much —as the reader would observe, if considerations of poetical and religious taste alike did not compel us to suppress the fourth and the last stanza—of the puerility and superstition which unfortunately to so great an extent characterize the teaching of the Church of Rome. The poem is entitled "The Three Kings," and is one of a group—Part II. of Faber's Hymns—on the "Sacred Humanity of Jesus:"—

Who are these that ride so fast o'er the desert's sandy road,
  That have tracked the Red Sea shore, and have swum the torrents broad;

Whose camels' bells are tinkling through the long and starry
    night —
For they ride like men pursued, like the vanquished of a fight?

Who are these that ride so fast? They are Eastern monarchs
    three,
Who have laid aside their crowns, and renounced their high degree;
The eyes they love, the hearts they prize, the well-known voices
    kind,
Their people's tents, their native plains—they've left them all
    behind.

The very least of faith's dim rays beamed on them from afar,
And that same hour they rose from off their thrones to track the
    Star.
They cared not for the cruel scorn of those who called them mad,
Messias' Star was shining, and their royal hearts were glad.

A speck was in the midnight sky, uncertain, dim, and far,
And their hearts were pure, and heard a voice proclaim Messias'
    Star;
And in its golden twinkling they saw more than common light,
The Mother and the Child they saw in Bethlehem by night!

And what were crowns, and what were thrones, to such a sight as
    that?
So straight away they left their tents, and bade not grace to wait;
They hardly stop to slake their thirst at the desert's limpid springs,
Nor note how fair the landscape is, how sweet the skylark sings!

Whole cities have turned out to meet the royal cavalcade,
Wise colleges and doctors all their wisdom have displayed;
And when the Star was dim, they knocked at Herod's palace gate,
And troubled with the news of faith his politic estate.

And they have knelt in Bethlehem! The Everlasting Child
They saw upon His mother's lap, earth's monarch meek and mild;
His little feet, with Mary's leave, they pressed with loving kiss,—
Oh, what were thrones! oh, what were crowns, to such a joy as
    this?

One little sight of Jesus was enough for many years,
One look at Him their stay and staff in the dismal vale of tears:
Their people for that sight of Him they gallantly withstood,
They taught His faith, they preached His word, and for Him shed
    their blood.

Ah me! what broad daylight of faith our thankless souls receive,
How much we know of Jesus, and how easy to believe!
'Tis the noonday of His sunshine, of His sun that setteth never;
Faith gives us crowns and makes us kings, and our kingdom is for
    ever!

Oh, glory be to God on high for these Arabian kings,
These miracles of royal faith, with Eastern offerings;
For Gaspar and for Melchior, and Balthazzar who from far
Found Mary out and Jesus by the shining of a Star!

The subsequent history of men upon whom so signal a favour had been conferred, and who had attained so grand and eminent a position, was certain to be of general interest and attraction. A work attributed to St. Chrysostom says that "after their return they continued serving God more than before, and instructed many by their preaching. And at last, when Thomas had gone into that province, they joined themselves to him, and were baptized, and became doers of his word." But tradition has a happy faculty of becoming more and more affluent with the course of years, and we have not only a collective account, but even short individual biographies, of the illustrious and sainted kings. Melchior, Gaspar, and Balthasar, are severally said, in almost identical expressions in the Cologne and German *Martyrologies*, to have been "kings and bishops in the East, and to have slept in the Lord after having first celebrated and partaken of the divine sacrifice." St. Melchior, again, is reported to have died at Sessania, in Arabia Felix, on the 1st January—which is his day, or one of his days, in the Roman calendar—aged 116 years; Gaspar is said to have died A.D. 109; and both, with Balthasar, are variously said to have obtained the crown of martyrdom, the "Chronicon" of Dexter having it that they suffered in A.D. 70.* It is fortunate, where there are so many discrepancies—and we have not nearly exhausted these—that the debateable matter is chiefly of sentimental rather than of practical importance. One other tradition and we have done, if not quite with the wise men, at least with Melchior, Gaspar, and Balthasar, kings, bishops, heroes, martyrs. It is said that their bodies were transported in the fourth century from Persia to Constantinople, where with great pomp and ceremonial they were placed in the Basilica of St. Sophia. From Constantinople they were removed to Milan by Bishop Eustorgius I., who deposited them in his cathedral. Here they reposed for six hundred and seventy years, until, in 1162, they were transferred to Cologne by order of the Emperor Frederick Barbarossa, who had taken and destroyed the city of Milan. Some critics, it is complained, have challenged the identity of the bodies of the three kings of Cologne; and the authority of the Church is handsomely pledged to the faithful for the genuineness of the relics. Whether these be genuine or not, there is no doubt that the magnificent memorial which enshrines them is the object of many a vow, and the goal of many a pilgrimage; and that the *Feast of the Three Kings*, having the twofold prestige of a *cultus* at once grand and local, yet ranks amongst the highest of the festivals of Cologne.

Whatever the quality, names, country, or history of the Magi may have been, it is for us to rejoice that with them we are admitted to the feet of the Infant Jesus. It is with them—as the first-fruits and representatives of a despairing Gentile world now first received to the fulness of the Hebrew promises, developed and spiritualized—that we join in an *Ave* to the Babe whose manifestation, if for the glory of Israel, was also for the enlightenment of the Gentiles. We owe the following short Epiphany salutation to the pen of Dean Alford:—

* *Acta Sanctorum.*

Thou that art the Father's Word,
Thou that art the Lamb of God,
Thou that art the Virgin's Son,
Thou that savest souls undone,
Sacred sacrifice for sin,
Fount of piety within;
  Hail, Lord Jesus!

Thou to whom Thine angels raise
Quiring songs of sweetest praise,
Thou that art the flower and fruit,
Virgin-born from Jesse's root,
Shedding holy peace abroad,
Perfect man and perfect God;
  Hail, Lord Jesus!

Thou that art the door of heaven,
Living bread in mercy given,
Brightness of the Father's face,
Everlasting Prince of Peace,
Precious Pearl beyond all price,
Brightest Star in all the skies;
  Hail, Lord Jesus!

King and spouse of holy hearts,
Fount of love that ne'er departs,
Sweetest life and brightest day,
Truest faith, and surest way
That leads onward to the blest
Sabbath of eternal rest;
  Hail, Lord Jesus!

We just now called the wise men the first-fruits and representatives of the entire Gentile world. The author of the poem which we are about to give deals with the circumstances of the visit to the cradle of the Saviour—the privileges which it symbolized, and the duties which it opened and enjoined—as if he and other Gentiles were present really and in person, where they were present only in a figure and by deputy. There is, in addition, a rendering of the sentiment of Simeon; so that it blends somewhat of the Presentation with the Epiphany. In his "Historical

Notes to the 'Lyra Germanica,' " the Rev. Theodore Kübler supplies us with a few particulars of John Rist, the author, of which we may do well to avail ourselves. "Rist was born on the 8th of March, 1607, in Ottensee, near Hamburgh, and was destined from his birth by his father to follow his profession as a clergyman. . . . Having finished his studies, he became minister at Wedel, near Hamburgh, where he laboured faithfully until his death. His pious zeal and poetical talents made him known far and wide, and brought him many honours and distinctions. He became poet laureate to the German Emperor, and was, by him, even raised to nobility. Some of his best hymns were composed on a hill near his village; many, however, were, as he used to say himself, 'pressed out of him by the dear cross' in the time of war, hunger, and pestilence. He died at sixty years of age, on the 31st August, 1667. His hymns number six hundred and fifty-eight; of which, however, as may be supposed, all are not equally good, for he composed many merely for the sake of composing."

In the "Lyra Germanica," from which we adopt this hymn, it is assigned to the year 1655. It has for its theme the "Epiphany," and for its motto the first verse of that marvellous chapter of Isaiah which forms the First Lesson for the day,—"Arise, shine; for thy light is come, and the glory of the Lord is risen upon thee."

> All ye Gentile lands, awake!
>   Thou, O Salem, rise and shine!
> See the day-spring o'er you break,
>   Heralding a morn divine,
> Telling, God hath called to mind
> Those who long in darkness pined.
>
> Lo! the shadows flee away,
>   For our light is come at length,
> Brighter than all earthly day,
>   Source of being, life, and strength!
> Whoso on this light would gaze
> Must forsake all evil ways.

MANIFESTATION OF THE LIGHT.

Ah, how blindly did we stray
   Ere shone forth that glorious Sun!
Seeking each his separate way,
   Leaving heaven unsought, unwon;
All our looks were earthward bent,
All our strength on earth was spent.

Earthly were our thoughts and low,
   In the toils of folly caught,
Tossed of Satan to and fro,
   Counting goodness all for nought;
By the world and flesh deceived,
Heaven's true joys we disbelieved.

Then were hidden from our eyes
   All the law and grace of God;
Rich and poor, the fools and wise,
   Wanting light to find the road
Leading to the heavenly life,
Wandered, lost in care and strife.

But the glory of the Lord
   Hath arisen on us to-day,
We have seen the Light outpoured
   That must surely drive away
All things that to night belong,
All the sad earth's woe and wrong.

Thy arising, Lord, shall fill
   All my thoughts in sorrow's hour;
Thy arising, Lord, shall still
   All my dread of Death's dark power:
Through my smiles and through my tears
Still Thy light, O Lord, appears.

Let me, Lord, in peace depart
   From this evil world to Thee;
Where Thyself sole brightness art,
   Thou hast kept a place for me:
In Thy shining city there
Crowns of light Thy saints shall wear.

We conclude our remarks and our poetical illustrations of the Epiphany with Milton's superb picture of the disarray wrought amongst the gods of the Gentile world by the Nativity of Christ. The verses which follow are a part of the great poet's *Ode* on that season; although there is perhaps a higher degree of fitness in applying the stanzas we transcribe from that production to the season of Epiphany, which was, relatively to the nations without the pale of Judaism, the time of the Incarnation. It is possible that Milton may have thought of the Epiphany as an incident of the Nativity, just as Baronius tells us, in his "Notes to the Martyrology," the Egyptians on one and the same day observed the birth and baptism of Christ; "the priests of that province," to quote Cassian in confirmation, "defining the day of Epiphany or baptism of the Lord as the day of his nativity *secundum carnem*." It is for us to breathe the prayer that all the heathendom yet rampant or sheltered within the microcosm of our hearts may shatter and fall, as in Milton's verses the divinities of the great world of paganism are seen to totter at the manifestation of the true God to a select and representative band of their unsatisfied worshippers.

        The oracles are dumb,
        No voice or hideous hum
Runs through the archèd roof in words deceiving.
        Apollo from his shrine
        Can no more divine
With hollow shriek the steep of Delphos leaving.
    No nightly trance or breathèd spell
Inspires the pale-eyed priest from the prophetic cell.

        The lonely mountains o'er,
        And the resounding shore,
A voice of weeping heard and loud lament;
        From haunted spring and dale,
        Edged with poplar pale,
The parting genius is with sighing sent;
    With flower-inwoven tresses torn,
The nymphs in twilight shade of tangled thickets mourn.

DISCOMFITURE OF THE HEATHEN DEITIES.

   In consecrated earth,
   And on the holy hearth,
The Lars and Lemures moan with midnight plaint;
   In urns, and altars round,
   A drear and dying sound
Affrights the Flamens at their service quaint;
 And the chill marble seems to sweat,
 While each peculiar power foregoes his wonted seat.

   Peor and Baalim
   Forsake their temples dim,
With that twice-battered god of Palestine;
   And moonèd Ashtaroth,
   Heaven's queen and mother both,
Now sits not girt with tapers' holy shine;
 The Lybic Hammon shrinks his horn,
 In vain the Tyrian maids their wounded Thammuz mourn.

   And sullen Moloch, fled,
   Hath left in shadows dread
His burning idol all of blackest hue;
   In vain with cymbals' ring
   They called the grisly king,
In dismal dance about the furnace blue;
 The brutish gods of Nile as fast,
 Isis, and Orus, and the dog Anubis, haste.

   Nor is Osiris seen
   In Memphian grove or green,
Trampling the unshowered grass with lowings loud:
   Nor can he be at rest
   Within his sacred chest;
Nought but profoundest hell can be his shroud:
 In vain with timbrelled anthems dark
 The sable-stolèd sorcerers bear his worshipped ark.

   He feels from Juda's land
   The dreaded Infant's hand,
The rays of Bethlehem blind his dusky eyn;
   Nor all the gods beside
   Longer dare abide,
Nor Typhon huge, ending in snaky twine;
 Our Babe, to show His Godhead true,
 Can in His swaddling bands control the damnèd crew.

Lent.

IT is observed by Philo Judæus that the Law "sets down every day as a festival;" the unfailing celebration of which, however, is to be assured only by a constant and uninterrupted perfection of virtue.* From the defect of the latter in human experience arises the frequent solution of the opportunity, and even of the faculty, of rejoicing. Granting that the life of perfect virtue would be a life of perfect pleasure and content, yet the life of imperfection, the only one of which we are actually aware, must be darkened by many a shadow, crossed and chequered by many a sorrow. The sin-laden individual must occasionally and of set purpose "afflict his soul," and sin-conscious communities, which are the aggregates of such individuals, will now and again assume the outward signs of a heart-seated penitence and self-deprecation.

The tendency to humiliation on account of sin has found historical exposition in all ages and amongst all peoples; and has manifested itself in every degree of mortification—from the sincere humiliation of repentance, and the desire to keep the inferior body in subjection to the superior soul, to a morose and sanguinary asceticism, the object of which was often, by external and mechanical processes, to *compel*

---

* *Treatise to show that the Festivals are Ten in Number.*

an abatement of the Divine wrath, or a bestowal of the Divine favour.

Traces of fasting, as a particular method of humiliation, are to be discovered in the records of nearly all the principal nations of the world. Now a fast was proclaimed as a state ceremonial for political purposes; now it was observed that a military expedition might be auspiciously initiated or triumphantly concluded; and again, that a social or municipal disaster might be averted, mitigated, or removed. Now a fast was dictated by the will or the necessities of the individual, whether king, emperor, magistrate, or citizen; and again, it was enjoined upon the members of a philosophical school or priestly college, or upon the aspirants after initiation into the various mysteries which the multiform *cultus* of Paganism so bountifully fostered.

The exceptionally occurring or seasonably recurring fasts of social exigencies or of religious privileges were by some of the choicer and severer spirits of the Greek philosophy, extended into a canonical rule and regimen. "Some of the Cynics fed upon nothing but herbs and cold water, living in any shelter that they could find, or in tubs, as Diogenes did."[*] Epicurus—a startling fact to those who are familiar chiefly with the degradation of his system and the abuse of his definitions—"was content with water and plain bread," to which, if cheese were at any time added, it was counted for a banquet.[†] It is more generally known that Pythagoras inculcated the observance of a perpetual Lent; and one account of the death of this philosopher, as given by Dicæarchus, and quoted by Diogenes Laërtius, is to the effect that "he died of starvation in or near the Temple of the Muses, at Metapontum, after having abstained from food for forty days."[‡]

The last few words are remarkable for bringing the idea

[*] Diogenes Laërtius. *Life of Menedemus.*
[†] Do. do. *Life of Epicurus.*
[‡] Do. do. *Life of Pythagoras.*

of fasting, or abstinence, into contact with that of a quadragesimal interval of time; and to this, as the reader may surmise, we shall very soon have occasion to recur. But in the next two or three short paragraphs we wish to trace generally the history of fasting amongst the Jews, who were given to its observance whenever they found themselves face to face with critical or disastrous circumstances (Judges xx. 26; 1 Sam. vii. 6, and xxxi. 13; 2 Sam. iii., 35; Is. lviii. 3-6).

The legislation of Moses was concerned as little as possible about fasts; and in the earliest times of the Jewish polity they were of desultory celebration, the spontaneous product and expression of the nation, the city, the family, or the individual. The great Lawgiver enjoined only one season of fasting, but that he inculcated under the severest of penalties and with the most solemn of sanctions (Levit. xxiii. 26-32). It occurred on the tenth day of the seventh month, a month which had been initiated by the Feast of Trumpets, and the fifteenth of which was to be the commencement of the Feast of Tabernacles.

It was not till the times of the Captivity that other anniversary fasts were added to the single one of Mosaic institution. These were held severally on the seventeenth day of the fourth month, Tammuz (July); the ninth day of the fifth month, or Ab (August); the third of the seventh month, or Tishri (October); and the tenth day of the tenth month, or Zebeth (January); and severally commemorated the capture of Jerusalem, the burning of the Temple, the death of Gedaliah, and the commencement of the attack on Jerusalem. There is a promise that all these fasts should, at some future period, "be to the house of Judah joy and gladness and cheerful feasts" (Zech. viii. 19). The period thus indeterminately promised of the Lord has not yet arrived, and His ancient and scattered people still continue to observe these yearly seasons as times of fasting and humiliation.*

* Jahn's *Biblical Archæology*.

SIGNIFICANCE OF THE QUADRAGESIMAL PERIOD. 125

The number forty, and the quadragesimal interval of time, have frequently been invested with a peculiar interest by the events connected with sacred history; a circumstance which did not escape the attention of the Fathers, or of the theologers only less ancient than they. The devoutness of the latter, combining with their tendency to the detection or invention of analogies and coincidences, habitually condescended to the minute, and did not always stop short of the trivial. The following are among the more relevant of their speculations in the sphere of our present enquiries:— The appositeness of the Christian Lent has been pointed by the fact that the world was drowned during forty days, and that it was after the ark had rested for a like interval on Mount Ararat that Noah sent forth the reconnoitring raven. To one or other of these intervals, tradition affixed a fast. Herrick, in his "Noble Numbers," sings:—

> Noah the first was, as tradition says,
> That did ordain a fast of forty days.

It was to a space of forty years that the wanderings of the Israelites in the desert were protracted; it was with forty stripes that the malefactor was to be beaten under the law of Moses; and the time of grace allowed to Nineveh for repentance was forty days, during which a fast was proclaimed that was to extend from the king downwards, not only to the meanest of his subjects, but to the very cattle, whose lives, indeed, along with the lives of their owners, were at stake in the threatened destruction.

But whilst these and other quadragesimal intervals may illustrate with more or less of relevancy and pertinence the existing institution of the Christian Lent, the period of abstinence acquires its most important significance when it is regarded as *en rapport* with the fasts of Moses and Elias, and its most Divine sanction when it is regarded as humbly imitative of the fasting of our Lord in the wilderness. There is a solemn warrant for the celebration of the last-mentioned fast in connection with the two former, when it is remembered that the conjunction of Moses and Elias with the Saviour is not arbitrary or capricious on the part of the Church. It was Moses and Elias, who, severally representing the Law and the Prophets, severally and together found themselves complete in the person of Jesus Christ, with whom they, and they only of all anterior saints, were associated in the splendours of " the Holy Mount"— an association which was one of the circumstances appealed to by Isidore of Seville, as proving the concord and agreement of the Gospel with the Law and the Prophets. " For the Law," he says, " is accepted in the person of Moses, the Prophets in the person of Elias, between whom Christ appeared glorious on the Mount of Transfiguration."* And he appeals for a dogmatic confirmation of what was thus symbolically rendered, to the words of St. Paul : " Now the righteousness of God without the law is manifested, being witnessed by the Law and the Prophets " (Rom. iii. 21).

But there are analogies of practice as well as of sentiment; and it has been rendered extremely probable by the elaborate researches of Bishop Hooper (Bath and Wells, 1703—1727), that " the derivation of our Christian Lent is from a like preparatory time of the Jews," which preceded their yearly Expiation. This preparatory time, which was one of solemn humiliation, as the bishop proves on the testimony of Jewish authors, began forty days before the Expiation; and the coincidence of its duration with that of the Christian Lent he shows not to be casual, nor "a single similitude," since " there were in the Christian religion many other like correspondences which must apparently be attributed to the same original."† The primitive Christians, in accordance with the precedent of the Jews, established a fast as a becoming preparation for the commemoration of the great Expiation

* *De Ecclesiasticis Officiis.*
† Bishop Hooper's *Discourse concerning Lent.*

for the sins of the whole world. That the Christian Lent, however, was not always of the length of forty days, and, indeed, not always of any uniform duration whatever, is a matter which we may defer for a sentence or two, until we have glanced at the obligation of fasting at all.

"The doctrine and practice of our Lord and His apostles respecting fasting may be thus described:—Our Saviour neglected the observances of those stated Jewish fasts which had been superadded to the Mosaic law, and introduced especially after the Captivity, to which the Pharisees paid scrupulous attention (Matt. xi. 18, 19); and He represented such observances as inconsistent with the genius of His religion (Matt. ix. 14-18; and parallel passages, Mark xi. 15-22; Luke v. 33-39). The practice of voluntary and occasional fasting He neither prohibited nor enjoined; He spoke of it, however, as being not unsuitable on certain occasions, nor without its use in certain cases (Matt. ix. 15; xvii. 21); He fasted Himself on a great and solemn occasion (Matt. iv. 2), and He warned His disciples against all ostentations and hypocritical observances of this kind (Matt. iv. 16-18). The doctrine of the apostles on this subject was to the same purport, neither commanding the practice of fasting, nor denouncing it as unlawful, unless either the observance or omission should involve a breach of some moral and Christian duty (Rom. xiv. 14-22; Col. ii. 16-23; 1 Tim. iv. 3-5). In practice the apostles joined fasting with prayer on solemn occasions (Acts xiii. 2, 3; xiv. 23)."*

But if no law was enacted by Christ or His apostles concerning fasts, there is enough to establish their occasional observance of them, if not to give colour to the hypothesis that such observance was implied or assured as a part of Christian discipline and experience (Matt. vi. 17, 18). Moreover, in some things the teaching of Christ assumed a *temporary* complexion, or was limited by a *tem-*

* Riddle's *Manual of Christian Antiquities.*

porary reticence (John xvi. 12, 13). It was under the dispensation of the Spirit that the disciples were to be guided into " all truth ;" and it is possible to argue, in accordance with what may be called a kind of "development theory," that, looking at the Pharisaic abuses and hypocrisies of contemporaneous fasting, this kind of self-mortification was one the enforcement of which He reserved to the compelling power of the Spirit over the individual conscience, and over the *communis sensus* of the Church. If fasting was observed by our Lord and His apostles, it is fair to infer, from such practical recognition, that at least it is to be considered as an acceptable service, whenever the conditions which are essential to a true fast are complied with. Fasting is objectionable when regarded as in itself efficacious and meritorious; becoming, when used as an instrument of self-control: objectionable, when it is looked upon as in itself constituting a claim for consideration and forgiveness; becoming, when it appears as a voluntary tribute of love, humbly and gratefully rendered by men who either feel that their sins are forgiven, or else trust that they may be forgiven, on grounds other than their own doings or sufferings. To it, as to other phenomena of Christian practice, we may apply the pregnant words of the dying Herbert: "It is a good work if it be sprinkled with the blood of Christ."

But whatever encouragement the New Testament may give to the occasional practice of fasting, or of uncommon abstinence from mere æsthetic pleasures, whether of the body or the mind, it furnishes no precept as to the time when such fasting should be celebrated. The particular season, the frequency, the manner, the degree, and the duration, are alike left to the spiritual discretion of the individual, who has to decide upon these in the light of such facts of health, temperament, and disposition as he can best judge of. But in the case of a general or corporate fast, the very idea bears with it a decision as to several of these points by some competent and recognised authority. The Church—meaning thereby the aggregate of its members—can celebrate a common or universal fast only by a decree of the Church; and the *set times* of such a fast—in default of the express indications of Scripture—are to be referred to the authority of the Church, as depending on this for their decent and orderly observance. George Herbert supplies us with a poetical enforcement of this principle in his poem on "Lent," that fast of forty days before Easter, which is still reckoned of special and singular obligation.

> Welcome, dear feast of Lent: who loves not thee,
> He loves not temperance or authority,
>   But is composed of passion.
> The Scriptures bid us fast; the Church says, now:
> Give to thy Mother what thou would'st allow
>   To every Corporation.
>
> The humble soul, composed of love and fear,
> Begins at home, and lays the burden there,
>   When doctrines disagree:
> He says, in things which use hath justly got,
> I am a scandal to the Church, and not
>   The Church is so to me.
>
> True Christians should be glad of an occasion
> To use their temperance, seeking no evasion,
>   When good is seasonable;
> Unless Authority, which should increase
> The obligation in us, make it less,
>   And Power itself disable.
>
> Besides the cleanness of sweet abstinence,
> Quick thoughts and motions at a small expense,
>   A face not fearing light:
> Whereas in fulness there are sluttish fumes,
> Sour exhalations, and dishonest rheums,
>   Revenging the delight.

> Then those same prudent profits, which the Spring
> And Easter intimate, enlarge the thing,
> > And goodness of the deed.
> Neither ought other men's abuse of Lent
> Spoil the good use; lest by that argument
> > We forfeit all our Creed.
>
> 'Tis true, we cannot reach Christ's fortieth day,
> Yet to go part of that religious way
> > Is better than to rest:
> We cannot reach our Saviour's purity;
> Yet are we bid "Be holy e'en as He."
> > In both let's do our best.
>
> Who goeth in the way which Christ hath gone,
> Is much more sure to meet with Him than one
> > That travelleth by-ways.
> Perhaps my God, though He be far before,
> May turn, and take me by the hand, and more,
> > May strengthen my decays.
>
> Yet, Lord, instruct us to improve our fast
> By starving sin, and taking such repast
> > As may our faults control:
> That every man may revel at his door,
> Not in his parlour; banqueting the poor
> > And among those his soul.

In the foregoing poem the idea of Lenten obligation is that of ecclesiastical appointment; but a Lent *of forty days* has been otherwise regarded as of apostolic institution. The latter theory has been chiefly confined to Roman Catholic advocates; some of whom, however, have so far modified it as to hold that Lent was "only such an apostolical rule or custom as left the church at liberty to alter it, as she did some other things upon just and proper occasions, and to abrogate it by introducing a contrary practice."* Such a qualification is very like a surrender of the position. On the other hand, it has been concluded

---

* Bingham's *Antiquities of the Christian Church*.

that the fast *of forty days* in Lent was not of apostolic institution, from the extreme probability, touching on certainty, that the Lenten fast was originally *of forty hours* merely, or the time during which our Saviour lay in the grave, that is, the Friday and Saturday before Easter. This was the time, the interval between His passion and His Resurrection, in which the Bridegroom was taken away from the disciples, "the children of the bridechamber," and in which it had been foretold or fore-enjoined that they should fast (Matt. ix. 15).

The practice of fasting, as it obtained in the second century, is incidentally, but in a way beyond challenge, because in a way of objection, established by Tertullian, who, whilst a follower of Montanus, reproached the Catholics that "they thought themselves obliged only to observe those two days in which the Bridegroom was taken away from them, and that these were the only legitimate fasts of Christians."* Still the practice was not uniform; and the want of uniformity was the occasion of a plentiful want of unanimity. Eusebius preserves a letter written to Pope Victor by Irenæus—Bishop of Lyons in the second century, and between whom and the apostle St. John, their common friend Polycarp, was a connecting link—in a spirit of accommodation worthy of his name, in which he pleads that the diversity of customs with regard to fasting should be allowed in the interests of peace, as being a diversity of already long-standing introduction, and one from which, in the generations of Christians that

---

* Tertullian, *De Jejuniis*. The Montanists understood the taking away of the Bridegroom in another sense for our Saviour's Ascension, or Assumption into Heaven, and therefore they kept one of their Lents or Fasts (for they had three in the year) after our Lord's Ascension, in opposition to the Church, which celebrated the whole time of Pentecost as a solemn festival. Montanists and Catholics agreeing on the reason of a fast, though they applied it to a different time according to their different apprehensions.—Bingham's *Antiquities*.

even to Irenæus and his contemporaries were ancestral, had been compelled a tribute to the unity of the faith.*

Down to the end of the fourth, and the beginning of the fifth century, the diversities were not less apparent. "In some churches," says Sozomen, "the interval called Quadragesima, which occurs before the festival of the Resurrection, and is devoted by the people to fasting, is made to consist of six weeks; and this is the case in Illyria and the western regions, in Libya, throughout Egypt, and in Palestine: whereas it is made to comprise seven weeks at Constantinople, and in the neighbouring provinces, as far as Phœnicia. In some churches, the people fast three alternate weeks, during the space of six or seven weeks; whereas in others, they fast continually during the three weeks immediately preceding the festival. Some people, as the Montanists, only fast two weeks."† Socrates bears like testimony; with the addition of showing further the varieties of manner, as well as of duration. "The fasts before Easter are differently observed. Those at Rome fast three successive weeks before Easter, excepting Saturdays and Sundays. The Illyrians, Achaians, and Alexandrians observe a fast of six weeks, which they term *the forty days' fast*. Others, commencing their fast from the seventh week before Easter, and fasting three five-days only, and that at intervals, yet call that time *the forty days' fast*.‡ It is indeed surprising that, thus differing

---

* Eusebius, *Ecclesiastical History*; B. v., c. 24.
† Sozomen, *Ecclesiastical History*; B. vii., c. 19.
‡ Our own term *Lent* does not carry with it any idea expressive of duration; but belongs to that class of appellations of the season which are taken from the time of year when it occurs. Of such also are the German *Lenz*, to which our own word is akin, and the Dutch and Flemish *Lente*, with which it is identical. There are other groups of names which refer to Lent as a season of fasting; in Russ, for instance, it is *Post*, or *Velekie Post*, the *Fast*, or the *Great Fast*; in Dansk and German respectively, it is *Fastetid* and *Fastenzeit*, both of which are equivalent to Fast-tide. In the Eastern Church it is

ORIGINAL DURATION OF LENT.

in the number of days, they should still give it one common appellation; but some assign one reason, some another, according to their several fancies. There is also a disagreement about abstinence from food, as well as the number of days. Some wholly abstain from things that have life; others feed on fish only of all living creatures; many, together with fish, eat fowl also, saying that, according to Moses, these were likewise made out of the waters. Some abstain from eggs, and all kinds of fruits; others feed on dry bread only; and others eat not even this; while others, having fasted till the ninth hour—three o'clock in the afternoon—afterwards feed on any sort of food without distinction. And among various nations there are other usages, for which innumerable reasons are assigned. Since, however, no one can produce a written command as an authority, it is evident that the apostles left each one to his own free-will in the matter, to the end that the performance of what is good might not be the result of constraint and necessity."*

It is most probable, therefore, that the quadragesimal fast was originally a fast of forty hours, which by gradual growth and extension, became protracted to a season of forty days. With the extension of duration, there seems to have been a corresponding extension of idea and significance; and that which was at first a fulfilment of the words of Christ that in His absence—interpreted as we have seen, as referring to His absence in the tomb, between His Crucifixion and His Resurrection—His disciples should mourn and fast, became a dutiful and sympathetic and isochronous commemoration of His Fasting and Temptation in the wilderness. To this the analogies of Moses and Elias were ready for applica-

simply Μεγάλη Νηστεία. Other designations are derived from its forty days' duration, as the Greek Τεσσαρακοστή, and the Latin *Quadragesima*, the Italian *Quaresima*, and the French *Carême*. This is the case in all the Romance languages, and the Celtic dialects.

* Socrates, *Ecclesiastical History*; B. v., c. 22.

tion; and these, together with the Jewish practice with which Bishop Hooper connected the origin of Lent, would naturally have the effect, when once the quadragesimal interval of forty hours had been exceeded, of producing and protracting the great Christian fast till it rested again and permanently in a quadragesimal interval of approximately the same number of days.

In the Eastern Church, Socrates and Sozomen have shown us that the days of Lenten abstinence were distributed over the seven weeks before Easter, from which all the Saturdays save one, and all the Sundays, were excepted, in order, in the words of St. Chrysostom, "that the souls of wayfarers along the Christian fast might be refreshed, as travellers intermitted their journeys at inns and stations." The Latin Church, however, reserving only the Sundays from the days of fasting, commenced its Lent with the sixth week before Easter. The practice of both communions so far agreed, that each reserved the Sunday, in what season soever it occurred, as an undivertible and unchangeable festival. "The Catholic Church, whilst it observes the forty days' fast before the Sacred Week, sets apart every Sunday as a glad and festive day on which no fasts are at any time observed; for it would be absurd to fast on the Lord's Day."*

It resulted from the reservation of the Sunday, or of the Saturday and Sunday, that in the case of each of the two communions, the number of clear fasting-days was thirty-six; a number which has been fondly dwelt on by Cassian and Isidore of Seville as being a tithe of the whole year. The Lenten fast continued to be actually of only thirty-six days' duration, till in the sixth century, Pope Gregory the Great, or alternatively Pope Gregory the Second in the eighth century, completed the full number of forty fasting-days; since the time of which addition,

* Epiphanius, *Expositio Fidei Catholicæ*.

ECCLESIASTICAL PENALTIES.

Lent has always dated its commencement from Ash-Wednesday.

The practice of fasting, which had at first been of voluntary observance in the Church, passed successively through the stages of pious and prevailing custom—to which, so late as the fourth century, the people were exhorted with entreaties—and finally of binding enactment. The Council of Orleans, A.D. 541, decreed that any one who should neglect to observe the stated times of abstinence, should be treated as an offender against the laws of the Church. The eighth Council of Toledo, A.D. 653, ordained that those persons who, without apparent necessity, should have eaten flesh during Lent, "should be deprived of it all the rest of the year, and should be forbidden to communicate at Easter." In the eighth century, fasting began to be regarded as a meritorious work; and the breach of its observance at the stated seasons, subjected the offender to excommunication. In the earlier part of the eleventh century, persons who ate flesh during the appointed time of abstinence, are stated by Baronius to have been punished with the loss of their teeth.

The first of the English kings to decree the observance of Lent in his dominions, was Earconbert, the seventh King of Kent (640—664), who, "of his supreme authority commanded the idols, throughout his whole kingdom, to be forsaken and destroyed, and the fast of forty days before Easter to be observed. And, that the same might not be neglected, he appointed proper and condign punishments for the offenders."[*] It was decreed by the Council of Trent, that confession should be enjoined as peculiarly fit and applicable to this season. "Grace," says the late Dr. Faber, in the spirit of his adopted Church, as illustrated in the last sentence—

"Grace is plentiful in Lent;"

a proposition which becomes wholesome and encouraging

[*] Bede's *Ecclesiastical History of England.*

when it is read simply as a particular statement of the general hortatory promise, "Seek, and ye shall find." The more abundant supplies await the more abundant supplications. The time of extraordinary contrition must be a time of extraordinary absolution; and Lent, by hypothesis, and ecclesiastical order, is such a time.

It is a characteristic of George Wither's "Hymns and Songs of the Church," that they exhibit in abstract almost the entire body of doctrine and the philosophy of the particular seasons about which they are conversant. The following poem on "Lent" is an example of his nearly exhaustive method:—

> Thy wondrous fasting to record,
>   And our rebellious flesh to tame,
> A holy fast to Thee, O Lord,
>   We have intended in Thy name:
> Oh, sanctify it, we Thee pray,
>   That we may thereby honour Thee,
> And so dispose us, that it may
>   To our advantage also be.
>
> Let us not grudgingly abstain,
>   Nor secretly the glutton play,
> Nor openly, for glory vain,
>   Thy Church's ordinance obey;
> But let us fast, as Thou hast taught,
>   Thy rule observing in each part,
> With such intentions as we ought,
>   And with true singleness of heart.
>
> So Thou shalt our devotions bless,
>   And make this holy discipline
> A means that longing to suppress,
>   Which keeps our will so cross to Thine;
> And though our strictest fastings fail
>   To purchase of themselves Thy grace,
> Yet they to make for our avail
>   (By Thy deservings) shall have place.
>
> True fasting helpful oft hath been,
>   The wanton flesh to mortify;

> But takes not off the guilt of sin,
>   Nor can we merit aught thereby:
> It is Thine abstinence, or none,
>   Which merit favour for us must,
> For when our glorioust works are done,
>   We perish, if in them we trust.

After such lines, the product of modern times and of the homebred muse, which set forth so well the spiritual uses and advantages of Lent, it may be of interest to revert to a more ancient statement of the practical benefits for the securing of which that season was instituted. "Why," asks St. Chrysostom, "do we fast these forty days?[*] Many, heretofore, were used to come to the Communion indevoutly and inconsiderately, especially at this time, when Christ first gave it to His disciples. Therefore, the fathers, considering the mischiefs arising from such careless approaches, meeting together, appointed forty days for fasting and prayer, and hearing of sermons, and for holy assemblies; that all men in these days being carefully purified by prayers and almsdeeds, and fasting, and watching, and tears, and confession of sins, and other the like exercises, might come according to their capacity with a pure conscience to the holy table."[†] And Cassian, who was a disciple of St. Chrysostom, and in whose time the term of Lent was still fixed at thirty-six days, has a kindred passage:—"So long as the perfection of the primitive Church remained inviolable, there was no observation of Lent; for they who fasted, as it were, all the year round, were not tied up by the necessity of this precept, nor confined within the strict bonds of such a fast, as by a legal sanction: but when the multitude of believers began to decline from the apostolic fervour of devotion, and to give themselves overmuch to worldly affairs; when, instead of

---

[*] Forty, nominally, and in round numbers.

[†] Chrysostom, *Orationes adversus Judæos*; Orat. 3.

imparting their riches to the common use of all (Acts iv.), they laboured only to lay them up and augment them for their own private expenses, not content to follow the example of Ananias and Sapphira (Acts v.), then it seemed good to all the bishops, by a canonical induction of fasts to recall men to holy works, who were bound with secular cares, and had almost forgotten what continence and compunction meant, and to compel them by the necessity of a law to dedicate the tenth of their time to God."*

The thoughts of Lent are not to terminate in a selfish solicitude for our own well-being, even when that solicitude takes the commendable form of humble and hearty confession with a view to the forgiveness of sin. Whilst men are prostrating themselves before the Throne of Justice, and lifting up streaming eyes to the Throne of Mercy, it especially becomes them to have a large-hearted care for the sorrows, and even a large-hearted charity for the offences of their brethren. In ancient times there was, during Lent, a *state* tenderness exercised towards the criminal. At this season, when men expected mercy and pardon from God, it seemed reasonable to them that they should exhibit more eminently than usual the quality of mercy towards their fellows. Upon this account the imperial laws forbade all prosecution of men in criminal actions, which might bring them to corporal punishment and torture, during this whole season. Two laws of the code of Theodosius the Great were enacted to this purpose :—" In the forty days, which by the laws of religion are solemnly observed before Easter, let the examination and hearing of all criminal questions be superseded" (Cod. Theod. l. 9. tit. 35, de Quæstionibus leg. 4); and, "in the holy days of Lent, let there be no punishments of the body, when we expect the absolution of our souls" (Do. leg. 5.). All public games and stage-plays were likewise prohibited, as well as the

* Cassian. *Collationes*, xxi., cc. 30 and 25.

celebration of all festivals, birth-days, and marriages, as being unsuitable to the grave solemnity of the Lenten fast.

That which was clemency in the government, appeared as charity in private life. The early Christians made a practice of giving to the poor the meat which they had denied to their own appetites. They devoted themselves to visiting the sick and the imprisoned, to entertaining strangers, and to reconciling differences. Most of these points are incorporated in a simple and energetic little poem of Robert Herrick's, who shows, as follows, how "To Keep a true Lent":—

> Is this a fast to keep
>   The larder lean,
>   And clean
> From fat of veals and sheep?
>
> Is it to quit the dish
>   Of flesh, yet still
>   To fill
> The platter high with fish?
>
> Is it to fast an hour,
>   Or ragged to go,
>   Or show
> A down-cast look, and sour?
>
> No: 'tis a fast, to dole
>   Thy sheaf of wheat,
>   And meat,
> Unto the hungry soul.
>
> It is to fast from strife,
>   From old debate,
>   And hate;
> To circumcise thy life.
>
> To shew a heart grief-rent;
>   To starve thy sin,
>   Not bin;
> And that's to keep thy Lent.

The Church points the propriety of the seasonable distribution of food to the poor, when, on the fourth Sunday in Lent, is read the Gospel which contains the narrative of the miracle which Jesus, on one occasion just before the Passover, wrought out of compassion to the faint and hungry thousands of His followers.

It will be observed that the acts of charity which, although always binding on the Christian, were reckoned to have a peculiar obligation in Lent, coincide almost literally with those deeds of mercy that were in the Last Judgment to secure the approbation of the Son of Man (Matt. xxv. 31-40). The late James Montgomery has a poem, as tender and beautiful as it is forcible, which points the moral of such good deeds :—" Inasmuch as ye have done it unto one of the least of these My brethren, ye have done it unto Me." The verses to which we allude, and which have for their subject "The Poor Wayfarer," are as follows :—

> A poor wayfaring man of grief
>   Hath often crossed me on my way,
> Who sued so humbly for relief
>   That I could never answer, Nay.
> I had not power to ask his name,
> Whither he went, or whence he came,
> Yet there was something in his eye
> That won my love, I knew not why.
>
> Once when my scanty meal was spread,
>   He entered ; not a word he spake :
> Just perishing for want of bread ;
>   I gave him all ; he blessed it, brake,
> And ate ; but gave me part again :
> Mine was the angel's portion then ;
> For while I fed with eager haste,
> That crust was manna to my taste.
>
> I spied him where a fountain burst
>   Clear from the rock ; his strength was gone ;

"THE POOR WAYFARER."

The heedless water mocked his thirst,
  He heard it, saw it hurrying on:
I ran to raise the sufferer up:
  Thrice from the stream he drained my cup,
Dipt, and returned it running o'er;
I drank, and never thirsted more.

'Twas night; the floods were out; it blew
  A winter hurricane aloof;
I heard his voice abroad, and flew
  To bid him welcome to my roof;
I warmed, I clothed, I cheered my guest,
Laid him on my own couch to rest;
Then made the hearth my bed, and seemed
In Eden's garden while I dreamed.

Stript, wounded, beaten nigh to death,
  I found him by the highway side:
I roused his pulse, brought back his breath,
  Revived his spirit, and supplied
Wine, oil, refreshment; he was healed:
I had myself a wound concealed;
But from that hour forgot the smart,
And peace bound up my broken heart.

In prison I saw him next, condemned
  To meet a traitor's death at morn:
The tide of lying tongues I stemmed,
  And honoured him 'midst shame and scorn:
My friendship's utmost zeal to try,
He asked, if I for him would die?
The flesh was weak, my blood ran chill,
But the free spirit cried, "I will."

Then in a moment to my view
  The stranger darted from disguise;
The tokens in His hand I knew,
  My Saviour stood before mine eyes!
He spake; and my poor name He named—
"Of Me thou hast not been ashamed;
These deeds shall thy memorial be;
Fear not, thou did'st them unto Me."

We have had occasion to notice that the Sundays which occur during the great quadragesimal period of humiliation are rather Sundays *in* Lent than Sundays *of* Lent. In the midst of the Fast, they form no part of it; and on them the Church continues without interruption to celebrate the Resurrection of the Saviour. Yet to any one observing the offices proper to these Sundays, it will be apparent that the general spirit of, so to say, the contextual days is upon them. Their rejoicing is done with evident trembling. There is in each the consciousness of the fast which was in force the day before, has been intermitted only for the Sunday, and is to be resumed on the morrow. In the order for Morning Prayer for the first Sunday in Lent, the Gospel is supplied by the narrative of the fasting and temptation in the wilderness, which leaves the Saviour as victor over the devil, and as enjoying the ministration of angels. The Gospels for the second and third Sundays are illustrative of the exercise of that power over diabolical agencies which Christ had first vindicated by His own personal supremacy. As we are invited hopefully to contemplate the fact that our High Priest "was in all points tempted like as we are, yet without sin;" so, conversely, the fact of our temptations at all points resembling His, is to be dwelt upon as one of the meditations very proper to the Lenten season. The following poem calls upon us to be aware of the armies of the Evil One contending against us and plotting within us for our discomfiture and destruction, and presents a vivid realization of those spiritual foes against whom the Christian is bound evermore to struggle. It is the production of Andrew, Archbishop of Crete, who was born at Damascus, about A.D. 640, and died near Mitylene, about the year 732. The most ambitious composition of this poet is the "Great Canon," which—partially used in the Eastern Church during other days of Lent—is sung right through on the Thursday of Mid-Lent week, called, on that account, the *Thursday of the Great Canon*. The *Great Canon* is, in its entirety, of great, and, for our purpose, of impracticable length. We transcribe a translation, from the late Dr. Neale's "Hymns of the Eastern Church," of a part of it called a "Stichera for the Second Week of the Great Fast."

> Christian! dost thou *see* them
> On the holy ground,
> How the troops of Midian
> Prowl and prowl around?
> Christian! up and smite them,
> Counting gain but loss:
> Smite them by the merit
> Of the Holy Cross!
>
> Christian! dost thou *feel* them,
> How they work within;
> Striving, tempting, luring,
> Goading into sin?
> Christian! never tremble!
> Never be downcast!
> Smite them by the virtue
> Of the Lenten fast!
>
> Christian! dost thou *hear* them,
> How they speak thee fair?
> "Always fast and vigil,
> Always watch and prayer?"
> Christian! say but boldly—
> "While I breathe I pray;"
> Peace shall follow battle,
> Night shall end in day.
>
> "Well I know thy trouble,
> O, my servant true;
> Thou art very weary,—
> I was weary too:
> But that toil shall make thee
> Some day all Mine own;
> But the end of sorrow
> Shall be near My throne."

The true use of Lent is, that its attendant contrition, charity, contemplation, and discipline should result in practical and discernible improvement and purification of the heart and the affections. Amongst the "Poems" of the late Dr. Faber we find one on "Lent," which sets forth the wholesome effect of that season upon the soul, which, if left to an uninterrupted succession of joyful commemorations, an unbroken series of festivals from which fasts should be excluded, would be liable to waywardness and wantonness. Dr. Faber is dramatic and personal in his method of exhibiting the chastening results of the Lenten period; and he seems to have been attracted to it by a kind of Spenserian emulation. We have religion and self-denial engrafted, as in the gorgeous allegories of the "Faerie Queene," upon a stock of chivalry. A Christian knight is represented as marching with a retinue, from whom he has assimilated some frivolity and contracted some stains in morals in the gaiety of a procession along the course of the Christian seasons, which, from the time of Christmas, have been unsaddened by a fast.

It is with this notice of a poem—which we regret not to be able to quote—devoted to the ideal *results* of Lent that it seems proper to bring to a close the present paper, in which we have sought to illustrate the various ideas and phases of the entire season. One day alone of Lent we reserve for separate and particular treatment; and the several poems which we set apart for the poetical illustration of this day are those which give utterance more singly and more fully than any we have hitherto quoted to that abasement, and rending, and contrition of heart which are so especially characteristic of Ash Wednesday.

Ash Wednesday.

FROM small and limited beginnings, and through the operation of a pious contagion, many of the existing celebrations of the Church have gradually spread into universality; with the attainment of which they became ripe for authoritative recognition and enactment. In proportion as the origin of these celebrations has been local and inconsiderable, the knowledge about them has been obscure, and the tracing of their precise history has been difficult or impossible. It is not every season that can, with the great festival of Easter, look down upon all posterior challenge from the unmoved base of apostolic institution. Already we have seen something, and hereafter we may see more, of the hopelessness of fixing to-day the exact birth-place or birth-time of various Christian commemorations.

The origin of Ash Wednesday, without being certain, is yet limited to a very small range of uncertainty. The traditions of its appointment oscillate only between the two popes, Gregory the Great and Gregory the Second, as its alternative authors; and between the sixth and eighth centuries as its alternative periods of first observance. Before the dedication of Ash Wednesday as the *Caput Jejunii*, the head or commencement of the Fast, this had begun on the first Sunday in Lent; and, regarded as a quadragesimal interval of forty days, had been only approximately observed.

ASH WEDNESDAY.

With the expansion of time, as we have seen already (page 133), there resulted a development of the doctrine and associations of the season. But it still remained that the radical idea of Lent was one of penitence, contrition, abasement and supplication. However complex and various the lessons of the great Fast may be, this survives above all, beneath all, and enfolding all. St. Chrysostom and Cassian gave prominence to the value of Lent as a season of preparation for the high communion of Easter. Still, as every form of preparation is founded on penitence, we never in the whole course of the Lenten fast get so far as a stage to which the necessity of penitence does not apply. It is ordered that every Collect peculiar to Lent is to be preceded by that for Ash Wednesday; which is humbly addressed to a sin-pardoning God, by his people "worthily lamenting their sins, and acknowledging their wretchedness." This is the key-note with which all subsequent intercession must be in accord; and by which even the gladsome strains of the Sundays in Lent are to be regulated.

Amongst writers who have investigated the origin, traditions, significance, and uses of Lent, there is no name of greater claim to honour and respect for the thoroughness of his work, than that of Bishop Hooper, who at the time of publishing his "Discourse concerning Lent" (1694), was Dean of Canterbury. We borrow from the Bishop a few of his concluding sentences, in which with an engaging combination of zeal and dignity, he enforces the peculiar lessons which the season of Lent should inculcate. "Were we," he says, "to celebrate the anniversary of our Lord's passion only, and with no respect to our sins since our baptism; yet we should come upon the solemn day too rashly and unworthily, if we did not appoint some others to go before it, and usher it in; and should seem to have too low thoughts of the sacred mystery, if we did not take care to rise up to its high consideration by the steps and ascents of some previous meditations. To the keeping of the great memorial rightly, such preparatory remembrances would be wanting: that we may bring to it a fuller and livelier perception of the *mercies of God in Christ;* may the better comprehend, *with all saints,* the dimensions of that surpassing, inestimable love; may more profoundly adore, more gratefully thank, and more zealously devote ourselves and our service; having beforehand endeavoured to confirm and actuate our faith, to raise and quicken our hope, and to oblige and inflame our charity. But such a preparatory season is still more needful for the other, the *penitential* part; that we should afore begin to recollect our past transgressions, to reflect upon their guilt, and to dispose our minds to an abhorrence of them: that we should beseech God humbly for His grace, to promote this holy work; should review our baptismal covenant, bewail its breaches, and repair them by confession to God, and restitution to men; renewing our vows, and mortifying our lusts, and recovering and improving our virtuous habits, against that Friday when we are solemnly to appear in the Divine presence, contrite and truly sorrowful for our sins, stedfastly resolved to forsake them, and as much as in us lies, qualified for their pardon. Thus would a preparation have been necessary to either of those offices apart; but much more justly will they expect it when joined together, when we are to be provided both fitly to contemplate the mystery, and effectually to be benefited by its expiation.

"For these holy and important purposes Lent is instituted; a solemn and large space of time; to be religiously employed by each private Christian at his discretion, as the condition of his soul shall require, and the circumstances of his worldly affairs shall permit. Accordingly, the first day of it gives warning of the then distant propitiation day, and calls us early to our duty; actually entering us on the godly work, by reflection on our sins, and acknowledgment of Divine justice; by fasting and prayer; and engaging us to go on, and to make use of the following intermediate season for the perfecting our repentance, and for our increase in the knowledge of the *cross of Christ*, that *wisdom and power of God*. A notice, very necessary to those who want a solemn monitor; and which, by the grace of God, may, some time or other, serve to awaken and reclaim them: but always acceptable and welcome to the good Christian; who, the more sensible he is of his own offences, and of the mercy of God in Christ, the more ready he will be to comply with the advice, and the more glad of the occasion."*

Thus the multiform duties and lessons of Lent are induced upon a foundation of penitence and contrition, the first stone of which is laid on Ash Wednesday. The sweetest flowers of Christian charity are to be unfolded from the bitter buds of Christian sorrow and humiliation. It is thus the peculiar concern of the poets of Lent in general, as of its first day in particular, to give form and utterance to the tearful agonies and the impassioned litanies of the sin-convicted and quickened spirit.

"Mortification," observes Bishop Jeremy Taylor, "is one half of Christianity; it is a dying to the world." As, in His first going up to the Passover, our Saviour scourged the traders who were polluting with their traffic and merchandize the temple of His Father, so it is incumbent upon His followers, by discipline, watchfulness, and self-mortification, to whip from their souls the old offending Adam.

Sir Archibald Edmonstone, in a poem on "Ash Wednesday," which occurs in his "Devotional Reflections in Verse," contemplates an entire people as falling, through covetousness and Mammonism, into the offence of temple defilement. In the spirit of the prophet Joel, from whom he adopts the motto for his verses (Joel ii. 15-17), he calls upon the Church to prostrate herself, with prayer and

* *Discourse concerning Lent.*

NATIONAL HUMILIATION.

fasting, in lamentation for the sins, and in mitigation of the penalties, of national pride, supineness, and alienation.

> Mourn ye o'er the nation's sin—
> Mourn His temple courts within;
> Priests and people, own the rod—
> Weeping, bow before your God.
>
> Queen of waters, veil thy pride,
> Boast not of thy commerce wide—
> That the sun doth never set
> On thy jewelled coronet;
>
> Boast not that thine ensigns tower,
> Boast not that thy foemen cower—
> Mourn and weep that thou canst bring
> No pure incense to thy King.
>
> All thy treasured gold is dross,
> All thy store is empty loss;
> Mammon reigns where God should dwell,
> As fiends haunt the hermit's cell.
>
> Church, our Mother, fast and pray,
> If thou judgment may delay!
> Princes, priests, and people all,
> Low before His footstool fall!
>
> Lenten time will soon pass by—
> Catch the moments as they fly;
> Fasting, praying, draw ye near—
> He is present, He will hear.

The true and efficient humiliation of a community can be assured only by the genuine humiliation of the individual. We quote a "Hymn to God the Father," which is one of the most valuable of the poetical legacies left to us by Dr. Donne, Dean of St. Paul's (1621-1631); whom his biographer, Izaak Walton, calls "a second St. Austin, for I think none were so like him before his conversion, none so like St. Ambrose after it; and if his youth had the infirmities of the one, his age had the excellencies of the other—the learning and holiness of both." Ben Jonson predicted that Donne would perish as a poet for want of being understood; and the latter has been represented as "imbued to saturation with the learning of his age;" as being " of a most active and piercing intellect—an imagination, if not grasping and comprehensive, most subtle and far-darting—a fancy rich, vivid, and picturesque—a mode of expression terse, simple, and condensed—and a wit admirable, as well for its caustic severity as for its playful quickness." To which praise it may be added that Donne was ever on the stretch and strain after conceits, and that his rhythm is too often chiefly remarkable for its ruggedness and tunelessness. The "Hymn to God the Father" is in the best manner of the author. A little stiff in its construction, it is admirable for the large inclusiveness of its confessions, which, it will be seen, take in every variety of personal sins and sins of example, as well as that only fatal sin of doubting that all sin is pardonable through the death of Christ. It was one of the most sacred delights of Dr. Donne to hear this "Hymn" sung by the choristers of St. Paul's, to " a most grave and solemn tune."

> Wilt Thou forgive that sin where I begun,
> Which was my sin, though it were done before?
> Wilt Thou forgive that sin through which I run,
> And do run still, though still I do deplore?
> When Thou hast done, Thou hast not done,
>   For I have more.
>
> Wilt Thou forgive that sin which I have won
> Others to sin, and made my sin their door?
> Wilt Thou forgive that sin which I did shun
> A year or two, but wallowed in a score?
> When Thou hast done, Thou hast not done,
>   For I have more.
>
> I have a sin of fear, that when I have spun
> My last thread I shall perish on the shore;

> But swear by Thyself that at my death Thy Son
> Shall shine as He shines now and heretofore;
> And having done that, Thou hast done—
> I fear no more.

The first of the foregoing stanzas offers an incidental disclaimer against the peril of inferring Divine forgiveness from human forgetfulness. Through the lapse of time merely, it is impossible that guilt should ever revert to innocence. The sins of a long past youth are as swift as if they were committed yesterday to overtake the palsied steps of a hardened old age. Not only do the undeplored offences of a hundred years stand simply unforgiven, but multiplied through the momentary repetitions of a century of impenitence. The greater guilt is the guilt of persistence.

In the French language there is extant a penitential "Sonnet," of disputed authorship, which, if some exception might be taken against it on the ground that it is slightly histrionic, is beyond doubt extremely forcible. It cannot be denied that its doctrine is as evangelical as its attitude and manner are dramatic. Twelve of its lines are taken up with an invocation of those Divine judgments which are in the last two lines turned aside by a valid deprecation. The thunders of God are challenged as *necessary* to His character for justice, and are then shown abruptly to be impossible or harmless, through the protective efficacy of the blood of atonement. The popularly reputed author of this "Sonnet" was Jacques Vallée des Barreaux, who was born at Paris, in 1602, achieved a composite fame as a "poet and Sybarite," and died at Chalons-sur-Saône, May 9th, 1673. He changed his residence with the seasons; and composed some verses, of which none remain but the remarkable "Sonnet" in question:—

> "Grand Dieu! Tes jugements sont remplis d'équité."

But his claim to the authorship of even this production has been contested in favour of an ecclesiastic named Louis

Irland de Lavau, who was born at Paris of a noble family in the former half of the sixteenth century, and who was a member and sometime director of the French Academy. That the "Sonnet" may want as little as possible of strangeness, it is no other than Voltaire who has questioned the title of Des Barreaux. "It is false," he says, "that this sonnet, *aussi mediocre que fameux*, was by Des Barreaux. Its true author was Abbé de Lavau, of which I have seen a proof in a letter of Lavau to the Abbé Sérvien." The subjoined version is transcribed from the "Foreign Sacred Lyre" of Mr. Sheppard, who disregards the fact that any other claimant to the authorship of the Sonnet has been put forward than M. Des Barreaux. Another translation is to be found in the "Remains" of Henry Kirke White.

> Great God, Thy judgments are supremely right;
> Thy joy is ever to forgive and spare:
> But such my guilt is, if Thy goodness e'er
> Me pardoned, it would wrong Thy justice quite.
>
> Yes, Lord, my bold revolts in Thy pure sight,
> Leave Power but choice of sufferings to prepare:
> Thine honour must forbid me bliss to share,
> Thy very clemency my doom shall write.
>
> Fulfil that doom, which vindicates Thy ways;
> Reject the tears which from these eyelids start;
> Crush; strike; 'tis time; the rebel's course arrest;
> Lost, Thy destroying justice I must praise.
> But—on what spot can Thy keen lightning dart,
> Not laved in life-blood from my Saviour's breast.

Scarcely less vivid than the foregoing lines, are those on "Wrestling Jacob," by Charles Wesley, the author of hymns of which some are unsurpassed by any in the language, and the younger brother of the famous John Wesley. Charles was born at Epworth, in Lincolnshire, December 18th, 1708. For many years he shared his brother's labours, voyages, and travels. "For the space of ten years," says a Wesleyan biographer, "we must admit that his ministry was like a flame of fire." He died March 29th, 1788, almost in the act of poetical composition:—

> In age and feebleness extreme,
> Who shall a helpless worm redeem?
> Jesus! my only hope Thou art,
> Strength of my fainting flesh and heart.
> Oh! could I catch a smile from Thee,
> And drop into eternity!

The poem quoted immediately below is one of hundreds, the production of Charles Wesley's impassioned and fervid muse; and it exhibits in an especial manner a certain startling but sublime audacity of faith. The struggle is graphically portrayed of the man of misery and sin with the Man in whose hands are blessings and forgiveness.

> Come, O thou Traveller unknown,
>   Whom still I hold, but cannot see!
> My company before is gone,
>   And I am left alone with Thee:
> With Thee all night I mean to stay,
> And wrestle till the break of day.
>
> I need not tell Thee who I am,
>   My misery and sin declare;
> Thyself hast called me by my name,
>   Look on Thy hands, and read it there!
> But who, I ask Thee, who art Thou?
> Tell me Thy name, and tell me now.
>
> In vain Thou strugglest to get free,
>   I never will unloose my hold!
> Art Thou the Man that died for me?
>   The secret of Thy love unfold:
> Wrestling, I will not let Thee go,
> Till I Thy name, Thy nature know.

ASH WEDNESDAY.

Wilt Thou not yet to me reveal
   Thy new, unutterable name?
Tell me, I still beseech Thee, tell:
   To know it now resolved I am:
Wrestling, I will not let Thee go,
Till I Thy name, Thy nature know.

'Tis all in vain to hold Thy tongue,
   Or touch the hollow of my thigh;
Though every sinew be unstrung,
   Out of my arms Thou shalt not fly:
Wrestling, I will not let Thee go,
Till I Thy name, Thy nature know.

What though my shrinking flesh complain,
   And murmur to contend so long?
I rise superior to my pain:
   When I am weak, then I am strong:
And when my all of strength shall fail,
I shall with the God-Man prevail.

My strength is gone, my nature dies;
   I sink beneath Thy weighty hand;
Faint to revive, and fall to rise;
   I fall, and yet by faith I stand:
I stand, and will not let Thee go,
Till I Thy name, Thy nature know.

Yield to me now, for I am weak,
   But confident in self-despair;
Speak to my heart, in blessings speak,
   Be conquered by my instant prayer!
Speak, or Thou never hence shalt move,
And tell me if Thy name is Love?

'Tis Love! 'tis Love! Thou diedst for me!
   I hear Thy whisper in my heart!
The morning breaks, the shadows flee;
   Pure universal Love Thou art!
To me, to all, Thy bowels move;
Thy nature, and Thy name, is Love!

My prayer hath power with God ; the grace
    Unspeakable I now receive ;
Through faith I see Thee face to face,
    I see Thee face to face, and live :
In vain I have not wept and strove ;
Thy nature, and Thy name, is Love !

I know Thee, Saviour, who Thou art ;
    Jesus, the feeble sinner's Friend !
Nor wilt Thou with the night depart,
    But stay, and love me to the end !
Thy mercies never shall remove,
Thy nature, and Thy name, is Love !

The Sun of Righteousness on me
    Hath rose, with healing in His wings ;
Withered my nature's strength, from Thee
    My soul its life and succour brings ;
My help is all laid up above ;
Thy nature, and Thy name, is Love !

Contented now, upon my thigh
    I halt, till life's short journey end ;
All helplessness, all weakness, I
    On Thee alone for strength depend ;
Nor have I power from Thee to move ;
Thy nature, and Thy name, is Love !

Lame as I am, I take the prey,
    Hell, earth, and sin, with ease o'ercome ;
I leap for joy, pursue my way,
    And as a bounding hart fly home !
Through all eternity to prove
Thy nature, and Thy name, is Love !

There is a very special ecclesiastical history attaching to Ash Wednesday ; by reserving which for the close of our remarks upon that day we have been able to present, with the least possible hiatus, the poetry of Ash Wednesday in contiguity with the poetry of Lent, of which, indeed, in everything but our formal treatment, it is a part.

Early in the practice of the Church—Bellarmine, on too slight or questionable evidence, would have us believe as early as the Council of Agde, A.D. 506—Ash Wednesday, *Dies cinerum*, was set apart for the public performance of penance. Yet not so as that this day was devoted to the granting of penance to the exclusion of other seasons. "It does not appear," says Bingham, "that, anciently, the time of imposing penance was confined to the beginning of Lent, but penance was granted at all times, whenever the bishop thought the sinner qualified for it; as St. Ambrose admitted Theodosius to penance at Christmas; and there are many examples of a like nature."*

Of the ancient discipline practised on Ash-Wednesday upon ecclesiastical offenders, we owe the following account to the canonist Gratian.—"On the first day of Lent, all penitents, who either then were admitted to penance, or had been admitted before, were to present themselves to the bishop, before the doors of the church, clothed in sackcloth, barefooted, and with eyes fixed on the ground, confessing themselves guilty, both by their habit and their looks; and this was to be done in the presence of the deans or arch-presbyters of the parishes, and the penitential presbyters, whose duty it was to examine diligently their conversation, and to enjoin them penance, according to the measure of their faults, by the degrees of penance that were appointed. After this, they introduced them into the church, where the bishop, with all the clergy, falling prostrate on the ground, sang the seven penitential psalms, with tears, for their absolution. Then the bishop, rising from prayer, gave them imposition of hands, sprinkled them with holy water, threw ashes upon their heads, and covered their heads with sackcloth, declaring, with sighs and groans, that, as Adam was cast out of Paradise, so they for their sins must be cast out of the church. Then the bishop commanded the inferior ministers to turn them out of the

* *Antiquities of the Christian Church.*

church doors; and all the clergy followed them, using this responsory, 'In the sweat of thy brow shalt thou eat thy bread; for dust thou art, and unto dust thou shalt return.' And all this was done to the end that the penitents, observing how great a disorder the holy Church was in by reason of their crimes, should not lightly esteem of penance."*

In course of time the penitential discipline of the first day of Lent so far relaxed as to become reduced to a common confession of all Christian people; and the ashes —obtained by burning the branches of palm or brushwood which had been used on Palm Sunday in the preceding year—were sprinkled indifferently over the heads of the officiating clergy and the whole congregation. And it is to that custom, which was at first one of a series of penitential ceremonies, that the name of Ash Wednesday— known by vernacular equivalents in most of the languages of Europe—is more palpably and popularly referred. In the Convocation which assembled in 1536, the twenty-eighth year of King Henry the Eighth, and which published articles of what Fuller calls a "medley religion," the custom of " giving of ashes on Ash Wednesday, to put in remembrance every Christian man in the beginning of Lent, and penance, that he is but ashes and earth, and thereto shall return," is encouraged as one of those "laudable customs, rites, and ceremonies which are not to be contemned and cast away, but to be used and continued, as things good and laudable to put us in remembrance of those spiritual things that they do signify, not suffering them to be forgotten, or to be put in oblivion, but renewing them in our memories from time to time. But none of these ceremonies have power to remit sin, but only to stir up our minds unto God, by whom only our sins be forgiven."†

* Gratian, *Concordia Discordantia Canonum.* Distinctio l., c. 64.
† Fuller's *Church History of Britain;* Book v., Century xvi.

It was beyond the power of those divines to whom it fell to complete the Reformation of the English Church, to revive the ancient discipline in that discriminating manner of observance which was its chief life and value. They contented themselves, therefore, with a protest in its favour in the preface to the office of Commination; the celebration of which, although left at other times to the discretion of the Ordinary, was expressly enjoined on the first day of Lent. "This office," says Mr. Palmer, "is one of the last memorials we retain of that solemn penitence. which during the primitive ages, occupied so conspicuous a place in the discipline of the Christian Church. In the earlier ages, those who were guilty of grievous sins were solemnly reduced to the order of penitents: they came fasting, and clad in sackcloth and ashes on the occasion, and after the bishop had prayed over them, they were dismissed from the church. They were admitted gradually to the classes of *hearers, substrati;* and *consistentes;* until at length, after long trial and exemplary conduct, they were again deemed worthy of full communion.

"This penitential discipline at length, from various causes, became extinct both in the Eastern and Western Churches; and from the twelfth or thirteenth century, the solemn office for the first day of Lent was the only memorial of this ancient discipline in the West. It seems that at least from about the eighth century, there was a solemn office for public penitents on the first day of Lent;* but in after ages this office was applied indiscriminately to all the people, who received ashes, and were prayed for by the bishop or presbyter.

"Thus the office lost its ancient character. The English Churches have long used this office nearly as we do at present, as we find almost exactly the same appointed for the first day in Lent in the missals of Salisbury and York, and in the MS. Sacramentary of Leofric, which was

* Marteno's *De Antiquis Ecclesiæ Ritibus.*

written for the English Church about the ninth or tenth century."*

As the Commination office is practically of only annual occurrence, it may not be out of place to set before the reader the precise terms of its preface, which is directed to be said by the priest at Morning Prayer, after the ending of the Litany. "Brethren, in the Primitive Church, there was a godly discipline, that, at the beginning of Lent, such persons as stood convicted of notorious sin, were put to open penance, and punished in this world, that their souls might be saved in the day of the Lord; and that others, admonished by their example, might be the more afraid to offend.

"Instead whereof (until the said discipline may be restored again, which is much to be wished), it is thought good, that at this time (in the presence of you all) should be read the general sentences of God's cursing against impenitent sinners, gathered out of the seven-and-twentieth chapter of Deuteronomy, and other places of Scripture; and that ye should answer to every sentence, *Amen*. To the intent that, being admonished of the great indignation of God against sinners, ye may the rather be moved to earnest and true repentance: and may walk more warily in these dangerous days: fleeing from such vices, for which ye affirm with your own mouths the curse of God to be due."

The spirit of the Church as exhibited in the Commination Office is not doubtful; it is one of faithful and yearning tenderness. The tears of pity and affection are in her eyes as she declares the curses which it was not herself who originated; and candour demands of her no vindication. Her true position is ascertained in a Sonnet for Ash Wednesday, on "God's judgments denounced against sinners in the Commination." It is by the late Bishop Mant,

* Palmer's *Origines Liturgicæ; or, Antiquities of the English Ritual.*

and is taken from that prelate's "Musings on the Church and her Services."

> No! deem it not the Church could e'er pursue
>   Her sons, though marked by many a crimson spot,
>   With prayer or wish for evil! Deem it not
> She bids thee e'er such prayer or wish renew!
> But well she knows that holy, just, and true
>   Are God's commands and menaces; and what
>   His word proclaims the wilful sinner's lot,
> She knows, and owns, and bids thee own it due.
>   "Cursed is the man who spurns Jehovah's will."
>   Doubt'st thou the sentence? Does it aught declare
> Which is not? aught which He shall not fulfil?
>   Confess the truth: pray God His flock to spare:
> And, warned thyself, and heedful of the ill,
>   Of sin, and sin's appointed doom, beware!

The poetry of the Commination is not very abundant, and we conclude our poetical illustrations of Ash Wednesday, by adding to Bishop Mant's Sonnet, another on "The Commination Service," which finds a place amongst the "Ecclesiastical Sonnets." of William Wordsworth.

> Shun not this Rite, neglected, yea abhorred,
> By some of unreflecting mind, as calling
> Man to curse man, (thought monstrous and appalling).
> Go then and hear the threatenings of the LORD;
> Listening within His Temple see His sword
> Unsheathed in wrath to strike the offender's head,
> Thy own, if sorrow for thy sin be dead,
> Guilt unrepented, pardon unimplored.
> Two aspects bears Truth needful for salvation;
> Who knows not *that*?—yet would this delicate age
> Look only on the Gospel's brighter page:
> Let light and dark duly our thoughts employ;
> So shall the fearful words of Commination
> Yield timely fruit of peace, and love, and joy.

Holy Week;

OR, PASSION WEEK.

AS the great Paschal Festival anciently carried its solemn joy over the seven days succeeding the day of the Resurrection, so it had a corresponding time of preparation, which was set apart for extraordinary and continued fasting and humiliation. That the Holy Week forms a part of Lent is a fact which it is fair to regard as a matter of the Calendar merely; for, irrespective of Lent, it would have its obligations, and when these are superinduced upon the existing sanctions of the Quadragesimal period, with the last days of which Holy Week coincides, a season of surpassing solemnity and significance is the result. The Sundays *in* Lent, as has been remarked in treating of that season, are not *of* Lent, being uniformly abstracted from the fast, as weekly commemorations of the Resurrection; and so, of Holy Week, we remark that, falling in Lent, it is *more* than Lent, by the introduction of other and overwhelming associations. The fast of Lent, commemorating especially the forty days' fasting and temptation which our Lord underwent in the wilderness at the outset of His ministry, surrenders, so to speak, its final period of seven days to receive the impressions of the last sorrowful events of His existence.

The observance of Holy Week is nearly as ancient as

that of Easter; and its rites of mourning and self-denial developed *pari passu* with the reverence and exultation which attached to that sublime anniversary. St. Chrysostom furnishes the following *rationale* of the observance of Holy Week, and the religious exercises which characterized the same in his time, when it was generally known as the Great Week:—" On this account we call it the Great Week, not because the days of this week are of longer duration than the days of others, for there are days which are longer than these; nor yet because they are more in number, for the days in every week, without exception, are seven; but because in it great things were accomplished for us by the Lord. For in this Great Week the long-standing tyranny of the devil was destroyed, death was extinguished, the strong man was bound, his goods were spoiled, sin was abolished, the curse was destroyed, Paradise was opened, heaven became accessible, men were associated with angels, the middle wall of partition was broken down, the barriers were taken out of the way, and the God of peace made peace between things above and things upon the earth;—therefore it is called the Great Week. And as it is the head of all other weeks, so the Great Sabbath is the head of this week, in which it bears the same relation to the other days as the head does to the rest of the body. Therefore, in this Week many persons increase their labours; some adding to their fastings, others to their holy watchings; others administer more abundant alms, and testify the greatness of the Divine goodness towards them by their anxiety to perform good works, and their solicitude after pious and holy living. As after the resurrection of Lazarus all the people of Jerusalem went forth to meet the Lord, and bore witness, by their multitude, that He had raised the dead—for the anxiety of the people going forth was a proof of the miracle—so now, also, the anxiety about this Great Week is a proof and a testimony of the great and perfect things which were done in it. For not from one city only—not from Jerusalem alone—do we go forth to meet Christ this day, but from all the world the myriad-membered Churches everywhere go forth to meet Jesus, not with waving palm-branches in their hands, but with alms, and brotherly love, and virtue, and fasting, and tears, and prayers, and vigils, and every kind of piety, which they offer to Christ the Lord.

"Not only *we* venerate this week, but the kings of this world of ours honour it with a set and purposed honour, making it a time of vacation from all civil business, that the magistrates, being free from the cares of office, may spend all these days in spiritual service. 'Let the doors of the courts,' say they, 'now be shut up; let all disputes and all kinds of contention and punishment cease; let the hands of the executioner be stayed for a little. Common blessings have been secured for us by the Lord; let some good be done by us, His servants.' Nor is this the only honour they show to this week, but they do one thing more no less considerable. The imperial letters are sent abroad at this time, commanding all prisoners to be set at liberty from their chains. For as our Lord, whilst he was in Hades, delivered all those who were detained by death, so the servants, according as it is in the power of each, should also, in imitation of the kindness of their Lord, loose men from their corporal bonds, when they have no power to relax the spiritual."[†]

During the Great Week, which we call Holy Week, or Passion Week, the acts of Lenten penitence and humiliation culminated in duration and severity. Prayer, whether public or private, was offered almost without intermission, and all the exercises and offices of religion were most devoutly observed. Fastings were multiplied in number, and intensified in rigour. Epiphanius assures us that in his

---

* *Homilia habita in Magnam Hebdomadam.* The sentiments of the above extract are substantially repeated by St. Chrysostom in *Homily* xxx.; *in Genesim* c. xi.

time—the fourth century—"all the faithful observed the Great Week ἐν ξηροφαγίᾳ, living on dry meats—that is, on bread and salt and water, which they used only in the evening; and that the more zealous and devout superadded two, three, and four days—some even the whole week—till cock-crowing on Sunday morning."[*]

"The Church of England," says Wheatly, "uses all the means she can to retain the decent and pious customs of Holy Week, and hath made sufficient provision for the exercise of the devotion of her members in public—calling us every day this week to meditate upon our Lord's sufferings, and collecting in the Lessons, Epistles, and Gospels, most of those portions of Scripture that relate to this tragical subject, to increase our humiliation by the consideration of our Saviour's; to the end that with penitent hearts, and firm resolution of dying likewise to sin, we may attend our Saviour through the several stages of His bitter passion.

"Our reformers did not much confine themselves to the Gospels appointed for this week by the ancient offices; but thought, as there was time enough to admit of it, it would be most regular and useful to read all the four Evangelists' accounts of our Saviour's passion, as they stand in order. To this end they have ordered St. Matthew's account on the Sunday, appointing the 26th chapter for the second Lesson, and the 27th, as far as relates to His crucifixion, for the Gospel. On Monday and Tuesday is read the story as by St. Mark; on Wednesday and Thursday, that by St. Luke; and on Good Friday, the 18th of St. John is appointed for the Second Lesson, and the 19th for the Gospel.

"The Epistles also that are now appointed are more suitable to the season than those that were found in older offices.

"As for the Collect, the same that is used on the Sunday

---

[*] *Expositio Fidei Catholicæ et Apostolicæ Ecclesiæ;* ¶ 22.

before is appointed (as indeed a very proper one) to be used on the four days following till Good Friday; on which day it is also appointed in the Liturgy of St. Ambrose, though in other offices it is found, as with us, upon the Sunday before."*

The custom just referred to, of publicly reading the history of the Passion of Christ on each of the days of this week, is stated by Durandus to have been instituted by Pope Alexander I. (A.D. 109-119). St. Chrysostom gives a striking reason for this public reading and exposition of the narrative of the Passion:—"Lest the heathen should say, 'You Christians know how to proclaim the notable miracles which Christ did, but you are silent about His degradation and death'—lest this should happen, the Church has appointed that on the eve of the Pasch, when men and women are present in great numbers in the congregation, all these particulars should be publicly read."†

We are not about to essay the task of characterising the impenetrable mystery, the divine pathos, the agony, and the wonder of the events of this week; but content ourselves with leaving them all but untouched in hands which alone could treat them with success—a success which after all must be limited by the conditions of human speech— the Spirit-guided hands of the holy Evangelists. Their narratives are, by hypothesis, momently available to each of our readers; and they have supplied the inexhaustible themes to which the Christian poets of all ages have tremblingly strung the trembling lyre. In the whole range of poetry there are no topics which are at once more attractive and more hopeless of competent illustration; and the authors of pieces which have won the tearful and thankful applause of their fellow-Christians would be

* *Rational Illustration of the Book of Common Prayer.*
† *Commentarius in Sanctum Matthæum Evangelistum;* Homilia lxxxviii.

amongst the first to confess their own shortcomings. All the poetry of the Passion is to be received and approved, not as being even approximately worthy, but as being the best which hearts can utter whose inarticulate love and weeping must be their ultimate expression of wonder and gratitude. Many are the poets who have knowingly and piously encountered failure in order to do such honour as they could to the overwhelming phenomena of Holy Week; but from them all we select, as representing the comprehensive and epitomizing method of treatment, the "Hymn" which occurs in the late Dean Milman's "Martyr of Antioch":—

> For Thou didst die for me, oh, Son of God!
> By Thee the throbbing flesh of man was worn;
> Thy naked feet the thorns of sorrow trod,
> And tempests beat Thy houseless head forlorn.
>   Thou, that wert wont to stand
>   Alone, on God's right hand,
> Before the Ages were, the Eternal, eldest born.
>
> Thy birthright in the world was pain and grief,
>   Thy love's return ingratitude and hate;
> The limbs Thou healedst brought Thee no relief,
>   The eyes Thou openedst calmly viewed Thy fate:
>   Thou, that wert wont to dwell
>   In peace, tongue cannot tell,
> Nor heart conceive the bliss of Thy celestial state.
>
> They dragged Thee to the Roman's solemn hall,
>   Where the proud Judge in purple splendour sate;
> Thou stoodst a meek and patient criminal,
>   Thy doom of death from human lips to wait;
>   Whose throne shall be the world,
>   In final ruin hurl'd,
> With all mankind to hear their everlasting fate.
>
> Thou wert alone in that fierce multitude,
>   When "Crucify Him!" yelled the general shout;
> No hand to guard Thee 'mid those insults rude,
>   Nor lip to bless in all that frantic rout;
>   Whose slightest whispered word
>   The Seraphim had heard
> And adamantine arms from all the heavens broke out.

They bound Thy temples with the twisted thorn;
  Thy bruised feet went languid on with pain:
The blood, from all Thy flesh with scourges torn,
    Deepened Thy robe of mockery's crimson grain;
        Whose native vesture bright
        Was the unapproached light,
The sandal of whose foot the rapid hurricane.

They smote Thy cheek with many a ruthless palm,
  With the cold spear Thy shuddering side they pierced;
The draught of bitterest gall was all the balm
    They gave, to enhance Thy unslaked, burning thirst:
        Thou, at whose words of peace
        Did pain and anguish cease,
And the long buried dead their bonds of slumber burst.

Low bowed Thy head convulsed, and, drooped in death,
  Thy voice sent forth a sad and wailing cry;
How struggled from Thy breast the parting breath,
    And every limb was wrung with agony.
        That head, whose veilless blaze
        Filled angels with amaze,
When at that voice sprang forth the rolling suns on high.

And Thou wert laid within the narrow tomb,
  Thy clay-cold limbs with shrouding grave-clothes bound;
The sealed stone confirmed Thy mortal doom,
    Lone watchmen walked Thy desert burial-ground,
        Whom heaven could not contain,
        Nor th' immeasurable plain
Of vast Infinity enclose or circle round.

For us, for us, Thou didst endure the pain,
  And Thy meek spirit bowed itself to shame,
To wash our souls from sin's infecting stain,
    To avert the Father's wrathful vengeance flame
        Thou, that could'st nothing win
        By saving worlds from sin,
Nor aught of glory add to Thy all-glorious name.

"The sixth week in Lent is, in all the Romance languages, as with us, *Holy Week*. The title Passion Week, so often bestowed improperly on it among ourselves, is in Russia given to it by right, *Strastnoe Nedevie*. The

Latin term, the Greater Week, *Hebdomada Major*, does not seem to have come into vernacular use. In old French it was called, as it sometimes is still, *La Semaine Peneuse*. So Hildebert begins a sermon on the Passion: 'Septimana ista, fratres carissimi, ex re nomen habens, vocatur laboriosa, vel, ut vulgo loquuntur, *a pœnâ, verbo rustico, pœnosa*.' The most beautiful term, however, as setting forth its abstraction from worldly labours, and its holy quiet, is that by which it is known in Germany and Denmark, the *Still Week*. In Germany it is also the *Marterwoche*, and *Car* or *Charwoche*, Suffering Week. In the East it is the *Great Week*, and each day has the same epithet, Great Monday, Great Tuesday, &c. Finally in many mediæval writers, it is the *Authentic Week*; in the sense, we suppose, of *the* week—the week that is a week indeed; and so we have found it named in a Mayence Missal of 1519. The Welsh call it *Wythnos y Grog*, the Week of the Cross. Tuesday was in Germany, for an unknown reason, called *Blue Tuesday*; Wednesday, *Krumm Mittwoche*, from the confusion (they say) of the Pharisees' Counsel. In Ireland, *Spy Wednesday*, with reference to Judas's mission." *

A week so sacred and so momentous could not, of course, long be restricted to an *aggregate* commemoration; and the piety of the faithful was prompt to individualize its several days, and to associate with each its own special event. It is, however, from the Wednesday in Holy Week that the commencement of the Passion is dated, as it was on this Wednesday that the Jews in their great Council agreed on their design to take away the life of Christ, by impeaching Him before Pontius Pilate. And from that circumstance it arose that every Wednesday, as well as Friday, was formerly kept as a fast-day.

We proceed to speak of the Thursday before Easter, or, as it is popularly called,

* Dr. Neale's *Church Festivals and their Household Words*.

MAUNDY THURSDAY.

Of this day, Dr. Neale, in his *Essays on Liturgiology*, remarks that, "it is rather singular that it should not have derived its vernacular name from its great institution, the Blessed Eucharist. It had, indeed, in mediæval Latin, the name, *The Birthday of the Chalice*. So Hildebert:—

> Hoc in Natali Calicis non est celebratum,
> Quando Pascha novum vetus est post Pascha dicatum.

"But in modern languages, this did not obtain. In Dansk we have the name of *Skiertorsdag*, as, in some parts of England, that of *Sheer Thursday*, from the old root *Skier*, signifying pain or affliction. In France it was simply *Jeudi Saint*, a term likely to be confounded with Ascension Day. In German it is *Grüne Donnerstag*, Green Thursday; the origin of the term is much disputed. It is probable, however, that the epithet is here to be taken in the sense of *unripe*, inasmuch as in Slavonia and Carinthia the day is called *Raw Thursday*, with what reference we are quite unable to explain. In Spain, as with us, it is *Juéves del Mandato*, from the performance of the *mandatum*, the washing of the feet. In Portugal, it is *Quinta Feira de Endoenças*, Sickness Thursday, on account of the consecration of the chrism for the unction of the sick. In Welsh, with reference to the mocking of our LORD, it is *Iau y Cablyd*, Thursday of Blasphemy. In Brunswick it was *Good Thursday*, and so Boniface IX. in a Bull, speaks of '*Bonam quintam feriam in Cœnâ Domini*.' The Swiss call it *High Thursday*. In some parts of Germany, and in France, *White Thursday*, from the white colour of that day only in Holy Week. In Austria, finally, it is *Antlatz-tag*, Remission Day, from the re-admission of penitents into the Church."*

* *Church Festivals and their Household Words.*

Although, as we have just said, by deputy of Dr. Neale, the modern vernacular names of Maundy Thursday are not derived from "its great institution, the Blessed Eucharist," it was far otherwise with the names by which it was anciently designated; for, as Mr. Riddle shows, "this day has been distinguished by several appellations alluding for the most part to the history or ceremonies attached to it. Such are (1) *Dies Cœnæ Dominicæ; Feria quinta in Cœna Dominica*, or *in Cœna Domini*. (2) *Eucharistia*, or *Dies Natalis Eucharistiæ*, with reference to Matt. xxvi., 26, 27; 1 Cor. xi., 24. (3) *Natalis Calicis*. (4) *Dies Panis*. (5) *Dies Lucis*—with allusion to the lights used at the institution of the Lord's Supper, or to the light of religious knowledge. (6) *Dies Mandati*—with reference to our Saviour's command to His disciples concerning the perpetual commemoration of His death, or to His 'new commandment,' to 'love one another.' (7) *Dies Viridium*. This title appears to have been adopted during the middle ages, but antiquarians have been much perplexed in their attempts to account for it. Perhaps it may have been given with reference to the appearance of Spring."†

The Thursday before Easter was a day occupied and crowded with momentous events, in the front of which, it may be repeated, was the celebration of the Passover by our Saviour with His disciples, and his institution of the Holy Eucharist. After the supper followed the washing of the feet of the disciples by their divine Master, who prayed for them and for all succeeding generations of the faithful. Then He instructed and edified them, warning them of the things which should come to pass in their experience, and of the circumstances which should attend His own death and resurrection. Withal He vouchsafed the promise of the Comforter. Then retiring to the garden of Gethsemane, He poured out His soul in prayer to His Father, and while so doing, was overtaken by that stupendous agony in which

† *Manual of Christian Antiquities.*

His sweat was, as it were, of blood. From this agony He recovered only to be betrayed by Judas, and forsaken in His extremity by all His disciples.

Of these events we select three for poetical illustration—the institution of the Lord's Supper, the washing of the feet of the disciples, and the agony in the garden. The following verses had their first publication in the Rev. Orby Shipley's "Lyra Eucharistica," and are a translation, in paraphrase, of a Sequence of the Sixteenth Century, which commences in the Latin original with the words *De Superna Hierarchia*. Their author, the Rev. Arthur M. Morgan, has since reproduced them in a volume of original and translated poems, bearing the title of "Gifts and Light: Church Verses" (1867).

From the most holy Place above,
   In the world's latter day,
The Wisdom true of GOD came down
   To guide us on our way.
Oh! we had ever longed for Him,
   And He at last was given,
Mary-the-Virgin's blessed CHILD
   JESUS, the mortal's Haven.

Great was He ever; great the name
   The holy Virgin won,
When by a miracle she rose
   Mother to such a SON:
He takes this lost world's sin away,
   Forward with might He goes,
And in the van of fainting men
   Doth put to flight their foes.

There was no sorrow in His home,
   There was no death on high;
He sought Him Flesh to sorrow in,
   A cross, that HE might die;
He was the righteous Lawgiver,
   And yet Himself He gave
To the stern Law's most bitter scourge,
   Us from its curse to save.

For, lo! the Lamb was lifted up
  Upon the cruel Tree,
And He for us was sacrificed,
  Incarnate Charity!
And thus our life was built again,
  Upon each infant brow
The Sign of Him Who saves is set,
  And Heaven is open now.

It was the night He was betrayed,
  When in the upper room,
With His loved Twelve He sate at meat,
  Knowing what soon should come;
He blessed and brake the Holy Bread
  And said—O hearken ye
Who doubt Him—" This My Body is;
  Do this, remembering Me.'

He ceased. Anon, He spake again,
  God's Holy Son and True,
And thus the Gift unspeakable
  Came in the Chalice too;
It had made glad man's heavy heart,
  But then His all it stood,
The drink of the New Paradise,
  The Word Incarnate's Blood.

This mystery is hid in God,
  This can none else explore;
Be thou content to wait awhile,
  Believe, embrace, adore;
But be thou ware to eat and drink,
  If slave to sin thou be,
Only the pure and guileless heart
  Can take it worthily.

Say, canst thou love as Peter loved?
  Behold the Love is here;
Art thou a Judas? in thy sins,
  Come not, O traitor, near;
This is the just man's Aliment,
  This arms him for the fray;
But whoso lacks a Wedding-robe
  Is the foe's certain prey.

Oh, save us from eternal wrath,
  Cloth us with chastity.
Thou hast restored the breach ; to Thee
  For health and Peace we come ;
Make us more worthy of Thy Gift,
  Bring us more near our home.

The poem in illustration of " Christ washing the Disciples' feet " is adopted from a Transatlantic author, George W. Bethune, and it occupies the first place in an interesting selection of Hymns, published in 1865, by the Religious Tract Society, under the title of " Lyra Americana."

O blessed Jesus! when I see Thee bending,
  Girt as a servant, at Thy servants' feet,
Love, loveliness, and might, in zeal all blending,
  To wash their dust away, and make them meet
To share Thy feast ; I know not to adore
Whether Thy humbleness or glory more.

Conscious Thou art of that dread hour impending,
  When Thou must hang in anguish on the tree ;
Yet, as from the beginning to the ending
  Of Thy sad life, Thine own are dear to Thee—
And Thou wilt prove to them, ere Thou dost part,
The untold love which fills Thy faithful heart.

The day, too, is at hand, when, far ascending,
  The human brow the crown of God shall wear,
Ten thousand saints and radiant ones attending,
  To do Thy will, and bow in homage there ;
But Thou dost pledge, to guard Thy Church from ill
Or bless with good, Thyself a servant still.

Meek Jesus! to my soul Thy spirit lending,
  Teach me to live, like Thee, in lowly love ;
With humblest service all Thy saints befriending,
  Until I serve before Thy throne above—
Yes ! serving e'en my foes, for Thou didst seek
The feet of Judas in Thy service meek.

  Thine is this marvel, blessed CHRIST,
    Thine would its sharers be ;

Daily my pilgrim feet, as homeward wending
  My weary way, are sadly stained with sin;
Daily do Thou, Thy precious grace extending,
  Wash me all clean without, and clean within,
And make me fit to have a part with Thee
And Thine, at last, in Heaven's festivity.

O, blessed name of **SERVANT**! comprehending
  Man's highest honour in his humblest name;
For Thou, God's Christ, that office recommending,
  The throne of mighty power didst truly claim;
He who would rise like Thee, like Thee must owe
His glory only to his stooping low.

The following lines on "Christ's Bloody Sweat" are transcribed from the "Mæoniæ" of Robert Southwell, to whom it may be forgiven that to so many of his expressions attaches more than a fair share of the quaintness of his time (1562-1595), when we consider that he among all modern Christian poets was, by reason of his own confinement, tortures, and execution, perhaps the best qualified to sympathise with his Master, and the best entitled to celebrate His unfathomable sufferings.

Fat soil, full spring, sweet olive, grape of bliss,
  That yields, that streams, that pours, that doth distil;
Untilled, undrawn, unstamped, untouched of press,
  Dear fruit, clear brooks, fair oil, sweet wine at will
Thus Christ prevents, unforced, in shedding blood,
The whips, the thorns, the nails, the spear, and rood.

He pelican's, He phœnix', fate doth prove,
  Whom flames consume, whom streams enforce to die;
How burneth blood, how bleedeth burning love?
  Can one in flame and stream both bathe and fry?
How could He join a phœnix' fiery pains,
In fainting pelican's still bleeding veins?

Elias once, to prove God's sovereign power,
  By prayer procured a fire of wondrous force,
That blood, and water, and wood did devour
  The stones and dust beyond all nature's course:

Such fire is love, that, fed with gory blood,
Doth burn no less than in the driest wood.

O, sacred fire! come, show thy force on me,
  That sacrifice to Christ I may return;
If withered wood for fuel fittest be,
  If stones and dust, if flesh and blood will burn,
I withered am, and stony to all good,
A sack of dust, a mass of flesh and blood.

One of Bishop Jeremy Taylor's "Festival Hymns" is conversant about the same subject—the agony in the garden; and although it is by its author, entitled "On Good Friday," it must be taken, if read on that day, as retrospective, and as more properly belonging to Maundy Thursday:—

  The Lamb is eaten, and is yet again
    Preparing to be slain;
  The cup is full and mixed,
  And must be drunk—
  Wormwood and gall,
To this, are draughts to beguile care withal;
  Yet the decree is fixed.
Double knees, and groans, and cries,
Prayers and sighs, and flowing eyes,
  Could not entreat.
  His sad soul sunk
Under the heavy pressure of our sin:
  The pains of death and hell
    About him dwell.
His Father's burning wrath did make
His very heart, like melting wax, to sweat
  Rivers of blood;
Through the pure strainer of His skin
  His boiling body stood,
    Bubbling all o'er,
As if the wretched whole were but one door
  To let in pain and grief,
  And turn out all relief.
O Thou, who for our sake
  Did'st drink up
  This bitter cup,

> Remember us, we pray,
> In Thy day,
> When down
> The struggling throats of wicked men
> The dregs of Thy just fury shall be thrown.
> Oh then
> Let Thy unbounded mercy think
> On us, for whom
> Thou underwentest this heavy doom,
> And give us of the well of life to drink. Amen.

The particular observance of Maundy Thursday is traceable to a very ancient period. So early as the fourth century it is known to have been commemorated by a solemn celebration of the Eucharist, which on this day was administered in the evening, in imitation of the communion of the apostles at our Lord's last supper. The twenty-ninth canon of the third Council of Carthage (A.D. 397) provides "that the sacrament of the altar should always be received by men fasting, one anniversary day being excepted, in which the last supper of the Lord is solemnly commemorated." The same custom is alluded to by St. Augustine, who observes that in some places the communion was administered twice on Maundy Thursday —in the morning, for the sake of such persons as were not able to keep the day as a fast; and in the evening, for the sake of those that fasted till that time, and then broke their fast by the reception of the elements.* In many places the day was distinguished by a *communio servorum*, in which, as the name indicates, it was the custom of slaves to communicate, who were not admitted to the Lord's table on the higher festivals, such as Easter, for which feast the non-servil emembers of the Church frequently reserved their communion.

Christ at His last supper not only washed the feet of the Twelve, but also gave them a command that they should

---

* *Epistola* 118; *Ad Januarium.*

perform the same office towards each other; and in literal obedience to this command, and in imitation of this example, it has been the custom in various ages for Christian princes, bishops, and others to wash the feet of some poor persons, or of their colleagues and fellows, on this day. It is this ceremony, indeed, which gives its vernacular name to the day, for it is this which constitutes the fulfilment of that command contained in the commencement of the first Antiphon, *Mandatum novum do vobis : ut diligatis invicem.* The custom of a literal compliance with the injunction to wash one another's feet—although much importance was attached to it in the Greek Church, and although its claims to even a sacramental sanction were sometimes agitated—does not appear to have become at any time quite universal in the Western Church. Yet the ceremony of washing the feet of the poor was long observed by the sovereigns of England. At the ceremony performed by Queen Elizabeth, at Greenwich, the feet of so many poor persons as there were years in the Queen's age were washed by the yeomen of the guard, and then washed and kissed by the Queen, with the sign of the cross. James the Second is said to have been the last king who observed this rite in person. Afterwards it was performed in the palace of Whitehall by the Archbishops of York, Lords Almoners, till A.D. 1731 at least. It has since been disused, though several of the minor parts of the office for it have been retained; and the alms which accompanied the ceremony of the washing are still distributed, the number of aged recipients, of either sex, of the sovereign's bounty—in money, clothes, and provisions—increasing by one every year with the increasing number of the years of Her Majesty's reign.

On Maundy Thursday, again, it was the custom for the candidates for baptism—*competentes*, as they were called—publicly to rehearse the Creed in the presence of the bishop or presbyters, at whose hands they likewise underwent an examination. This is certified for us by the forty-sixth canon of the Council of Laodicea—held in the course of the fourth century—which fixes this *redditio symboli* to the fifth day of the Great Week, as well as by Theodorus Lector, who writes that "Timotheus, Bishop of Constantinople, ordered the Creed to be recited in every Church assembly, which formerly had been recited only once in every year, to wit, on the day of the Great Parasceve, or Preparation of the Passion of our Lord, in the course of the catechizing of the candidates for baptism by the bishop."[*]

One other custom observed on Maundy Thursday may be recorded in the words of Wheatly:—" On this day the Penitents, that were put out of the Church upon Ash Wednesday, were received again into the Church, partly that they might be partakers of the Holy Communion, and partly in remembrance of our Lord's being on this day apprehended and bound, in order to work our deliverance and freedom (Innocent. Epist. ut citat ab Ivo, part 15, cap. 40, et a Bachardo, l. 18., c. 18.).

"The form of reconciling penitents was this: the bishop went out to the doors of the church, where the penitents lay prostrate upon the earth, and thrice, in the name of Christ, called them, *Come, come, come, ye children, hearken to me; I will teach you the fear of the Lord.* Then, after he had prayed for them, and admonished them, he reconciled them, and brought them into the church. The penitents thus received, trimmed their heads and beards, and laying off their penitential weeds, reclothed themselves in decent apparel.

"It may not be amiss to observe, that the church-doors used to be all set open on this day, to signify that the penitent sinners, coming from north or south, or any part of the world, should be received to mercy, and the Church's favour."[†]

---

[*] *Ecclesiastical History*; Lib. ii., c. 52.
[†] *Rational Introduction of the Book of Common Prayer.*

GOOD FRIDAY.

> Oh! for a pencil dipped in living light,
> To paint the agonies that Jesus bore!
> Henry Kirke White; *The Christiad*.

THIS momentous day—a day on which the principle of "utter self-sacrifice" was shown to be nothing less than *Divine*—derives its appellation "from the blessed effects of our Saviour's sufferings, which are the ground of all our joy; and from those unspeakable good things which He hath purchased for us by His death, whereby the blessed Jesus made expiation for the sins of the whole world, and by the shedding of His own blood obtained eternal redemption for us (Heb. ix., 12.)."*

Dr. Neale claims for *Good Friday* that it "is another example of an English appellation that surpasses in beauty the vernacular terms of other languages, except the Flemish, where it is also used. But that we are so completely used to it, we should probably feel what a touching acknowledgment is the name of the work accomplished on that day. In some parts of England it is *Char-Friday*, that is, *Passion Friday;* a name also in use in Germany. There, however, it is usually called *Still Friday*. Denmark has a far less appropriate name, *Long Friday*. It is not a mark of very high devotion, that the length of the office should be that which has given the title to the day. *Black Friday*, a name common over Southern Germany, gives the popular view of the season, and *Holy Friday* is the somewhat commonplace title adopted in most of the Romance languages. In Welsh, it is *Gwener y Corglith*, Friday of the Lesson of the Cross."†

The commemoration of our Saviour's sufferings has been kept up from the very first age of Christianity, and was

---

* Nelson's *Festivals and Fasts*.
† Neale's *Church Festivals and their Household Words*.

always observed as a day of the strictest fasting and humiliation; not that the grief and affliction therein expressed by the faithful arose from the loss they sustained, or from any indignation against our Saviour's mortal persecutors, but from a sense of the guilt of the sins of the whole world, as the cause that drew upon Him the painful and shameful death of the Cross. The sympathetic despair of Christendom seems in some places to have been carried out to the length of closing the churches altogether during the whole of Good Friday, as if there were no heart left either for the service of praise or for prostration on account of sin. Everywhere, indeed, the offices for the Day, where these had not been stayed by a hopeless silence, manifested the prevailing feeling by the most sombre symbols of grief and desolation.

Historically, the sufferings of what Wither calls "the insufferable passion of Jesus" anticipated the dawn—sorrow broke upon the divine Victim before the struggling light of a sun whose beams were presently to be eclipsed as if in horror and affright. The remarks we made upon the impossibility of worthily treating or describing the various events of Holy Week in general, press upon us with greater force than ever, when it falls to us to invite a consideration of the phenomena of Good Friday. The poetry of the Day, and of its several events is extremely wealthy; and we cannot pretend to exhaust it, even representatively, in our illustrations. One circumstance is so intimately connected with another, one topic so interestingly involved with another, and the great doctrine of the Day so informs everything related to it, that we can make little attempt at even so much as precise historical arrangement, and must be content with offering a few poems which will illustrate, with a loose or approximate sequence, some of the great occurrences of the day. Where these are so many and so various, we naturally hurry to the catastrophe, or to the circumstances immediately preceding or leading up to it.

The procession to Calvary seems to have had a great attraction for the mind of Robert Herrick, who in his "Noble Numbers," devotes four or five poems to the subject, the largest of which is called "Rex Tragicus, or Christ going to His Crosse." This, however, we pass by to transcribe a simple and shorter piece which bears a kindred title, and paraphrases " His Saviour's Words, going to the Crosse."

> Have, have ye no regard, all ye
> Who passe this way, to pitie me,
> Who am a man of miserie!
>
> A man both bruised and broke, and one
> Who suffers not here for mine own,
> But for my friends' transgression!
>
> Ah! Sion's daughters, do not feare
> The crosse, the cords, the nailes, the speare,
> The myrrhe, the gall, the vinegar;
>
> For Christ, your loving Saviour, hath
> Drunk up the wine of God's fierce wrath;
> Onely, there's left a little froth,
>
> Lesse for to tast, then for to shew,
> What bitter cups had been your due,
> Had He not drunk them up for you.

In a little poem, "'Twas I that did it," which occurs in Dr. Horatius Bonar's "Hymns of Faith and Hope," the author reviews generally the persecuting incidents of the Day, for the purpose of founding on each act of barbarity a personal accusation of complicity with the Jews in the despite done to the Saviour in His arraignment, mocking, scourging, and crucifixion.

> I see the crowd in Pilate's hall,
> I mark their wrathful mien;
> Their shouts of " Crucify " appal,
> With blasphemy between.
>
> And of the shouting multitude
> I feel that I am one;
> And in that din of voices rude,
> I recognize my own.

I see the scourges tear his back,
  I see the piercing crown;
And of that crowd who smile and mock
  I feel that I am one.

Around yon cross, the throng I see,
  Mocking the Sufferer's groan,
Yet still my voice it seems to be—
  As if I mocked alone.

'Twas I that shed the Sacred Blood,
  I nailed Him to the tree;
I crucified the Christ of God,
  I joined the mockery.

Yet not the less that blood avails
  To cleanse away my sin,
And not the less that cross prevails
  To give me peace within.

The same spirit, the same contrite tendency to convict oneself of being the cause of Christ's suffering, animates the verses "To the Instruments of the Passion of Jesus," which we transcribe from "Hymns and Verses on Spiritual Subjects: Being the Sacred Poetry of St. Alphonso Maria Liguori, Founder of the Congregation of the Most Holy Redeemer. Translated from the Italian, and edited by Robert Aston Coffin, Priest of the congregation of the most Holy Redeemer."

O ruthless scourges, with what pain you tear
My Saviour's flesh so innocent and fair!
Oh, cease to rend that flesh divine,
  My loving Lord torment no more;
Wound rather, wound this heart of mine,
  The guilty cause of all He bore.

Ye cruel thorns, in mocking wreath entwin'd,
My Saviour's brow in agony to bind,
Oh, cease to rend that flesh divine,
  My loving Lord torment no more;
Wound rather, wound this heart of mine,
  The guilty cause of all He bore.

> Unpitying nails, whose points with anguish fierce,
> The hands and feet of my Redeemer pierce!
> Oh, cease to rend that flesh divine,
> > My loving Lord torment no more;
> Wound rather, wound this heart of mine,
> > The guilty cause of all He bore.
>
> Unfeeling lance, that dar'st to open wide
> The sacred temple of my Saviour's side
> Oh, cease to wound that flesh divine,
> > My loving Lord insult no more;
> Pierce rather, pierce this heart of mine
> > The guilty cause of all He bore.

Having now fully arrived at the foot of the cross, we are in a position to take advantage of a description of the external phenomena in which a sympathetic universe is seen exhibiting its astonishment at the fact of the Author of all life being just at the point of death. The writer of the following stanzas was Giles Fletcher—to whom we have devoted a few biographical words in our remarks on Ascension-Day—and the poem from which they are taken, was published in 1610, under the title of "Christ's Victory and Triumph." The stanzas in question form a part of the third Canto, which sets forth "Christ's Triumph over Death."

> See where the Author of all life is dying:
> O fearful day! HE dead, what hope of living?
> See where the hopes of all our lives are buying:
> O cheerful day! they bought, what fear of grieving?
> LOVE love for hate and death for life is giving!
> Lo, how His arms are stretched abroad to grace thee,
> And, as they open stand, call to embrace thee:
> Why stayest thou then, my soul? O fly, fly, thither haste thee!
>
> His radious head with shameful thorns they tear,
> His tender back with bloody whips they rent,
> His side and heart they furrow with a spear,
> His hands and feet with riving nails they tent,
> And, as to disentrail His soul they meant,
> They jolly at his grief, and make their game
> His naked body to expose to shame,
> That all might come to see, and all might see that came.

Whereat the Heaven put out his guilty eye,
That durst behold so execrable sight;
And sabled all in black the shady sky;
And the pale stars, struck with unwonted fright,
Quenchèd their everlasting lamps in night:
And at His birth as all the stars Heaven had
Were not enow, but a new star was made:
So now both new and old and all away did fade.

The mazèd angels shook their fiery wings
Ready to lighten vengeance from God's throne:
One down his eyes upon the Manhood flings,
Another gazes on the Godhead, none
But surely thought his wits his own.
Some flew to look if it were very HE;
But when God's arm unarmèd they did see,
Albe they saw it was, they vowed it could not be.

The sadded air hung all in cheerless black,
Through which the gentle winds soft sighing flew,
And Jordan into such huge sorrow brake,
(As if his holy stream no measure knew)
That all his narrow banks he overthrew;
The trembling earth with horror inly shook,
And stubborn stones, such grief unused to brook,
Did burst, and ghosts awaking from their graves 'gan look.

The wise philosophers cried, all aghast,
"The God of nature surely languishèd;"
The sad centurion cried out as fast,
"The Son of God, the Son of God, was dead!"
The headlong Jew hung down his pensive head
And homewards fared; and ever as he went
He smote his breast half-desperately bent;
The very woods and beasts did seem His death lament.

The several utterances of Jesus as He hung upon the cross have been fruitful themes for exposition, poetical and otherwise; and especially that appeal of mystery and agony which seems to point to a severance, in the article of death, of the two Natures which in life had jointly occupied the tabernacle of His flesh. The Deathless and the Divine must leave the human to the lonely despair and abandonment of the moment when the Son, as human, is about once for all to stoop to enter that region of death and shadows which simply *is not* in the presence of the Eternal Source of Life.

The following poem, "Juxta Crucem," appeared in the "Churchman's Family Magazine" for August, 1865, and is conversant about the short interval between the death of Christ, and the taking down of His body from its shameful exaltation. At the foot of the cross, it is necessary to picture the Virgin Mother, whose "dolours" having at length attained their culmination, are now on the eve not merely of abatement, but of glorious transformation.

> And is it thus determines Prophecy?
> Ends thus the clue that, threading all the maze
> Of the world's life from dawn to Calvary,
> Was the lone guide of countless darkest days?
>   Must Israel here the book of Love upfold;
>   And curse with bitter tears the promises of old?
>
> Tended to this the mocking Gabriel's voice?
> Was it for this the flower of heaven came down,
> Proclaiming peace and bidding earth rejoice,
> Because an heir was born to David's crown?
>   And did the hood-winked Magi from afar
>   Bring gifts in vain, and trust a vagrant wanton star?
>
> Did Simeon dote? and did the Baptist dream?
> Where are the realm, the glory, and the light?
> What boots the Dove-descent amid the gleam
> Of God upon the river-font, if night—
>   If night like this appal the cowering day,
>   And shattering earth reel on uncertain of her way?
>
> Where is the triumph of the wilderness?
> Where is the might the tempter's might that foiled?
> Where now the healing? where the power to bless,
> That slew the slayer, and the grave despoiled;
>   That loosed from Nature's stole the badge of hell;
>   And walked the conscious sea in pomp of miracle?

Where is the pageant of the mountain height—
The sun-like glory of the shining face ;
The raiment white and glistering as the light ;
The saintly congress ; and the words of grace
    That fell approving from the o'ershadowing cloud,
    Whilst the disciples' heart with awe and rapture bowed ?

Where are the glad hosannas and the psalms ?
The praise to David's Son that thousands sing ?
The state, the following, and the scattered palms,
That deck the route of Zion's meekest King ?
    Where are the lips and hands that homage pay,
    The plaudits and the shouts that fill the ear of day ?

"Where ?" ask the platters of the shameful crown ;
"Where ?" ask the ribald tongues of them who smote ?
"Where ?" ask the ruffian courtiers, kneeling down ;
"Where ?" asks the winner of the seamless coat ;
    "Where ?" ask the scornful echoes of the deep ;
    Base hearts of those who flee ; true hearts of those who weep.

Shall we with felons seek for majesty ?
And shall we call the cursed tree a throne ?
Is Godhead seen in utter agony ;
And Sonship in a last forsaken groan ?
    And should the purple of a monarch's pride
    Be taken from the opened wardrobe of his side ?*

Nature tries her poor best to mete thy dole,
Thou blameless mother of thy Lord and Head ;
Earth quakes, the day retires, and thunders roll,
And troubled graves give up their holy dead.
    Ah ! thou who in great hopes lived erst apart,
    Despair not, though the sword of Simeon pierce thine heart.†

Thy Son's " 'tis finished" was the close of shame :
Thy hold is on the pillar of His might ;
Henceforth thou changest the all-mother's name,‡
And art the gate of universal light :
    For food immortal is that flesh and blood ;
    The Tree of Life is graft into the Holy Rood.

---

* " Opening the purple wardrobe of his side."—*Crashaw.*
† " Yes, a sword shall pierce through thy own soul also."—*Luke* ii 35.
‡ " Mutans nomen Evæ."—*Ancient Hymn,* " De Beatâ Virgine."

It would, perhaps, be impossible to sum up the picturesque circumstances of splendour and abasement arising from the neighbourhood of Natures in the person of Christ, more effectively and more popularly than in the late Dr. Milman's well-known lines on "The Crucifixion:"—

> Bound upon the accursed tree,
> Faint and bleeding, who is *He*?
> By the eyes, so pale and dim,
> Streaming blood and writhing limb,
> By the flesh with scourges torn,
> By the crown of twisted thorn,
> By the side so deeply pierced,
> By the baffled burning thirst,
> By the drooping death-dewed brow;
> Son of Man! 'tis Thou! 'tis Thou!
>
> Bound upon the accursed tree,
> Dread and awful, who is *He*?
> By the sun at noonday pale,
> Shivering rocks, and rending veil,
> By earth that trembled at *His* doom,
> By yonder saints who burst their tomb,
> By Eden, promised, ere He died,
> To the felon at His side;
> Lord! our suppliant knees we bow;
> Son of God! 'tis Thou! 'tis Thou!
>
> Bound upon the accursed tree,
> Sad and dying, who is *He*?
> By the last and bitter cry,
> The ghost given up in agony;
> By the lifeless body laid
> In the chambers of the dead;
> By the mourners come to weep
> Where the bones of Jesus sleep:
> Crucified! we know Thee now;
> Son of man! 'tis Thou! 'tis Thou!
>
> Bound upon the accursed tree,
> Dead and awful, who is *He*?
> By the prayer for them that slew,
> "Lord! they know not what they do!"

> By the spoiled and empty grave,
> By the souls He died to save,
> By the conquest He hath won,
> By the saints before *His* throne,
> By the rainbow round *His* brow—
> Son of God! 'tis Thou! 'tis Thou!

The last few lines of the preceding poem have, in fact, carried us over the sadness of the Passion to the joys of Easter and the glories of the Ascension. It is necessary for us, therefore, to retrace our steps for the few minutes which we wish either to spend beside the Tomb, or to occupy with a very few observations on

EASTER-EVE; OR, HOLY SATURDAY.

OF this day, Dr. Neale remarks that it "has in few modern languages any more recondite name than in our own. In Portugal it is *Sabbado de Alleluia*, from the triumphant resumption of the Alleluia in the first Vespers of Easter. In some parts of Germany it is *Judas Saturday*. In the East, in the same way as the rest of the week, it is *Great Saturday*, except among the Armenians, who call it *Burial Saturday*." *

Great Saturday, or the *Great Sabbath*, was the only Saturday which the Eastern Churches, and some of the Western, observed as a fast. All other Sabbaths, about which the hallowing effect of Jewish associations, especially amongst the Oriental Christians, still lingered—all other Sabbaths, even those in Lent—were observed as festivals, together with the Lord's Day. "But this *Great Sabbath* was observed as a most solemn fast, which some joined with the fast of the preceding day, and made them both but one continued fast of superposition; and they who could not thus join both days together without some refreshment, yet observed the Saturday with great strictness, holding out their fast till after midnight, or cock-crowing

---

* *Church Festivals and their Household Words.*

in the morning, which was the supposed time of our Lord's Resurrection." * The Church might well be exceptionally humbled in her observance of this Day, for it was the day of the utter humiliation of her Lord, during all the hours of which He lay, as to His body, in the grave, and as to His soul, sojourned in the place of the departed.

The poetry of Holy Saturday is, therefore, essentially the poetry of the tomb. It is thus that George Herbert moralizes over the "Sepulchre:"—

> O blessed Body! whither art Thou thrown?
> No lodging for Thee, but a cold hard stone?
> So many hearts on earth, and yet not one
>   Receive Thee?
>
> Sure there is room within our hearts good store;
> For they can lodge transgressions by the score;
> Thousands of toys dwell there, yet out of door
>   They leave Thee.
>
> But that which shows them large, shows them unfit.
> Whatever sin did this pure rock commit,
> Which holds Thee now? who hath indited it
>   Of murder?
>
> Where our hard hearts have took up stones to brain Thee,
> And, missing this, most falsely did arraign Thee;
> Only these stones in quiet entertain Thee,
>   And order.
>
> And as of old, the Law by heavenly art
> Was writ in stone; so Thou, which also art
> The letter of the Word, find'st no fit heart
>   To hold Thee.
>
> Yet do we still persist as we began,
> And so should perish, but that nothing can,
> Though it be cold, hard, foul, from loving man
>   Withhold Thee.

The only other poem which we offer as illustrative of *Burial Saturday*—to adopt for a moment the Armenian

* Bingham's *Antiquities of the Christian Church*.

name—is one which regards the grave of the Saviour as a place of rest after His work and Passion. The author of the poem is S. Franck; and its theme is "Easter Even." It is given in the following English version in Miss Winkworth's "Lyra Germanica," where it takes its motto from the Gospel for the Day:—"And Joseph wrapped the body in a clean linen cloth, and laid it in his own new tomb, which he had hewn out in the rock."

"Solomon Franck was born on the 6th March, 1659, in Weimar, and was afterwards secretary to the Consistory in the same town, where he died on the 11th June, 1725. Nothing further is known of his life. He was a pious man, who early learned to pray with Moses, *So teach us to number our days that we may apply our hearts unto wisdom.* For he composed many hymns on death and heaven; and in his hymn-writing aimed at following the example of Rist. This hymn, addressed to "Jesus in the Grave," is one of seven Passion hymns in the second volume of Franck's poems, published in 1716."*

>Rest of the weary! Thou
>Thyself art resting now,
>Where lowly in Thy sepulchre Thou liest:
>From out her deathly sleep
>My soul doth start, to weep
>So sad a wonder, that Thou Saviour diest!
>
>Thy bitter anguish o'er,
>To this dark tomb they bore
>Thee, Life of life—Thee, Lord of all creation!
>The hollow rocky cave
>Must serve Thee for a grave,
>Who wast Thyself the Rock of our Salvation!
>
>O Price of Life! I know
>That when I too lie low,
>Thou wilt at last my soul from death awaken;

* Rev. Theodore Kübler's *Historical Notes to the Lyra Germanica.*

Wherefore I will not shrink
From the grave's awful brink;
The heart that trusts in Thee shall ne'er be shaken.

To me the darksome tomb
Is but a narrow room,
Where I may rest in peace from sorrow free:
Thy death shall give me power
To cry in that dark hour,
O Death, O grave, where is your victory?

The grave can nought destroy,
Only the flesh can die,
And e'en the body triumphs o'er decay:
Clothed by Thy wondrous might
In robes of dazzling light,
This flesh shall burst the grave at that last Day.

My Jesus, day by day,
Help me to watch and pray,
Beside the tomb where in my heart Thou'rt laid.
Thy bitter death shall be
My constant memory,
My guide at last into Death's awful shade.

Of all the vigils of the Church the most famous was that between the *Great Sabbath* and Easter-Day; for it was the expectation of the rising Saviour. "This is the night," Lactantius says, "which we observe with a *pervigilium*, or watching all night, for the advent of our King and God: of which night and its observance there is a twofold reason to be given—for in this night our Lord resumed His life after His Passion; and in the same night He is expected to return to receive the Kingdom of the World. For He is our Liberator, and Judge, and Avenger, and King and God, whom we call Christ."*

St. Jerome mentions "a tradition among the Jews that Christ would come at midnight, as He did upon the Egyptians at the time of the Passover; and thence," he

---

* *Divinæ Institutiones;* Lib. vii., De Vita Beata, c. 19.

says, "I think arose the Apostolic custom not to dismiss the people on the Paschal vigil before midnight, expecting the coming of Christ: after which time, presuming upon security, they kept the day a festival." *

This night was also famous above all others as a season for the Baptism of Catechumens, who were thereby rendered eligible to partake of the Holy Eucharist on Easter-day; for our observations on which Festival we defer any further remark upon the illuminations or other symbolical expressions of the joy attendant upon this as the greatest of the Baptismal seasons.

* *Commentarius in Evangelium Matthæi;* Lib. iv., c. xxv., v. 6.

Easter Day.

THE festival of Easter is at once a distinctively Christian institution, and a perpetuation of a Hebrew anniversary. It is, so to say, a new and more glorious edition of the Jewish Passover; and may, in this sense, date its first origin from the time when Moses made it incumbent upon his people annually to commemorate the safety of the youth of Israel from the angelic vengeance that smote down the first-born of Egypt. From that period to the present there has been no considerable solution of its observance. The Apostles who merged their Judaism in the broader waters of Christianity, carried into their developed faith their reverence for a feast that after the Crucifixion had a twofold significance, of which the later-acquired was infinitely the more glorious, because the more spiritual. They enjoined likewise upon their followers the celebration of the *renewed* Passover; so that it is one of the singular honours of Easter, that it alone—whilst the earliest or Apostolic authority for the celebration of other Christian seasons is to be approximately established by inference and varying probabilities—rests upon absolute Scripture precept and Apostolic injunction:—" Christ our Passover is sacrificed for us, therefore let us keep the feast" (1 Cor. v., 7, 8).

There is not, then, as there never has been, any room for dispute about the origin of the Paschal festival; although when we turn to the *time* at which it was thought the festival ought to be kept, we shall find a plentiful divergence of custom and opinion. The followers of St. John and St. Philip on the one side were early at variance with the followers of St. Peter and St. Paul on the other. When Polycarp, Bishop of Smyrna, and representative of the Jewish and other Asiatic Churches, visited Rome in A.D. 158, he and Anicetus, Bishop of the latter city, mutually endeavoured to win over each other to their respective usage. There was no conversion, however, and there was no quarrel. "Like stout champions both kept their ground; and like good Christians kept also the peace of the Church."

But the charitable agreement to differ could not be secured for ever; and intolerance on one side and the other, in spite of the noble protest of Irenæus, presently manifested itself. The question of the time for celebrating Easter continued to agitate Christendom till, in the year 325, the Emperor Constantine summoned the Council of Nicæa, one of the cardinal objects of which was to procure the uniformity of Easter practice. The account of the Paschal dispute occupies a considerable space in the pages of all ecclesiastical historians, from Eusebius downwards; and Bingham may especially be mentioned as having treated the matter with his usual learned exhaustiveness. The whole question is readily accessible in almost any degree of detail to which an enquirer may desire to pursue it. We thankfully take advantage, when it becomes necessary to present an abstract of what is now at best a rather dry and flavourless topic, of a pen which is accustomed to impart animation to subjects little susceptible of living or pictorial treatment. The principal landmarks are preserved, and they are all that is necessary. "The first of the two questions which remained (after the settlement of the creed) for the decision of the Council of Nicæa—the first in importance, if not in order of discussion—was the ques-

tion of Easter. It was the most ancient controversy in the Church. It was the only one which had come down from the time when the Jewish and Christian communities were indistinguishable. It was the only one which grew directly out of events in the Gospel History. Its very name (the 'Quartodeciman,' the 'Fourteenth-day' con-controversy) was derived, not from the Christian or Gentile, but the Jewish calendar. The briefest statement of it will here suffice. Was the Christian Passover (for the word was still preserved, and by the introduction of the German word 'Easter,' we somewhat lose the force of the connection) to be celebrated on the same day as the Jewish, the fourteenth day of the month Nisan, or on the following Sunday? This was the fundamental question, branching out into others as the controversy became entangled with the more elaborate institution of the Christian fast of forty days, as also with the astronomical difficulties in the way of fixing its relations to the vernal equinox. On one side were the old, historical, apostolical traditions; on the other side, the new, Christian, Catholic spirit, striving to part company with its ancient Jewish birth-place. The Eastern Church, at least in part, as was natural, took the former, the Western the latter, view. At the time when the Council was convened at Nicæa, the Judaic time was kept by the Churches of Syria, Mesopotamia, Cilicia, and Proconsular Asia; the Christian time by the Churches of the West, headed by Rome, and also, as it would seem, the Eastern Churches of Egypt, Greece, Palestine, and Pontus. It was a diversity of practice which probably shocked the Emperor's desire for uniformity almost as much as the diversity of doctrine. The Church appeared (this was the expression of the time) 'to go halting on one leg.'*
'The sight of some Churches fasting on the same day when others were rejoicing, and of two Passovers in one

---

* *Ath. ad Afros.*; c. 5: ἐχώλευε.

year, was against the very idea of Christian unity.' 'The celebration of it in the same day as was kept by the wicked race that put the Saviour to death was an impious absurdity.' The first of these reasons determined that uniformity was to be enforced. The second determined that the elder, or Jewish, practice must give way to the Christian innovation.

"We know nothing of the details of the debate. Probably, the combined influence of the churches of Rome and of Egypt, of Hosius and of Eusebius, backed by the authority of the Emperor, was too great for resistance. . . . The observance of Easter, from that time, was reduced to almost complete uniformity. Cilicia had already given way before the decree was issued. Mesopotamia and Syria accepted the decree, at a solemn Council held at Antioch within twenty years (Tillemont, vi., 666).

"Three small sects,[*] indeed, in each of those provinces still maintained their protest against the innovation of the Nicene Council as late as the fifth century, almost after the fashion of the modern Dissenters of Russia; abjuring the slightest intercourse with the established Churches which had made the change, and ascribing the adoption of the Nicene Decree to the influence of the Emperor Constantine fixing the day to suit the Emperor's birth-day, much as the corresponding communities in Russia ascribe the alterations against which they protest to the influence of Peter. But these were isolated exceptions. Through the rest of the Church the Jewish observance died out. Whatever subsequent troubles arose concerning the observance of Easter had no connection with this original diversity; and the Nicene Council may fairly claim the credit of having extinguished at least one bitter controversy, which had once seemed interminable, and of laying down

[*] The Novatians of Constantinople (Soc. v. 21), the Audians in Mesopotamia (Epiph. Hær. 70), the remaining Quartodecimans in Asia Minor (*ib*. 50).

at least one rule which is still observed in every Church, East and West, Protestant and Catholic.

"Even in details, the mode of observance which still prevails was then first prescribed. Besides the original and more important question, whether the Paschal Feast should be observed on the Jewish or the Christian day, had arisen another question, occasioned by the difficulty of rightly adjusting the cycle of the lunar year; from which it resulted, that, even amongst those who followed the more general Christian practice, Easter was observed sometimes twice or three times, sometimes not at all. It was now determined, once for all, that the Sunday should be kept which fell most nearly after the full moon of the vernal equinox. For the facilitation of this observance, two measures were taken; one of which is remarkable as still guiding the calculations of Christendom, the other as having given rise to an important custom, long since obsolete.

"The table of the Golden Number in the Prayer Book first originated in the Council-chamber of Nicæa. When the task of adapting the cycle of the lunar year to the Paschal question was proposed, the Council would naturally turn to the most learned of its members to accomplish the work. That member was unquestionably Eusebius of Cæsarea (Tillemont, vi., 668), who devoted himself to the work, and in the course of it composed an elaborate treatise on the Paschal Feast, which he presented to his Imperial master, who gratefully acknowledged it as a gigantic, almost inconceivable, enterprize; and gave orders, that, if possible, it should be translated into Latin, for the use of the Western Church.

"Whilst this work was preparing, the Council looked to another quarter for immediate and constant help. If Eusebius of Cæsarea was the most learned individual at hand, the most learned body represented at Nicæa was the Church of Alexandria. It is interesting to see how the ancient wisdom of Egypt still maintained its fame, even in

Christian theology. By a direct succession, the bishops of Alexandria had inherited the traditions of astronomical science that first appear in the fourteenth century before the Christian era, on the painted ceilings of the temples of Thebes. On them, therefore, was imposed the duty—it had already existed as a custom—of determining the exact day for the celebration of each successive Easter; and of announcing it for each following year, by special messengers, sent immediately after the Feast of Epiphany to all the towns and monasteries within their own jurisdiction, as well as to the Western Church through the Bishop of Rome, and to the Syrian Church through the Bishop of Antioch.

"The first result of this arrangement is known to us in the 'Festal,' or 'Paschal' Letters of Athanasius, who succeeded to the see of Alexandria the year after the decision of the Council. From that year, for a period of thirty years, these Letters (preserved to our day by the most romantic series* of incidents in the history of ancient documents) exhibit to us the activity with which, amidst all his occupations, Athanasius carried out the order which he had heard, as a deacon, enjoined by the Council on his aged master Alexander. The Coptic church still looks back with pride to the age when its jurisdiction was thus acknowledged by all Christian sees." †

The decree of the Council of Nicæa was not potent enough to compel an absolute uniformity; but those persons who refused to comply with it were accounted as schismatical, and worthy of ecclesiastical censure. Henceforth, they were to be found in the 'Black-book that registered heretics,' under the names of Quartodecimani, Tessarescædekatitæ, Audiani, Protopaschites, and others.

"Besides the difference about keeping Easter on the Lord's-day, there was another, which, though of less

* Dr. Cureton's *Preface to " The Festal Letters of Athanasius."*
† Stanley's *Lectures on the History of the Eastern Church.*

moment, yet sometimes very much embarrassed and troubled the Church. That was a dispute among those who agreed to observe the festival on no other but the Lord's-day; for though they all unanimously combined in this, yet it was not so easy to determine on what Lord's-day it was to be held, because it was a moveable feast, and because sometimes it happened that the Churches of one country kept it a week or a month sooner than others, by reason of their different calculation."* This difference, as Dean Stanley has just indicated, arose from the employment of different cycles, the number of years in which ranged from eight to eighty-four. And although the greater number of these cycles disappeared after the Council of Nicæa, there yet remained a sufficient ground of diversity in the fact that the Roman Church proceeded by the old Jewish cycle of eighty-four years till A.D. 525, when Dionysius Exiguus brought the Alexandrian cycle of nineteen years into general use in the West. Meanwhile the Churches of France and Britain adhered to the old Roman rule; and it required the lapse of nearly three centuries from the date last mentioned to establish the new canon among them. In the achievement of this there were considerable struggle and difficulty, which were intermittent over about two hundred years. Augustine, in 602, just failed of persuading the British bishops to conform to the Roman practice; and in 628 the Churches of Britain refused to submit their Paschal calculations to the authority of Pope Honorius. At a conference between the English and Scottish bishops, held at Whitby in 664, a decision was arrived at in favour of observing the Roman method in Great Britain; and this method was conformed to by one Church after another, until in the year 800 the uniformity of the observance of the Paschal Feast was completed in these Islands by the winning over of the Welsh to the dominant practice. The

* Bingham's *Antiquities of the Christian Church.*

various anomalies attendant upon diversity thus finally determined; and it could no longer happen, as it had happened formerly, that, of members of the same household, some, through the adoption of one canon, should be celebrating Easter, whilst others, through their adherence to another canon, should have only lately entered upon the penitential austerities of Lent.

It was anciently the custom to include fifteen days in the whole solemnity of the Pasch—*i.e.*, the week before Easter Sunday and the week following it, the one of which was called Pascha σταυρώσιμον, the *Pasch of the Crucifixion*, and the other Pascha ἀναστάσιμον, the *Pasch of the Resurrection*. The general name *Pascha*, from the Hebrew *Pesach*, which signifies the *Passover*, comprised both these seasons. For the Christian Passover includes as well the Passion as the Resurrection of our Saviour, who is the true Paschal Lamb, or Passover that was sacrificed for us. And therefore, though our English word *Easter* be generally used only to signify the Resurrection, yet the ancient word *Pascha* was taken in a larger sense to denote as well the *Pasch of the Crucifixion* as the *Pasch of the Resurrection*.[*]

The word Pascha is perpetuated in divers forms as the modern name of the Great Festival. In Italian it appears as *Pasqua*, in Spanish as *Pascua*, in Portuguese as *Pascoa*, in French as *Pâque*, in Swedish and Danish respectively as *Paask* and *Paaske*, and in Welsh as *Pasg*. For our own word *Easter*, various derivations have been suggested. One writer would refer it to the Anglo-Saxon *Yst*, a storm; and an antiquary of the last century would, in a kindred spirit, refer it to the seasonable prevalence of *Easterly* winds. An old mediæval book of devotion suggests its derivation from *Astur* or *Astre*, the hearth, which at Easter was thoroughly cleansed from smoke stains and the black winter brands, in order to be gaily arrayed with fair flowers and strewn with

[*] Bingham's *Antiquities of the Christian Church*.

green rushes. More piously *Aster* has been deduced from the East, "because as there the sun ariseth—who, as it were, dies in his setting—so here the Sun of Righteousness, which is Christ, who, as it were, sets in His death, and rises again." Other etymologers recognise the "obvious root" of the word in the Anglo-Saxon *Ostre*, to rise, or the German *Erstand*, Resurrection, and are content with so "significant and natural a derivation;" whilst others, again, headed by the Venerable Bede, contend that the word comes from the name of the ancient goddess, *Eostre* (the Ashtaroth, or Astarte, of the Phœnicians), whose feast, falling in April, coincided generally with the Paschal celebration. It happens thus, as in the case of so many of our most familiar names, that a large choice is offered to the discretion of the individual. It is right, in conclusion, to compare *Easter* with its German cognates. *Ostern* and *Oster-tag*.

The Fathers of the Church have vied with each other to shower upon this festival the abundance of exulting and affectionate epithet, and to exhaust in its favour the pregnancy of thought, and the vigour, copiousness, and elasticity of language. It is the great day—the day of days—the lady and queen of days; it is the highest of feasts—the chief and sovereign of all festivals. It is the bright Sunday—God's Sunday—*Dominica Gaudii*, the Lord's day of joy. In the words of Gregory Nazienzen, it is "God's own Easter day, the Easter in honour of the Trinity, feast of feasts, solemnity of all solemnities, so far passing all other feasts holden not only by or for men, but even those held in honour of Christ Himself, as the sun doth surpass and excel the stars."[*] St. Chrysostom styles it "the desirable feast of our salvation, the day of our Lord's Resurrection, the foundation of our peace, the occasion of our reconciliation, the end of our contentions and enmity with God, the destruction of death, and our victory over the Devil."[†] In the

[*] Oratio xlv.; *In Sanctum Pascha*.   [†] *In Sanctum Pascha Concio*.

fervid hyperbole of our own George Herbert, it is the only day in the calendar:—

> Can there be any day but this,
> Though many suns to shine endeavour?
> We count three hundred, but we miss:
> There is but one, and that one ever.

The primitive Church distinguished Easter by the solemn celebration of the Lord's Supper, and especially by selecting it as the principal season of the three—Epiphany and Pentecost being the other two—which were solemnly dedicated to the baptism of catechumens. The spiritual joy of the season manifested itself in political, civil, and domestic amenities. The Emperors Theodosius and Valentinian, "in honour of the Paschal feast," enacted the opening of the prisons to all except the vilest and most incorrigible of criminals. This was done, as St. Chrysostom informs us, in order that the Emperors "might imitate as far as in them lay, the example of their Lord and Master. For, as He delivered us from the grievous prison of our sins, and made us capable of enjoying innumerable blessings, so ought we in like manner, as far as possible, to imitate the mercy and kindness of our Lord." *

Easter was one of the times which private Christians in like manner chose for extraordinary efforts of charity and benevolence; for hospitality and alms-giving, and for the manumission of slaves. So that Gregory Nyssen could exclaim—"There is no one so forlorn and miserable as not to find relief by the magnificence of this great festival; for at this time the prisoner is loosed, the debtor is set at liberty, and the slave has his freedom granted him by the kind declaration (ἀγαθῷ καὶ φιλανθρώπῳ κηρύγματι) of the Church.† Other

---

* Homily xxx.; *In Genesim*, c. 11.
† *In Sanctum Pascha.* Oratio iii.; *De Sacro festo Paschæ et de Resurrectione, habita in magna die Dominica.*

and divers observances, ecclesiastical and social, conspired to uphold the glories of the day; so that the later popular fancy which made the sun dance for joy on Easter morning is rather to be taken as an exaggerated expression of a reasonable piety than shamed by the easy harshness of the word superstition.

The glad solemnities of Easter were not confined to the one day; the whole succeeding week was kept in the strictest manner as appertaining to the same festival. Religious assemblies were held daily for prayer, for preaching, and for receiving the holy communion. The sanctity of the season was enforced by the decrees of several Councils; and whilst it lasted, all public games and spectacles were prohibited, and all ordinary proceedings at law were intermitted. From Easter Eve,* when the Competentes were baptized, until the Sunday in Albs, the eve of which, Alcuin observes, was called the "close of Easter," the new-made Christians, wearing their white robes, and with lights before them, came each day to church, and the whole week was known by the name of the "Neophytes' octave." The first Sunday after Easter was variously named Low Sunday, Quasimodo, and *Dominica in Albis*. The last title is more fully written *in albis depositis*, because on that day the neophytes, the newly-baptized or illuminated, laid aside their white baptismal garments, and delivered them up to the repository of the Church.

Various particulars might be mentioned in illustration of the habit in the early Church of throwing the sanctity and

* Easter Eve is remarkable as having been the only Jewish seventh day which was eventually retained by the Christian Church. It was known as the Great Sabbath, and the Holy Sabbath, and was celebrated with singular devotion, with solemn watchings, and with a blaze of illuminations whether in churches or in private houses. At Constantinople night is said to have been turned into day by the clustering all over the city of lighted torches, or rather *pillars* of wax.— *Eusebius de Vita Beatissimi Imperatoris Constantini*; L. iv., c. 22.

blessing of Easter on the days that followed it. The second Council of Macon, (585) and the Constitutions of Egbright (740) appointed that all the days of Easter week should be observed with equal solemnity. In the Spanish Church Easter is continued till after Whitsuntide, a fact which is in accordance with the declaration of St. Ambrose, that "our ancestors have delivered unto us all the fifty days ending in Whitsunday to be celebrated as a continued Easter."* Tertullian also mentions that these days were spent in holy joy and exultation. The early Christians stood during prayers through all that time, and are represented by St. Chrysostom and Tertullian as looking up into heaven with arms extended at length, and their hands upraised, as if they were malcontent that they could not fly even up to heaven. The Council of Tours, in 813, ordered that prayers should be said kneeling, except at Easter and on Sundays.

In primitive times it was the practice among Christians of all Churches to use to each other on Easter morning the glad salutation, "Christ is risen," to which the response was, "Christ is risen indeed;" or alternatively, "And hath appeared unto Simon." In the Greek Church, which has been conservative of several ceremonies that have lapsed in other communions, the interchange of these salutations is still perpetuated, and they are happily amplified in the letter, and happily rendered in the spirit, by the Rev. Phipps Onslow, who contributes the following poem to the Rev. Orby Shipley's " Lyra Mystica," where it has for its title " The Salutation of the Greek Church on Easter Day:"—

> Spring-tide birds are singing, singing,
>   For the daybreak in the East;
> Silver bells are ringing, ringing,
>   For the Church's glorious Feast.

* *Expositio Evangelii secundum Lucam*; L. viii., c. 25.

EASTER SALUTATION.

CHRIST is risen! CHRIST is risen!
  Sin's long triumph now is o'er;
CHRIST is risen! Death's dark prison
  Now can hold His Saints no more.
    CHRIST is risen! risen, Brother!
    Brother, CHRIST is risen indeed!

Holy Women sought Him weeping,
  Weeping at the break of dawn;
Sought their LORD where He lay sleeping,
  In the love of hearts forlorn,
Life for death on death's throne meeting,
  Joy for sorrow, faith for fear;
For their tears, the Angels greeting —
  CHRIST is risen! He is not here!
    CHRIST is risen! risen, Brother!
    Brother, CHRIST is risen indeed!

Loved Apostles, scarce believing
  In His triumph o'er the grave,
Hear the tale amid their grieving,
  Hasten eager to the Cave.
Find the folded grave-clothes lying,
  Death's unloosed and shattered chain:
Find Him gone, Death's power defying,
  From the Cavern sealed in vain.
    CHRIST is risen! risen, Brother!
    Brother, CHRIST is risen indeed!

Mary comes, a refuge seeking
  For her mourning and her shame,
Lo! a well-known voice is speaking,
  Lo! the Master calls her name.
First, the life o'er sin victorious,
  She who wept for sin, adored;
For her tears, the mission glorious
  To announce the Risen Lord.
    CHRIST is risen! risen, Brother!
    Brother, CHRIST is risen indeed!

For her tears, O glad reversing
  Of the Woman's work of old,
Glorious tidings now rehearsing;
  For the tale in Eden told,

EASTER DAY.

Woman's voice that tale supplying,
  Brought in death by Satan's lie ;
Woman's voice is now replying—
  CHRIST is risen! we shall not die.
    CHRIST is risen! risen, Brother!
    Brother, CHRIST is risen indeed!

Where the noon-tide rays are falling
  On the rugged mountain side,
Brethren journey, sad recalling
  How He loved, and how He died.
He is with them! He is hearing
  How their trust and hope had fled,
To their loving faith appearing
  In the Blessing of the Bread.
    CHRIST is risen! risen, Brother!
    Brother, CHRIST is risen indeed!

Flashing back the sunset glory,
  Burns a casement high and dim,
There the Ten, on all His Story
  Sadly dwelling, speak of Him.
He is there! the Light that never
  Into twilight fades away,
Day-star of the dawn that ever
  Breaks into the perfect Day!
    CHRIST is risen! risen, Brother!
    Brother, CHRIST is risen indeed!

Saints! your Cross in patience bearing,
  Mourners! stained with many a tear,
Penitents! in sorrow wearing
  Darkest weeds of shame and fear,
CHRIST is risen! lose your sadness,
  Joying with the joyous throng,
Faithful hearts will find their gladness
  Joining in the Easter song.
    CHRIST is risen! risen, Brother!
    Brother, CHRIST is risen indeed!

CHRIST is risen! CHRIST the Living,
  All His mourners' tears to stay,
CHRIST is risen! CHRIST forgiving,
  Wipes the stain of sin away.

> CHRIST is risen! CHRIST is risen!
> Sin's long triumph now is o'er;
> CHRIST is risen! Death's dark prison
> Holds His Faithful never more.
> CHRIST is risen! risen, Brother!
> Brother, CHRIST is risen indeed!

" Our Church, supposing us as eager of the joyful news as were the primitive Christians, is loath to withhold from us long the pleasure of expressing it; and, therefore, as soon as the Absolution is pronounced, and we are thereby rendered fit for rejoicing, she begins her offices of praise with anthems proper to the day, encouraging her members to 'keep the feast.'" And with this and other texts she incorporates the very phrase we have just seen rendered in verse:—" Christ is risen from the dead, and become the firstfruits of them that slept."*

The homiletic and general literature of Easter is, if we may use the expression, of a peculiarly prismatic character. It is, to use another phrase which may require indulgence, remarkably polygonal. Its central fact is arrived at by an infinite number of approaches, and viewed from an infinite variety of aspects. And from the earliest Christian ages the preacher and the poet have delighted to illustrate every corner of the subject; which, amongst others, is susceptible of an *anticipatory* treatment, when looked at in the light of type, analogy, and prophecy.

But the prime idea of Easter is that of rejoicing; and in much of the poetry of this season we see the singers contented to be exultingly dazzled by the full stream of achromatic and unbroken light. The glory and the joy are too splendid for analysis. The poetry of this kind does not so much exhibit the *Hallelujah* for a frequent *refrain*, as present the characteristics of a Hallelujah in paraphrase. The monotone is a single altissimo of triumph and doxology:—

---
* Wheatly's *Rational Illustration of the Book of Common Prayer*.

'Tis the day of Resurrection:
　　Earth! tell it out abroad!
The Passover of gladness!
　　The Passover of God!
From Death to Life eternal,—
　　From this world to the sky,
Our CHRIST hath brought us over,
　　With hymns of victory.

Our hearts be pure from evil,
　　That we may see aright
The Lord in rays eternal
　　Of Resurrection-light:
And, listening to His accents,
　　May hear, so calm and plain,
His own—*All Hail!*—and, hearing,
　　May raise the victor strain!

Now let the heavens be joyful!
　　Let earth her song begin!
Let the round world keep triumph,
　　And all that is therein:
Invisible and visible
　　Their notes let all things blend;
For CHRIST the LORD hath risen—
　　Our Joy that hath no end.

The author of the foregoing specimen of the ecstatic order of Easter poetry—which we have borrowed from Dr. Neale's "Hymns of the Eastern Church"—was St. John Damascenus, who flourished in the eighth century. Although he has the double honour of being "the last but one of the Fathers of the Eastern Church, and the greatest of her poets," but little is known of his personal history. "That he was born of a good family at Damascus—that he made great progress in philosophy—that he administered some charge under the Caliph—that he retired to the monastery of S. Sabas, in Palestine—that he was the most learned and eloquent writer with whom the Iconoclasts had to contend—that, at a comparatively late period of life, he was ordained priest of the Church of Jerusalem, and that he died after 754, and before 787, seems to comprise all that has reached us of his biography." For his defence of Icons he was distinguished by the title of "The Doctor of Christian Art." His three Great Canons are those on Easter, the Ascension, and St. Thomas's Sunday. The poem just quoted is the first ode, ἀναστάσεως ‘ημέρα, of the Canon for Easter Day, called the Golden Canon, or the Queen of Canons.

Kindred in spirit, but with a little more diffuseness, is Luther's hymn on "Easter Day," for an English version of which we are indebted to Miss Winkworth's "Lyra Germanica."

> In the bonds of death He lay,
>   Who for our offence was slain,
> But the Lord is risen to-day,
>   Christ hath brought us life again.
> Therefore let us all rejoice,
> Singing loud with cheerful voice
>   Hallelujah!
>
> Of the sons of men was none
>   Who could break the bonds of Death;
> Sin this mischief dire had done,
>   Innocent was none on earth;
> Wherefore Death grew strong and bold,
> Death would all men captive hold.
>   Hallelujah!
>
> Jesus Christ, God's only Son,
>   Came at last our foe to smite,
> All our sins away hath done,
>   Done away Death's power and right,
> Only the form of Death is left,
> Of his sting he is bereft;
>   Hallelujah!
>
> 'Twas a wondrous war, I trow,
>   When Life and Death together fought;
> But Life hath triumphed o'er his foe,
>   Death is mocked and set at nought;

> Yea, 'tis as the Scripture saith,
> Christ through death has conquered Death.
> > Hallelujah!
>
> Now our Paschal Lamb is He,
> And by Him alone we live,
> Who to death upon the tree,
> For our sake Himself did give.
> Faith His blood strikes on our door,
> Death dares never harm us more.
> > Hallelujah!
>
> On this day, most blest of days,
> Let us keep high festival,
> For our God hath showed His grace,
> And our Sun hath risen on all,
> And our hearts rejoice to see
> Sin and night before Him flee.
> > Hallelujah!
>
> To the supper of the Lord
> Gladly will we come to-day,
> The word of peace is now restored,
> The old leaven is put away.
> Christ will be our food alone,
> Faith no life but His doth own.
> > Hallelujah!

In the following Sapphics, entitled "The Lord is risen," and taken from the Rev. Gerard Moultrie's "Hymns and Lyrics for the Seasons of the Church," we arrive at a still further stage of discursiveness. The central splendour trails more and more the clouds of glorious circumstance.

> Bright beams the Morn of Easter o'er the nations!
> Earth from her slumber rises, and in triumph
> Welcomes the dawning Day-Star of the morning:
> > The Lord is risen!
>
> Fresh bloom the flowers around the grave of JESUS,
> Pressed to intenser scent, as forth advancing
> Those beloved footsteps come, and, from the death-shade
> > The Lord is risen!

Fear and amazement fill the vaults of Hades,
God-man hath burst the brazen bars asunder,
And through the open gates the cry swells louder,
  The Lord is risen!

Risen with glory beaming round His forehead
Damp with the dews of death and desolation,
Crowned with the thorny garland of His Passion,
  The Lord is risen!

King of the purple robe He comes in triumph,
With the reed sceptre never to be broken;
Bearing the smoking flax of His Atonement,
  The Lord is risen!

Crowned with the deathless diadem of glory,
Which the fierce sons of Adam wove to crown Him
On the earth-shaken morn of coronation;
  The Lord is risen!

Awe-struck the sun hath hid his face at noon-day,
As the Lord spread His arms to bless the Nations;
Weary those arms have rested from their labours;
  The Lord is risen!

Calvary's shades have fled: the earthquake slumbers
In the deep silent lull of Easter even,
And from the dewy night the dawn grows brighter:
  The Lord is risen!

Hark! His returning footsteps! Alleluia!
Light from the tomb is beaming! Alleluia!
Adam wins back the garden! Alleluia!
  The Lord is risen!

Earth's myriad voices thunder "Alleluia!"
Heaven's choir responsive echoes "Alleluia!"
Death is defeated! God reigns, "Alleluia!"
  The Lord is risen!

Of all the phenomena and circumstances with which, looking at the Resurrection of Christ in its objective or historical aspect, the Easter poet is conversant, the first and most salient is the birth of a celestial victory from a temporary infernal triumph. The Easter sun stirred the tearful Church to a joy more astounding than that to which the dawnings of life stirred up the wondering Adam; for the change was not from non-existence merely, but from all that was antagonistic to existence. But yesterday the Christian, with bowed head and bended knees, was fascinated by the agony of the Passion, and the despair of the Grave. To-day all is changed for erectness and jubilance, and deathless expectation. The leap is from the bottom of the abyss to a more than Alpine summit. The tomb itself is become the birth-place and cradle of immortality.

The historical accessories of the Resurrection are pregnant with a happy symbolism. The time was at the dawning of the year, and before the dawning of the day; and it was on account of this latter circumstance that the Eastern Church kept up its Easter-Eve observances until after midnight, about which hour it was, tradition said, that the Divine Event took place. The Evangelists, by various expressions, severally give countenance to this tradition; which, together with their testimony, appears to have been present to the mind of George Herbert, when, in the poem on "Easter," from which we have already quoted, he sings:—

> I got me flowers to strew Thy way;
> I got me boughs off many a tree:
> But Thou wast up by break of day,
> And brought'st Thy sweets along with Thee.

The Resurrection thus stood at the head of both the daily and the annual cycle of life. Man and Nature were on the point of commencing a new period of strength, beauty, and vitality. With the Paschal poets, all the lower forms of creation share in the victory of a typical humanity. The earth returns with smiles the kisses of the Spring; conflict becomes gentle, and stability is added to the things of peace; in the air is a greater lightness and liveliness; a vaster clearness and intensity is in the skies; and in the sea more rest. The deadness and dreariness of Winter are forgotten in the greenness of leaves and the varied hues of flowers; in the song of the bird, the voice of the turtle, the lowing of the ox, the gambol of the lamb.

As an example of the kind of poetry which delighted in singing of the Easter aspects of nature, we transcribe from the "Voice of Christian Life in Song" a translation of a part of a hymn of Venantius Fortunatus, which Daniel characterizes as a "very sweet poem, representing Nature renewing her birth in the spring-time, as welcoming the risen Christ." The stanzas which immediately follow have been sung for more than ten centuries as a triumphal Paschal hymn. Venantius Fortunatus, who was the last great representative of Latin poetry in Gaul, was born A.D. 530, and was a member of a considerable family of Italy. He died at Poitiers—of which see he had late in life been appointed bishop—early in the seventh century. He was a man of great culture and of general esteem, numbering among his friends the most illustrious names in the ecclesiastical annals of his time. He had the reputation of being the first poet of his age; and he is said by Paulus Diaconus to have composed hymns for all the festivals of the year. His other best known poems are the Passion hymns *Vexilla Regis* and *Pange Lingua*.

> Hail, festal day! ever exalted high,
> On which God conquered hell, and rules the starry sky,
>   Hail, festal day! ever exalted high.
>
> See the fresh beauty of the new-born earth,
> As with the Lord, His gifts anew come forth,
>   Since God hath conquered hell, and rules the starry sky.
>
> Christ, after suffering, vanquished Satan's powers,
> Thus dons the groves its leaves, the grass its flowers;
>   Hail, festal day! ever exalted high.
>
> He burst the bands of hell, through heaven ascending,
> Sea, earth, and sky, to God their hymns are sending,
>   Since God hath conquered hell, and rules the starry sky.

The Crucified reigns God for evermore,
All creatures their Creator now adore;
   Hail, festal day! ever exalted high.

The changing months, the pleasant light of days,
The shining hours, the rippling moments praise,
   Since God hath conquered hell, and rules the starry sky.

Christ, Maker and Redeemer—Health of all—
Only begotten Son— on Thee we call;
   Hail, festal day! ever exalted high.

Thou, seeing man sunk in the depths forlorn,
To rescue man, Thyself as man wast born;
   For God hath conquered hell, and rules the starry sky.

Author of Life! Death's garments round Thee lay;
To save the lost, Thou treadest Death's dark way;
   Hail, festal day! ever exalted high.

Let Faith to the sure promise lift her eyes;
The third day dawns, Arise, my Buried! rise,
   For God hath conquered hell, and rules the starry sky.

From hell's imprisoned shades strike off the chain,
And those who perish from the depths regain.
   Hail, festal day! ever exalted high.

Bring back Thy face, that all its light may see,
Bring back the Day, which died to us with Thee,
   Since God hath conquered hell, and rules the starry sky.

Countless the hosts Thou savest from the dead;
They follow free where Thou, their Lord, hast led.
   Hail, festal day! ever exalted high.

Taking Thy flesh again, to heaven Thou farest;
Mighty in battle, glorious spoils Thou bearest,
   For God hath conquered hell, and rules the starry sky.

These, and such as these, were circumstances that occurred in the fixed order of times and seasons; although they had imported into them a fuller significance from the fact of their coincidence with the Resurrection of Christ. But there were other phenomena, peculiar and proper to this as a unique season, upon which the Easter muse has lovingly lingered:—The coming up of departed saints from their graves; the futile precautions of the chief priests and Pharisees, who, having in vain sealed a stone and set a watch at the tomb of Jesus, bribed the soldiers to report that the disciples had carried off the body of their risen Master; the great earthquake, and the coming down of the Angel of the Lord from heaven; the rolling back of the stone from the door of the sepulchre; the quaking of the keepers at the angelic vision, and the bewildered joy of the two Maries at the angelic message; the appearance of Christ Himself to the women, to Peter, to the travellers to Emmaus, to the Ten, and, afterwards, to the Eleven in the "upper room"; the incredulity, and at length the satisfied faith, of Thomas; the legacy of peace, and the inspiration of the Holy Ghost. Such, and so various are the salient features of one or more of which the Easter poets have essayed the description; and some of them are presented by Dean Alford in an "Easter Ode":—

> The calm of blessed night
>   Is on Judæa's hills;
> The full-orbed moon, with cloudless light,
>   Is sparkling on their rills:
> One spot above the rest
>   Is still and tranquil seen,
> The chamber, as of something blest,
>   Amidst its bowers of green.
>
> Around that spot, each way,
>   The figures ye may trace
> Of men-at-arms, in grim array,
>   Girding the solemn place:
> But other bands are there—
>   And, glistening through the gloom,
> Legions of angels, bright and fair,
>   Throng to that wondrous tomb.
>
> "Praise be to God on high!
>   The triumph-hour is near;
> The Lord hath won the victory,
>   The foe is vanquished here!

Dark Grave, yield up the dead—
Give up thy prey, thou Earth;
In death He bowed His sacred head—
He springs anew to birth!

Sharp was the wreath of thorns
Around His suffering brow;
But glory rich His head adorns,
And angels crown Him now.
Roll yonder rock away
That bars the marble gate;
And gather we in bright array
To swell the Victor's state!"

"Hail! hail! hail!
The Lord is risen indeed!
The curse is made of none avail;
The sons of men are freed!"

The appearance of the risen Saviour to the Disciples is the subject of a poem, entitled "Easter Day: the Evening Benediction," which is adopted from the Rev. Canon Oakeley's "Lyra Liturgica; or, Reflections in Verse for Holy Days and Seasons."

'Mid the hushed echoes of the Upper Room,
The chosen Ten had met that First Day's eve;
'Twixt dawning gladness poised and passing gloom,
Too firm to doubt, too fearful to believe.

Could they review those three eventful Days—
With sorrows fraught and memories unblest;
Their Lord's rebuke, their own half-loyal ways—
And quite their hearts of grief and shame divest?

Could they forget their failing, and their flight,
One comrade's weakness, and another's crime;
And all the wonders of that former Night—
Its acts of winning love, its words sublime?

Yet joy would flash across their pensive talk,
As one was fain with surety to declare,
How CHRIST was seen upon the earth to walk—
He was alive, but still He was not *there*.

"THE EVENING BENEDICTION."

The Paschal moonlight through the lattice gleamed,
  Silvering the shades of Evening's dreamy hour,
When on their sight a more than vision beamed,
  No sleight of eye, no freak of fancy's power.

A glorious form into their presence came,
  Piercing with arrowy force the bolted door;
In grace the same, in aspect not the same,
  With Him who blessed their acts so oft before.

All saw Him changed—how changed! but chiefly he
  Who at the Supper leaned upon His Breast,
And watched on Calvary's steep the Agony
  That o'er His frame its harrowing trace impressed.

Sorrow is past, and death. What is He now?
  No flower so beautiful, no sun so bright;
The note of empire sits upon His brow,
  His form is circled with a vest of light.

Yet hardly dared they hope the vision true,
  Till to the fulness of their joy they woke,
As the known accents, "Peace be unto you!"
  From Him who gives the peace He proffers, broke.

Dear to the exile are the songs of home;
  To captives, dear the message of release;
But dearest to the burdened Christian come
  From Jesus' lips His promises of peace.

Such the calm joy Thou givest, Lord, to-night,
  To all who bow before Thine altar-throne,
And seek the grace of that celestial rite,
  Which pours Thy benediction on Thine own!

Which knits in privilege as in degree,
  Us with Thy children of the olden time,
Since Thou art One with all, and all with Thee,
  In this Thy Church's age, as in her prime.

We, too, are gathered in our Upper Room
  (Thy Church), with grateful hearts, but records sad;
Come in our midst, O Risen Saviour, come,
  And bless us with Thine Hand, and make us glad!

> Lo! Thou art here. Hence, doubt; hence, vain alarms;
>   Let carking cares and envious whispers cease;
> CHRIST bears us in His everlasting Arms.
>   And lifts His voice on high, and sheds His peace.
>
> This morn, with loving hearts and conscience pure,
>   We met Him at His sacramental Feast;
> This eve He comes our pardon to assure,
>   And shadow forth the image of our rest.

The whole body of Paschal doctrine is set forth in the fifteenth chapter of St. Paul's First Epistle to the Corinthians, and its moral and spiritual significance, as affecting Christian conduct, is fully exhibited, amongst other places, in the Epistle to the Colossians, from the third chapter of which the Epistle for the day is taken. It was impossible that every aspect of Easter should not at least be intimated wherever one was poetically exhibited. The doctrinal and the didactic have thus appeared in the historical poems which we have already placed before the reader. It remains for us to offer two or three other poems which refer severally to the Resurrection hopes of the Christian individual, and of the Church, the Christian corporation. The first, entitled "The Resurrection," we owe to Friedrich Gottlieb Klopstock, the author of the "Messiah;" who, besides his larger poem, left a number of odes, "the general character of which," says Mr. Nind, the translator of the "Odes of Klopstock, from 1747 to 1780," "is to promote humanity, friendship, patriotism, and religion. Nor ought it to be forgotten, that at a time when an eclectic scepticism was supposed to be the badge of genius and philosophy—when the tide of infidelity was billowing up Europe—he planted the Cross above the waves, and sang to his fellow-countrymen, GOD THE REDEEMER." The following, from among the spiritual songs of Mr. Nind's volume, has appeared in other versions; and a rendering of it, at once smoother and more paraphrastic, occurs in the "Lyra Sacra" of the Rev. Bourchier Wrey Savile.

Yes! thou wilt rise, wilt rise as Jesus rose,
  My dust, from brief repose:
    Endless to live
  Will He who made thee give.
    Praise ye the Lord.

Again to bloom the seed the sower sows:
  The Lord of harvest goes
    Gathering the sheaves
  Death's sickle reaps and heaves.
    Praise ye the Lord.

Oh! day of thankfulness and joyful tears,
  The day when God appears!
    When 'neath the sod
  I have slept long, my God
    Will wake me up.

Then shall we be like unto them that dream,
  And into joy supreme
    With Jesus go.
  The pilgrim then shall know
    Sorrow no more.

Ah! then my Saviour me shall lead in grace
  To the Most Holy Place,
    If Him I serve
  This side the veil, nor swerve.
    Praise ye the Lord.

The Resurrection of Jesus was the Great Charter of humanity. Man, contemplating this most magnificent of events, becomes irradiate with a light that never was on sea or shore. Feelings of a mysterious grandeur struggle in his soul; for it is on this Day that his soul first *ascertains* the fact of her immortality—a fact which had been but feebly lighted by the Old Testament, left in doubt by Plato, denied by Epicurus, or perverted by Pythagoras into a mongrel metempsychosis. The universality of the Resurrection hope is set forth in Crashaw's "Easter Day," a short ode, which occurs in his volume called "Steps to the Temple."

Rise, Heir of fresh Eternity
    From thy virgin-tomb:
Rise, mighty Man of Wonders, and Thy world with Thee,
    Thy tomb, the universal East,
        Nature's new womb;
Thy tomb, fair Immortality's perfuméd nest.

Of all the glories make noon gay,
    This is the morn;
This Rock buds forth the fountain of the stream of day.
    In joy's white annals live this hour,
        When Life was born;
No cloud scowl on his radiant lips, no tempest lour.

Life, by this light's nativity,
    All creature's have.
Death only by this day's just doom is forced to die;
    Nor is Death forced; for he may lie
        Throned in Thy grave—
Death will on this condition be content to die.

The late Dr. Isaac Williams, author of "The Cathedral," and the ζ of "Lyra Apostolica," published in 1849 a volume entitled "The Altar: or, Meditations in Verse on the Great Christian Sacrifice." From this volume we take our last poetical illustration of Easter. It is in the form of a Sonnet, and has for its theme:—"If we have been planted together in the likeness of His death, we shall be also in the likeness of His Resurrection."

Christ rises!—not alone, with Him His own
    Are rising from their graves, and burst the veil,
    And look again on this their earthly jail,
Even as the moon doth not arise alone,
But watchful sentinels attend her throne,
    Yet love that they themselves should fade and fail,
    In her surpassing lustre, dim and pale.
'Tis thus when Christ within the soul made known
    His glorious Resurrection shall declare,
His love and light shall dissipate the gloom;
Nor shall He thither unattended come,
But all the graces with Him make their home,

> When He the darkness of the soul lays bare,
> Fain to vouchsafe His gracious presence there.

"The Resurrection once believed," to conclude with the words of the late Professor Archer Butler, "who *can* believe it, and not acknowledge that it alters the whole complexion of his existence; that he has sprung at one bound from dust to angels; that he stands on the great platform of immortal natures, can see below him the whole universe, above him nothing but his God? Shall we not then awake, and know ourselves the immortals that we are? This world is but the womb of eternity. The Father, who has regenerated, has regenerated that He may immortalize. Sooner shall He yield His heavenly throne than hold it and forsake us; sooner shall God be no longer God, than 'the children of God' fail to be 'the children of the Resurrection.' Behold! we stand alone in creation; earth, sea, and sky, can show nothing so awful as *we* are! The rooted hills shall flee before the fiery glance of the Almighty Judge; the mountains shall become dust, the ocean a vapour; the very stars of heaven shall fade and fall as the fig-tree casts her untimely fruit! yea, 'heaven and earth shall pass away:' but the humblest, poorest, lowliest among us is born for undying life. Amid all the terrors of dissolving nature, the band of immortals shall stand before their Judge. He has made you to be sharers of His own eternity; the most incomprehensible of His attributes is permitted in its measure to be yours. Alone in a world of weak and fading forms,—with all perishable, even to the inmost folds of the fleshly garment that invests you,—with the very beauty of nature dependent on its revolutions, its order the order of successive evanescence, its constancy the constancy of change,—amid all this mournful scenery of death, you alone are deathless. In the lapse of millions of ages hence, for aught we can tell, it may be the purpose of God that all this outward visible universe shall gradually give place to some new creation;

that other planets shall circle other suns; that unheard-of forms of animated existence shall crowd all the chambers of the sensitive universe with forms of life unlike all that we can dream of; that in slow progression the universal cycle of our present system of nature shall at length expire:—but even then no decay shall dare to touch the universe of souls. Even then there shall be memories in heaven that shall speak of their little speck of earthly existence as a well-remembered history; yea, that shall anticipate millions of even such cycles as this, as not consuming even the first glorious minute of the everlasting day! For these things ye are born; unto this heritage are ye redeemed. Live, then, as citizens of the immortal empire. Let the impress of the eternal country be on your foreheads. Let the angels see that you know yourselves their fellows. Speak, think, and act, as becomes your high ancestry; for your Father is in heaven, and the First-born of your brethren is on the throne of God. Oh! as you read and hear of these things, strain your eyes beyond the walls of this dim prison, and catch the unearthly light of that spiritual world where the perfected just are already awaiting your arrival." *

* Sermon on *The Power of the Resurrection*.

The Ascension-Day.

IT was the fond custom of heathen nations whose origin was veiled in obscurity, to claim a descent from ancestral gods, or an ascent from the soil of the country which they occupied; and the practice is not entirely without its parallel in the assumed derivation of Christian seasons. Although no mention of the celebration of the feast of Ascension occurs in the writings of the earliest fathers, as Justin Martyr, Cyprian, and Clement of Alexandria; and although Origen omits it from his list of the Christian festivals,* it is claimed by St. Augustine as one of those solemn anniversaries, which, being observed through all the Church, were to be referred, on account of their universality, to the appointment of the Apostles themselves, or to the authority of general Councils.† From the fact of certain immunities to slaves being provided for at the recurrence of Ascension-day, by the *Apostolical Constitutions* (Lib. viii., c. 33), it has been concluded that it was established not later than the second half of the third century. Its commemoration is recognized by St. Chrysostom among the other principal holydays of the Crucifixion, the Passion, the Resurrection,

---

* *Contra Celsum;* Lib. viii., c. 22.
† *Epistola; Ad Inquisitiones Januarii;* Ep. liv.

and the Pentecostal outpouring of the Holy Spirit; and he styles it "the illustrious and refulgent day of the Assumption of the Crucified."* St. Augustine speaks of it as "the day on which we celebrate the Ascension of our Lord to Heaven."†

The Council of Agde, A.D. 506, and the Council of Orleans, A.D. 511, severally made decrees to enforce, under heavy ecclesiastical penalties, the regular and decent observance of this festival.‡ And in the previous century, Proclus, Archbishop of Constantinople, who died in 447, in his enumeration of the five great festivals, gave the fourth place to that which "declared the ascent into Heaven of Him who was our Firstfruit."§ The fact of the primitive obscurity of the festival of the Ascension may be understood from the probability of its having to achieve a gradual emergence into individuality and pre-eminence above the rest of the fifty days which, intervening between the Resurrection and the outpouring of the Holy Spirit, were all grouped together in one extended season of Pentecost. On this quinquagesimal duration of the period was the boast of Turtullian founded, when, addressing his heathen opponents, he challenged them:—"Gather all the festivals of the Gentiles, and put them together into one sum; they will not be able to rival this single one of Pentecost."‖ The dawning of the more particular distinction of the day of Christ's Ascension may, as Joachim Hildebrand infers from the manner of its mention by St. Augustine, be fixed in the early part of the fourth century.¶

In the *Apostolical Constitutions* the day of our Lord's

* Homily, *In Ascensionem Domini nostri Jesu Christi*.
† Sermo, *De Ascensione Domini*.
‡ Labbé's *Sacrosancta Concilia*.
§ Oratio iii. *De Incarnatione Domini*.
‖ *De Idololatria*: c. xiv.
¶ *De Diebus Festis Libellus: Festum Ascensionis*.

Assumption into Heaven is called τὴν ἀνάληψιν; and more fully in an Oration ascribed to Epiphanius, τὴν ἀνάληψιν τοῦ Κυρίον ‘ημων Ιησοῦ Χριστοῦ. Another title for this day which was anciently in considerable vogue was Ἐπισωζομένη, ἡμέρα ἐπισωζομένης, or σωζομένης; for the reason, as has been generally supposed that the Ascension was the completion of the work of human redemption, and of the whole polity and economy of the Christian system. The words of St. Chrysostom favour this hypothesis:—" On this day the reconciliation between God and man is perfected; on this day the ancient enmity is destroyed, and the protracted war concluded; on this day a marvellous and unexpected peace is restored to us. * * * * * * * * After God in His anger had destroyed man and beast from off the earth by a universal deluge, we, who had been shown to be unworthy to be lords of earth, are exalted to the hope of Heaven; we, who were not fit to receive dominion below, are advanced to a kingdom which is above. We ascend higher than the heavens, and take possession of a royal throne; and that very nature of ours, against which the cherubim were set to guard the gate of Paradise, is this day set above the cherubim."[*] Amongst the moderns, Ascension-day has no great variety of vernacular names. In Germany it is known as *Himmelfahrtstag;* and sometimes as *Non-tag*, because nones were kept with singular splendour, out of respect to a tradition that at this hour our Lord ascended to Heaven. In some parts of the south of France it was termed *Bread-Thursday*, from a distribution of bread which was then made to the poor; whilst in England it is popularly known as Holy Thursday.

Ascension-Day is one of the twelve feasts which—the Paschal Feast standing alone and above all—the Oriental church calls by the name of Great, in contradistinction to the other classes known respectively as Middle and Little.

[*] Homily, *In Ascensionem Domini Nostri Jesu Christi.*

It is one of the seasons at which the English Church especially enforces upon its members the duty of receiving the Holy Communion; and it is one of the six Holydays for which proper liturgical offices are appointed.

Although, as we have seen, it began to assume a more strictly defined individual life late in the third, or early in the fourth, century, Ascension-day was never less than a time for the delivery of special discourses, having for their object the exhortation of the faithful to lift up their souls to accompany the ascended Christ to the heavenly places where His power and glory were manifested. The honours paid to the Ascension came gradually to include observances which to an educated spiritual taste appear to overstep the marches that separate piety from superstition and burlesque. "As for any such ridiculous pageantry," are the words of Bingham, "as has been used in some places to represent Christ's Ascension in the church, by drawing up an image of Christ to the roof of the church, and then casting down the image of Satan in flames, to represent his falling as lightning from Heaven, with abundance more of the same kind (which the curious reader may find described by Hospinian* out of Naogeorgus), the ancient Church was wholly a stranger to it; this being the invention of later ages, when superstitious ceremonies had debased religion into sport and ridicule, and made the great things of God's Law look more like ludicrous pomp and comedy, than venerable mysteries of the Christian faith."†

Foreshadowings of the Ascension of Christ are to be found in various typical representations and prophetic utterances recorded in the Old Testament Scriptures; and these the several offices for the day of its commemoration set forth with a singular completeness. The ascent of Moses to the Mount in order to receive from God the Law which was to be the rule of Israel, finds its antitype in the

* *De Festis Christianorum.*
† *Antiquities of the Christian Church.*

Ascension of Christ in order that from the heights of His glory He might dispense "a new law, the law of faith." This latter Ascension was further and recurrently represented "by the High Priest's being appointed once every year to enter into the Holy of Holies; which showed that the High Priest of the good things to come, by a greater and more perfect tabernacle not made with hands, was to enter into the holy place, having obtained eternal redemption for us (Heb. ix, 11, 12), all the Jews believing that the tabernacle did signify this world, and the Holy of Holies the highest heavens. Wherefore, as the High Priest did pass through the rest of the tabernacle, and with the blood of the sacrifice enter into the Holy of Holies, so was the Messias to offer up Himself a sacrifice to pass through all the courts of this world, and with His blood to enter into the highest heavens, the most glorious seat of the majesty of God."*

It would be difficult to demonstrate fully the relation of type and antitype between the translation of Enoch, the fiery *rape* of Elijah, and the Ascension of Christ. Yet these are events which have ever been objects of legitimate comparison—a comparison that has generally taken the complexion of a contrast of which all the stupendous circumstances were on the side of a greater and unique glory to the Saviour of mankind. Enoch was "taken;" Elijah was carried upwards; but Christ, *propriâ virtute*, perforce of His divine nature, Himself ascended. *They* owed their elevation to an agency external to themselves; He owed His to His own inherent power. "It is to be expressly noted," says Gregory the Great, "that Elias is said to have ascended in a chariot, that it might be openly and abundantly demonstrated that even a righteous man requires assistance foreign to himself. The aids which Elias received, he received at the hands of angels, for not even to the

* Nelson's *Companion for the Festivals and Fasts of the Church of England.*

aërial heaven, encumbered as he was by the infirmity of his nature, could he possibly ascend by himself. But our Redeemer, not in a chariot, not by the ministration of angels, was raised up to heaven, because He who had made all things was naturally borne above all things by His own native power and virtue."*

The essential superiority of the Ascension of Christ is further pointed by a quaint and curious speculation of Benedict XIV, who therein presumably represents the current opinion of his time (1740—1758). This speculation, which an all but exhaustive geographical discovery has at present routed, would seem to have been based upon a fanciful application of a passage in the prophet Malachi (iv. 5, 6). "In the Old Testament," says Pope Benedict, "we are told that Elias was carried away into heaven. Now there is an aërial heaven, and there is an ethereal heaven. The aërial heaven is that which is nearest to the earth; whence we speak of the fowls of heaven, because we see them flying about in the air. Elias, therefore, was taken up into the aërial heaven, in order that he might be speedily conducted to some remote and secret region of the earth, where he should live in great quietness both of body and spirit, until at the end of the world he should return and discharge the debt he still owes to death. For he has deferred death, not evaded it. But our Redeemer, by not deferring death, has overcome it; by His Resurrection has consumed and destroyed it; and by His Ascension has declared the splendour of His Resurrection."†

With the Ascension, the whole sphere of Christ's activity as the Saviour of mankind was perfected; the whole cycle of the work of atonement was complete. Beginning in heaven, it had there its consummation. When our Lord had accomplished the objects of His life, He laid it down; when He had accomplished the objects of His death, He

* *XL Homiliæ in Evangelia; Hom. XXIX, In Ascensione Domini.*
† *De Festis Domini Nostri Jesu Christi.*

rose again; and when He had accomplished the objects of His Resurrection, He ascended to resume His intermitted grandeur—the same divine pomp which He had with the Father before the world began—the same, but with an eternal difference. St. Bernard thus calls the feast of Ascension "the consummation and the complement of all other solemnities—the happy closing of the whole of the itinerary of the Son of God. For He who descended is the same as He who this day ascended above all heavens, that He might perfect all things (Ephes. iv. 10)."* But in an especial manner the Ascension was the complement of the Resurrection; and these two together make up one God-like procession from the unfathomed abyss to the approachless height. Earth was simply the halting-place; and the quadragesimal delay was simply the interval between the extremes of subjection to death on the one hand, and the power of dispensing life on the other. Rightly estimated, it may be said that the Resurrection was the greater miracle of the two. It was less astonishing, if we may so reverently phrase it, that He who by His own power forced the unwilling gates of death and the tomb from *within*, should pass through the open gates of expectant heaven from *without*.

The poetry of the Ascension has not concerned itself so much with the typology as with the prophecy of the Old Testament; and the language of the latter has supplied the Christian imitator with his grandest, his most vivid and most fervid images. The spirit of the Psalmist affords, up to this moment, the most elevated inspiration of the baptised muse. The soul of David still vibrates through the songs that record the ascending triumphs of the Son and the Lord of David.

The circumstances attending the Ascension divide themselves very naturally into the circumstances severally on earth and in heaven. The former of course refer to the

* Sermo ii.; *In Ascensione Domini.*

phenomena of the parting below; the latter, of the reception above. The difference of place was great; the difference of time, although at a minimum, was yet sufficient to give the idea of sequence. There was at least the difference of past and present; of the *was* and the *is*, the *then* and the *now*.

The scene of the Ascension was the Mount of Olives, distant eastward from Jerusalem about five or eight furlongs, according as the measurement was taken to the base or the summit. To this Mount it was that our Lord was accustomed to retire for prayer and contemplation after the public services of the day; from it, weeping, He pronounced the impending destruction of the City; and at its foot lay the garden which was the place of His agony.*
It was in the act of benediction, and whilst promising the descent of the Holy Spirit, that a cloud received Him out of the sight of His assembled friends and followers, to whom, whilst still they looked after their ascending Master, angels appeared to give assurance of a like glorious return for the Judgment of the world.

> Now that Death by death hath found its ending,
>   Thou dost call to Thee Thy loved Eleven,
> And from holy Olivet ascending
>   On a cloud art carried up to Heaven.
>
> O that wondrous Birth! that wondrous Rising!
>   That more wondrous mounting to the sky!
> So Elias, earthly things despising,
>   In a fiery chariot went on high.
>
> Parted from Him, still they watched His going:
>   "Why stand gazing thus?" the Angel said—
> "This same JESUS, all His glory showing,
>   Shall return to judge the quick and dead."

---

* The footprints of our Lord on the Mount of Olives were said, by a tradition mentioned by Pope Benedict XIV., to be indelible by any force or pressure that could be brought to bear upon them. They were even reported to have remained fresh and distinct after all the trampling of the horse and foot of the besieging army of Titus.

ST. JOSEPH OF THE STUDIUM.

The foregoing is the fifth Ode, Νεκρώσας τὸν θάνατον, of the *Canon for Ascension* of St. Joseph of the Studium, who is known as the most prolific of Eastern hymn-writers. Dr. Neale calls the *Canon for Ascension*, "the crowning glory of the poet Joseph;" and says that in it the author "has with a happy boldness entered into the lists with S. John Damascene, to whom, on this one occasion, he must be pronounced superior." "A Sicilian by birth, Joseph left his native country on its occupation by the Mahometans in 830, and went to Thessalonica, where he embraced the monastic life. Thence he removed to Constantinople; but, in the second Iconoclastic persecution, he seems to have felt no vocation for confessorship, and went to Rome. Taken by pirates, he was for some years a slave in Crete, where he converted many to the faith; and, having obtained his liberty, and returned to the Imperial city, he stood high in the favour first of S. Ignatius, then of Photius, whom he accompanied into exile. On the death of that great man he was recalled, and gave himself entirely to Hymnology."*

The Latin hymn *Æterne Rex Altissime* was not in any considerable vogue in the ages nearest to its production. It is extant, however, in more than one version, varying in length as well as in particular turns of expression; and it occurs in the *Roman Breviary* as an Ascension hymn for Matins. Daniel, in his "Thesaurus Hymnologicus," gives it a place—in a twofold form—amongst a group of anonymous hymns which he assigns to a period between the sixth and the ninth century. The English translation here offered is taken from the Rev. Edward Caswall's "Lyra Catholica." It owes its order in our series of examples of Ascension poetry to the affinity which its ending displays to the conclusion of the Ode of St. Joseph of the Studium—both coinciding in referring to the second coming of Christ as a Judge.

* *Hymns of the Eastern Church.*

THE ASCENSION-DAY.

O Thou eternal King most high!
    Who didst the world redeem;
And conquering Death and Hell, receive
    A dignity supreme.

Thou, through the starry orbs, this day
    Didst to Thy throne ascend;
Thenceforth to reign in sovereign power,
    And glory without end.

There, seated in Thy majesty,
    To Thee submissive bow
The Heaven of Heavens, the spacious earth,
    The depths of Hell below.

With trembling there the angels see
    The changed estate of men;
The flesh which sinned by Flesh redeemed;
    Man in the Godhead reign.

There, waiting for Thy faithful souls,
    Be Thou to us, O Lord!
Our peerless joy while here we stay,
    In Heaven our great reward.

Renew our strength; our sins forgive;
    Our miseries efface;
And lift our souls aloft to Thee,
    By Thy celestial grace.

So, when Thou shinest on the clouds,
    With Thy angelic train,
May we be saved from vengeance due,
    And our lost crowns regain.

Glory to Jesus, who returns
    Triumphantly to Heaven;
Praise to the Father evermore,
    And Holy Ghost be given.

The Twenty-fourth is one of the Psalms which the Church has made proper to the commemoration of the Ascension; and the fine poetical imagery of its latter part has been vigorously rendered in evangelical paraphrase by Charles

Wesley, whose muse is almost unexampled in its impassioned fervour and in the unfaltering boldness of its expressions of love and confidence. The hymns of Charles Wesley remain to evidence the probability of the opinion delivered on his ministry by one of his biographers, to the effect that "for the space of ten years, it was like a flame of fire." It is probable that, like the Seventy-eighth, another of the Psalms proper to Ascension-day, the Twenty-fourth Psalm was composed by the royal poet on the joyous occasion of the bringing of the Ark of the Covenant from the house of Obed-Edom into the city of David, and into the house prepared for it on Mount Sion.* In the Christian adaptation of the enthusiasm of David, "our blessed Redeemer is represented as rising in His triumphal chariot, leading captive the powers of Hell, arriving at the portals of the celestial city. Attendant angels chant His praises, and demand on His behalf that the gates shall be thrown wide open, that the everlasting doors shall be lifted up, and that He shall be solemnly ushered into those mansions which He claims as His own. The enquiry is thus raised, *Who is this King of Glory?* In reply, His name is given, and some of His exploits are enumerated. A second enquiry and a second reply lead to a confirmation of the former statement, with additional titles and dignities bestowed upon Him; the last being the highest and most glorious of all, and involving absolute, supreme, and eternal Deity—*God over all, for ever blessed.* The whole subject, when thus applied to the Ascension of the Lord Jesus, and His reception in the abodes of endless bliss, is invested with the deepest importance, and exhibits all the beauty and sublimity which characterize poetry of the highest order. One might indeed say, without any impropriety, that the Jewish bard is here excelled by the Christian poet: because

* "This Psalm alludes so very plainly to Christ's Ascension, that Theodore says, it was actually sung on that occasion by a choir of angels that attended Him." Wheatly's *Common Prayer.*

the latter, guided by the superior light of the Gospel dispensation, and enjoying in the largest measure the gifts of the Holy Spirit, understood these divine mysteries far better than even the favoured son of Jesse could understand them in his day."*

> Our Lord is risen from the dead;
>   Our Jesus is gone up on high!
> The powers of Hell are captive led,
>   Dragged to the portals of the sky;
> There His triumphant chariot waits,
>   And angels chant the solemn lay:
> Lift up your heads, ye heavenly gates;
>   Ye everlasting doors, give way!
>
> Loose all your bars of massy light,
>   And wide unfold the ethereal scene;
> He claims these mansions as His right;
>   Receive the King of Glory in!
> Who is the King of Glory? Who?
>   The Lord that all our foes o'ercame;
> The world, sin, death, and hell o'erthrew:
>   And Jesus is the Conqueror's name.
>
> Lo! His triumphal chariot waits,
>   And angels chant the solemn lay:
> Lift up your heads, ye heavenly gates;
>   Ye everlasting doors give way!
> Who is the King of Glory? Who?
>   The Lord, of glorious power possessed;
> The King of saints, and angels too,
>   God over all, for ever blessed!

Our next example of Ascension poetry fills up the grand outline of Charles Wesley with a particularity of detail the suggestion of which is to be traced to the *Te Deum*. But before it proceeds to describe the reception of Christ

---

* *Wesleyan Hymnology: or a Companion to the Wesleyan Hymn Book.* By William Pennington Burgess, *Wesleyan Minister*, 1845.

in heaven, it depicts the sympathy of terrestrial Nature with the triumph of the Lord of earth and heaven. The author of this piece was Giles Fletcher, nephew of Richard Fletcher, Bishop of London, and younger brother of Phineas Fletcher, the very ingenious poetical allegorist of the "Purple Island." Giles Fletcher was born in 1588, or a year or two earlier, and educated at Westminster and at Trinity College, Cambridge, of which he was chosen Fellow. Fuller describes him as "one equally beloved of the *Muses* and the *Graces*, having a sanctified wit, witness his worthy poem entituled "Christ's Victory," made by him —being but Bachelor of Arts—discovering the piety of a saint and divinity of a doctor. He afterwards applied himself to school-divinity (cross to the grain of his genius as some conceive), and attained to good skill therein. When he preached at *St. Maries* his prayer before his sermon usually consisted of one entire allegory, not *driven* but *led* on, most proper in all particulars. He was at last (by exchange of his living) settled in *Suffolk*, which hath the best and worst airs in *England*, best about *Bury*, and worst on the sea-side, where (at Alderton) Master Fletcher was beneficed." * Here, Fuller proceeds to inform us, his career was cut short about the year 1623; his death being accelerated by the unkindness at once of the atmosphere and the people.

In 1610 Fletcher published at Cambridge his great poem entitled "Christ's Victory and Triumph," which, although never enjoying popular appreciation commensurate with its deserts, affords instances of bold and graphic personification, and abounds in majestic passages. It consists of four Cantos, the subjects of which are respectively (1) Christ's Victory in Heaven; (2) Christ's Triumph on Earth; (3) Christ's Triumph over Death; and (4) Christ's Triumph after Death. The stanzas which follow are extracted from the last of these Cantos.

* *History of the Worthies of England.*

Toss up your heads, ye everlasting gates,
And let the Prince of Glory enter in:
At whose brave volley of siderial states,
The sun to blush, and stars grow pale were seen;
When, leaping first from Earth, He did begin
    To climb His angels' wings, then open hang
    Your crystal doors,—so all the chorus sang
Of heavenly birds, as to the stars they nimbly sprang.

Hark how the floods clap their applauding hands,
The pleasant valleys singing for delight,
And wanton mountains dance about the lands,
The while the fields, struck with the heavenly light,
Set all their flowers a-smiling at the sight;
    The trees laugh with their blossoms, and the sound
    Of the triumphant shout of praise that crowned
The flaming Lamb, breaking through Heaven hath passage found.

Out leap the antique patriarchs, all in haste,
To see the powers of Hell in triumph led,
And with small stars a garland interchased
Of olive-leaves they bore to crown His head,
That was before with thorns degloried:
    After Him flew the prophets brightly stoled
    In shining lawn, and wimpled manifold,
Striking their ivory harps strung all in cords of gold.

To which the saints victorious carols sung,
Ten thousand saints at once, that with the sound
The hollow vaults of Heaven for triumph rang:
The cherubim their clamours did confound
With all the rest, and clapt their wings around:
    Down from their thrones the dominations flow,
    And at His feet their crowns and sceptres throw;
And all the princely souls fall on their faces low.

Nor can the martyrs' wounds them stay behind,
But out they rush among the heavenly crowd,
Seeking their Heaven out of their Heaven to find,
Sounding their silver trumpets out so loud,
That the shrill noise broke through the starry cloud,
    And all the virgin souls, in pure array,
    Came dancing forth and making joyous play;
So Him they led along into the courts of day.

So Him they led into the courts of day,
Where never war, nor wounds abide Him more,
But in that house eternal peace doth play,
Acquieting the souls, that new before
Their way to Heaven through their own blood did score,
   But now estranged from all misery,
   As far as Heaven and Earth discoasted lie,
Swelter in quiet waves of immortality.

A simple, single treatment of a divine subject is a rarity. The scheme of salvation, whilst presenting an aggregate of events, is yet at the same time a unity; and it is difficult to set a part in motion without agitating the whole. It is difficult, again, to find an historical fact severed from the doctrine which it suggests; or to find the exhibition of a doctrine detached from the fact on which it is based. In the poem which follows, Dr. Monsell, the well-known author of "Spiritual Songs for the Sundays and Holydays throughout the Year," whilst covering generally the same ground as we have just seen occupied by Giles Fletcher, goes lightly over parts which the latter has most elaborated, and presents, delicately and naturally, a modification of Christ's reception in heaven which had not occurred to Fletcher—the surprise of the angelic inhabitants of heaven at the insensate ignorance and the truculent ingratitude of earth. Further, in his verses on Ascension-day, to which he gives the appropriate title of "The Link with Heaven," Doctor Monsell goes beyond Fletcher in glancing at that intercession which is the continuous occupation of the glorified Priest and Victim.

Rise, my soul! to Heaven ascend,
Follow Christ, thy Lord and Friend,
He is gone into the skies,
Follow Him with straining eyes.
Though He seem from thee to part
Follow Him with faithful heart;
Sense may fail, and sight grow dim,
But still faith can follow Him.

He hath fought, and He hath won,
He His glorious work hath done;
He is now gone up on high,
Captive leads captivity;
Taking to the mercy-seat
Wounded hands, and weary feet,
Bleeding brow, and wounded side—
Thus returns the Crucified!

Heaven, though earth had made Him mourn,
Stoops to welcome His return;
God's own chariots are at hand,
Twenty thousand near Him stand,
Thousand thousand angels wait
Lowly on His royal state;
Backward angel hands have rolled
For His entrance gates of gold.

Yet those glorious guards of light
Blush to see that shameful sight,
Horrified at human sin,
Blush to let the Conquerer in;
Him, the Eternal One, the Holy,
Him, the Saviour meek and lowly,
Stained with travail, tears, and toil—
Wounds! His only seeming spoil!

But therein His glory lies—
Mystery of mysteries!
That despoiled humanity,
Angels wondering weep to see,
Is the great Redeemer's crown,
Which triumphant He lays down,
And before His Father's throne
Claims all nations as His own.

He—whose faintest sigh or thought
Legions had around Him brought,
When on earth His petty foes
In their wretched wrath arose—
Comes not now for vengeance pleading,
But for mercy interceding,
And, by His own grief and loss,
Pleads His prayer upon the cross.

Gifts, the best that Heaven can pour
Out of Its exhaustless store,
Hallowed days and happy hours,
Kindly sunshine, gracious showers,
Nevermore for souls to cease,
Till the blessedness of peace,
Re-uniting sinful men,
Bring them back to God again;—

These He asks for, these obtains!
These His glories! these His gains!
'Twas for these His wounded feet
Hastened to the mercy-seat;
'Tis for these that there He stands,
Holding out His piercèd hands,
Earth to save, and Heaven to move,
And for hatred gives back love.

"Headstone" of the wondrous plan!
Perfect God! and perfect man!
In the ascended Saviour met,
On the throne of judgment set,
Mighty in His power to bless,
Almighty in His tenderness,
All that man can want in need,
Man to feel—and God to plead.

The benefits of the Ascension of Christ do not determine in His own person; it is something more than the cold glitter of a selfish glory that falls on the procession where captivity is seen led as a captive. It is the Brother of mankind who is seated on the eternal throne; it is our nature which He has carried into heaven. A part of ourselves has departed thither; a sinless type of humanity that still sympathises with the sorrows and the frailties of His sin-laden followers. "If any man sin, we have an Advocate with the Father, Jesus Christ the righteous" (1 John ii. 1). "We have not an High Priest which cannot be touched with the feeling of our infirmities; but was in all points tempted like as we are, yet without sin" (Hebrews iv. 15).

THE ASCENSION-DAY.

Where high the heavenly temple stands,
The house of God not made with hands,
A great High Priest our nature wears,
The Patron of mankind appears.

He who for men in mercy stood,
And poured on earth His precious blood,
Pursues in heaven His plan of grace,
The Guardian God of human race.

Tho' now ascended up on high,
He bends on earth a brother's eye,
Partaker of the human name,
He knows the frailty of our frame.

Our fellow-sufferer yet retains
A fellow-feeling of our pains;
And still remembers in the skies
His tears, and agonies, and cries.

In every pang that rends the heart,
The Man of Sorrows had a part!
He sympathizes in our grief,
And to the sufferer sends relief.

With boldness, therefore, at the throne
Let us make all our sorrows known,
And ask the aids of heavenly power,
To help us in the evil hour.

On the subject of the intercession of Christ there is perhaps little more, and little better, to be said than is expressed in the foregoing hymn. Its reputed author was the Rev. John Logan, a clergyman of the Church of Scotland, who, born about the year 1748, died in London, December 28th, 1788.* In 1781, he published a volume of

* The authorship of the hymn in question has been challenged on behalf of a young poet named Michael Bruce, who died at the age of twenty-one, and whose poems were edited by Logan; who, by injudiciously or unfairly mingling some of his own compositions with those of Bruce, published what was in fact a miscellany of joint production.

Poems, of which the first edition was exhausted in a few months after publication. But from the time of his early university life, his poetical and critical abilities had won respect and attention; so that when the General Assembly of his Church appointed a Committee for the revision of its psalmody, Logan was named as a member. In this capacity he was very active, not only revising and improving some of the old versions, but adding others of his own production. The collection of "Translations and Paraphrases" which was the result of the labours of the Committee, was put forth in 1781, by authority of the General Assembly; and the poem above quoted is one of the Paraphrases, which at that time tended to enrich a service of praise which is yet kept meagre out of set and jealous purpose.

From brotherhood to co-inheritance the progress is easy and natural. As Christ did not proceed to Heaven to glorify Himself merely, so He did not ascend thither merely to make more easy or more holy the earthly state of His followers. He went as the "First-born among many brethren" (Rom. viii., 29). The celestial law of primogeniture makes all for the advantage of the younger members of the family. On the Elder is laid the toil, the pain, the suffering, the conflict; and when He alone has won the victory, then its results are thrown open to the enjoyment of the later-born. "The Ascension of Christ is the great pledge and proof of our eternal state; our nature is for ever identified with His, so that as long as He is *man*, we must be happy, as one *with Him*. The great value of this transcendant fact is, not merely that it is an example of

The Hymn is the last poem in Logan's volume alluded to in the text; but in spite of this direct claim, it has been lately asserted by a very exact and well-informed author, that "this exceedingly touching and much-prized hymn is erroneously attributed to Logan. It is by Michael Bruce."—*Singers and Songs of the Church*. By Josiah Miller, M.A., 1869.

our future ascension, but that it is our ascension *begun*—we in Him having risen to Heaven, we in Him being at this time present before God, we in Him being united with the eternal plans and procedures of Heaven, so that we are for ever blended with Christ—His property—His purchased possession—the very members of His body."*

After such burning words, the last of Dr. Donne's series of seven "Holy Sonnets," which is devoted to the "Ascension," seems almost prosaic:—

> Salute the last and everlasting day,
> Joy at the uprising of this Sun, and Son,
> Ye, whose true tears of tribulation
> Have purely washed or burnt your drossy clay;
> Behold the Highest, parting hence away,
> Lightens the dark clouds, which He treads upon,
> Nor doth He by ascending show alone,
> But first He, and He first, enters the way.
> O strong ram, which has battered Heaven for me,
> Mild Lamb, which with Thy blood hast marked the path,
> Bright torch, which shinest, that I the way may see,
> Oh! with Thy own blood quench Thy own just wrath:
> And if Thy Holy Spirit my muse did raise,
> Deign at my hands this crown of prayer and praise.

Other poetical illustrations of Ascension-day, which might be given if we could proceed without reference to the conditions of space, open up a vision of the time when anticipation shall have become changed into fruition—a vision of the white-robed and palm-waving "multitude which no man could number" (Rev. vii., 9).

But the enjoyment of Heaven, so far as the followers of Christ on earth are concerned, is for the present limited to faithful expectation; and for each one, fruition is postponed for an unknown and indefinite, if for a short, period. It is for each to fix his heart where his treasure

---

* *Sermons Doctrinal and Practical.* By the Rev. William Archer Butler, M.A.—*The Ascension.*

is laid up already, to set his affections on things above, and to cultivate those dispositions which are in conformity with his hopes. Love is here the sum of all duties; and love is the very atmosphere of the place where are prepared the "many mansions" and the crowns of gold. Heaven itself is reached on the wings of holy and affectionate longing. Dr. Watts, in a poem which occurs in his *Horæ Lyricæ*, and which is entitled "Ascending to Christ in Heaven," gives vent to a sacred impatience to join the Saviour in the realms of celestial beatitude.

> 'Tis pure delight, without alloy,
>   Jesus, to hear Thy name:
> My spirit leaps with inward joy,
>   I feel the sacred flame.
>
> My passions hold a pleasing reign,
>   While Love inspires my breast,
> Love, the divinest of the train,
>   The sovereign of the rest.
>
> This is the grace must live and sing,
>   When faith and fear shall cease,
> Must sound from every joyful string
>   Through the sweet groves of bliss.
>
> Let life immortal seize my clay;
>   Let Love refine my blood;
> Her flames can bear my soul away,
>   Can bring me near my God.
>
> Swift I ascend the heavenly place,
>   And hasten to my home;
> I leap to meet Thy kind embrace,
>   I come, O Lord, I come.
>
> Sink down, ye separating hills,
>   Let Guilt and Death remove:
> 'Tis Love that drives my chariot wheels,
>   And Death must yield to Love.

"Christ," says St. Augustine, "is in Heaven, we upon the earth. Is He, as it were, far from us? The answer is, He is absent. If the question be asked with regard to space, He is remote: but let Charity be interrogated—He is with us."* If we know Him no longer after the flesh, if we know Him not of sensible perception or miraculous vision—still we apprehend Him by a deeper, a better, an inward and abiding sense. Though on the right hand of God, He is not the less with us, for God Himself is with us, and we "are the temples of God," by the indwelling of the Spirit. It is to the guidance of the Comforter that we are to look for help and meetness during the interval that separates this world from the next. Even in the absence of Christ from us and in our exile from Him, we are not bereaved: He hath bequeathed us His peace, and hath promised us His Spirit. The expectation of this Gift makes the following Sonnet on "Ascension" a fitting conclusion to our present subject. It is taken from "The Altar" of the late Dr. Isaac Williams, where it has for a motto the parting words of Elijah to Elisha:—"If thou see me when I am taken from thee, it shall be so unto thee: but if not, it shall not be so" (2 Kings ii., 10):—

> As from an Exile's sad and ruined coast,
>   They who would send one to prepare a home
>   In happier climes, where they themselves would come,
> And watch him in departing; yet, when lost,
> Miss his protecting hand, and feel then most
>   Bereaved; so we, where clouds the skies illume,
>   Watch Him ascend, and feel an evening gloom
> Steal o'er us on our way by shadows crossed.
>   But if our hearts we wean from things of sense,
>   And cleanse our eyes by faith and abstinence
>   To see Him still in His departing hence,
> The mantle of His peace shall on us rest;
> His Spirit's double portion fill our breast;
> And we even by His absence be more blest.

* Sermo, *De Ascensione Domini.*

Pentecost;

OR, WHITSUNDAY.

THE feast of Pentecost is one of those seasons in which Christianity is discovered palpably placed *en rapport* with Judaism, by the coincidence of their anniversaries. The free maturity of the "man in Christ Jesus" is seen prepared and provided in the cradle of prohibitions, and the swaddling-bands of a minute ceremonial. The liberty of the Gospel is traced to the sometime fetters of the Law; the thunder-cloud and menace of Sinai become irradiate with the peaceful glory of Mount Sion.

As on the fiftieth day after the celebration of the Jewish Passover, was ordained that greater feast which, taking its name from the period of its occurrence, was instituted for the national expression of gratitude on account of the ingathering of the fruits of harvest, and for a perpetual memorial of the promulgation of the Law of Moses; so on the fiftieth day after Easter, the Christian Passover, is celebrated Whitsunday, the Christian Pentecost, in joyful commemoration of the sealing of the Gospel by the descent of the Spirit, of the promulgation of the new Law of Love, and of the endless harvest of the saved who then began to be incorporated into the Church.

The Fathers, with one accord, point out this coincidence, and some of them eloquently dilate upon it. "We celebrate Pentecost," St. Augustine says, "that is, the fiftieth day after the Passion and Resurrection of the Lord, because in it, according to His promise, He sent unto us the Holy Spirit, the Comforter (Acts ii., 1-4); and because the event of this day was presignified by the Passover of the Jews, when, on the fiftieth day after the feast of the slain Lamb, Moses received on the Mount the Law written by the Finger of God (Ex. xix. and xxxi). Read the Gospel, and observe that the Holy Spirit is there called the Finger of God" (Luke xi., 20).*

To a statement of the same connection between the two dispensations, Leo the Great appends a doctrine of capital importance. "As to the Hebrew people," he says, "just delivered from the bondage of the Egyptians, on the fiftieth day after the sacrifice of the Lamb, the Law was given on Mount Sinai (Ex. xix., 17), so after the Passion of Christ, in which the true Lamb of God was slain, on the fiftieth day from His Resurrection, the Holy Spirit entered into the Apostles and the whole body of the faithful (Acts ii., 3), that the earnest enquirer might understand that the elements of the Old Testament subserved to the principles of the Gospel, and that the Second Covenant was established by the same Spirit by which the First was instituted."†

The term Pentecost is of two-fold significance; it is both a day and a series of days—a diurnal and a cyclic anniversary. Its first appearance in ecclesiastical history is in the latter character, when, as we have already seen while treating of Ascension-day, it comprehended that quinquagesimal interval which, commencing at Easter, came to a close with the day we now name Whitsunday. That this was the sense in which it was understood by Tertullian is evident from the manner of his mention of it as more than outmeasuring in dignity and duration the aggregate of the fes-

* *Contra Faustum Manichæum;* Lib. xxxii., c. 12.
Sermones de Pentecoste; Sermo 1., c. 1.

tivals of Heathendom;* and again when he speaks of it as "a very large space of time appointed by the Church for the administration of baptism (Acts ii.), during which season not only was the Resurrection of the Lord frequently demonstrated to the Disciples, but the grace of the Holy Spirit was first poured out upon them."† A like conclusion as to the ancient customary duration of Pentecost is to be arrived at from a decree of the Council of Elvira (A.D. 303 or 309), which was framed against an obnoxious custom that had originated in some part of Spain, of anticipating the day—or, which is the same thing, of abridging the season—of Pentecost by celebrating it on the fortieth, instead of the fiftieth day after Easter. The Council of Elvira protested against this abuse, and enacted (Canon xliii.) that any one who was guilty of the practice, and refused to conform to catholic usage, should be dealt with as the bringer in of a new heresy.

Following the Jewish custom of commencing and ending a cyclic festival with a degree of solemnity greater than that attaching to the average run of the days which composed it, the primitive Christians distinguished with peculiar honour the first and the fourth week of the Pentecostal season. But the whole time of its duration was regarded as one prolonged day of sacred joy and festivity, during which, indeed, it was anciently forbidden to observe a fast or to bend the knee in prayer, as Tertullian and Epiphanius severally inform us. "We hold it a wickedness," observes the former, "to fast on the Lord's-day, or to worship kneeling. We rejoice in the same immunity from Easter even to Pentecost."‡ And Epiphanius writes to the same effect:—" During the fifty days of Pentecost neither are the knees to be bent, nor is a fast to be proclaimed."§ The Council of Nicæa applied its authority to establish the uni-

---

* *De Idololatria*, c. 14.   † *De Baptismo* c. 19.
‡ *De Corona Militis*, c. 3.   § *Expositio Fidei Catholicæ*, c. 22.

versality of the practice,* not so successfully, however, as to convince St. Augustine that a uniform observance had been secured;† whilst Cassian more expressly cites the monks of Syria as habitual offenders against the rule, although their neighbours, the Egyptians, were very precise and punctual in its observance.‡ St. Ambrose, in his time, spoke of the custom in question as an ancestral one:— "We have received by tradition from our fathers that all the fifty days of Pentecost are to be observed as Paschal days. . . . Throughout these fifty days the Church allows no fast, but holds them all as if they were one continued Lord's-day."§

But no statement of the unbroken festivity of Pentecost is to be taken without qualification. For, not to mention the appointment as vigils of the eves of Ascension and Whit-Sunday, there arose in the middle of the fifth century a custom of setting apart the three days immediately preceding Ascension-Day as *Litany* or *Rogation* days. This custom was introduced by Mamercus, Bishop of Vienne, who, out of gratitude for the success of the intercessions which had cleared his diocese of several direful evils that afflicted it, appointed these days to commemorate the deliverance of his flock, and as a perpetual preparation for the coming feast of Ascension. Litanies, or Rogations, were not new to the Church in the time of Mamercus, but it

* The twentieth and last canon re-established the uniformity of the usage which obtained in former ages of praying upright, and not on the knees, on Sundays and the fifty days of the Paschal season. This canon is omitted, however, in the version of the Western Church, and the practice seems to have been confined to the Orientals, notwithstanding that Irenæus had assumed to trace its origin to the Apostles.

† "As to our standing to pray during these days and all Lord's-days, I know not whether the custom be generally observed."— *Epistola* 119 or 55, c. 17.

‡ *Collatio* xxi., c. 11.

§ *Expositio Evangelii Secundum Lucam*, c. xvii., v. 4.

was he who first fixed them to these particular days; and the observance of them gradually obtained amongst the Churches in the West until the era of the Reformation, which frowned upon the public processions by which their supplications had been accompanied.

The twenty-seventh Canon of the first Council of Orleans, A.D. 511, appointed that they should be yearly observed; and the thirty-third Canon of the Council of Mayence, A.D. 813, ordained various acts of penitence and deprecation as proper to this *triduum*, which was to be a season of "abstinence and not of joy." The Rogation fast in the season of Pentecost was, however, a thing unknown to the Greek Church, which always preserved unbroken the festival character of the period. In the Church of England it was thought fit to continue the observance of these days as private fasts. There is no office appointed for the Rogation days in the book of Common Prayer; but among the Homilies there is one designed for the improvement of these days. The requisitions of the Church are "abstinence," and "extraordinary acts and exercises of devotion." Perambulations were in many parishes observed on the Rogation days; during which, as ordained by an Injunction of Queen Elizabeth, the curate was "to admonish the people to give thanks to God in the beholding of God's benefits, for the increase and abundance of His fruits upon the face of the earth, with the saying of the 104th Psalm." George Herbert's "Country Parson" is represented as a great lover of these quasi-religious processions, which he well knew how to turn to the pious purposes just mentioned; and Izaak Walton, in his "Life of Hooker," has a pleasant picture of the latter upon his annual perambulations, for the keeping-up of which he was a staunch advocate, and during which he would vary as grave and gay, facetious and didactic, but above all exhorting his parishioners then present "to meekness and mutual kindness and love."

The custom of singing "Hallelujah" was in some Churches peculiar to the period of Pentecost,[*] during which divine service and the sacrament of the Lord's Supper were daily celebrated. Devout exercises of all kinds were enjoined, and the season was specially set apart to the public reading of the Acts of the Apostles, as is declared in the sixty-third *Homily* of St. Chrysostom, in the course of which he propounds and discusses the question, "Why are the Acts of the Apostles read in Pentecost?" He shows that at every season such portions of Scripture were read as particularly related to that season. Thus on the day of our Lord's Passion, all such Scriptures were read as had any relation to His crucifixion; on the Great Sabbath, or Saturday before Easter, all such portions as contained the history of His betrayal, crucifixion, death, and burial; and on Easter-day, such passages as gave an account of His Resurrection. And if any objection seemed to lie against the commemoration of events at Pentecost which in fact took place only after the season of Pentecost had fully ended, that objection was to be met with the fact that the miracles of the Apostles contained in the book of the Acts were the great demonstration of our Lord's Resurrection, to give men the evidences and proofs of the holy mystery, which was the completion of their redemption. The universality of the custom further appears from St. Augustine,[†] and from Cassian;[‡] whilst the fourth Council of Toledo, A.D. 633, either conjoined with this practice, or substituted for it, the public reading of the book of the Revelation. The seventeenth Canon of that Council enjoined "under pain of excommunication, the reception of the Apocalypse as divine, and

---

[*] St. Augustine, *Epistola* 119 or 55, c. 17.

[†] "It was the custom of the Church to commence the reading of the Acts of the Apostles with Easter Sunday."—*Sermo* cccxv.; *In Solemnitate Stephani Martyris.*

[‡] *De Cænobiorum Institutis;* Lib. ii., c. 6.

its reading in the churches from Pasch to Pentecost, during divine service."*

Although such were the sacred engagements that gave a distinctive character to the Pentecostal anniversary, it is not to be supposed that there was anything like a total cessation of labour, especially amongst the poorer classes, throughout the fifty days of its duration. Even the courts of law were shut only during the first week after Easter, and with the close of that week pleadings and trials were resumed. Secular amusements, however, were, by the pious care of the younger Theodosius, forbidden throughout the entire season—such as the public games, and the diversions of the theatre and circus; "because this was a time of more solemn worship, when the minds of Christians ought to be wholly employed in the service of God, and in commemorating those wonderful miracles that were wrought in confirmation of the Gospel by the hand of the Apostles."† It was quite in keeping with such legislation that Pentecost should be one of the seasons peculiarly recommended for the extraordinary exercise of works of charity and beneficence; as, for instance, almsgiving and the manumission of slaves.

As early as the time of Tertullian, Easter and Pentecost were severally illustrated by the solemn public baptisms of the Church, out of regard to the great events of the Resurrection, and the Descent of the Holy Spirit; to which the Greek Church early, and the Latin Church some ages later, added the Epiphany as a third, in honour of the baptism of Jesus, the commemoration of which was included in the anniversary of His manifestation. So far as Pentecost was concerned, it owed its importance as a baptismal season to a desire to commemorate the baptism of "the three thousand this day baptized by the Apostles (the first Christians that ever were). In memory of that baptism

* Labbé, *Sacrosancta Concilia.*
† Cod. Theod., l. 15, tit. 5, de Spectaculis, leg. 5.

the Church ever after held a solemn custom of baptizing at this feast. And many, all the year round, reserved themselves till then (those except, whom necessity did cause to make more haste)."*

At length the honours which had been anciently distributed over the Pentecostal season came to be attracted and appropriated to the day itself which was eponymous of that season. More than one anniversary of the Church have been subjected to a disintegrating process, the result of which has been to reduce the unit of commemoration to a single day in substitution for any more extended period. The ordinary days of such periods were left unmarked; but with each day in which a special characteristic could be discovered, a separate idea was identified. One important commemoration formerly embraced within the season of Pentecost was the memorial day of our Lord's Ascension; and it is probable that the appearance of the latter as a distinct festival coincided in point of time with the appearance of the memorial *day* of Pentecost. The same act of analysis would affect all the days of the season that were capable of an independent existence or worthy of an egregious distinction.

As a day, Pentecost was remarkable—as it had been as a season—for the solemn administration of baptism. The jealousy with which the Latin Church long regarded the intrusion of a third season—that of Epiphany—to share with Easter and Pentecost in the public dispensation of this sacrament, is pointed by a letter written about the middle of the fifth century by Pope Leo the Great to the Bishops of Sicily.† Pope Gelasius the First, who was elected to the see of Rome A.D. 492, was equally solicitous for the exclusive baptismal honours of Easter and Pente-

---

* Bishop Andrewes' *Sermons on the Sending of the Holy Ghost;* Sermon viii.

† Epistola xvi.; *Ad Universos Episcopos per Siciliam constitutos.*

cost, and forbade the Bishops of Lucania and Sicily to allow the administration of baptism at any season other than these, except in cases of the most urgent necessity.[*]

Pentecost was also distinguished as one of the three seasons at which it was incumbent on the faithful to communicate. The eighteenth Canon of the Council of Agde (A.D. 506) ordained that "laymen who did not communicate at Christmas, Easter, and Pentecost, should forfeit all claim to the title of Catholic Christians."

The joy of the day of Pentecost further found expression in the decoration of the houses and churches with flowers and green boughs. This is one of the minutiæ which helped to connect the Pentecost of the Law with that of the Gospel, being derived, as Buxtorf the elder informs us, from the Jews, who, "in honour of the giving of the Law, strewed the floors of their houses, the streets, and the synagogue, with grass; wove all round their windows festoons of boughs and roses and other flowers; and wore green garlands upon their heads, because at that season when the Law was given on Sinai, everything was green and blooming."[†]

Other and more questionable observances of the day were gradually incorporated with the Pentecostal offices, of a like character to those we saw attaching to Ascension; and *àpropos* of which observances it may be said that there are facts in the Christian economy which can only be done *divinely*, if their safety, dignity, and reverence are to be preserved. These facts have been once so done; and, being past, are for ever incapable of human reproduction. The dramatic representation of them necessarily degenerates into travesty and burlesque.

With some such reflections as the above it must be that we contemplate the histrionic effects by which it was

[*] Epistola ix. *Ad Episcopos Lucaniæ.* c. 9.
[†] *Synagoga Judaica.* Caput xx.; *De Judæorum Pentecoste.*

attempted to imitate the phenomena of the day of Pentecost. "Because," writes Durandus, "it is said in the pro-Epistle: *And suddenly there came a sound from heaven as of a rushing mighty wind, &c.*, in order to represent this, it is the custom in some churches to accompany the singing of the sequence [Veni Sancte Spiritus] with the blare of trumpets. . . . Flames of fire are cast down from the roof, because the Holy Spirit descended upon the disciples in fiery tongues; and flowers of various kinds are scattered on every side as a sign of joy and to denote the diversity of tongues and gifts (virtutum). Doves also are sent flying through the church, and the despatch of these birds figuratively expresses the sending of the Holy Spirit."[*] And Joachim Hildebrand records that "on the day of Pentecost, the *pontificii* are accustomed to send forth white doves, bound with cords, through the churches, and in the middle to suspend a wooden dove as a symbol of the Holy Spirit. But this," he concludes, "is certainly superstition."[†] Thomas Kirchmeyer—or Naogeorgus, as he rather rudely Hellenized his name—states the same fact, but with a satirical moralising which is all his own:—

> "In Pentecoste mites albæque columbæ,
> Funiculis leviter vinctæ, mittuntur ab alto:
> Lignea postremo cælo dependet eodem.
> Cernis ut idolis ludant, doceantque popellum,
> Non secus ac pupis teneræ assuevere puellæ!"[‡]

Barnaby Googe thus renders the above in English:—

> "On Whitsunday whyte pigeons tame in strings from heaven flie,
> And one that framed is of wood still hangeth in the skie.
> Thou seest how they with idols play, and teach the people too;
> Non otherwise than little gyrls with puppets use to do."

Variations of these customs have obtained in England

[*] *Rationale Divinorum Officiorum*, Lib. vi., c. 107. *De die Sancto Pentecostes.*
[†] *De Diebus Festis Libellus. Festum Pentecostes.*
[‡] *Regnum Papisticum.* A.D. 1553.

no less than in continental countries, and have been attended with more or less of circumstantial pomp and pageant.

The date of the first institution of Pentecost has been much debated; and various theories with reference to its origin have been broached, impugned, and defended. Of all these the boldest is that of St. Ambrose, who refers the institution of the Pentecostal feast—in the sense of a quinquagesimal interval—to the Saviour Himself, saying that "the Lord had appointed that for forty days we should fast, and that during fifty days we should rejoice." A second theory refers the introduction of the festival to the Apostles; and it is enforced, *inter alios*, by St. Hilary,* Epiphanius,† and Polydore Vergil, who says that they are deluded, who, in the face of the twentieth chapter of the Acts, deny that Pentecost was a feast of Apostolic observance.* The hypothesis of Apostolic institution is of course mainly sustained by the account of St Paul's journey to Jerusalem in order that he might keep the feast of Pentecost in that city. The hypothesis can be held, however, only on the condition that St. Paul celebrated the feast of Pentecost as a *Christian* anniversary; and this is the very thing which to candid criticism has seemed left in doubt. We know that St. Paul countenanced the Christian perpetuation of some Jewish ordinances, whenever he could regard them as otherwise indifferent, according as they seemed expedient or not. He may, therefore have adjudged his assisting at a Jewish festival to be one of those proceedings which were rendered expedient by the general advis-

---

* "The celebration of Pentecost was solemnly ordained by the Apostles, so that during these fifty days no one should either prostrate himself in prayer, or should mar by fasting the festivity of this spiritual beatitude." *Prologus in Librum Psalmorum*, c. 12.

† *Adversus Octoginta Hæreses.* Hæres. 75, c. 7.

‡ *De Inventoribus Rerum*, Lib. vi. c. 8.

ability of keeping up or of manifesting the *catena* which connected the Law with the Gospel. If it had been the Christian feast that he wished to observe, he, who had so fully entered into the spirituality of a dispensation which, even whilst respecting them, rose superior to considerations of times and places, might have celebrated Pentecost with equal validity in Asia or at Jerusalem. It may be permitted, with Joachim Hildebrand,* to discover a sufficient reason for St. Paul's visit to Jerusalem at this season in his zeal to instruct in the principles of the faith of Christ the immense numbers of Jews then gathered together, according to wont, in the metropolis of their nation and their religion.

Another theory is advanced by persons who claim for Pentecost an institution of slightly later date than the time of the Apostles, and affirm their position by the fact that although it is mentioned by such early writers as Irenæus, Justin Martyr, and Origen, Tertullian stops short with asserting for the festival an ecclesiastical, and not an Apostolic, initiation. Even when such writers as these do name it, it is to be remembered that they speak of the quinquagesimal period between Easter and Pentecost, and not according to later usage, of the day merely. In the modern sense of a festival day, we repeat that it is safe to believe that Pentecost began to be observed when, the *season* of Pentecost beginning to be disintegrated, an opportunity was given for Ascension-day and the day we now call Whitsunday to achieve a separate existence. The glory of each of these days arose as the glory of the period declined—that is, very late in the third, or early in the fourth century. In the time of St. Augustine it is clear that Pentecost as a festival day had already been, if not long, at least fully, established, for he mentions it amongst those feasts which Christians were in the habit of celebrating all

* *De Diebus Festis Libellus. Festum Pentecostes.*

the world over; and it is named as a day by Paulinus, Bishop of Nola (409—431) :—

> Hoc* solemne dies sequitur: septem numeramus
> Hebdomadas, et lux populis festiva recurrit,
> Qua Sanctus quondam cœlo demissus ab alto
> Spiritus ignito divisit fulmine linguas. †

But if it is difficult to fix with certainty the date of the first appearance of Pentecost as a daily festival, it is almost as bewildering to attempt to fix the origin of its popular name of Whitsunday. L'Estrange conjectures that it was Huit Sunday, as if the eighth Sunday after Easter. ‡ A manuscript in the Bodleian Library derives it from the custom of giving white meat, the milk of the flock and the herd, to the poor on this day; and it is otherwise supposed that it may have been so called because all persons were required to pay their tithe of young before that day, or in default to become liable to the *wite* or mulct. Wheatly thinks "it was styled *Whit-Sunday* partly because of those vast diffusions of light and knowledge which were then shed upon the Apostles in order to the enlightening of the world; but principally from the white garments which they that were baptized at this time put on." Verstegan suggests the

---

* That is, *Pascha*.

† *Natales Sancti Felicis:* Carmen ix.

‡ "This day is called Whitsunday by reason, say some, of the white garments then put on by them who were at this time baptized, the probability whereof, as I cannot absolutely deny, so it may be free for me to offer mine own conjecture, differing from it, and then I would rather derive it from the French word *huict*, which signifieth *eight*, and then *Whitsunday* will be *Huict Sunday*, the eighth Sunday, recounting from *Easter*, which all men will yield to be the first, and that this conceit may pass the better, let me further it not only with an argument from the consonancy of the words *huict* and *whit*, which sound exactly alike, but also from another word of the same denomination, used in our law, I mean *utas*, which is no more but the *huictas*, in Latine, the *Octavo*, of the anteceding Feast." L'Estrange's *Alliance of Divine Offices*.

original to be *Wied* or *Witen* Sunday, i.e., Holy Sunday.*
Brady mentions a contention of some authorities "that the
original name of this season of the year was WITTENTIDE,
or the time of choosing the WITS or WISEMEN to the WIT-
TENAGEMOTE, FOLK-MOTES, or conventions of our Saxon
ancestors;"† an etymology which had been substantially
put forward more than four centuries before Brady advanced it. In a manuscript poem by Richard Rolle, or de
Hampole, the author of the *Pricke of Conscience*, who died
1348 or 1349, occur the following lines:—

> "This day Whitsonday is cald,
> For wisdom and wit sevene fald
> Was yoven to the Apostles as this day,
> For wise in alle thingis wer thay,
> To spek withouten mannes lore
> Al manner langage everiwhore."

The same view was taken by John Mirkus, a canon of
the monastery of Lilleshal, who compiled out of the *Le-
genda Aurea* a volume entitled *Liber Festivalis*, which,
under the care successively of Caxton and Wynkyn de
Worde, went through several editions in the latter part of
the fifteenth century. "Good men and wymmen"—so
runs a passage in the edition of 1496—"this day is called
Wytsondaye by cause the Holy Ghoost broughte wytte and
wysdom in to Cristis discyples, and soo by their prechying
after in to all Cristendom."

Upon this point, however, Dr. Neale is pretty nearly as
decisive as he is decided. "It is curious," he writes, "that
this name should be so mistaken. It is neither *White*

* "*Wihed*, or *Wied*. Sacred, we say yet hallowed for halihwied,
also we hereof retain the name of Whitsonday, which more rightly
should be written Wied-Sonday, that is, Sacred-Sonday, so called by
reason of the descending down of the Holy Ghost, &c." Verstegan's
*Restitution of Decayed Intelligences: The Antiquity and Propriety
of the Ancient English Tongue.* 1673.

† *Clavis Calendaria; or, Compendious Analysis of the Calendar.*
1812.

Sunday (for, in truth, the colour is red), nor *Huit* Sunday, as the eighth after Easter; but simply by the various corruptions of the German *Pfingsten*, the Danish *Pintse;* the various patois *Pingsten, Whingsten,* &c., derived from Pentecost. The corruption is easy and plain enough: if more proof were wanted, note—

"1. That as it is not Easter Sunday, but Easter *Day,* so it is not Whit Sunday, but Whitsun *Day.*"

"2. Although the barbarous corruptions of Whit Monday and Whit Tuesday are now in vogue (they do not occur in the Prayer-Book), yet no one ventures to speak of Whit Week, Whit-tide, or Whit-holidays, but Whitsun Week (just as *Pfingsten Woche* in German), &c. If the derivations were from White, was it utterly impossible that the unmeaning syllable should here have got in? Who ever heard of Easter-sun Week, or Easter-sun holidays?"

"The Romance languages have, for the most part, vernacularized the Latin name. But in Spain the day is usually called the *Fiesta del Espirito Santo,* and in Portugal *Pascoa do Espirito Santo.* In Italy it is *Pasqua Rosata,* because the roses are now in full flower."*

The history of the morning of Pentecost is given in the second chapter of the Acts of the Apostles; all the rest of which book may be considered as an edifice erected on the miraculous outpouring of the Spirit as on a necessary foundation. The most salient events of this, the birth-morning of a new dispensation, are presented in simple epitome in a hymn often attributed to St. Ambrose, one version of which occurs in the *Roman Breviary,* where it is set down for Whitsunday at Matins. There is also an older version extant; and Daniel gives both in his "*Thesaurus Hymnologicus,*" with the remark that the *Hymnus de die Pentecostes,* commencing *Jam Christus astra ascenderat,* is found in very few of the more ancient Breviaries.

* Dr. J. M. Neale's *Essays on Liturgiology and Church History: Church Festivals, and their Household Words.*

The English translation which follows is taken *verbatim* from the Rev. E. Caswell's "Lyra Catholica."

Above the starry spheres,
To where He was before,
Christ had gone up, soon from on high
The Father's Gift to pour.

And now had fully come,
On mystic circle borne,
Of seven times seven revolving days,
The Pentecostal morn:

When, as the Apostles knelt,
At the third hour in prayer,
A sudden rushing sound proclaimed
The God of glory near.

Forthwith a tongue of fire
Alights on every brow;
Each breast receives the Father's light,
The Word's enkindling glow.

The Holy Ghost on all
Is mightily outpoured,
Who straight in divers tongues declare
The wonders of the Lord.

While strangers of all climes
Flock round from far and near,
And with amazement all at once
Their native accents hear.

But Judah, faithless still,
Denies the Hand Divine;
And madly jeers the saints of Christ,
As drunk with new-made wine.

Till Peter, in the midst
Stood up, and spake aloud:
And their perfidious falsity
By Joel's witness showed.

Praise to the Father be!
Praise to the Son who rose!
Praise, Holy Paraclete, to Thee,
While age on ages flows!

Bishop Jeremy Taylor, in a poem "On the Feast of Pentecost, or Whitsunday," turns into a prayer a simple statement of the descent of the tongues on the heads of the Apostles:—

> Tongues of fire from heaven descend
> With a mighty rushing wind,
>   To blow it up and make
>   A living fire
> Of heavenly charity, and pure desire,
> Where they their residence should take.
> On the Apostles' sacred heads they sit
> Who now like beacons do proclaim and tell
>   The invasion of the host of hell;
>   And give men warning to defend
> Themselves from the enraged brunt of it.
> Lord, let the flames of holy charity,
>   And all her gifts and graces slide
>   Into our hearts and there abide:
> That thus refined, we may soar above
> With it into the element of love,
>   Even unto Thee, dear Spirit,
> And there eternal peace and rest inherit. Amen.

Very early in this paper we made a remark to the effect that Pentecost was a festival of common commemoration to both Judaism and Christianity. In each dispensation its claims to honour rested in part upon the felt and directly apprehended presence of the Deity for the purpose of promulgating a Law. The different circumstances of the two theophanies have been, from the first ages of Christianity, a theme for thankful and trembling exultation. Both Laws were given, as the Fathers, and especially St. Jerome, delighted to point out, on the fiftieth day after the Passover; one on Sinai, the other on Mount Sion. There the mountain quaked; here, the house of the Apostles. There, amid flaming fire and lightnings, spake the thunder and the stormy tempest; here, with the vision of fiery tongues, came the sound of a great wind. There the voice of the trumpet uttered aloud the words of the

Law; here, the trump of the Gospel thundered on the lips of the Apostles.*

The lines on "Whitsunday," in the "Christian Year," may be taken, with the least possible reservation, whether in point of time or language, as the finest picture in verse of the above-contrasted phenomena of Sinai and of Sion:—

>When God of old came down from Heaven,
> In power and wrath He came;
>Before His feet the clouds were riven,
> Half darkness and half flame.
>
>Around the trembling mountain's base
> The prostrate people lay;
>A day of wrath, and not of grace;
> A dim and dreadful day.
>
>But when He came the second time,
> He came in power and love,
>Softer than gale at morning prime
> Hovered His holy Dove.
>
>The fires that rushed on Sinai down
> In sudden torrents dread,
>Now gently light, a glorious crown,
> On every sainted head.
>
>Like arrows went those lightnings forth,
> Winged with the sinner's doom;
>But these, like tongues, o'er all the earth,
> Proclaiming life to come;
>
>And as on Israel's awe-struck ear,
> The voice exceeding loud,
>The trump, that angels quake to hear,
> Thrilled from the deep, dark cloud.
>
>Lo! when the Spirit of our God
> Came down His flock to find,
>A voice from Heaven was heard abroad,
> A rushing, mighty wind.

* St. Jerome's *Epistola ad Fabiolam*; *Mansio* 12.

> Nor doth the outward ear alone
>   At that high warning start;
> Conscience gives back the appalling tone;
>   'Tis echoed in the heart.
>
> It fills the Church of God; it fills
>   The sinful world around;
> Only in stubborn hearts and wills
>   No place for it is found.
>
> To other strains our souls are set:
>   A giddy whirl of sin
> Fills ear and brain, and will not let
>   Heaven's harmonies come in.
>
> Come, Lord; come Wisdom, Love, and Power,
>   Open our ears to hear;
> Let us not miss the accepted hour;
>   Save, Lord, by Love or Fear.

The principal—that is, the doctrine-carrying—circumstances of the morning of Pentecost have been mentioned in the preceding examples of Whitsunday verse; but there are, of course, many of a more minute or incidental character, of which we can scarcely offer so much as a suggestion. Amongst the minor *memorabilia*, however, it may be observed, that it was because Pentecost was one of the three grand seasons on which all the males of Israel were required to present themselves before the Lord in the place of His sanctuary—"one of their great Panegyries or Generals," as L'Estrange claims to call them—that the now fully-inspired[*] Apostles met with an audience collected "out of every nation under heaven."

There are a few questions which are chiefly important because, historically speaking, they have been thought to be important; and which considerable debate and discus-

---

[*] The act of inspiration recorded John xx. 22, 23, may be regarded partly as prophetical, partly as a symbol and an earnest of that which was soon to be realized.

sion have been unable conclusively to settle. One of these is concerned about the number of persons affected by the descent of the Holy Spirit; though a very colourable exegesis favours the idea that the number and the persons were the same "hundred and twenty" who are spoken of in Acts i., 15. Other enquiries have had for their object to discover whether the "cloven tongues" were of real, natural fire, or not; and, with regard to the use of the gift of tongues, whether all the hearers understood at once, each in his own language, the self-same utterance of the Apostles, or whether the latter, with an unlimited command of tongues, appealed separately and consecutively to each section of their audience in its own vernacular. As to the locality of the "upper room," it is probable that it may have been in the house of Mary, the mother of that John who was surnamed Mark, and who was afterwards the companion of Paul and Barnabas.* The hour of the day is fixed by the sacred narrative itself; and tradition seems on the whole to point to the conclusion that in the particular year of the descent of the Holy Spirit, the Hebrew Pentecost fell to be celebrated on a Christian Sunday.

The feast of Pentecost is one emphatically in honour of the third Person in the Trinity, and the day of His de-

---

* Benedict xiv.: *De Festis Domini Nostri Jesu Christi; De Festo Pentecostes.*—In this connection it may be noticed that there exists an old tradition, preserved or re-asserted by Nicephorus, Venerable Bede, Mede, and Bishop Pearson, to the effect that the "upper room" (Acts i., 13) on the top of Mount Sion was distinct from the Temple, and the scene of all the great events of the last Passover, the institution of the Lord's Supper, the appearance of the Saviour on the night of His resurrection to St. Thomas, His ordination of the Apostles, the election of St. Matthias, the appointment of the seven deacons, the consecration of St. James, the assembly of the first Apostolic Council, and of the Descent of the Holy Spirit; so that it was, in fact, the first Christian Church, in the sense of a house of assembly, on earth.

scent, was, in the language of Gregory Nazienzen[*] and others, 'ημερα Πνευματος, the day of the Holy Ghost. The poets of Whitsunday have delighted to identify the person of the Holy Spirit, and to trace the history of His operations up to this the climax of His Self-revelation. He it is who is the great Life-giver; the pulse and the heart of nature; the spring and fountain of all existence. He it is who, brooding over the abyss, impregnated it with the seeds of a multiform and infinite vitality. He it is who searcheth all things, and declareth even the deep things of God, revealing the same to holy men—to Apostles and to Prophets. He it is who dwells in the bodies of believers as in a temple, by which indwelling they who were sometime dead in sin are regenerated to a life of holiness. He it is by whom the Son was conceived when He would become incarnate; and He it is who like a Dove descended upon Him at His baptism. He is the Comforter, the Spirit of Truth, and the Guide into all Truth. He, the same Spirit, it is, by whom was given to one of the Apostles the Word of Wisdom and Knowledge; to another, the gifts of healing; to another, the working of Miracles; to another, Prophecy; to another, the discovering of Spirits; to another, divers kinds of Tongues; and to another, the Interpretation of Tongues, dividing to every man severally as He would. He is the Spirit of Liberty, of Goodness, Righteousness, Truth, Love, Joy, Peace, Long-suffering, Gentleness, Faith, Meekness, and Temperance. He it is who maketh intercession with groanings that cannot be uttered; who strengthens the weakness of the saints, who illuminates their darkness, helps their infirmities, quickens their zeal, retrieves their backslidings, and purifies them in obeying the Truth.

Gifts and blessings such as these would naturally be the objects of a sacred and constant cupidity; and we find that

[*] Oratio 44; *De Pentecoste.*

hymns combining praise and prayer to the Holy Spirit as their Divine source and channel, have from the infancy of the dispensation He inaugurated, been of almost uninterrupted production. Two of these are appointed alternatively to be sung as antiphons in the offices for the "Ordering of Priests," and "the Consecration of Bishops." The hymns referred to are of the simplest construction and language, as indeed are most of the litanic verses which invoke the Holy Spirit—such, for instance, as the "Prose" or Sequence, *Veni Sancte Spiritus*, which is now given in the Roman Missal, to be said or sung after the *Graduale* in the mass for Whitsunday, and which, being better known than authenticated, has been variously referred to Notker; to Robert II, King of France; to Hermannus Contractus; to Stephen Langton; and to Pope Innocent III. The period represented by this uncertainty of authorship ranges from the tenth century to the thirteenth.

To say that Pentecostal hymns, upon a superficial comparison with their subject, frequently appear tame and prosaic, is probably to praise their good taste without really accusing their poetic merit. There are themes where too free an activity of the Muse would be an impertinent *bustle* of the Muse; and whenever the earthly sings of the heavenly, it is necessary that words should be simple and few, if they would also be well chosen. It is impossible to celebrate any but the incarnate Person of the Godhead except on a purely celestial table-land, where, because it is so uniformly lofty, we are almost unconscious of the elevation. The following well-known rendering of the *Veni Creator Spiritus* is not so much a translation as a paraphrase; and is, we need scarcely say, from the pen of John Dryden.

It is the same hymn which, simply translated, is one of those just referred to as forming part of the offices used in the English Church, either for admission to, or for promotion in, Holy Orders. It shares what would seem to be the common fate of early Pentecostal hymns, and its authorship seems to be one of the questions which time has rendered insoluble. It has been referred to Alcuin, the preceptor, friend, and *deliciæ* of the Emperor Charlemagne; Daniel ascribes it to Charlemagne himself;[*] Palmer, probably following Gavantus and Merati, speaks of it as generally referred to St. Ambrose;[†] Mone attributes it to Gregory the Great;[‡] whilst Bässler quotes it, not imprudently, amongst the "Hymni Ἀδέσποτοι" of the eighth century.[§] Rabanus Maurus, not to attempt to exhaust the list, has also been named as its probable author.

> Creator, Spirit, by whose aid
> The world's foundations first were laid,
> Come, visit every pious mind;
> Come pour Thy joys on human kind;
> From sin and sorrow set us free,
> And make Thy temples worthy Thee.
> O source of uncreated light,
> The Father's promised Paraclete!
> Thrice holy fount, thrice holy fire,
> Our hearts with heavenly love inspire;
> Come, and Thy sacred unction bring
> To sanctify us, while we sing.
> Plenteous of grace, descend from high,
> Rich in Thy sevenfold energy!
> Thou strength of His Almighty hand,
> Whose power doth heaven and earth command;
> Proceeding Spirit, our defence,
> Who dost the gift of tongues dispense,
> And crown'st Thy gift with eloquence.
> Refine and purge our earthly parts;
> But, O, inflame and fire our hearts!
> Our frailties help, our vice controul,
> Submit the senses to the soul;
> And when rebellious they are grown,
> Then lay Thy hand, and hold them down.

---

[*] *Thesaurus Hymnologicus.*   [†] *Origines Liturgicæ.*
[‡] *Hymni Latini Medii Ævi.*   [§] *Auswahl Altchristlicher Lieder.*

Chase from our minds the infernal foe;
And peace, the fruit of love, bestow;
And, lest our feet should step astray,
Protect and guide us in the way.

Make us eternal truths receive,
And practice all that we believe;
Give us Thyself, that we may see
The Father, and the Son, by Thee.

Immortal honour, endless fame,
Attend the Almighty Father's name;
The Saviour Son be glorified,
Who for lost man's redemption died;
And equal adoration be,
Eternal Paraclete, to Thee!

The more lively members of the Church have in almost every age, short of the earliest, cast a wistful and reverted eye in the direction of the miraculous gifts of the Spirit. Often it has happened that, in the too keen search after special endowments, the meteor has been taken for the calm clear light of heaven; and thousands have thought no operation so wild, and no instrument so vulgar, as not to be the competent vehicles of supernatural gifts and virtues. The longing expressed in the following verses by George Herbert, on "Whitsunday," for a revival of extraordinary spiritual achievement, is of the calmly earnest, as distinguished from the fanatic order, and seems to embody a kind of meek and pious protest against the long withdrawal of the more powerful and external manifestations of the Holy Spirit.

Listen, sweet Dove, unto my song,
And spread Thy golden wings in me;
Hatching my tender heart so long,
Till it get wing, and fly away with Thee.

Where is that fire which once descended
On Thy Apostles? Thou didst then
Keep open house, richly attended,
Feasting all comers by twelve chosen men.

  Such glorious gifts Thou did'st bestow,
  That the earth did like a heaven appear:
  The stars were coming down to know
If they might mend their wages, and serve here.

  The sun, which once did shine alone,
  Hung down his head, and wished for night,
  When he beheld twelve suns for one
Going about the world, and giving light.

  But since those pipes of gold, which brought
  That cordial water to our ground,
  Were cut and martyred by the fault
Of those who did themselves through their side wound;

  Thou shutt'st the door, and keep'st within;
  Scarce a good joy creeps through the chink:
  And if the braves of conquering sin
Did not excite Thee, we should wholly sink.

  Lord, though we change, Thou art the same;
  The same sweet God of love and light:
  Restore this day, for Thy great name,
Unto his ancient and miraculous right.

When God and man are made *at one* by the sacrifice of Christ, every aspect of the Deity becomes one of love and benevolence. The Father Himself loveth those for whom the Son has died; and the operation of the Spirit, "proceeding from the Father and the Son," is a direct one of pity and of comfort on the minds of the faithful. It is in this light that we understand an address to the Holy Spirit under circumstances when, without it, we should expect a prayer rather to Him who had known in His own person what it was to suffer and to die, and who now and ever lives to bear a part in the anguish of His brethren. Herrick's "Litany to the Holy Spirit" needs no word of introduction; the deep pathos with which he so simply invests the trembling soul, and the infinite tenderness which he imputes to the "Sweet Spirit," leave criticism on one side. It may be said, however, that the "Litany" was well remembered in the rural parish of Dean Prior—

the living of which had been held by the author a hundred and fifty years before—in the beginning of the present century, having been handed down traditionally even by the poor who had never learned to read or write.

In the hour of my distress,
When temptations me oppress,
And when I my sins confess,
  Sweet Spirit, comfort me!

When I lie within my bed,
Sick in heart, and sick in head,
And with doubts discomforted,
  Sweet Spirit, comfort me!

When the house doth sigh and weep,
And the world is drowned in sleep,
Yet mine eyes the watch do keep,
  Sweet Spirit, comfort me!

When the artless doctor sees
Not one hope, but of his fees,
And his skill runs on the lees,
  Sweet Spirit, comfort me!

When his potion or his pill,
Has, or none, or little skill,
Meet for nothing but to kill,
  Sweet Spirit, comfort me!

When the passing-bell doth toll,
And the furies in a shoal
Come to fright a parting soul,
  Sweet Spirit, comfort me!

When the tapers now burn blue,
And the comforters are few,
And that number more than true,
  Sweet Spirit, comfort me!

When the priest his last hath prayed,
And I nod to what is said,
Because my speech is now decayed,
  Sweet Spirit, comfort me!

When, God knows, I'm tossed about,
Either with despair or doubt;
Yet, before the glass be out,
    Sweet Spirit, comfort me!

When the tempter me pursu'th
With the sins of all my youth,
And half damns me with untruth,
    Sweet Spirit, comfort me!

When the flames and hellish cries
Fright mine ears, and fright mine eyes,
And all terrors me surprise,
    Sweet Spirit, comfort me!

When the Judgment is revealed,
And that opened which was sealed;
When to Thee I have appealed,
    Sweet Spirit, comfort me!

The poetry of Whitsuntide is not concerned alone with the attributes and operations of the Holy Spirit; there is from these a reflex glory which falls upon the day itself, and invests it with a splendour that makes it remarkable even amongst the highest of Christian anniversaries. It is regarded as the birth-day of the Church, the day of the coronation of the Saviour, who then gave the last miraculous touch to that work for which He had come down to earth. It was the first grand day of the authoritative preaching of the Gospel; the day on which the Apostles first opened their commission in the hearing of the people. It was the Epiphany of the Holy Spirit, whereon He visibly descended in the stead of Christ to take the charge of His orphan Church, which now first learned the Song of Moses and of the Lamb—the feast of the Law and Spirit both—in the harmony of heaven. It was the reversion of the confusion of Babel, all tongues being hallowed to God's own purpose (Rev. v., 9; vii., 9, 10; xiv., 6). It was the day of the work of the Holy Spirit in the soul, by whose "intervention we are united and incorporated into

Christ Himself, being made living Members of His Body, partaking a common Life and Sense with Him; by it we are compacted into the same spiritual Edifice, dedicated to the Worship and Inhabitation of God; our Bodies and Souls are made Temples of His Divinity, Thrones of His Majesty, Orbs of His celestial Light, Paradises of His blissful Presence."*

It was the day of the introduction into the world more specially His own, of the same Spirit of order as had already moved in the beginning to evolve the physical *cosmos*. Dr. Isaac Williams devotes the first of a pair of Whitsunday Sonnets to a statement of this analogy. It is from the "Altar," and has for its motto:—"Their eyes saw the majesty of His glory, and their ears heard His glorious voice."

> "Let there be Light!" God said: and at the sound,
>   With varied order, beautiful and young,
>   From the dead formless void Creation sprung;
> And sea and land, with their alternate bound;
> And shining worlds that range the blue profound,
>   With hills and woods, and beasts the hills among,
>   And painted birds that in the forest sung,
> And flowers of scent, and hue that decked the ground,
> And seas and streams where roamed the finny herd.
> But how much more when that creative Word,
>   The Gift Unspeakable on man conferred,
> Was seen in flaming tongues that came to sight,
> And heard in rushing winds of viewless might,
> Saying to man's dark soul, "Let there be Light!"

The second of the pair of Dr. Williams's Sonnets on "The Descent of the Holy Ghost" is a companion one to the first, in much the same sense that the pictured "Peace" of Sir Edwin Landseer is a companion to his "War." The instant execution of the *Fiat Lux* in the natural world, as compared with the age-by-age deferred fulfilment of the

* Dr. Isaac Barrow's *Whitsunday Sermon: Of the Gift of the Holy Ghost.*

same *Fiat* in the spiritual world, is startling, humiliating, and confounding. The progress of modern evangelization is so inconsiderable that the mind is thrown back almost violently on its very reserves of faith, if it would cleave to the conviction that the same Christ as of old, by the same Spirit as of old, is with His ambassadors "even unto the end of the world."

And yet there need be no surprise at the *pace* of operations conducted by an Almighty Worker, with whom a day and a thousand years are convertible durations. It is for man to hasten, who fears to grow old ere his task be begun, or to die before it be completed; not for Him, who, having the universe for a stage, and eternity for a working-day, is independent of the trivial conditions of time and space. Certainly if there be, anything adapted to put to proof the power of Omnipotence, it might well be reckoned to be the subjection of a world so populous with souls. Nature is soft and fictile. The granite, the marble, the diamond, yield to mortal skill and power; and Will is the one really stubborn thing in the universe. The subordination of the universal aggregate of wills to the universal Will—this is, if we may say it, the labour and the triumph of God. To His Omnipotence, such a triumph would be, if He so willed it, the fruition of a moment. But His law is a law of growth; His results are those of development, not of revolution. The process of ripening is long or short, just in proportion to the time during which the state of perfect maturity, without decay, is to continue. It is the same law under which the oak that rules the greenwood for a thousand years occupies longer in *becoming* than a violet or a gourd; and under which the building of a Church for eternity requires a larger period than to create a world that shall endure for an æon.

To some such effect as this is the burden of Dr. Williams's second Sonnet, the motto of which is the appropriate one:—"The vision is yet for an appointed time, but at the end it shall speak and not lie; though it tarry, wait for it; because it will surely come, it will not tarry."

> "Let there be Light!" Dead matter heard of old,
>   When the foundations of the world were laid,
>   And even in hearing instantly obeyed.
> But twice nine hundred years have onward rolled,
> Since with His gifts and graces manifold
>   The Spirit hath gone forth, with light arrayed,
>   And the Almighty fiat hath been said;
> Then why is the fulfilment yet untold?
>   There was of days a numbering and delay,
> When rose this visible scene of earth and sky,
> Which hastes so fast to fade away and die:
>   To the All-wise it needs a longer day,
>   From the soul's endless ruin and decay,
> To form a world for immortality.

Still, the inspiration of Pentecost, the "rushing mighty wind," once set in motion, ceases not, in the face of what let and hindrance soever, to blow hither and thither throughout the earth; whilst prayerful zeal looks for a speedy and decisive cast of that divine alchemy which shall transmute the iron of the present age into the glory of an endless "golden year." With such an aspiration, the expression of which we owe to Mr. J. W. Hopkins, junior, an American writer, we close our examples of the poetry of Pentecost. The verses are entitled, "The Rushing Mighty Wind," and occur in "Lyra Americana," published in 1865 by the Religious Tract Society.

> Blow on, thou mighty Wind,
>   And waft to realms unbounded
> The notes of faith and hope and tender love
>   The Gospel trump hath sounded.
>   Those sweetly piercing tones,
> That charm all wars and tears and groans,
>   Through earth and sea and sky
> Upon thy rushing wings shall fly:
> Therefore, thou mighty Wind, blow on.

"THE RUSHING MIGHTY WIND."

Blow on, thou mighty Wind;
    For tempest-tossed and lonely,
The Church upon the rolling billows rides,
    And trusts in thy breath only.
    She spreads her swelling sails
For thee to fill with favouring gales,
    Till, through the stormy sea,
Thou bring her home where she would be;
Therefore, thou mighty Wind, blow on.

Blow on, thou mighty Wind,
    On hearts contrite and broken,
And bring in quickening power the gracious words
    That JESU's lips have spoken.
    Lo! then, from death and sleep,
The listening soul to life shall leap;
    Then love shall reign below,
And joy the whole wide world o'erflow:
Therefore, thou mighty Wind, blow on.

To GOD, the FATHER, SON,
    By all in earth and heaven,
And to the HOLY SPIRIT, Three in One,
    Eternal praise be given:
    As once triumphant rang
When morning stars together sang;
    Is now, as aye before,
And shall be so for evermore,
World without end Amen Amen.

Trinity Sunday.

Holy, holy, holy, Lord God Almighty!
　Early in the morning our song shall rise to Thee;
Holy, holy, holy! merciful and mighty!
　God in three Persons, blessed Trinity!

Holy, holy, holy! all the saints adore Thee,
　Casting down their golden crowns around the glassy sea;
Cherubim and Seraphim falling down before Thee,
　Which wert and art and evermore shall be!

Holy, holy, holy! Though the darkness hide Thee,
　Though the eye of sinful man Thy glory may not see,
Only Thou art holy, there is none beside Thee,
　Perfect in power, in love, and purity!

Holy, holy, holy, Lord God Almighty!
　All Thy works shall praise Thy name in earth and sky and sea,
Holy, holy, holy! merciful and mighty!
　God in three Persons, blessed Trinity!

　　　　　　　　　　　　　Bishop Heber.

S compared with the generality of ecclesiastical anniversaries, the Feast of the Holy Trinity was of late introduction; and it was not indeed, till the fourteenth century that its observance was authoritatively decreed by Pope John XXII. (1316—1334) to be binding on the universal Church.* Yet in

---

* Benedict XIV.: *De Festis Domini Nostri Jesu Christi; De Festo Sanctissimæ Trinitatis.*

place after place, and in age after age, the Church had been preparing, by divers local offices and desultory practices, to adopt a commemoration which had slowly developed from the baptismal formula:—"In the name of the Father, and of the Son, and of the Holy Ghost." This formula had very early dictated the terms of a liturgical doxology; and the antiquity of the *Gloria Patri, &c.*, is understated when it is referred—as some have referred it—to the Council of Nicæa. Of the Council of Nicæa, the more probable merit is that of appending the clause, "As it was *in the beginning;*" a clause conceived in opposition to the Arians, who heretically held that the Father had begotten the Son *in time,* and that there had consequently been a time when the Son was not. In its second Canon the Council of Narbonne (A.D. 589) decreed the chanting of the *Gloria Patri* at the close of each Psalm, and after each division of the longer Psalms; and the Canon was so generally honoured by the Church, that Alexander II. in the eleventh century cited its universality as a reason why a special commemoration of the Trinity was not necessary to the perpetuation of the orthodox belief.

It has sometimes been contended that the festival in question had its origin in the sixth century, on the strength of the fact that it then became the practice to sing a certain Preface in honour of the Trinity, the author of which was Pope Pelagius II. (A.D. 578—590). But the argument derived from this circumstance has the flaw of proving too much; in so far that, as we learn from Micrologus, the Preface composed by Pelagius was used on any and every Lord's-day indifferently, and was not confined to a particular Sunday.*

It is affirmed by Durandus that Pope Gregory IV. "instituted a feast not only in honour of the Apostles and

---

* Micrologus: *De Ecclesiasticis Observationibus; De Officio Sanctæ Trinitatis.*

Martyrs, but also of the Holy Trinity, and of Angels, and generally of all Holy Confessors, male and female."* But such a statement seems scarcely compatible with the facts which follow, or even with another assertion of Durandus himself to the effect that in his own time—the latter part of the thirteenth century—the commemoration of the Trinity, though a frequent, was not a universal custom; which would scarcely have been the case if the anniversary had been decreed so long before from the papal chair.† Rupert, Abbat of the monastery of Duitz, in the neighbourhood of Cologne, who died A.D. 1135, writes that it was a settled custom in his time "both in the morning and evening offices, to set forth the name and glory of the same holy and undivided Trinity, in whose name on the Sunday following the advent of the Holy Spirit, the Apostles began to teach."‡ Rupert's testimony is not inconsistent with that of Potho, who in A.D. 1152, was Abbat of Prüm, a monastery of Rhenish Prussia, in the Diocese of Treves, and who speaks of the Festival of the Trinity as one of the *novæ celebritates* of his age. "We wonder," he says "why it has seemed good *at this time*, in some monasteries, to fall off from their excellent rule by the introduction of certain novel celebrations. Can it be that we are more learned or more devout than our fathers? * * * * For what cause, then, has the celebration of these festivals been introduced, viz., that of the Most Blessed Trinity, and that of the Transfiguration of our Lord?"§

When the innovation, the informal establishment of which Potho thus met with rebuke, had been proposed to Pope Alexander II. (1061-74) for his sanction, it had been received by that pontiff with an indifference that was in

* *Rationale Divinorum Officiorum; De Festo Omnium Sanctorum.*
† "In plerisque locis, in octava Pentecostes, fit festum sanctæ Trinitatis." *Rationale; De die Dominica Sanctæ Trinitatis.*
‡ *De Divinis Officiis;* Lib. xi., c. 1.
§ *De Statu Domus Dei, sive Ecclesiæ;* Lib. 3.

fact disfavour. One of his *Decretals*, which is sometimes erroneously attributed to Alexander III. (1159—81), witnesses that "the Festival of the Most Holy Trinity, with varying customs in various places, was by some persons observed on the octave of Pentecost, and by others on the Sunday next before the Advent of our Lord. The Roman Church did not observe it at any special time in this manner, because day by day the *Gloria Patri, &c.* was chanted, and other like things pertaining to the praise of the Trinity."* The attitude of the Pope is thus represented by Micrologus:—" Pope Alexander, of pious memory, in answer to a question about a special anniversary of the Holy Trinity, replied that according to the Roman order there need be no day specially dedicated to the solemnity of the Holy Trinity, nor of the Holy Unity, particularly as on every Lord's day, and even daily, the memory of both was celebrated." † Against which rendering of Alexander's meaning, Benedict XIV. enters his protest:—" This Feast Alexander II. did not disapprove in that *Decretal*, as Micrologus seems to have thought; for the Supreme Pontiff says only that no certain precise day was prescribed by the Roman Church, to which the peculiar worship of the Most Holy Trinity should be attached."

The zeal and piety of many Christians, whether as groups or individuals, had, so early as the eighth and ninth centuries, yearned for the consecration of a fixed and particular day on which to contemplate the mystery of the Holy Trinity. In a letter cited by Benedict XIV. and addressed by Carturflus to Charlemagne, about the year 800, the writer appeals to his sovereign "to appoint, in conjunction with the Synod of the Franks, one day in the year in honour of the Holy Trinity, and of the Unity, and of Angels, and of all Saints." And it is known that

* *Titulus* ix: *De Feriis*.
† *De Ecclesiasticis Observationibus*; c. 60.

Stephen, Bishop of Liege, who died A.D. 920, ordered the composition of an Office of the Most Holy Trinity.

Two or three further particulars about the institution of the Festival of the Trinity are supplied in one of the valuable notes with which Dr. Waterland has illustrated Wheatly's treatise on the Book of Common Prayer. "Durandus sets this festival as high as Gregory IV., A.D. 834. Gervase of Canterbury (who lived about A.D. 1200), informs us that Thomas à Becket, soon after his consecration, A.D. 1162, instituted this festival in England. Quesnel informs us of an *Officium pro festo Sanctissimæ Trinitatis*, extant in a MS. Breviary for the use of the monks of Mount Cassin—the age about 1086. And this is the oldest certain authority I have met with, except Berno Augiensis, who mentions it (*De Rebus ad Missam Spectantibus*). He flourished about A.D. 1030, so that the festival is certainly near seven "—it would now be more correctly written, *eight*—" hundred years old."

After the feast in honour of the Trinity had thus been celebrated in a loose and desultory manner, without uniformity of time, or universality of place, but with a growing determination to both, it was, as we have seen, finally extended to Rome, whence its observance was, in the fourteenth century, ordained upon the Church at large. The day to which it was henceforth fixed in the Western communion was the first Sunday after Pentecost ; a day which in the Greek Church is appropriated to the festival of All Saints, whilst the Monday in Whitsun week is set apart for the commemoration of the doctrine of the Most Holy Trinity.

But at whatever stage of its progress from its earliest parasitic introducton—on the octave of Pentecost, and as dependent on that Feast—to the time of its authoritative promulgation and universal observance, the Festival of the Trinity was never anything less or other than a solemn protest against idolatry or Arianism. "After Arius," says George Wither, in the compendious preface to his poem on Trinity Sunday—" after Arius, and other heretics, had broached their damnable fancies, whereby the faith of many, concerning the mystery of the Blessed Trinity, was shaken, divers good men laboured in the rooting out of those pestilent opinions: and it was agreed upon by the Church, that some particular Sunday in the year should be dedicated to the memory of the Holy Trinity, and called Trinity Sunday, that the name might give the people occasion to enquire after the mystery. And moreover, (that the pastor of each several congregation might be yearly remembered to treat thereof, as necessity required) certain portions of the Holy Scripture, proper to that end, were appointed to be read publicly on that day. In some countries they observed this institution on the Sunday next before the Advent; and in other places the Sunday following Whitsunday, as in the Church of England."*

The *rationale* of the institution of Trinity Sunday may be further stated in the words of Bishop Sparrow:— "There were who objected, that because on each day (and especially Sundays) the Church celebrates the praises of the Trinity, in her Doxologies, Hymns, Creeds, &c., therefore, there was no need of a feast on one day for that which was done on each. But yet the wisdom of the Church thought it meet, that such a Mystery as this, though part of the Meditation of each day, should be the chief subject of one, and this to be the day. For no sooner had our Lord ascended into Heaven, and God's Holy Spirit descended upon the Church; but there ensued the notice of the glorious and incomprehensible Trinity, which before that time was not so clearly known. The Church, therefore, having solemnised in an excellent order all the high Feasts of our Lord, and after, That of the descent of God's Spirit upon the Apostles, thought it a thing most seasonable to conclude these great solemnities with a Festival of full, special, and express Service to the Holy and Blessed

* *Hymns and Songs of the Church.*

Trinity."* Much the same view is taken consentaneously by Durandus and Joachim Hildebrand, both of whom—ascribing the Feast of the Nativity to the Father, as a manifestation of His divine Paternity; the Paschal Feast to the Son, who in that season finished the work of Redemption; and the Feast of Pentecost to the Holy Spirit, who was then fully revealed in His outpouring upon the Apostles —enforce the propriety of the institution of a Festival in honour of the Most Holy and Adorable Trinity.

The late appearance of Trinity Sunday amongst the settled Holydays of the Church is to be readily understood in the light of the unique character of that celebration. It is not, as other feasts, the commemoration of an event—not the memorial of a phase of divine, or angelic, or saintly activity or passion. It is rather the commemoration of a systematised result of many separate and several facts of revelation—of the nexus and relation of several simple propositions, each of which, involving the Infinite and the Self-Existent, involves also the unthinkable and the incomprehensible. In its ontological doctrine, there is nothing necessarily of human interest. Reason is dazzled and transcended; the festival is a festival of faith, of orthodoxy, of a creed.

Thus it is that we account for the late rise of Trinity Sunday above the ecclesiastical horizon; for an orthodox creed is, historically speaking, the consequence of heresy and infidelity. Christianity, in the earliest ages, was not exclusively, or even chiefly, dogmatic; one comprehensive proposition which took the form of a postulate, was necessary to its adoption. Assent was demanded to the fact that Christ was the Son of God; and in this postulate was contained the germ of all orthodox belief. Creeds were not so much chosen by the Church, as forced upon her; and

* *Rationale upon the Book of Common Prayer of the Church of England.*

the former, as various schools of heresy arose, condescended upon details to an extent which a more wholesome state of faith had not found necessary. The history of anti-christian or heretical speculations may be generally traced in the development of the barest symbol of belief into the elaborate formulæ of the creed known as the Athanasian—a creed which Dr. Waterland praises as " the best exposition (for its compass) of the doctrines of the *Trinity* and *Incarnation*, that we shall anywhere meet with."*

The difficulties and apparent antitheses of the doctrine of the Trinity, and the spirit in which they should be approached, are ably and eloquently set forth by Dr. Barrow in a Sermon which he preached on Trinity Sunday, in the year 1663. " That there is one Divine Nature or Essence, common unto Three Persons incomprehensibly united, and ineffably distinguished; united in Essential Attributes, distinguished by peculiar Idioms and Relations; all equally infinite in every divine Perfection, each different from other in order and manner of subsistence; that there is a mutual Inexistence of one in all, and all in one; a Communication without any Deprivation or Diminution in the Communicant; an Eternal Generation, and an Eternal Procession, without Precedence or Succession, without proper Causality or Dependence; a Father imparting His own, and the Son receiving His Father's Life, and a Spirit issuing from both, without any division, or multiplication of Essence : These are Notions which may well puzzle our Reason in conceiving how they agree, but should not stagger our Faith in assenting that they are true; upon which we should meditate, not with hope to comprehend, but with disposition to admire, veiling our Faces in the Presence, and prostrating our Reason at the Feet of Wisdom so far transcending us."†

* *The Case of Arian Subscription Considered.*
† Sermon entitled *A Defence of the Blessed Trinity.*

It is well to let our speculation stay at the limit to which revelation has conducted us. In the region of the Infinite, at least, man can originate nothing; safely to *combine* is a strain upon his utmost powers. And we cannot hold it otherwise than a pious vice of the intellect to seek for illustrations of the Trinity in vegetation or mathematics. The ultimate revelation of God is a Self-revelation; the ultimate knowledge of God is a Self-knowledge. God has no analogue but Himself. We cannot see the Supreme Centre of act and thought reflected into intelligibility in the mirror of a shamrock; when the Sun has done his best as a prism, we cannot effect an analysis of the Divine Nature; nor can we, by the aid of an equilateral triangle, ascertain the mode of a modeless Existence. Yet as all analogies must halt somewhere—for if they did not, they would cease to be analogies, and become identities —we have no wish to exclude these symbols from their place in the education of the popular mind; but to press their value too far, to cast in the earthern frame of Nature the master-keys that profess to fit the wards of Deity, is to do violence even to our own intelligible laws of thought, and to intrude a misapprehension where before was nothing worse than non-comprehension. There are secrets of the Divine nature which are, and must be, for ever unrevealed; because, by the mere force of *quantity*, they are for ever unrevealable. Neither the wrath of God nor the grace of God can ever impart to any intelligence but His own, a comprehensive knowledge of Himself. Millions of æons will not suffice to compress the ocean into anything less than the ocean;* and after an eternity of contempla-

---

* "St. Augustine tells us"—no one knows *where*, but the legend has a grander significance than could result from a mere literal authenticity —"St. Augustine tells us that while busied in writing his Discourse on the Trinity, he wandered along the sea-shore [at Centum Cellæ, now Civita Vecchia] lost in meditation. Suddenly he beheld a child, who, having dug a hole in the sand, appeared to be bringing water from the

tion, there will still remain the exhaustless charm of being lost in the Infinite. In the following poem for "Trinity Sunday," which forms one of George Wither's "Hymns and Songs of the Church," the author judiciously refrains from pressing the Sun into the service of ontological exposition; he is content with citing him as an illustration of the Deity in action.

> Those, oh, thrice holy Three in One,
> Who seek Thy nature to explain,
> By rules to human reason known,
> Shall find their labour all in vain;
> And in a shell they may intend
> The sea, as well, to comprehend.
>
> What, therefore, no man can conceive,
> Let us not curious be to know;
> But when Thou bid'st us to believe,
> Let us obey, let reason go:
> Faith's objects true, and surer be,
> Than those that Reason's eyes do see.
>
> Yet, as by looking on the sun,
> (Though to his substance we are blind),
> And by the course we see him run,
> Some notions we of him may find:
> So, what Thy brightness doth conceal,
> Thy word and works in part reveal.
>
> Most glorious Essence, we confess,
> In Thee, (whom by our faith we view),
> Three Persons, neither more or less,
> Whose workings them distinctly shew:
> And sure we are, those Persons Three
> Make but One God, and Thou art He.

sea to fill it. Augustine enquired what was the object of his task? He replied that he intended to empty into this cavity all the waters of the great deep. 'Impossible!' exclaimed Augustine. 'Not more impossible,' replied the child, than for thee, O Augustine! to explain the mystery on which thou art now meditating!'" Mrs. Jameson's *Sacred and Legendary Art*.

The sun a motion hath, we know,
Which motion doth beget us light;
The heat proceedeth from those two,
And each doth proper acts delight:
The motion draws out time a line,
The heat doth warm, the light doth shine.

Yet, though this motion, light, and heat,
Distinctly by themselves we take,
Each in the other hath his seat,
And but one sun we see they make:
For whatsoe'er the one will do,
He works it with the other two.

So in the Godhead there is knit
A wondrous threefold true-love knot,
And perfect union fastens it,
Though flesh and blood perceive it not;
And what each Person doth alone,
By all the Trinity is done.

Their work they jointly do pursue,
Though they their offices divide;
And each One by Himself hath duo
His proper attributes beside:
But One in substance They are still,
In virtue One, and One in will.

Eternal all the Persons be,
And yet Eternal there's but One;
So likewise Infinite all Three,
Yet Infinite but One alone:
And neither Person aught doth miss,
That of the Godhead's Essence is.

In Unity and Trinity,
Thus, oh, Creator! we adore
Thy ever-praised Deity,
And Thee confess for evermore,
One Father, One begotten Son,
One Holy Ghost, in Godhead One.

It is not, then, to Nature that we look for such an impress of the Divine seal, as of old the mind of man presented in the Golden Age; nor, indeed, as it brokenly reflects it in these times of iron, the results of an alchemy read backwards. God dwells, or finds the nearest approach to analogy, in the moral nature, and in the thought and speech of man; which, if they cannot contain or comprehend the boundless—in other words, be themselves properly divine—are yet greater than all possible or conceivable limitations. The boast of Protagoras is half a truth: Man *is*, negatively, the measure of the universe.*

At such a goal do we arrive in the "Search after God," a poem which occurs in Thomas Heywood's "Hierarchie of the Blessed Angells; their Names, Orders, and Offices" (1635). The nine Books into which the "Hierarchie" is divided treat of (1) Seraphim, (2) Cherubim, (3) The Thrones, (4) The Dominations, (5) The Vertues, (6) The Powers, (7) The Principats, (8) The Archangell, (9) The Angell. Each book is followed by "Theological philosophical, moral, poetical, historical, apothegmatical, hieroglyphical, and emblematical observations to the further illustration of the former (foregoing) Tractate." The "Search after God" is a poetical "meditation" upon the first book, and is called in the metrical argument of the author—

"A Quære made the world throughout,
To find the GOD of whom some doubt."

The "Meditations" generally are thoroughly religious, experimental, and often profound. The author's verse is deficient in harmony; but his directness, earnestness, and solemnity frequently carry him far in the direction of the sublime. Heywood was an actor, and of so great fecundity as a writer of plays, that, for prolific production, his name must be placed soon after that of Lope de Vega on the

* "Man is the measure of all things: of those things which exist as he is, and of those things which do not exist as he is not."—Diogenes Laërtius: *Life of Protagoras*.

roll of dramatic authors. He claims to have had "an entire hand, or at least a main finger," in no fewer than two hundred and twenty plays, of which only twenty-three have survived to our time. Of these, perhaps the best known is "A Woman Killed with Kindness," which was produced in the year 1617. Little is known of the events of Heywood's life. The date of his birth, which occurred about the year 1575, is only approximately ascertained; but it appears that he was a native of the county of Lincoln, and a sometime Fellow of Peterhouse, Cambridge. His last work, which was an "Actor's Vindication," was published in 1658, and there is every reason to believe that he died soon afterwards. So much is due to be said of the dramatic and histrionic author of so learned and pious a treatise as the "Hierarchie," and of so just and graphic a poem as the "Search after God."

> I sought Thee round about, O Thou my God!
>   To find Thy abode.
> I said unto the Earth, "Speak, art thou He?"
>   She answered me,
> "I am not." I enquired of creatures all,
>   In general
> Contained therein: they with one voice proclaim,
> That none amongst them challenged such a name.
>
> I asked the seas, and all the deeps below,
>   My God to know.
> I asked the reptiles, and whatever is
>   In the abyss;
> Even from the shrimp to the Leviathan
>   Enquiry ran:
> But in those deserts which no line can sound,
> The God I sought for was not to be found.
>
> I asked the air, If that were He? but know
>   It told me, No.
> I, from the towering eagle to the wren,
>   Demanded then,

If any feathered fowl 'mongst them were such?
   But they all, much
Offended with my question, in full quire
Answered, "To find my God I must look higher."

I asked the heavens, sun, moon, and stars; but they
   Said, "We obey
The God thou seek'st." I asked what eye or ear
   Could see or hear;
What in the world I might descry or know,
   Above, below:
With an unanimous voice all these things said,
"We are not God, but we by Him were made."

I asked the world's great universal mass,
   If that God was?
Which with a mighty and strong voice replied,
   (As stupified),
"I am not He, O man! for know that I
   By Him on high
Was fashioned first of nothing, thus instated
And swayed by Him, by whom I was created."

I did enquire for Him in flourishing peace,
   But soon 'gan cease:
For when I saw what vices, what impurity,
   Bred by security,
(As pride, self-love, lust, surfeit, and excess),
   I could no less
Than stay my search; knowing where these abound
God may be sought, but is not to be found.

I thought then I might find Him out in war;
   But was as far
As at the first; for in revenge and rage,
   In spoil and strage,
Where unjust quarrels are commenced, and might
   Takes place 'bove right;
Where zeal and conscience yield way to sedition,
There can be made of God no inquisition.

I sought the court; but smooth-tongued Flattery there
        Deceived each ear:
In the thronged city there was selling, buying,
        Swearing, and lying;
In the country, craft in simpleness arrayed:
        And then I said,
"Vain is my search, although my pains be great;
Where my God is there can be no deceit."

All these demands are the true consideration,
        Answer and attestation
Of creatures touching God; all which, accited,
        With voice united,
Either in air or sea, the earth or sky,
        Make this reply:
"To rob Him of His worship none persuade us,
Since it was He, and not our own hands made us."

A scrutiny within myself I then
        Even thus began:
"O man, what art thou?"—What more (could I say)
        Than dust and clay?
Frail, mortal, fading, a mere puff, a blast
        That cannot last;
In a throne to-day, to-morrow in the urn;
Formed from that earth to which I must return.

I asked myself what this great God might be
        That fashioned me?
I answered, The All-Potent, solely immense,
        Surpassing sense;
Unspeakable, Inscrutable, Eternal,
        Lord over all;
The only Terrible, Strong, Just, and True,
Who hath no end, and no beginning know.

He is the Well of Life, for He doth give
        To all that live
Both breath and being: He is the Creator
        Both of the water,

Earth, air, and fire: of all things that subsist,
    He hath the list;
Of all the heavenly host, or what earth claims,
He keeps the scroll, and calls them by their names.

And now, my God, by Thy illumining grace,
    Thy glorious face
(So far forth as it may discovered be)
    Methinks I see;
And though Invisible and Infinite
    To human sight—
Thou, in Thy mercy, justice, truth, appearest,
In which to our frail senses Thou com'st nearest.

O make us apt to seek, and quick to find,
    Thou God, most kind!
Give us love, hope, and faith in Thee to trust,
    Thou God, most just!
Remit all our offences, we entreat,
    Most good, most great!
Grant that our willing though unworthy quest
May, through Thy grace, admit us 'mongst the blest.

The theme of the Trinity is one which surpasses the whole power of song, whether of mortal or immortal natures. If the subject be considered in itself, it excludes the ideas of circumstance and accident; of analysis; and, strictly speaking, of illustration; and the true attitude of the soul seems to be one of voiceless worship. After essaying the futility of language and the slightness of the muse, Sir John Beaumont, the author of the "Ode of the Blessed Trinity" which we are about to present to the reader, would leave the sublime mystery to "humble silence" and "still devotion." Sir John was the elder brother of Francis Beaumont, the famous dramatic poet, and was born in the year 1582, at Belton, in Leicestershire. He was created a baronet by Charles I., in 1626, the second year of that monarch's reign; and died in 1628, so escaping the dark days that were in store for Church and

State. "The former part of his life," says Antony à Wood, "he successfully employed in poetry, and the latter he as happily bestowed on more serious and beneficial studies; and had not death untimely cut him off in his middle age, he might have proved a patriot, being accounted at the time of his death a person of great knowledge, gravity, and worth."*

    Muse, thou art dull and weak,
    Oppressed with worldly pain:
    If strength in thee remain
    Of things divine to speak,
Thy thoughts awhile from urgent cares restrain,
And with a cheerful voice thy wonted silence break.

    No cold shall thee benumb,
    Nor darkness taint thy sight;
    To thee new heat, new light,
    Shall from this object come,
Whose praises if thou now wilt sound aright,
My pen shall give thee leave hereafter to be dumb.

    Whence shall we then begin
    To sing or write of this,
    Where no beginning is?
    Or, if we enter in,
Where shall we end? The end is endless bliss—
Thrice happy we, if well so rich a thread we spin!

    For Thee our strings we touch,
    Thou that art Three and One,
    Whose essence, though unknown,
    Believed is to be such;
To whom whate'er we give, we give Thine own,
And yet no mortal tongue can give to Thee so much.

    See how in vain we try
    To find some type to agree
    With this great One in Three,
    Yet none can such descry:
If any like, or second, were to Thee,
Thy hidden nature then were not so deep and high.

  * *Athenæ Oxonienses.*

  Here fail inferior things—
  The sun, whose heat and light
  Make creatures warm and bright,
  A feeble shadow brings:
The Son shows to the world His Father's might,
With glorious rays fro' forth, our fire, the Spirit, sings.

  Now to the topless hill
  Let us ascend more near,
  Yet still within the sphere
  Of our connatural skill;
We may behold how in our souls we bear
An understanding power joined with effectual skill.

  We cannot higher go
  To search this point divine;
  Here it doth chiefly shine
  This image must it show:
These steps, as helps, our humble minds incline
To embrace these certain grounds which from true faith must flow.

  To Him these notes direct,
  Who not with outward hands,
  Nor by His strong commands,
  Whence creatures take effect;
While perfectly Himself He understands,
Begets another Self with equal glory deckt.

  From these, the Spring of Love,
  The Holy Ghost proceeds,
  Who our affection feeds
  With those clear flames which move
From that eternal Essence which them breeds,
And strikes into our souls as lightning from above.

  Stay, stay, Parnassian girl,
  Here thy descriptions faint;
  Thou human shapes canst paint
  And canst compare to pearl
White teeth, and speak of lips which rubies taint,
Resembling beauteous eyes to orbs that swiftly whirl.

  But now thou may'st perceive
  The weakness of thy wings;

And that thy noblest strings
To muddy objects cleave:
Then praise with humble silence heavenly things,
And what is more than this, to still devotion leave.

Contemplating the Trinity in Its Essence, and apart from Its relations to anything else, and forgetting even its own being, its own joys or sorrows in such contemplation, the soul, if it will break silence, can do so only in the language of praise and adoration. Its most fitting utterance is a rhapsody, a series of ecstatic ejaculations which do not presume to systematic coherence, and which have for their aim the expression of thanks to God for the existence and the fact of His "great glory," rather than for any manifestation, however gracious, of the same. Of this order of poetry, the following "Prayer to the Three Persons of the ever-blessed Trinity" may be taken as nearly representative. Its author was Hildebert, Archbishop of Tours, whose life extended from about the year 1057 to 1134; and in Bässler's *Auswahl Altchristlicher Lieder*, it is characterized as *Oratio Devotissima*. The subjoined English version is from the vivid pen of Dr. Kynaston, and is to be found in his "Occasional Hymns":—

To The FATHER.

A et Ω magne Deus.

First and Last of faith's receiving,
Source and sea of man's believing,
God, Whose might is all-potential,
God, Whose Truth is Truth's essential,
God supreme in Thy subsisting,
God in all Thy seen existing!
Over all things, all things under,
Touching all, from all asunder;
Centre, but Thyself excluded,
Compassing, and yet included;
Over all, and not ascending,
Under all, but not depending;

Over all, the world ordaining,
Under all, the world sustaining;
All without, in all surrounding,
All within, in grace abounding;
Inmost, yet not comprehended;
Outer still, and not extended;
Over, yet on nothing founded,
Under, but by space unbounded;
Omnipresent, yet indwelling,
Self-impelled, the world impelling;
Force, nor Fate's predestination
Sways Thee to one alteration;
Ours to-day, Thyself for ever,
Still commencing, ending never;
Past with Thee is Time's beginning,
Present all its future winning;
With Thy counsel's first ordaining
Comes Thy counsel's last attaining;
One the light's first radiance darting
And the elements' departing.

To The SON.

Nate, Patri coæqualis.

Next in Revelation's sequel,
Co-eternal Son, co-equal,
Father's Light, and Father's feature,
All-creating, yet a creature,
With our flesh Thyself enduing,
All our righteousness ensuing;
With immortal glory shining,
Yet to death and time declining;
Man and God united ever,
God in Man confounded never.
Not Thyself to flesh converting,
All the Godhead still asserting;
All the God to manhood taking,
Yet the manhood not forsaking;
One with God by conformation,
Less than God by Incarnation;
Man in substance of Thy Mother,

TRINITY SUNDAY.

Yet than God Thyself no other.
Thus two Natures' wondrous union
Stands in unimpaired communion;
What He was ere worlds were dated,
That He was on earth created;
He our only Mediator,
None but He our Legislator;
Born for us, and circumcised,
Dead, and buried, and baptized;
Fell on sleep, to hell descending,
Rose again to life unending;
Thence to Judgment comes to call men
Who Himself was judged for all men.

To The HOLY GHOST.
Paracletus increatus.

God, of Glory unabated,
Not begotten, nor created,
Spirit, Son or Father neither,
Yet proceedest Thou from either,
From no heavenly source exterior,
With no quality inferior,
From Eternity no lower,
Substance, Majesty, or Power.

Father One in Gospel-story,
One the First-begotten's Glory,
One the Holy Ghost's Procession,—
Three, but One to Faith's confession
Each Himself is God alonely,
Yet not Three, but One God only.
In this Oneness, worshipped truly,
Three in One I worship duly;
In their Persons ever Three,
In their Substance Unity;
None of Whom is less than other,
None is greater than another:
In each One no variation,
Into each no transmutation;
Each is God, and yet no blending,
Everlasting without ending.
      Amen.

The foregoing lines are conceived in the spirit of Synesius, a famous and rather mystical Greek hymnographer, who died A.D. 430, and who crowded his hymns with epithet, if not with epigram. Somewhat of the manner of the same writer may be discovered in the first part of the following hymn on "The Most Holy Trinity;" whilst further on its author, Canon Oakeley, proceeds, in addition to praising the essential glory of the Deity in repose, to praise It as manifested in the joint or several activities of Its Persons.

God! of life, and light, and motion,
Cause and Centre, Fount and Home;
Limitless and tideless Ocean;
Past and present and to come;

Unbeginning as Unending,
Uncontrolled by time or space;
Undefined, yet Unextending;
Boundless, yet in every place.

Self-existent; Uncreated,
Underived, evolved of none;
In sublimest peace instated,
Perfect in Thyself alone;

With unclouded vision seeing,
Spread o'er one eternal page,
All the mysteries of Being,
Traversing the course of age;

Every art of man detecting;
Sketched in form or shaped in fact;
All his cherished plans inspecting,
Locked in heart or bared in act;

Loving all and all befriending
With a love as deep as wide;
And to meanest creatures bending
Low, as if were none beside.

God the Father whose relation
With the sole-begotten Son,
By a mystic generation,
Stood ere Time had learned to run;

God the Son! by the supernal
Ever with the Father bound;
In the glorious folds eternal
Of one single Nature wound;

God the Spirit! Stream Vivific
Ceaselessly by Both outpoured,
And in Union Beatific
Equally with Both adored:

God the Father, Son, and Spirit!
Three in One, and One in Three,
Thine united glories merit
Thanks and praise continually;

Praise to Thee and adoration
On Thy Festival be done,
For the blessed Incarnation
Of the co-eternal Son.

For the coming of the Spirit,
For the grace of saintly life!
For the joys that saints inherit
When they cease from earthly strife.

More than all the praise unending
Paid throughout the Church to Thee,
For the Majesty transcending
Of thy Triune Deity!

Sun of splendour, never waning,
Fount of sweetness, never dry,
Staff of comfort, all sustaining,
Ever Blessed Trinity.

It is almost impossible to find a hymn which does not suggest, or contain, even if at the same time it appears to conceal, a prayer. It is not only that it is the Infinite, and the infinitely happy, holy, and perfect Being, who is adored; but the beings who offer their adoration are either, as men, poor and blind, sinful and miserable, or, at best, as angels, are chargeable "with folly," the dwellers in a heaven which is unclean. When, therefore, the Divine nature is thought of by men afflicted with the burden of their own, it is intelligible that even the purest adoration of the Trinity should attract and assume a colour from the sorrows and the sins of earth. The men who have celebrated in hymns the glorious attributes of the Deity, have, through the instant and simultaneous conviction of their own weakness and guilt, degraded, almost of necessity, to the less glorious occupation of prayer. Every ascription of praise has contained, at least implicitly, a supplication. It is thus that we read the incidental, but regretful allusion to the sin-caused disabilities of mankind, in that sublime hymn of Bishop Heber's which stands at the head of this paper.

But there are other and more cheerful circumstances to which Heber gives prominence; and which are brought out in the verses almost immediately to follow, from the pen of Charles Wesley. Man is not the only worshipper in the synagogue of earth, or in the temple of the universe. Once he was the priest as well as the lord of the world; and once again, as a king and priest unto God, he becomes the mouth-piece of nature in the world-wide liturgy. Not man alone, but all the works of the Lord, praise the Lord, in all worlds, and under all regimes and dispensations. From the darkest speck of matter, or from the heaviest clod, up to the most huge and resplendent of suns or the most ethereal and brilliant of intelligences—all confess, articulately or not, the Thrice Holy:—

>   Holy, holy, holy, Lord,
>   God the Father, God the Word,
>   God the Comforter, receive
>   Blessings more than we can give:
>   Mixed with those beyond the sky,
>   Chanters to the Lord Most High,
>   We our hearts and voices raise,
>   Echoing Thy eternal praise.
>
>   One, inexplicably Three,
>   One, in simplest Unity,
>   God, incline Thy gracious ear,
>   Us, Thy lisping creatures, hear:

Thee while man, the earth-born, sings,
Angels shrink within their wings;
Prostrate Seraphim above
Breathe unutterable love.

Happy they who never rest,
With Thy heavenly presence blest!
They the heights of Glory see,
Sound the depths of Deity!
Fain with them our souls would vie;
Sink as low, and mount as high;
Fall o'erwhelmed with love, or soar;
Shout, or silently adore!

"It is very meet, right, and our bounden duty, that we should at all times, and in all places, give thanks unto Thee, O Lord, Almighty, Everlasting God; Who art one God, one Lord; not one only Person, but Three Persons in one Substance. For that which we believe of the glory of the Father, the same we believe of the Son, and of the Holy Ghost, without any difference or inequality. Therefore, with Angels and Archangels, and with all the company of heaven, we laud and magnify Thy glorious Name; evermore praising Thee, and saying, Holy, Holy, Holy, Lord God of hosts, heaven and earth are full of Thy glory: Glory be to Thee, O Lord Most High."

St. Andrew's Day.

November 30.

THE earlier religious life of this Apostle affords a proof of the perfect adaptation of the preaching of John the Baptist to the task of training his disciples to the recognition of Jesus as "The Lamb of God."

St. Andrew was a native of Bethsaida, a city of Galilee, and was the son of Jonas, and the brother of Simon Peter, though whether he was older or younger than that apostle has never been fully ascertained. The probabilities, however, may be said, on the whole, to favour the supposition that he was junior to St. Peter. He is commonly spoken of by the Fathers and ancient writers as "the first-called Disciple," though he can have no exclusive right to such a title, to the prejudice of that unnamed disciple—believed to be St. John—by whom he was accompanied when the Baptist drew their joint attention to the passing Saviour. A distinction which may be more readily substantiated for St. Andrew is that he was the first of all the Apostles to commence the work of evangelization :—" He first findeth his own brother Simon, and saith unto him, we have found the Messias, which is, being interpreted, the Christ" (John i., 41). The vocation of Andrew and Peter to the Apostolate, however, did not take place till about a year after their first introduction to Jesus Christ; and during that interval it would seem that they occupied themselves in their ordinary pursuits, seeing that it was from the actual employments of the net and the boat that they were finally called upon to become "fishers of men."

Modified by such considerations, we may read the words of Wheatly, to the effect that, as St. Andrew "was the first that found the Messiah (John i., 38), and the first that brought others to Him (John i., 42), so the Church, for his greater honour, commemorates him first in her anniversary course of holy-days, and places his festival at the beginning of Advent as the most proper to bring the news of our Saviour's coming."*

One of the distinctive lessons of St. Andrew's career attaches to this period of his life, and is of course to be read as encouraging generally the spirit which is concerned for the widest diffusion of the Gospel throughout the world; and, more particularly, the spirit which prompts individuals, without having received from God and the Church the commission to minister in the ranks of ordained men, to regard themselves as centres of a domestic and *neighbourly* propaganda, and so to order their life and conversation as to "adorn the doctrine of God our Saviour" in deeds aptly done and words fitly spoken.

In a poem for St. Andrew's Day, which occurs in Dr. Monsell's "Spiritual Songs," where it is entitled "Domestic Care," the author gives prominence to the circumstance of the special fitness of this festival for considerations of family interest. The verses, it will easily be recognized, are founded upon the narrative of the Evangelist St. John i., 40-42.

* *Rational Illustration of the Book of Common Prayer.*

"DOMESTIC CARE."

What day in all the year than this
More meet to bring domestic bliss
   In praise before the Lord?
Or if we have domestic care,
To lay it before God in prayer,
   And search His answering Word.

We think of one this blessed day
Who followed Christ without delay,
   And, full of holy fear,
First his own brother Simon sought,
And him to Jesus meekly brought,
   In brotherhood more dear.

The youthful convert, fain to prove
The blessings of his new-found love,
   First seeks his own abode;
And the dear brother of his heart
Persuades to choose the better part,
   And give himself to God.

No triumphs of maturer years,
Won for the cross in toil and tears,
   Will ever seem so fair,
As that one gain—a brother found!
And doubly, as a brother, bound
   This new-born bliss to share.

Are there for us some brethren dear,
Near to our hearts, but not so near
   To God as they should be?
For whom we know no peace or rest
Until they choose the thing that's best,
   And Christ's salvation see?

Or are there those, whom we have borne
Upon our hearts, till their return
   To Him, from Whom they strayed,
Has been to prayer the best reply,
The Saviour's tenderest sympathy
   In mercy could have made?

> Then let us come, and one and all
> Use this glad Christian festival
>   For special prayer and praise ;
> Prayer for the lost to be restored,
> Praise for the loved ones whom the Lord
>   Hath brought back to His ways.
>
> And as the rolling year brings round
> The memory of some lost one found,
>   Some loved one gone astray ;
> Let each domestic grief, or joy,
> Our heart's best Faith and Love employ
>   On each St. Andrew's Day.

As compared with the generality of festivals observed in honour of Saints, the dedication of a day to the memory of St. Andrew is of more than average antiquity; and its institution may be pretty exactly referred to A.D. 358, in which year his remains, together with those of St. Luke, were, by order of the Emperor Constantius, transferred to Constantinople, and there deposited in the great church which had been erected to the honour of the twelve Apostles.* Over and above the reason which Wheatly has given for the commemoration of St. Andrew at the head of Advent, it has been held that he owes his present position in the Calendar to the fact that the translation of his relics to Constantinople was completed on the 30th of November, which is also alternatively regarded as the anniversary of his *Nativity* or martyrdom.

On the division of the world among the Apostles, it fell by lot to St. Andrew to undertake Scythia and the neighbouring countries as his province.† He then first travelled through Cappadocia, Galatia, and Bithynia, the inhabitants of which he instructed in the faith of Christ, passing all along the Euxine Sea, and so into the solitudes of Scythia,

---

* St. Jerome: *De Viris Illustribus.* Baronius: *Annales Ecclesiastici,* A.D. 358.

† Eusebius: *Ecclesiastical History;* Lib. iii., c. 1.

where his fervent zeal and his invincible courage triumphed over difficulties the most disheartening, and hazards the most perilous.

In the course of his travels he preached the Gospel at Sebastopol, Cherson, and Sinope. Thence going to Byzantium, he instructed the people in the knowledge of the Christian religion, founded a church for Divine worship, and ordained Stachys, the "beloved Stachys" of St. Paul (Rom. xvi., 9), first bishop of that place. Being banished from Byzantium, St. Andrew removed to Argyropolis, whence, after sojourning there for two years, he set out upon his travels through Thrace, Macedonia, and Thessaly, and arrived finally at Patræ, a city of Achaia, where he was so wonderfully successful that Ægeas, the Proconsul, condemned him to be first scourged and then crucified. This sentence, cruel enough in itself, was rendered still more atrocious by the peculiar aggravation of its circumstances. Seven lictors by turns exhausted their strength on the naked body of the Apostle; after which the Proconsul, enraged at the invincible patience and constancy of St. Andrew, gave orders for the carrying out of the second part of the sentence. In order that the death of this most brave and inflexible martyr might be as lingering and painful as possible, he was not nailed, but fastened with cords to the cross, which was of the kind called *decussate*, in the form of the letter X, and popularly known by the name of St. Andrew.

When he was being conducted to execution, and had come within sight of the cross on which he was to suffer, he apostrophized it as follows:—"Hail, precious Cross, that hast been consecrated by the Body of my Lord, and adorned with His limbs as with rich jewels. I come to thee exulting and glad; receive me with joy into Thine arms. O good Cross, that hast received beauty from our Lord's limbs, I have ardently loved thee. Long have I desired and sought thee; now thou art found by me, and art made ready for my longing soul. Receive me into thine arms, taking me from among men, and present me to my Master; that He who redeemed me on thee, may receive me by thee."

The Venerable Bede has left a pharaphrase of the address of "St. Andrew to his Cross," which has been translated as follows by the Rev. Dr. Kynaston:—

> "Cross, whereon my Saviour bled,
> Dying to redeem our loss,
> Now with living trophies spread,
> Welcome, welcome, happy Cross!
>
> "Sickening once with hope delayed,
> Paling all our hearts with gloom,
> Then a Tree of Life displayed,
> Budding with eternal bloom.*
>
> "Cross, thy loving arms' embrace
> Clasps my Saviour to my soul,
> Heaven to bring us face to face,
> Rending wide from pole to pole.
>
> "Where to buy me Jesus died,
> How shall I, poor serf, recline,
> To Thy gaging standard tied
> Measure all His love with mine?"
>
> Thus, his cross beholding nigh,
> With its horns athwart the sky,
> Andrew spake,—then doff'd his vest
> Ere they lift him to his rest.

St. Andrew lingered on the cross for two days, during which he failed not in prayers and exhortations for the spread and establishment of the faith for which he so magnanimously suffered; and when, in the meanwhile, great importunities were used with the Proconsul for the sparing of the Apostle's life, he, on his part, earnestly entreated our Lord that he might then depart, and seal his confes-

---

* Prov. xiii. 12; Num. xvii. 10.

sion of the Faith with his blood. In this prayer he was graciously heard; and the much-enduring martyr at length entered into rest. Neither the day nor the year of the passion of St. Andrew has been precisely ascertained; but respectable authorities have decided in favour of November 30th, A.D. 69.

The body of St. Andrew, having been taken down from the cross, was embalmed and honourably interred by Maximilla, the wife of the Proconsul; and it lay in the tomb which her piety had prepared, until, as has just been said, it was transferred to Constantinople, and deposited in the Church of the Apostles, in the year 358.

We have already poetically illustrated that spirit of zeal and fraternal affection which led St. Andrew to spread the tidings of the Saviour as soon as He was discovered, and to make his brother Simon the first object of his solicitude. It remains to pay the tribute of a verse to that amazing and stupendous fortitude which bore the Apostle through an agony of two days' duration, every moment of which must have been a crisis of suffering.

We connect with this last scene of St. Andrew's life a poem which has no nominal or titular relation to the Apostle; but at least it offers a magnificent exposition of that faith and constancy of which he was so illustrious an example—of faith and constancy in circumstances trying beyond conception to the solitary human soul—the shivering of the elements, "the wreck of matter, and the crush of worlds." The poem we allude to is Campbell's "Last Man," in which, it may be said without prejudice to the stirring patriotism of his favourite lyrics, the author seems to have uttered all the concentrated grandeur of his intellect and imagination.

> All worldly shapes shall melt in gloom—
> The Sun himself must die,
> Before this mortal shall assume
> Its immortality!

ST. ANDREW'S DAY.

I saw a vision in my sleep,
That gave my spirit strength to sweep
   Adown the gulf of time!
I saw the last of human mould,
That shall creation's death behold,
   As Adam saw her prime.

The Sun's eye had a sickly glare,
   The earth with age was wan;
The skeletons of nations were
   Around that lonely man!
Some had expired in fight— the brands
Still rested in their bony hands—
   In plague and famine some:
Earth's cities had no sound or tread,
And ships were drifting with the dead
   To shores where all was dumb!

Yet prophet-like that lone one stood,
   With dauntless words and high,
That shook the sere leaves from the wood,
   As if a storm passed by;
Saying, "We are twins in death, proud Sun;
Thy face is cold, thy race is run,
   'Tis mercy bids thee go:
For thou ten thousand thousand years
Hast seen the tide of human tears,
   That shall no longer flow.

What though beneath thee man put forth
   His pomp, his pride, his skill;
And arts that made fire, flood, and earth
   The vassals of his will?
Yet mourn I not thy parted sway,
Thou dim, discrownèd king of day;
   For all those trophied arts,
And triumphs that beneath thee sprang
Healed not a passion or a pang
   Entailed on human hearts.

Go, let oblivion's curtain fall
   Upon the stage of men,
Nor with thy rising beams recall
   Life's tragedy again:

Its piteous pageants bring not back,
Nor waken flesh upon the rack
   Of pain anew to writhe;
Stretched in diseases' shapes abhorred,
Or mown in battle by the sword,
   Like grass beneath the scythe.

Even I am weary in yon skies
   To watch thy fading fire:
Test of all sumless agonies,
   Behold not me expire:
My lips that speak thy dirge of death,
Their rounded gasp and gurgling breath,
   To see thou shalt not boast.
The eclipse of nature spreads my pall—
The majesty of darkness shall
   Receive my parting ghost!

This spirit shall return to Him
   That gave its heavenly spark;
Yet think not, Sun, it shall be dim,
   When thou thyself art dark!
No! it shall live again and shine
In bliss unknown to beams of thine,
   By Him recalled to breath,
Who captive led captivity,
Who robbed the grave of victory,
   And took the sting from death!

Go, Sun, while mercy holds me up
   On Nature's awful waste,
To drink this last and bitter cup
   Of grief that man shall taste—
Go, tell the night that hides thy face,
Thou sawest the last of Adam's race,
   On earth's sepulchral clod,
The darkening universe defy
To quench his immortality,
   Or shake his trust in God!

St. Thomas the Apostle.

DECEMBER 21.

We saw Thee not, when Thou didst tread,
   O Saviour, this our sinful earth ;
Nor heard Thy voice restore the dead,
   And wake them to a second birth ;
But *we believe* that Thou didst come,
And quit for us Thy glorious home.

We were not with the faithful few,
   Who stood Thy bitter cross around,—
Nor heard Thy prayer for those who slew,
   Nor felt that earthquake rock the ground ;—
We saw no spear-wound pierce Thy side ;—
Yet *we believe* that Thou hast died.

No angel's message met our ear
   On that first glorious Easter-day,—
' The Lord is risen, He is not here;
   Come see the place where Jesus lay ! "
But *we believe* that Thou didst quell
The banded powers of Death and Hell.

We saw Thee not return on high,—
   And now, our longing sight to bless,
No ray of glory from the sky
   Shines down upon our wilderness ;
Yet *we believe* that Thou art there,
And seek Thee, Lord, in praise and prayer.

                                  Rugby Hymn Book.

S T. THOMAS, whose name, whether in its original form, or in that of its Greek equivalent, Didymus, signifies "a Twin," was probably a native of Galilee, and a fisherman; "for when St. Peter, after our Saviour's resurrection, thought fit to return to his former profession of fishing, to relieve his present necessities, Thomas bore him company."*

It is open to remark that the Disciples, from different circumstances and from different causes, varied in their courage and devotion. Nearly every one of them in his turn shone forth with a greater brilliancy than the average run of his brethren; and nearly every one of them in his turn was dimmed by a passing cloud which did not eclipse the light of the others. On only one critical occasion did the same fault exhibit itself, for a short time, as a universal epidemic, when it is written of them that "all the disciples forsook Him and fled" (Matt. xxvi., 56). This is, perhaps, the only instance in which cowardice or self-seeking prudence on the part of the immediate Disciples of Christ, attained the proportions of absolute unanimity; whilst in other cases, there was always a larger or smaller number whose opinion could be brought to bear in the interests of right and justice upon the temporary representatives of excessive calculation, carnal ambition, or unenlighted and exclusive zeal.

It was at a moment when the Disciples were giving expression to an unbecoming anxiety for their Master's safety and their own, that Thomas stepped to the front with a grandeur of courage which ought to be at least as immortal as his reprobated scepticism—a scepticism which, reprobated as it may be, is yet one of the treasures of the Christian evidences.

The Evangelist St. John records that Jesus had been threatened with stoning by the Jews assembled at Jerusalem at the feast of the Dedication; from whose fury

* Nelson's *Festivals and Fasts*.

he escaped beyond Jordan, to the site of the earliest ministry of John the Baptist. Here it was that a message reached Him from Bethany, to the effect that Lazarus, his friend, and the brother of two other friends, was sick; and He proposed to go to visit him. The Disciples, with a lively memory of their recent danger at Jerusalem, from which Bethany was not quite two miles distant, dissuaded Him from taking a step which they represented as fraught with peril. Then the magnanimity and unselfishness of Thomas broke forth in words that showed no limit in the way of love and devotion: "Let us also go, that we may die with Him" (John xi., 16). How splendid an aspiration!—splendid, according to its light; splendid in any case, if not fully informed!* It has been the dearest aspiration of hundreds of years of Christian chivalry; and yet, astounding as it may seem, this privilege of dying with Christ—in His fellowship, in His immediate neighbourhood, and simultaneously with Him—was conferred only on a felon, whose conscience, springing to life in all but the article of death, confessed the righteousness of the doom that gave him to the cross. Yet in deep truth, the death which St. Thomas afterwards did really die, was a demonstration of a grander order of devotion than even this one of dying with the Saviour. To die as Thomas had expressed his readiness to die, would have been to die cheered with the society of men who for the same purpose ran the same risks and shared the same hopes,—whatever in their then stage of

* Thomas has been undeservedly unfortunate in his reputation; in modern times he has generally been regarded as a model of infidelity, whilst some of the ancients regarded his name as a byword of cowardice. "The Disciples all feared the attack of the Jews," says St. Chrysostom, "and Thomas most of all: on which account he said, 'Let us go, that we may die with Him.' Some, indeed, say that he was ready to die; but this is a misconception: for he spake rather out of fear, as if he wished to alarm the others with a certain fatality."— *Homily* lxii.; *On the Gospel of St. John.*

Christian development these hopes may have been; would have been to die ennobled by the conviction that each was at least attesting his devotion to a Friend and Teacher. But to St. Thomas, the reality of death, as we shall have occasion to see in the course of a paragraph or two, wore a much more cold, grim, and lonely aspect; without tangible supports, and without society; in the midst of a strange civilization and a strange heathenism; more remote than any previous Christian martyr from the centres of the Christian life and the Christian faith.

The poem "On St. Thomas" which occurs in Bishop Ken's "Hymns for the Festivals" is of sixteen stanzas, and is devoted to a kind of narrative illustration of the salient points in the Apostle's career. From the commencement of this poem we take so much as has reference to the courageous readiness of St. Thomas to sacrifice his life with and for his Master.

> When Jesus notice gave
> Of Lazarus sleeping in his grave;
> And that, to wake his friend,
> His course should towards Judæa tend;
> His votaries to dissuade Him strait combined
> Since there the Jews His stoning had designed.
>
> Blest Thomas, who well knew
> The rage of the malicious Jew,
> Who in like fate resolved
> His votaries all should be involved;
> To run the danger with his Lord was bent,
> Rather than hinder His benign intent.
>
> This was his brave reply :—
> " O let us go, and with Him die;
> Him we for Master chose
> And of our lives let Him dispose;
> The radiant gates of Heaven are open set,
> Thrice happy those who early entrance get!"

> Blest Saint, by Jesus taught,
> Of things below to value nought;
> With Love, which casts out fear,
> To your Redeemer to adhere;
> May I, like you, the world and life despise,
> And live to God perpetual sacrifice!

The other occasion on which St. Thomas occupies a prominent position in the narrative of the Evangelist is that whereon he is seen hesitating to believe the Resurrection of Jesus Christ on any evidence short of his own senses. This has frequently been spoken of as "a grievous fall;" and the sceptical Apostle has been pilloried as an object of pious horror by faultless Christians who complacently feel assured that they would have exhibited a more ready acquiescence in the testimony of the rest of the Disciples. But, indeed, of no one of the Disciples can it be confidently affirmed that he would have acted in any other manner than did Thomas, if he had been the one, out of the whole number, from whom ocular demonstration of the resurrection of Christ had been withheld. Was St. Thomas really more incredulous than the rest of the Apostles? If we would do him justice, we must confess that we are in no position to answer the question. St. Thomas, in the very depths of his scepticism, asked for no more sensible proof of his Master's resurrection than his fellow-disciples had already enjoyed. The blessing pronounced by Christ upon those "who have not seen, and yet have believed," was not applicable to any one of the Apostles; for all, except Thomas, had already been forced into a belief upon evidence which was too palpable to allow of what in strictness could be called faith. Perhaps for them the only possible exercise of faith was in trusting in the reality of Christ's death; and the fault of Thomas—which, if we could read the hearts of the others, may not have been his fault alone—lay in not yielding his assent to Christ's resurrection on higher grounds than mere external evidence, whether of others, or of his own senses. He ought to have had the witness within himself; he ought to have trusted that the predictions of Christ would be fulfilled, and that His rising again was, in the spiritual fitness of things, at once a certainty and a necessity.

The value of the temporary doubt of Thomas was the probable evidence it affords of the independent way in which conviction was attained by each mind concerned in authenticating the Resurrection of our Lord. The cunning devisers of a fable would hardly have ventured to invalidate it so much as to allow that it was, or ever had been, possible for one person out of eleven to hesitate about receiving its most significant particular. *Now* we know that evidence was duly weighed before being pronounced decisive. Some such view of the question, and one which should again become prominent in human thought, was very intelligibly prevalent in the earlier times of Christianity. Thus St. Augustine says that the doubt of St. Thomas "was not the expression of one denying, but of one enquiring; whose enquiry became the instruction of the Church. . . . O happy ignorance, which taught the ignorant, which convinced the unbelieving! O blessed unbelief which has for so many ages fought for the faith!"* And Gregory the Great, speaking of the same subject, varies rather the words than the sentiment:—"The infidelity of Thomas profits more to our faith than the faith of the believing disciples; because whilst he is brought back to faith by touching, our minds, casting aside all doubt, are confirmed and established in the faith."†

It is not forbidden to regard the singular condescension of Christ on the occasion of St. Thomas's unbelief as a tribute to the singular devotion which the Apostle had formerly manifested upon the occasion we have already referred to, of the journey to Bethany in the face of a

* *Sermones de Tempore: De Pascha.*
† *XL Homilia in Evangelia: Hom.* xxvi. *: John* xx., 19—31.

very probable death. And it may be said, in addition, that if Christ went more out of His way—so to speak—to convince St. Thomas, the latter in his turn went further out of *his* way in his subsequent preaching of Christ than any other of the Apostles. We are not anxious, except upon compulsion, to say anything in depreciation of the sometimes maligned character of a chivalrous and not unreasonable Disciple. We may sum up the two instances of St. Thomas's prominence in the New Testament by praising that fine courage which, whilst he thought of Christ as Friend and Instructor only, made him willing to die; and that pious submission to evidence and conviction, which, Divinity once being proved, made him the foremost to adore.

However cold and repellent as an end, Scepticism is a valuable instrument in the investigation of truth. Without it faith would be divorced from reason; and would as a consequence degenerate into credulity and superstition. The ideal Reason, whilst it knows itself too well to quarrel with the mysterious and the incomprehensible—whilst it knows, in fact, that there are many things which it *ought* not to understand, even while it accepts them—must still give forth a clear protest against the attempt of an uninstructed piety to assimilate absurdities.

Abraham Cowley is the name of a poet (1618—1667) whose popularity, once so wide spread and remarkable, is now barely sustained by the respectability of his character as a Christian. Hazlitt said of him that he was " a writer of great sense, ingenuity, and learning; but as a poet his fancy is quaint, far-fetched, and mechanical. Most of his pieces—his *Anacreontics* excepted—should be read for instruction, not for pleasure." The last is not quite a valueless characteristic for a philosophic poet; and it is perhaps exemplified in the following lines on " Reason: the use of it in Divine Matters;" of which, however, the concluding simile is very natural and very beautiful.

Reason is the Moses that conducts to Canaan, and points it out; Faith is the Joshua that secures the possession of the Promised Land :—

> Some blind themselves, 'cause possibly they may
>   Be led by others a right way;
> They build on sands, which if unmoved they find,
>   'Tis that there was no wind.
> Less hard 'tis not to err ourselves, than know
>   If our forefathers erred or no,
> When we trust men concerning God, we then
>   Trust not God concerning men.
>
> Visions and inspirations some expect
>   Their course here to direct;
> Like senseless chymists their own wealth destroy,
>   Imaginary gold t' enjoy:
> So stars appear to drop to us from sky,
>   And gild the passage as they fly;
> But when they fall, and meet the opposing ground,
>   What but a sordid slime is found?
>
> Sometimes their fancies they 'bove reason set,
>   And fast, that they may dream of meat;
> Sometimes ill spirits their sickly souls delude,
>   And bastard forms obtrude;
> So Endor's wretched sorceress, although
>   She Saul through his disguise did know,
> Yet, when the devil comes up disguised, she cries,
>   "Behold the god's arise!"
>
> In vain, alas! these outward hopes are tried;
>   Reason within 's our only guide;
> Reason, which (God be praised!) still walks, for all
>   Its old original fall;
> And, since itself the boundless Godhead joined,
>   With a reasonable mind,
> It plainly shows that mysteries divine
>   May with our reason join.
>
> The holy Book, like the eighth sphere, does shine
>   With thousand lights of truth divine;
> So numberless the stars, that to the eye
>   It makes but all one galaxy.

> Yet reason must assist too; for in seas
>   So vast and dangerous as these,
> Our course by stars above we cannot know,
>   Without the compass too below.
>
> Though Reason cannot through Faith's mysteries see,
>   It sees that there and such they be;
> Leads to heaven's door, and there does humbly keep,
>   And there through chinks and keyholes peep;
> Though it, like Moses, by a sad command
>   Must not come into the Holy Land,
> Yet thither it infallibly does guide,
>   And from afar 'tis all descried.

After the Ascension of Christ, the Apostolic province assigned to St. Thomas was Parthia; and in discharge of his commission, as we are told by St. Jerome, he published the glad tidings of salvation to the Parthians, the Medes, the Persians, the Carmanians, the Hyrcanians, the Bactrians and the Magi.* It is further said by St. Chrysostom—or some other, the author of the *Homilies on St. Matthew's Gospel*—that St. Thomas also baptized those Magi, who, guided by a star, found Christ at Bethlehem; and that he ordained them as his colleagues in preaching the Word.† St. Thomas is said, in addition, to have "washed the Æthiopians white;" by which is evidently meant that he converted them to Christianity.

There is a well-established tradition that St. Thomas penetrated as far as India, in which country, by the common consent of historians, his martyrdom took place, after he had visited the island of Taprobane—Ceylon or Sumatra?—and been attended everywhere with signal success. The precise circumstances of his death vary somewhat in the hands of various narrators; but the fact common to all is that he sealed his testimony with his blood. After he had converted great numbers of the Indians, including many

---

* St. Jerome: *De Vitis Apostolorum.*
† See page 115.

of their princes and nobles, it appears that the Brahmins, jealous of the wonderful success of the Apostle, fell upon him as he was engaged in prayer; and that whilst the others assailed him with stones and darts, one of their number despatched him by thrusting him through with a spear. This event took place on the coast of Coromandel, at Meliapour—or Calamina, as it is called by St. Jerome,* and the *Breviarium Romanum*—a town near Madras. His body was taken up by his disciples and buried in a church which he had lately built, and which was afterwards re-constructed on a scale of considerable magnificence.

There is a tradition which Joachim Hildebrand refers to Rufinus, that the body of St. Thomas was transferred from India, and, with the consent of the Emperor Alexander Severus, buried, about A.D. 230, at Edessa, in Mesopotamia; "in which city," says Socrates, "there is a splendid church —Μαρτύριον—dedicated to St. Thomas the Apostle, wherein, on account of the sanctity of the place, religious assemblies are incessantly held."† On the other hand, it is stated that the relics of St. Thomas were discovered, in A.D. 1517 or 1521, beneath the ruins of an immense church at Meliapour; and that, having been placed in a shrine enriched with silver, they were subsequently taken to Goa, and deposited in a church dedicated in his honour. At various intervals since the days of the Apostle, the "Christians of St. Thomas" have challenged the attention of the European traveller and historian. Their locality is the southern part of India; and they boast, or boasted, of an ancient tradition that "Thomas the Apostle sojourned amongst them, teaching them, and incorporating them into Churches."

It is impossible to establish the first institution of the Festival of St. Thomas at a period earlier than the eleventh

* "Dormivit in civitate Calamina, quæ est Indiæ." *De Vitis Apostolorum.*

† *Ecclesiastical History;* Book iv., c. 18.

century; and no conclusive reason has been assigned for the 21st of December as the day of commemoration. In England, at least, there seems to have been a disposition to hail such a celebration as early as A.D. 883; in which year " Marinus the Pope sent *lignum Domini* to King Alfred; and that same year Sighelm and Athelstan carried to Rome the alms which the King had vowed to send thither, and also to India, to St. Thomas and to St. Bartholomew."*

We have mentioned the far travel of St. Thomas in the discharge of his Apostolic commission; and it has never been forgotten to his praise in the Church, that he outdid all his fellows in the breadth of a field of labour which embraced almost the whole of the Eastern world. To him, " his Lord and his God" was at once Father and Fatherland; and from Him, he could never be remote. Space, time, and circumstance were swallowed up in one abiding, living, encompassing Presence. Madame de la Mothe Guion, the friend of Fénélon, and the persecuted of Bossuet and Louis XIV., devotes one of her hymns to the theme that "The soul that loves God finds Him everywhere." It is one of many of her productions, the translation of which we owe to the sympathetic inspiration of Cowper. Sustained by "the combined force of much grace, and much imagination," Madame Guion reposed in a region of lofty mysticism. " She grasped the central truth that God is love, and in this love she rested; she was content to be nothing that He might be all; and in His will, hers was, she believed, absorbed."†

> Oh Thou, by long experience tried,
> Near whom no grief can long abide;
> My Love! how full of sweet content
> I pass my years of banishment!
>
> All scenes alike engaging prove
> To souls impressed with sacred love!

* *Anglo-Saxon Chronicle.*
† *Voice of Christian Life in Song.*

Where'er they dwell, they dwell in Thee;
In heaven, in earth, or on the sea.

To me remains nor place nor time;
My country is in every clime;
I can be calm and free from care
On any shore, since God is there.

While place we seek, or place we shun,
The soul finds happiness in none;
But with a God to guide our way,
'Tis equal joy to go or stay.

Could I be cast where Thou art not,
That were indeed a dreadful lot;
But regions none remote I call,
Secure of finding God in all.

My country, Lord, art Thou alone;
Nor other can I claim or own;
The point where all my wishes meet;
My Law, my Love; life's only sweet!

I hold by nothing here below;
Appoint my journey, and I go;
Though pierced by scorn, opprest by pride,
I feel Thee good—feel nought beside.

No frowns of men can hurtful prove
To souls on fire with heavenly Love;
Though men and devils both condemn,
No gloomy days arise from them.

Ah, then! to His embrace repair;
My soul, thou art no stranger there;
There Love divine shall be thy guard,
And peace and safety thy reward.

The Conversion of St. Paul.

JANUARY 25.

Whose is that sword—that voice and eye of flame—
That heart of inextinguishable ire?
Who bears the dungeon keys, and bonds, and fire?
    Along his dark and withering path he came—
Death in his looks, and terror in his name,
Tempting the might of Heaven's eternal Sire.
    Lo! the Light shone!—the Sun's veiled beams expire—
A Saviour's self a Saviour's lips proclaim!
    Whose is yon form, stretched on the earth's cold bed,
With smitten soul and tears of agony
Mourning the past? Bowed is the lofty head—
Rayless the orbs that flashed with victory.
Over the raging waves of human will
The Saviour's spirit walked—and all was still.

Thomas Roscoe.

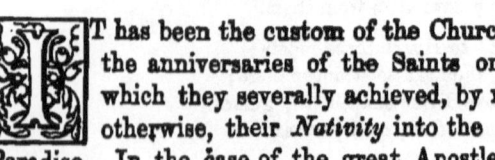IT has been the custom of the Church to celebrate the anniversaries of the Saints on the days on which they severally achieved, by martyrdom or otherwise, their *Nativity* into the glad world of Paradise. In the case of the great Apostle of the Gentiles, however, an exception has been made; and his Conversion is the surpassing fact in his history which it has seemed good to commemorate. For this exception three definite reasons are alleged by Durandus :—" (1) For the sake of the example of St. Paul's conversion; lest any sinner should despair of pardon, when, after such offences

as those of which he had been guilty, St. Paul was chosen to be a vessel of mercy. (2) For the sake of giving expression to a special gladness; for as the Church suffered the greatest of grief in the season of his persecuting fury, so she had the utmost cause for joy in his conversion. (3) For the sake of the miracle which the Lord showed in him, seeing that from having been the most cruel of persecutors, St. Paul was made the most faithful of preachers."*

These points are substantially presented in the following poem by George Wither, in whose volume of "Hymns and Songs of the Church," it bears the title of the "Conversion of St. Paul."

> A blest conversion and a strange
>   Was that when Saul a Paul became;
> And, Lord, for making such a change,
>   We praise and glorify Thy name;
> For whilst he went from place to place
>   To persecute Thy truth and Thee,
> And running to perdition was,
>   By powerful grace called back was he.
>
> When from the truth we go astray,
>   Or wrong it through our pointed zeal,
> Oh, come and stop us in the way,
>   And then Thy will to us reveal.
> The brightness show us from above,
>   Which proves the sensual eyesight blind;
> And from our eyes those scales remove
>   That hinder us Thy ways to find.
>
> And as Thy blessed servant Paul,
>   When he a convert once became,
> Exceeded Thy apostles all
>   In painful preaching of Thy name;
> So grant that those who have in sin
>   Exceeded others heretofore,
> The start of them in faith may win—
>   Love, serve, and honour Thee the more.

* *Rationale Divinorum Officiorum.*

CONVERSION OF ST. PAUL.

The conversion of St. Paul is believed to have taken place within the same ecclesiastical year as the Crucifixion of our Lord, and the stoning of Stephen, the Protomartyr; but the institution of a day in its honour cannot be accurately traced further back than the time of Innocent III., who wished it to be made, what it had not yet become, a festival of universal obligation. The proof of this statement is easy and conclusive; for an *Epistle* of Innocent III., dated March, 1198, is yet extant, in which, addressing the Bishop of Worms, the Pontiff complains that "the feast of the Conversion of St. Paul was not celebrated in the diocese of Worms, although the anniversary of his Passion was there solemnly observed."* On vaguer evidence, Cardinal Baronius contends that the festival had been observed so early as the time of St. Augustine, and that after the ninth century it had gradually grown into disuse. But it is contrary to all we know of the vitality of festivals once established, to suppose that a commemoration of so illustrious a Christian teacher as St. Paul should ever have lapsed through the lukewarmness of Christendom to his memory. In the thirteenth century the festival was in a fair way to be generally observed, as appears from the twenty-first decree of the Council of Cognac (A.D. 1254); whilst in England its celebration had already been ordained in the eighth statute of the Council of Oxford, which met at the summons of Stephen Langton, Archbishop of Canterbury, A.D. 1222.

The fortunes of the day in our own calendar—together with those of the festival of St. Barnabas, the other extraordinary member of the Apostolic College—form the subject of a lengthy and interesting note in Wheatly, which is as follows:—" St. Paul and St. Barnabas were neither of them inserted in the table of holy-days prefixed to the calendar, till the Scotch Liturgy was compiled, from whence they were taken into our own at the last review; nor were

---

* *Decretales:* Lib. I; *Epistola* XLIV.

they reckoned up among the days that were appointed by
the Act, in the fifth and sixth year of King Edward VI., to
be observed as holy-days; though it is there expressly
enacted that no other day but what is therein mentioned
shall be kept, or commanded to be kept, holy. However,
the names of each of them were inserted in the calendar
itself, and proper services were appointed for them in all
the Common Prayer Books that have been since the Reformation. And in the first book of King Edward they are
both red-letter holy-days: though in the second book (in
which the other holy-days are also printed in red letters)
the conversion of St. Paul is put down in black, and
St. Barnabas is omitted. But this last seems to have been
done through the carelessness of the printer, and not
through design; proper second Lessons being added in the
calendar against the day. The reason of their being left
out of the table of holy-days was, because if they fell upon
any week-day, they were not to be observed as *days of
obligation*, or by ceasing from labour, nor to be bid in the
church. Their proper offices might be used, so they were
not used solemnly, nor by ringing to the same, after the manner used on high-holy-days. The reason why they were not
high-holy-days, I suppose, was, because the Conversion of
St. Paul did always, and St. Barnabas did often, fall in term-
time; during which time and the time of harvest, *i. e.* from
the first of July to the twenty-ninth of September, it
was ordained in Convocation by the authority of King
Henry VIII., in 1536, that no days should be observed as
holy-days except the feast of the Apostles, of our Blessed
Lady, and St. George, and such feasts as the King's judges did
not use to sit in judgment in Westminster-hall. The days
in the terms in which the judges did not use to sit were
the feasts of the Ascension, of St. John the Baptist, of All
Saints, and of the Purification. By the feasts of the
Apostles, I suppose, the twelve only were meant; and
therefore, St. Paul and St. Barnabas were excluded. But

as they are inserted now in the table of holy-days, which, with the whole Liturgy, is confirmed by the Act of Uniformity, they are both of them days of equal obligation with the rest."*

The book of the *Acts of the Apostles* enters so fully into the Christian activity of St. Paul, and he himself is so frequent in autobiographic passages throughout his various *Epistles*, that it is well to leave almost utterly untouched a life which is at once so accessible and so little susceptible of treatment at anything like a medium length.

After the events recorded in the inspired narrative, it is related that St. Paul, having been restored to liberty at the end of his two years' imprisonment at Rome, prepared for the execution, in its widest sense, of his commission as the Apostle of the Gentiles. Whither he at first directed his course, has not been made absolutely certain. During the interval of eight years which elapsed between his two appearances at Rome, he is said to have "extended his labours to the utmost bounds of the Western world," which would naturally include our own island. "There is very good and sufficient evidence, built on the testimony of ancient and credible writers, with a concurrent probability of circumstances, that there was a Christian Church planted in Britain during the Apostles' times. Eusebius, a learned and inquisitive person, affirms, in his third book of *Evangelical Demonstration*, that some of the Apostles preached the Gospel in the British Islands. Theodoret, another learned and judicious historian, expressly names the Britons among the nations converted by the Apostles; and says, in another place, that St. Paul brought salvation to the islands that lie in the ocean (*Tom. i. in Psal.* 116). St. Jerome testifies, that St. Paul, after his imprisonments, preached the Gospel in the Western parts (*Hierom in Amos;* c. 5); by which the British Islands were especially understood; as will appear by the following testimony of

* Wheatly: *Rational Introduction to the Book of Common Prayer.*

Clemens Romanus, who saith, 'St. Paul preached righteousness through the whole world, and in so doing went to the utmost bounds of the West' (*Epist. ad Corinth.*); which necessarily includeth the British Islands, as is plain to those who knew how the phrase, 'the utmost bounds of the West,' was used by the historians and poets of those times."*

Upon St. Paul's return to Rome, about the eighth or ninth year of the reign of Nero, he is said to have drawn upon himself the fury of that cruel Emperor, either by joining with St. Peter in procuring the fall of Simon Magus, or by effecting the conversion of one of Nero's female favourites. The Apostle was apprehended, tried, and sentenced to death. As a Roman citizen, he might have claimed—unless his crimes were assumed to have been of a most heinous and aggravated kind—exemption from the preliminary torture of the scourge; although Cardinal Baronius relates that in one of the churches of Rome, the pillars were long afterwards exhibited to which both St. Peter and St. Paul were said to have been bound whilst they were scourged. On his way to execution the holy Apostle was the means of converting no fewer than three of his guard; and these men, within a few days after, by the Emperor's order, became martyrs for the faith. The place of St. Paul's execution was the Aquæ Salviæ, at a distance of three miles from Rome, where, after some time spent in solemn preparation, he cheerfully gave his neck to the fatal stroke. As a Roman, he might not be put to the servile and opprobrious death of crucifixion; and he therefore suffered decapitation, which was considered a more noble form of execution. St. Paul was buried in the Via Ostiensis, about two miles from Rome; and over his grave, about A.D. 318, Constantine the Great, at the instance of Silvester, Bishop of Rome, built a stately church, which he adorned with superb

---

* Nelson's *Festivals and Fasts of the Church of England.*

gifts, and enriched with noble endowments. The Emperor Theodosius, however, thought this church too mean for the memory of so great an Apostle, and caused it to be taken down, and another, more noble and magnificent still, to be erected on its site.

As the Apostle of the Gentiles, St. Paul has naturally been very highly and very widely venerated. In the old English calendar, as still in the Roman, his *Nativity* as a martyr was observed, jointly with that of St. Peter, on the 29th of June; his Conversion being kept in them, as in the present English calendar, on the 25th of January. His association with St. Peter was based upon the supposed fellowship of the two Apostles in their death, which, say some writers, took place on the same day and in the same year; whilst others, cleaving to the identity of the day, interpose an interval of one or more years between the two martyrdoms. "Certainly," says Dr. Cave, "if St. Paul suffered not at the very same time with St. Peter, it could not be long after, not above a year, at most. The best is, which of them soever started first, they both came at last to the same end of the race: to those palms and crowns which are reserved for all good men in Heaven, but most eminently for the martyrs of the Christian faith."*

St. Paul offers many attractions to the Christian muse, whether we have regard to his character, which was so noble and so manifold; to his life, which was so picturesque and so eventful; to his boldness, which was so constant and so uncalculating; to his sympathies, which were so ready and so catholic; to his sufferings, which were so numerous and so severe; or to his teaching, which was so powerful and so profound. Yet it remains that his conversion is the critical event of his life, as it is the theme of his festival; for on his conversion depends all his succeeding exploits and experiences. As Innocent III. puts it, in

* Cave's *Antiquitates Apostolicæ; Life of St. Paul.*

the *Epistle* to which we have already alluded:—" The glorious passion of St. Paul would have been impossible, unless his conversion had first been effected." We conclude our remarks upon a festival in honour of an event which to cultivated minds ranks among the dearest of the historical evidences of Christianity, with a poem on the "Conversion of St. Paul," by Dr. Monsell, in whose volume of "Spiritual Songs" it occurs.

> Saviour, when our souls would trace
> All the wonders of Thy Grace,
> And by sweet experience prove
> How, through the power of mighty love,
> Hardened hearts perverse and proud,
> Can before thy cross be bowed,
> Be Thy great Apostle Paul
> Type and Teacher of it all!
>
> Greater difference cannot be,
> Than in Saul and Paul we see;
> He—who Christ and Christ's abhorred—
> Lowly breathes—" Who art Thou, Lord?"
> He—who calmly stood and owned
> Those who holy Stephen stoned—
> Trembling and astonished too,
> Sighs, " What wilt Thou have *me* do?"
>
> Grace his soul with blessings reaches;
> He, who persecuted, preaches;
> He, who with the bigot's rod
> Chastened once the Church of God,
> Takes up now the insulted Cross,
> Counts as nought its shame and loss,
> And, before he lays it down,
> Wins a martyr's palm and crown!
>
> Such God's glorious power of old!
> And the story still is told
> Every year, that brings again
> This high festival to men;

THE CONVERSION OF ST. PAUL.

These glad tidings to proclaim,
Jesus Christ is still the same,
Still the same, He changes never,
Yesterday, to-day, for ever!

That, which humbled to the knee,
The proud-hearted Pharisee—
That, which pardoned all the wrong,
He had done to Christ so long—
That, which with its soft control
Soothed to love his stubborn soul—
Still remains; it changes never!
Yesterday, to-day, for ever!

Blessed Saviour, when we stray,
Meet us on our will-ward way,
Meet, and plead with us, till we
Yield, repent, and turn to Thee,
And beneath the beaming grace
Of Thy reconcilèd face,
Like the great Apostle, prove
Converts to Thy gentle love.

The Presentation of Christ

IN THE TEMPLE,
COMMONLY CALLED
THE PURIFICATION OF ST. MARY THE VIRGIN.
FEBRUARY 2.

THERE have been celebrated, with more or less of universality, at least half-a-dozen festivals in commemoration of events connected with the Blessed Virgin. Of these, four are mentioned by Durandus, with the remark that a holiday in honour of Mary occurred in each of the four quarters of the year, to wit, her Annunciation, Assumption, Nativity, and Purification; to which list may be added her Visitation and Conception. The observance of the last-mentioned festival was of ancient date in the Eastern Church, and became obligatory in that communion about the middle of the twelfth century; although in the Western Church it required three hundred years more to advance to the same degree of universality. Its introduction into Britain has been inconclusively referred to St. Anselm, Archbishop of Canterbury, about the year 1150; whilst by the eighth statute of the Council of Oxford, A.D. 1222, its celebration, which occurs December 8th, was expressly left without authoritative sanction to the option of the faithful.*

* "Statuimus quod festa subscripta sub omni veneratione serventur, videlicet * * * omnia festa Beatæ Mariæ, præter festum Conceptionis, cujus celebrationi non imponitur necessitas." Labbeus, *Sacrosancta Concilia*.

The Nativity of the Virgin, September 8th, was a festival unknown in the time of St. Augustine; although the *Sacramentary* of Gregory the Great (590-604) contains a special office for it. Its institution has been attributed to Servius, Bishop of Rome, about A.D. 695; and in the time of St. Bernard the feast was of general observance throughout Christendom.

The feast of the Visitation of the Blessed Virgin Mary, July 2nd, which was first instituted by Pope Urban VI., in the year 1389, and confirmed by the Council of Basle, A.D. 1431, had for its object the commemoration of the visit of Mary to her cousin Elizabeth, immediately after the Annunciation of the birth of the Redeemer.

The Assumption of the Blessed Virgin finds its place in the Roman Calendar on the 15th of August; and is reckoned the greatest of all her festivals, as being the consummation of them. "This feast of her Assumption was celebrated with the utmost solemnity at Jerusalem, in the fifth and sixth ages, as appears from the life of St. Theodosius."*

Of the various commemorations of the Blessed Virgin, the Church of England retains only those two, which, while they have a very close relation to herself, do yet more peculiarly belong to her Divine Son; of which, without excluding her, He is the chief and central figure. These two are the Annunciation and the Purification; the latter of which—the one more immediately concerning us at present—has for its alternative title, the Presentation of Christ in the Temple. The very names mark out the Purification as what Bishop Sparrow calls a "double feast, partly in memory of the Virgin's Purification (this being the fortieth day after the birth), which she observed according to the Law (Leviticus xii., 4), though she needed it not: but chiefly in memory of our Lord's Presentation in the Temple, which the Gospel commemorates." †

* Alban Butler's *Lives of the Saints.*
† *Rationale upon the Book of Common Prayer.*

The Feast of the Purification does not claim to be of the remotest Christian antiquity; for even if a confessedly spurious *Homily* of St. Chrysostom were conceded to be genuine, it would not necessarily authenticate the observance of the day any earlier than the beginning of the fifth century. But in the time of St. Chrysostom there is express reason for concluding that this feast had not originated; and the only very colourable doubt is whether, according to some authorities, it was first instituted in the time of the Emperor Justin, or, according to more numerous ones, in the reign of his nephew and successor, Justinian the First. Cardinal Baronius, indeed, would claim for Pope Gelasius (492-496) the establishment of this feast, in substitution for the pagan *Lupercalia;* but although it is probable that Gelasius may have wished to establish it, he does not appear to have been able to carry his desire into execution, from the default of imperial consent and co-operation.

Whatever provincial vogue the feast of the Purification may have enjoyed, it would seem that the occasion of its attaining an œcumenical celebration was a fierce and fatal plague at Constantinople, which, happening in the fifteenth year of the Emperor Justinian (A.D. 542), deepened an impression which had been widely spread, seven years previously, by the portentous earthquakes at Pompéiopolis, in Mysia. "At Constantinople, a great mortality having arisen, the solemnity of the Purification of the Blessed Mary was appointed, which in Greek is called 'ὑπαπαντή, *i.e., obviatio;* because on that day Simeon *met* the Lord on His way to be presented in the temple; and so the mortality ceased."[*] So writes Sigebert, a Benedictine monk of the convent of Gembloux (A.D. 1030-1112); whose evidence is more than fortified by the earlier testimony of Paulus Diaconus, who records that "in the fifteenth year of Justinian there was a great mortality at Byzantium,

[*] Sigebert of Gembloux: *Chronicon* A.D. 542.

and in the same year the *Hypapante* of the Lord had its origin, so that it was celebrated at Byzantium on the second day of the month of February." *

Opinions vary as to the origin of the particular form which the celebration of the festival assumed. The earlier ritualists are pretty unanimous in referring the illuminations which attended it to a desire on the part of the Christian bishops to lure their people from the commemoration of the search of Ceres after her daughter Proserpine, when the latter had been carried off by Pluto, or of the quinquennial lustrations held in honour of Februa, the mother of Mars—a desire to be explained, on the principle that it was expedient to amalgamate and to *baptize* such heathen observances as might innocently be perpetuated, and to invest them with a new and spiritual significance. "With the heathen," says Joachim Hildebrand, summing up the case of previous opinions, although not with approval—"with the heathen, Proserpine, the spouse of the infernal deity, was honoured; but with us, in her stead, Mary, the spouse of the God of Heaven. With the heathen, Februa, who was the mother of the god of war; but with us Mary, the mother of the God of peace, was worshipped. With the heathen, the honour was paid to an infernal court; with us to the queen of angels: and so this pagan feast is converted into the Feast of the Purification of Mary."† L'Estrange more piously derives the "custom of bearing tapers lighted in procession on this day, from a desire to imitate the five wise virgins, represented in the parable (Matthew xxv.), as St. Bernard delivereth; or to put Christians in remembrance of Christ, the spiritual light, of whom Simeon did prophesy, as is read in the Church on that day."‡ Later authorities, as Dean Stanley, have seen in the custom a probable reminiscence

---

* *Historia Miscella*; Lib. xvi.
† *De Festis Diebus Libellus: Festum Purificationis Mariæ.*
‡ *Alliance of Divine Offices.*

of the circumstances of worship in the darkness of the catacombs; whilst others, again, have recognized in it nothing more than a particular instance of that tendency to regard lights as a natural and obvious expression of warmth and joy, which is to be traced in all symbolical religions.

The possibility of so many reasons—which, if different, are not mutually exclusive or contradictory—being given for an ecclesiastical ceremony, is an argument for the possibility of their historical concurrence; so long as one is not insisted on to the detriment or prejudice of others. The simplest of events are not the products of the simplest causes; and a course once determined upon has a wonderful facility in the way of aggregating incentives, as a fact once accomplished has a wonderful facility in the way of precipitating explanations.

The custom of consecrating wax-tapers has been ordinarily regarded as one initiated by Pope Sergius the First (687—701), of whom the *Ordo Romanus* says, that "he added Litanies to the Feast of *Hypante*, and holy candles" —a statement which it is difficult, however, to conciliate with the fact that the blessing of candles was not unknown in the year 665. A solution of the question may possibly be arrived at by regarding Sergius as the first pontiff who gave the practice the sanction of his chair. The same pope is recorded to have instituted processions at other anniversaries of the Virgin—the Annunciation, namely, and the Nativity.

According to the transcendental symbolism of Durandus, the lighted torches carried by the faithful in procession were for a sign that they bore the divinity as well as the humanity of Christ, as Simeon did when he took in his arms the illustrious Babe. The wax, taken from the bee, was a type of the humanity assumed from the Virgin; the light, of the divinity, for "our God is a consuming fire." Again, the burning taper represented faith and good works; for as the light could not exist without the co-efficiency of flame and taper, "so faith without works is dead also."

In the spirit of what we may call a mere practical symbolism, the same author gives six reasons for the processional carrying of burning torches and tapers :—" (1) That each individual might illuminate himself, thereby professing that his deeds were done in the light, and lay open to the gaze of others. (2) That the Christian religion might improve upon the ceremonial illuminations of the Gentiles * * * for which purpose Pope Sergius appointed the Festival of the Purification in honour of the Mother of our Lord, at which processions should be made, that the people at large, carrying burning tapers in their hands, should march through the churches in memory of the heavenly kingdom, when all the elect, coming to meet the Bridegroom with the resplendent lamps of good works, should with Him hereafter take part in the celestial nuptials. (3) That thus we might imitate the prudent virgins, of whom the Blessed Virgin is the chief, so that, keeping alight in our hearts the lamp of chastity, we might be worthy with them to enter into the temple of glory, to the presence of the true Bridegroom. (4) Because the Light, which, according to Simeon, was to lighten the Gentiles, was on this day presented for us; so that this procession signifies that which the Virgin Mary, Joseph, and Simeon made to the temple. (5) To commemorate the humanity and the divinity of Christ, as aforesaid. (6) To shew forth the purity of the Virgin, lest anyone, hearing of her purification, should venture to think it was necessary for her. Therefore we carry lighted candles, as if the Church said by that act:—' The Blessed Virgin needs no purification; for she is altogether bright, altogether splendid.' For these reasons it is that candles are enjoined."*

We have from St. Bernard of Clairvaux (1091-1153) an account of the processions in which he was accustomed to join a hundred and fifty years before the time of Durandus—who died A.D. 1296—which offers such variety of

* Durandus : *Rationale Divinorum Officiorum.*

phenomena and *rationale* from the foregoing quotation that we venture to transcribe it. It is taken from one of a group of three *Sermons* delivered by St. Bernard on the Purification of the Blessed Virgin Mary, and has for its more immediate subject the "Order and mode of the Procession of Christ to the Temple." "By Joseph and Mary," says the preacher, "by Anne and Simeon, a procession was formed, which to-day through the four quarters of the globe with solemn rejoicings is commemorated. Because, therefore, we ourselves are about to-day to arrange a festive procession, over and above the wont of other solemnities, I do not think it useless to investigate a little more closely its method and order. For we are about to march in procession two and two, holding candles in our hands, and these lighted, not with fire taken at random, but with fire which has first been consecrated in the church by priestly benediction. Of those who shall take part in our procession, they that go out first shall return last: and we shall sing in the way of the Lord, for great is the glory of the Lord. It is not without a purpose that we proceed two and two, for so the Holy Gospels testify that the disciples were sent forth by the Saviour, to the praise of brotherly love and social life. Our procession would be marred and disturbed if any one walked in it unaccompanied." We carry lights in our hands, St. Bernard goes on substantially to say, to signify that our lights should shine before men; and in memory of those wise virgins who went to meet their Lord with their lamps alight and burning. And from this usage, and the many lights set up in the church this day, it is called Candelaria, or Candlemas. The candles are lighted with holy fire, to show that all our works should be done in the holy fire of charity. They that go out first return last, to teach humility (Philippians ii., 3). We sing in the way, for the reason that God loveth a cheerful giver. The Procession itself is to teach us that we ought not to stand idle in the way of life, but to proceed from virtue to virtue; not looking back to that which is behind, but reaching forward to that which is before.*

From the fact that the Purification is a "double feast," combining honour to the Mother with adoration to the Son, it has very naturally been debated which of these was the predominant intention at the time of its first institution. Which was the substantial and primary idea, and which the secondary and accidental? Was the festival established, in the first instance, for the worship of Jesus, and presently warped by the attraction of a too prevailing Mariolatry; or was it, established in the first instance as a venerating memorial of the Virgin, modified by the prominence given in it to the infinite glory and grandeur of the Child? We think Bingham has put the case impartially, if not in a quite impartial spirit; only it should be remembered, *per contra*, that the analogies in heathen worship, from which the Purification cannot be disassociated, point to the festival as if its institution had been conceived directly in honour of the Virgin. But taking the signification of the earliest name of the Feast, apart from a consideration of the circumstances attending, possibly, its earliest celebration, Bingham's argument is not more short than conclusive. "Baronius," he says, "would have the Feast first instituted in honour of the Virgin Mary, which the very name of *Hypapante* confutes, which signifies the coming of Simeon to *meet* the Lord in His temple, according to the revelation made to him, 'that he should not see death till he had seen the Lord's Christ;' and the Greeks always reckoned it among those festivals which they called *Festa Dominica*, festivals appointed in honour of our Lord, as Leo Allatius himself informs us."†

Besides the name of *Hypapante*, *Festum Occursus*, the Feast of the Meeting, which by the Latins was corrupted

* St. Bernard: Sermon *De ordine et modo processionis Christi in Templum.*

† *Antiquities of the Christian Church.*

into *Hypante*, its most frequent mediæval name, the Feast was known as *Festum Purificationis Mariæ; Festum Presentationis;* and *Festum Simeonis*, and *Simeonis et Annæ*. "The Purification was, in one sense, to the West, what the Epiphany was to the East, and has usually received its name from the multitude of tapers employed in the office, with reference, primarily, to the light to lighten the Gentiles, which was then manifested by the mouth of Simeon. The French Church calls it *La Chandeleur;* in Spain and Portugal, it is the *Candelaria;* in Basque, *Ganderailu;* in Denmark, it is the *Kyndelmisse;* in Germany, the *Lichtmesse;* in Suabia, *Kerzweihe*, or *Kerzmesse;* in Belgium, the *Kersdag*. In Welsh, it is *Gwyl Vairy Canwyllau*, the Festival of Mary of the Candles; in Manx, for a reason we cannot explain, it is *Laa'l Moirrey my Giangle*, the Day of Mary's being tied or secured. By the Russian Church it is called *Srietenie*, the vernacular equivalent for the Greek *Hypapante;* in the north of Italy it was often termed *St. Simeon's Day;* in France, the name was, in many instances, the same as that in our Calendar, the Presentation. We also meet with that of *Susception Day*."* We may complete the list with our own familiar *Candlemas;* and with another, the *Wives' Feast*, for which we are indebted to Brady's "Clavis Calendaria."

The special virtue which all ages have consented to praise in the conduct of the Virgin Mary, was her humility in complying with a Law to which she was not obnoxious. This Law required the mother of a son to separate herself from the public congregation for forty days after the birth, and at the end of that period to present an offering proportioned to her means, with which the priest was to make atonement before the Lord; whilst the son, if a first-born, was to be presented in the Temple, and a ransom, the price of which did not vary with the parents' circumstances, was to

* Dr. J. M. Neale's *Essays on Liturgiology and Church History: Church Festivals and their Household Words.*

be paid in his behalf to the priest. "The Mother, superior to the Law, subjected herself to the Law; higher than the Temple, she went up to the Temple."* "Undoubtedly," exclaims Pope Benedict XIV., "a profound humility impelled this most holy woman, that she should submit to the requirements of the Law, by which she was not bound."† But the question arises, was an act of humiliation, which was unnecessary, politic, or sincere, or faithful? And how could it be reconciled with her belief in her Son's destiny on the one hand, and on the other with that prudence which would shun the hazard of compromising His prospects and her own character, that she should ostensibly impute to herself and to Him the sinful disabilities of ordinary conception and parturition? To which it may be answered, *inter alia*, that, as the Virgin was not at that time free to promulgate her Son's pretensions, it was expedient that she should in all things comport herself as the ordinary mother of an ordinary child; and with regard to the Child, it was His mission, as had already been shown in His reception of the right of circumcision, to fulfil all righteousness, to satisfy, before He abrogated, the minutest demands of that ceremonial Law under which He was born. The matter is thus lucidly put by Neander: —" Forty days after the birth of the infant Jesus, His parents carried Him to the Temple at Jerusalem, in order to offer, according to their means, the prescribed sacrifice for the purification of Mary, and to pay the usual ransom for their first-born. This appears strange, in view of the extraordinary circumstances that preceded and followed the birth of the Child, which, one might suppose, would make it an exception to ordinary rules. The points which the Levitical law had in view seem not to have existed here; so remarkable a birth might have precluded the necessity of the Levitical purification. The ransom which

---

* *Acta Sanctorum: De Hypapante Domini.*
† *De Festis Beatæ Mariæ Virginis.*

had to be paid for other first-born sons, in view of their original obligation to the priesthood, could hardly be necessary in the case of an infant who was one day to occupy the Summit of the Theocracy. It would be natural to suppose that Mary must have hesitated, and laid her scruples before the priests for decision before she could make up her mind to perform these ceremonies. But we cannot judge of such extraordinary events by common standards. Mary did not venture to speak freely in public of these wonderful things, or to anticipate the Divine purposes in any way; she left it to God to educate the Child, which had been announced to her as the Messiah, so as to fit Him for His calling, and, at the proper time, to authenticate His mission publicly and conspicuously."*

> Pure and spotless was the Maid
>   That to the Temple came,
> A pair of turtle-doves she paid,
>   Although she brought the Lamb.
> Pure and spotless though she were,
> Her body chaste, and her soul fair,
>   She to the temple went
>   To be purified
>   And tried,
> That she was spotless and obedient;
> O make us to follow so blessed precedent,
>   And purify our souls, for we
>   Are clothed with sin and misery.
>   From our conception
>   One imperfection,
>   And a continued state of sin,
>   Hath sullied all our faculties within,
>   We present our souls to Thee
>   Full of need and misery:
>   And for redemption a Lamb
>   The purest, whitest that e'er came
>   A sacrifice to Thee,
>   Even He that bled upon the tree.

* Neander's *Life of Jesus Christ*.

The foregoing poem, of which the quaintness of the style and expression is equal to the beauty of the thought, is from the "Festival Hymns" of Bishop Jeremy Taylor, and is written, as well as entitled, "On the Purification of the Blessed Virgin."

It is not all, nay, it must be that it is very few, persons who share in that most gracious and instinctive humility which the conduct of the Blessed Virgin exemplifies. With most people that, which with her was a *connatural* endowment, is the result of sharp and long-continued discipline; and the pride of the heart has, generally speaking, a constant tendency to reassert itself, whenever the disciplinary action of Providence is withdrawn. This fact was known to none better than to the author of the "School of the Heart," whoever he may have been, whether Francis Quarles or Christopher Harvey.* The poem immediately following is taken from the work just mentioned; and is therein called "The Humiliation of the Heart."

So let it be,
 Lord, I am well content,
  And Thou shalt see
   The time is not misspent,
Which Thou dost then bestow, when Thou dost quell
And crush the heart where pride before did swell.

 Lord, I perceive,
  As soon as Thou dost send,
   And I receive
    The blessings Thou dost lend,
Mine heart begins to mount, and doth forget
The ground whereon it goes, where it is set.

 In health I grew
  Wanton, began to kick,
   As though I knew
    I never should be sick.
Diseases take me down, and make me know,
Bodies of brass must pay the debt they owe.

* See page 88.

"HUMILIATION OF THE HEART."

If I but dream
    Of wealth, mine heart doth rise
With a full stream
    Of pride, and I despise
All that is good, until I wake and spy
The swelling bubble pricked with poverty.

A little wind
    Of undeserved praise
Blows up my mind,
    And my swoln thoughts do raise
Above themselves, until the sense of shame
Makes me condemn my self-dishonoured name.

One moment's mirth
    Would make me run stark mad,
And the whole earth,
    Could it at once be had,
Would not suffice my greedy appetite,
Didst Thou not pain, instead of pleasure, write.

Lord, it is well
    I was in time brought down,
Else Thou canst tell,
    Mine heart would soon have flown
Full in Thy face, and study to requite
The riches of Thy goodness with despite.

Slack not Thine hand,
    Lord, turn Thy screw about:
If Thy press stand,
    Mine heart may chance slip out.
O quast it into nothing, rather than
It should forget itself, and swell again.

Or if Thou art
    Disposed to let it go,
Lord, teach mine heart
    To lay itself as low
As Thou canst it: that so prosperity
May still be tempered with humility.

> Thy way to rise,
> Was to descend; let me
> Myself despise,
> And so ascend with Thee.
> Thou throw'st them down that lift themselves on high,
> And raisest them that on the ground do lie.

If for a very short time we regard that aspect of the "double feast" in which it is viewed as the Presentation of the Infant rather than as the Purification of the Mother, we see, generally, with Bishop Sparrow, that it was the offering by our Saviour of "Himself, a living Oblation for us, that so the whole obedience of His life might be ours;"[*] and more particularly, that it was the third in a series of manifestations of which the other two had been made at Bethlehem forty days before, severally to pastoral simplicity and to Magian wisdom. It was, as is well said in the *Acta Sanctorum*, "the complement of the Epiphany by reason of Simeon's song." Yet this is only half the truth; inasmuch as it refers only to that part of the Song of Simeon which mentions the Saviour as a "Light to lighten the Gentiles." On the same ground, the Purification was also the complement of the Angelic message. The glad tidings of the Angel, catholic as heaven or earth or goodwill, would yet have a certain practical limitation in that they must, from the circumstances of the Shepherds, their locality and nationality, be promulgated chiefly, if not exclusively, to Jews, and even of them only to such as were dwellers within a confined and difficult district; whilst the "exceeding great joy" of the Wise Men at the leading of the Star, and their discovery of the divine Infant, could, by reason of their rapid flight homewards after their gifts and prostration, be communicated only to the Gentiles, their fellow-countrymen. In the Purification it was, that, from the mouth of an aged Hebrew, just and devout, waiting only his peaceful departure to a world where distinctions

---

[*] *Rationale upon the Book of Common Prayer.*

and privileges of race were to be unknown, was announced the advent of that " Salvation which God had prepared *before the face of all people;* to be a Light to lighten the Gentiles, and to be the glory of His people Israel."

It is this " Light of the Gentiles," in that *distributed phase* in which He is the " true Light, which lighteth *every man* that cometh into the world "—it is this Light in the aspects it presents to each individual soul, which is the subject of a poem recognised by the pious popular heart as perhaps the gem of " Lyra Apostolica." Our readers will for the most part be aware that it is from the pen of Dr. J. H. Newman.

> Lead, kindly light, amid the encircling gloom,
>   Lead Thou me on!
> The night is dark, and I am far from home—
>   Lead Thou me on!
> Keep Thou my feet; I do not ask to see
> The distant scene,—one step 's enough for me.
>
> I was not ever thus, nor prayed that Thou
>   Shouldst lead me on.
> I loved to choose and see my path; but now,
>   Lead Thou me on!
> I loved the garish day, and spite of fears,
> Pride ruled my will: remember not past years.
>
> So long Thy power hath blest me, sure it still
>   Will lead me on,
> O'er moor and fen, or crag and torrent, till
>   The night is gone;
> And with the morn those Angel faces smile
> Which I have loved long since, and lost awhile.

We have already alluded to the fact of the Presentation being regarded as the complement of the Epiphany of Christ. The idea has not been limited to particular times and places. It is at least as old as Ephraim Syrus, as is evidenced by the poem we are about to quote from that grand old Syrian monk, the original of which poem, along with a German version, occurs in Daniel's "Thesaurus Hymnologicus;" and a German version of which is also given by Ferdinand Bässler, in his "Auswahl Altchristlicher Lieder." The author of "The Voice of Christian Life in Song" supplies the following unpretending English translation. The title given to the poem in the last-named volume is less extensive than the ground which the poem in fact covers—"The Star of Bethlehem." Daniel's description of it is at once larger and more precise; he entitles it "In Epiphania et Præsentatione Domini:"—

A star shines forth in heaven suddenly,
A wondrous orb, less than the sun, yet greater:—
Less in its outward light, but greater in
Its inward glory, pointing to a mystery.
That morning star sent forth its beams afar
Into the land of those who had no light,
Led them as blind men by a way they knew not,
Until they came and saw the Light of men,
Offered their gifts, received eternal life,
Worshipped, and went their way.
Thus had the Son two heralds,—one on high,
And one below. Above, the star rejoiced;
Below, the Baptist bare Him record:
Two heralds thus, one heavenly, one of earth;
That witnessing the nature of the Son,
The majesty of God, and this His human nature.
O mighty wonder! thus were they thy heralds,
Both of His Godhead and His manhood.
Who held Him only for a Son of earth,
To such the star proclaimed His heavenly glory
Who held Him only for a heavenly Spirit,
To such the Baptist spoke of Him as man.
And in the holy temple Simeon held the babe
Fast in his aged arms, and sang to Him,—

"To me, in Thy mercy,
    An old man, Thou art come;
Thou layest my body
    In peace in the tomb.

  Thou soon wilt awake me,
   And bid me arise;
  Will lead me, transfigured,
   To paradise."

Then Anna took the babe upon her arms,
And pressed her mouth upon His infant lips;
Then came the Holy Spirit on her lips,
As erst upon Isaiah's, when the coal
Had touched his silent lips, and opened them;
With glowing heart she sang,

  O Son of the King!
   Though Thy birthplace was mean,
  All-hearing, yet silent;
   All-seeing, unseen;
  Unknown, yet all-knowing;
   God, and yet Son of man!
    Praise to Thy name."

We complete our poetical illustrations of the Feast of the Purification with a poem from Dr. Monsell's "Spiritual Songs for the Sundays and Holidays throughout the Year," in which the narrative element is piously and unaffectedly combined with the didactic. The poem is entitled "Daily Prayer."

  The days of separation past,
   Commanded by the Word,
  The Virgin Mary brings her child,
   To offer to the Lord.

  Thanksgivings for His wondrous love
   Her grateful thoughts employ,
  For blessings spared, and bliss bestowed,
   Life, and a mother's joy!

  Through childbirth she hath safely past,
   Through fear of worldly shame,
  Her body kept from grief and harm,
   Her purity from blame.

  And now she comes, her vows to pay,
   His law her sacred guide,
  Her glorious Infant in her arms,
   Her husband by her side.

More than a mother's common joy
  Her thoughtful heart beguiled,
For to her breast, she knew she prest
  More than a common child.

The Hope of all the ends of earth
  Then on her bosom lay,
Whom saints had sought, while Prophets taught
  The coming of His day.

She knew the prize, for which all eyes
  So long had strained, was won,
And how "that Holy Thing" was both
  Her Saviour and her Son.

O wondrous mingling of the love
  A mother only knows,
With the deep reverence, which a soul
  Upon its God bestows!

Her arms His cradle—while His grace
  Sustains her, lest she fall;
He draws from her life's daily food,
  She draws from Him her all!

No glory of the days of old,
  When great Jehovah bowed
Beneath the Temple gates of gold,
  And entered in a cloud,

Was equal to that gentle light
  Of reconciling Love,
Which now, through all the Holy Place,
  Comes beaming from above.

God's rising Sun, on Israel's cloud
  Its rainbow hues hath thrown,
A light to lighten Gentile homes,
  The glory of His own.

But who were they, that knew that Light,
  And, in that crowding throng,
Saw Jesus, in that little babe,
  So meekly borne along?

Who realized the blessed hope
  Which had their hearts beguiled,
And " Israel's consolation " saw
  In that long-looked-for Child?

They who, in holy commune, long,
  With their dear God, had kept,
And, wakeful, watched the break of dawn,
  While all around them slept.

They who, with aged eyes, had searched
  Deep through the Sacred Word,
And caught each sign, whose Light divine,
  Told of their coming Lord.

They who, with fastings and with prayers,
  Both night and day did crave
To see the Lord's salvation here,
  Before they saw the grave :—

They coming in—as was their wont
  In bygone anxious days—
Found Jesus there ; thenceforth their prayer
  Was changed to songs of praise.

So keep us ever waiting, Lord,
  In daily prayer for Thee :
For who can say what hour we may
  Thy second Advent see?

This Word, at least, is fixed and sure,
  That they who seek to gain
Thy glad salvation for their souls—
  Shall never seek in vain.

The long delays of weary days,
  In Thy good time shall cease ;
Some blessed morn Thou wilt return,
  And we "depart in peace."

The picturesque grouping suggested by the circumstances of the Presentation and Purification has attracted the genius of the Christian painter no less than the inspiration of the Christian poet—the Temple and its accessories; the Holy Family, Joseph, Mary, and the Babe; Anna, the devout prophetess; and the God-instructed Simeon, whose ecstasy is either a pleasant or a portentous enigma to the ministering priest, and to the more or less interested spectators. And the sum of the lessons which the poets of the "double feast" inculcate is this—that in humility, obedience, and docility, we should imitate the Virgin; that we should imitate Christ in that reverence for Law which led Him as a helpless child into a fane of which he was the Divinity;* that, with Anna, we should be constant in prayer and self-repression; and that, finally, as Simeon took up Jesus in his arms, we should so receive Him into our hearts, that at all times it may be said of Him and them, " the Lord is in His holy temple."

* "Hodie Templi Dominum in Templum Domini Virgo Mater inducit." St. Bernard: *First Sermon on the Purification.*

St. Matthias.

February 24.

"THE date of the introduction of this festival is involved in considerable obscurity. It appears to have been established in the Greek Church in the course of the eleventh century. It was, perhaps, *partially*, observed in the West before that time, but it is entirely omitted in many ancient calendars. Dr. Waterland observes, in a MS. note on Wheatly, 'The oldest authority I have yet met with is the Calendar in Athelstan's *Psalter*, Cotton Libr. A.D. 703.'" *

The observance of the Day among ourselves has been attended with some confusion. The Common Prayer Book of Queen Elizabeth directs that, in Leap years, an intercalary or additional day should be supplied between the twenty-third and the twenty-fourth of February; and hence St. Matthias's Day, which in common years was observed on the twenty-fourth of February, was in Leap years celebrated on the twenty-fifth. But in the review of our Liturgy it was thought more proper to add a twenty-ninth day to February; so that now, there being no variation of the days, this festival must always keep to the twenty-fourth of that month. In the Greek church, the Day of St. Matthias is observed on the ninth of August.

Although Matthias was not an Apostle of the first election, immediately called and chosen by our Saviour, and although

---

* Riddle's *Manual of Christian Antiquities.*

his name does not emerge into notice before the occasion of the solemn service held between the Ascension of Christ and the outpouring of the Holy Spirit, for the appointment of a successor to the traitor Judas, Eusebius quotes from the *Hypotyposes* or *Institutions* of Clement of Alexandria, a very decided and reasonable opinion that not only Matthias, but Barsabas, the unsuccessful candidate with him for the honour of the Apostolate, was one of the seventy disciples whom Christ commissioned to be the heralds of His own approach throughout the cities of Judæa (Luke x., 1—16).* So much, indeed, is clearly to be inferred from the expression of St. Peter, that the choice of a new Apostle should be made from amongst those "men which have companied with us all the time that the Lord Jesus went in and out among us, beginning from the baptism of John, unto that same day that He was taken up from us" (Acts i., 21, 22).

The allusions to St. Matthias in the New Testament are of the scantiest; but from other authorities it is safe to believe that he was a member of a noble family of the tribe of Judah, and that from his early childhood he had been carefully instructed in the divine law.

Part of the doctrine of the Festival of St. Matthias is a warning and a terror. His introduction into the Apostolate reminds us of a previous miserable secession; his promotion, of a voluntary degradation, and perdition. The living and faithful Apostle is a substitute for a self-slain traitor. The literal sin of Judas does not admit of repetition. Only once was it within the possible of an unutterable Baseness to betray an unutterable Friendship; and to-day even covetousness itself, if it could become incarnate, could not palpably make merchandise of the Son of Man. Yet in more subtle forms is the betrayal of the Saviour of every-day recurrence. It requires for this purpose no overt treason, no active sacrilege, no malicious

* Eusebius : *Ecclesiastical History; Book* ii. c. 1.

opposition. The Master may be sacrificed afresh by omission not less than by commission; the folded arm may betray as surely as the kiss and the open hand. Luxury and sloth are as effectual bribes as thirty poor pieces of silver; and of such bribes whose hands are clean? It is not for us, from any cause soever, to void the work which Providence has committed to our trust. Neither from disloyalty nor faintness of heart have we any right to enter into the unblest rest of an anticipated Sabbath. It is not for us to hang back as cowards when doughtier champions are leading the attack upon the powers of evil. It is not for us, hesitating and uncertain between the poles of pity and fastidiousness, to forbear the touch that might carry health to the plague-stricken. But if we do so forbear, we may be sure that God has agents in reserve. Nature is wealthy, and no one man is necessary to her processes; she did not groan to fashion even him who may seem the most indispensable. The task and the sphere which may appear the most personal and proper to the possessor of certain gifts and capabilities, are equally proper and personal to scores of yet undeclared competitors. It may be that in the prodigality of Nature, and her carelessness of the individual, men may be superseded in the very occupation to which her finger seemed especially pointing them. Merely to be superseded, therefore, when it does not arise from our own consent or complicity, whether of action or supineness, does not imply fault or disgrace, and duty is clear without the impediment of such calculations. We are to see that no man take our crown, at least of will and of effort; we are to be careful that of us the fearful voice should never be heard by way of censure and complaint, "His bishoprick let another take."

The same retrospective glance at Judas which formed the motive of the just-preceding paragraph, is exemplified in a poem entitled "Self-Condemnation," of which "holy George Herbert" is the author.

> Thou who condemnest Jewish hate,
> For choosing Barabbas a murderer
>   Before the Lord of glory;
> Look back upon thine own estate,
> Call home thine eye (that busy wanderer)
>   That choice may be thy story.
>
> He that doth love, and love amiss,
> This world's delights before true Christian joy,
>   Hath made a Jewish choice:
> The world an ancient murderer is;
> Thousands of souls it hath and doth destroy
>   With her enchanting voice.
>
> He that hath made a sorry wedding
> Between his soul and gold, and hath preferred
>   False gain before the true,
> Hath done what he condemns in reading:
> For he hath sold for money his dear Lord,
>   And is a Judas-Jew.
>
> Thus we prevent the last great day,
> And judge ourselves. That light which sin and passion
>   Did before dim and choke,
> When once those snuffs are ta'en away,
> Shines bright and clear, even unto condemnation,
>   Without excuse or cloak.

A more modern rendering of the humble self-consciousness of the foregoing poem is given in a few verses which occur in the "Churchman's Family Magazine" for March, 1866, where, with reference to St. Mark xiv. 18, 19, they bear the title, "Who is the Traitor?"

> Last at supper with my Lord,
>   Ere yet was broke the Paschal bread,
> Ere yet the healing wine was poured—
>   The food by which a world is fed;
> A trouble that was almost gloom
>   Hung care upon the face divine:
> "A traitor lifts his hand of doom
>   Upon the table, near to Mine."

So spake the Ruler of the Feast,
  And smote the guests with sudden dread;
Till one who leaned on Jesus' breast
  Raised his but now reclining head.
Could it be self-distrust that made
  Him put a question in reply;
Was Love of loss of love afraid,
  That he should murmur, "Is it I?"

Who was a Rock for steadfastness,
  Who was for zeal a very flame,
Next asked the question, fearing less
  Than Love to earn a traitor's name.
No doubt did that frank forehead wear;
  Nor dimmed that eye of loyalty;
No faltering was there in the clear
  Brave voice that uttered, "Is it I?"

Then he who once, when danger hung
  Threatening above his Master's path,
Still to His perilous fortunes clung,
  And dared the fierce Judæans' wrath;
Who to his fellows: "Let us go
  Where He will lead, and with Him die!"
Abased his voice, and, trembling, low
  Demanded, wondering, "Is it I?"

The wise and watchful who had read
  The signs by which the Christ was shown,
And by the Law and Prophets led,
  Had all fulfilled in Jesus known;
Who, guileless, bade a guileless friend
  Draw to the new-found Saviour nigh,
In words where shame and sorrow blend,
  Now tearful asks, "Lord, is it I?"

He who, immersed in sordid gain,
  Braved all the public scorn of old;
Then, all things braving else, was fain
  To close his books, and leave his gold
Mindful perchance of former days
  Sacred to base cupidity,
Fears more than others fear, and prays
  A deprecation, "Is it I?"

> So one, and other. Yet no sign—
> > Love still shall keep its hold on love;
> > Zeal still shall burn with fires divine;
> > > Weakness lean on the Strength above:
> > Self-sacrifice itself shall gain,
> > > And Constancy shall keep its vow;
> > Devotion piety retain—
> > > And none be answered, "It is thou!"
> > So one, so most. If none of these
> > > Shall be the traitor to his Lord,
> > I bow my head upon my knees
> > > And dare not breathe the testing word;
> > For all my sins in judgment rise;
> > > And conscience wails a bitter cry;
> > And shame and tears conceal mine eyes:
> > > "Lord, save Thou help me, it is I!"

The first period of the ministry of St. Matthias was spent in Judæa, which is said by some to have fallen to him as his province at the division of the world made by the Apostles after the descent of the Holy Spirit. Thence he is affirmed to have passed into Macedonia; whilst Sophronius relates that he traversed a considerable part of the outlying districts of (the Asian) Æthiopia. In all his labours he was distinguished for his zeal, activity, courage, and success. Concerning the death of St. Matthias, many conflicting opinions have found currency; and the theory that he died a natural and peaceful death has not altogether wanted for supporters. Julius Africanus, who identifies the Apostle with a certain Abdias, or Obadiah, records that he was beheaded at Naddarer, a large city of Æthiopia; but he cites as a prelude to this martyrdom, so grotesque an exercise of miraculous power in a presumed contest with the magicians Zaroe and Arphaxad, as lays his narrative open to the suspicion of having been a later invention. And Nicephorus, varying his narrative from that of Julius, yet invalidates his statements by bringing forward such particulars as are contradictory to accounts which are more worthily received, and more conclusively authenticated. Again, St. Matthias is said to have been seized in Galilee, about A.D. 62, whilst on his way to Jerusalem, and to have been carried before Ananias, the High Priest, who had, some time previously, ordered the execution of St. James the Just, and who now caused St. Matthias to be beheaded with a battleaxe. Still another version, given in the Greek *menæa*, and corroborated by several ancient Breviaries, assigns Cappadocia as the country of his martyrdom, the mode of which is further said to have been crucifixion; so that, as Judas was hanged upon a tree, his more faithful successor resembled our Lord in the instrument and manner of his passion. The day of the death of St. Matthias is with more unanimity stated to have been the 24th of February; and it is frequently stated that his body, having been kept a long time at Jerusalem, was translated to Rome by Helena, the mother of the Emperor Constantine the Great, and by her placed in a tomb of porphyry, and deposited in the Church of Santa Maria Maggiore, where the head of the Apostle is still exhibited, in defiance of a rival claim set up in behalf of Treves for the possession of his relics.

A festival, one of whose leading ideas is the casting down of one Apostle, and the setting up of another to a bishopric in that world-wide province of which Christ is Metropolitan, offers a very fitting occasion for a consideration of the qualities requisite in those to whom is "given the ministry of reconciliation." The following poem from the "Christian Year" is suggested by the text, Acts i. 21, 22 :—

> Who is God's chosen priest?
> He who on Christ stands waiting day and night,
> Who traced His holy steps, nor ever ceased,
>   From Jordan banks to Bethphage height :
>
> Who hath learned lowliness
> From his Lord's cradle, patience from His Cross ;
> Whom poor men's eyes and hearts consent to bless ;
>   To whom, for Christ, the world is loss ;

Who both in agony
Hath seen Him, and in glory ; and in both
Owned Him divine, and yielded, nothing loth,
Body and soul, to live and die,

In witness of his Lord,
In humble following of his Saviour dear:
This is the man to wield the unearthly sword,
Warring unharmed with sin and fear.

But who can e'er suffice—
What mortal—for this more than angels' task,
Winning or losing souls, Thy life-blood's price?
The gift were too divine to ask,

But Thou hast made it sure
By Thy dear promise to Thy Church and Bride,
That Thou, on earth, wouldst aye with her endure,
Till earth to Heaven be purified.

Thou art her only spouse,
Whose arm supports her, on Whose faithful breast
Her persecuted head she meekly bows,
Sure pledge of her eternal rest.

Thou, her unerring guide,
Staying her fainting steps along the wild ;
Thy mark is on the bowers of lust and pride,
That she may pass them undefiled.

Who, then, uncalled by Thee,
Dare touch Thy spouse, Thy very self below?
Or who dare count him summoned worthily,
Except Thine hand and seal he show?

Where can Thy seal be found?
But on the chosen seed, from age to age,
By Thine anointed heralds duly crowned,
As kings and priests, Thy war to wage?

Then fearless walk we forth,
Yet full of trembling, Messengers of God :
Our warrant sure, but doubting of our worth,
By our own shame alike and glory awed.

Dread Searcher of the hearts,
Thou who didst seal by Thy descending Dove
Thy servants' choice, O help us in our parts,
Else helpless found, to learn and teach Thy love.

The Annunciation of The Blessed Virgin Mary.

MARCH 25.

IF the various theories which have been held concerning the origin of this Festival were equally trustworthy, it might be credibly authenticated that it was instituted in every century from the third to the seventh, both inclusive. Benedict XIV., willing to believe in the genuineness of a *Homily* attributed to Gregory Thaumaturgus, and professing to have been written in the third century, claims for a Feast so ancient the prestige of Apostolic tradition.* Hospinian, in like manner, accepting the genuineness of a *Homily* ascribed to Athanasius, favours the opinion that this Festival was already in existence in the year 340.† Of both these *Homilies*, L'Estrange roundly says that "in regard they are both impostures, the youngest being A.D. 600, he will not urge them." Cardinal Baronius, in his *Notes* to the *Roman Martyrology*, points out an anachronism which forbids him to refer the latter of the two *Homilies* to Athanasius; for the author of that *Homily* disputes

---

* *De Festis Beatæ Mariæ Virginis.*
† *De Origine Festorum Christianorum: De Annunciationis B. Mariæ Festo.*

against Nestorius, who lived a long time after Athanasius. The *Homily*, therefore, is more colourably ascribed to St. Cyril, who about the year 430, wrote in refutation of Nestorianism; or, again, to "Maximus, or some other, after the time that the Monothelite heresy appeared in the world, which was in the seventh century."* The author of the *Homily*, whoever he may have been, calls the Feast of the Annunciation the primary one, and very venerable; but expressly affirms—and this is a significant fact when speculating upon the probable origin of the Feast—that it was established as one of the festivals of our Lord, and not of the Virgin. Taking this as true, the possibility of the existence of the Annunciation as a *Festum Dominicum* in the fourth century, is not destroyed by that decree—the fifty-first—of the Council of Laodicea,† which ordained that "the Quadragesimal Feast should not be interrupted by the commemorations of Martyrs and Saints; and that, if these fell to be observed in Lent, they should be confined to the Sabbaths and Lord's-Days." By such a decree, a *Festum Dominicum* would not be affected; and there is no proof that the Feast of the Annunciation did not even then exist in that character. If, on the other hand, it be maintained that it was from the beginning a Feast of the Virgin, then it follows that it must have been introduced at some time in the long interval between the Council of Laodicea and the Council in Trullo, A.D. 692, which in its fifty-second canon, whilst renewing the aforesaid prohibition of Laodicea, does so with this difference, that it " ordains the celebration, all through Lent, of the mass of the presanctified, except on Saturdays, Sundays, and the day of the Annunciation."

* Bingham's *Antiquities of the Christian Church*.
† The date of this Council is disputed, and each of several years have been assigned to it from A.D. 314 to 399. In the *Sacrosancta Concilia* of Labbeus, it is put down, without question or alternative, for the year 320.

This decree shows, says Bingham, "that by this time it had become a noted festival; and, therefore, we may date its original from the seventh century." * But such a conclusion hardly savours of Bingham's accustomed sagacity: "for the Council in Trullo," as Benedict XIV. points out, "speaks not of the institution of a festival; but presumes it to be flourishing, and to have been instituted long before."†

Thomassin and L'Estrange go even beyond Bingham, inasmuch as they deny the existence of any trustworthy document about the Feast in question before the Council in Trullo, from which Bingham dates it. Mr. Riddle's account is more in the direction of both ingenuity and generosity. "Augusti," he says, "thinks that this festival may have been observed in the time of the Council of Laodicea, only that it was observed as one of those which related to our Blessed Lord, and not as a Saint's Day. It is, indeed, expressly called one of our Lord's Festivals in the *Homily* ascribed to Athanasius. It is probable that, after the fifth century, when the respect paid to the Virgin Mary greatly increased in consequence of what passed during the Nestorian controversies, this festival was expressly referred to the honour of that Saint, and its observance was fixed to the 25th of March. This arrangement was not adopted at first by the Spanish and Oriental churches, but afterwards it became universal. If these views be correct, the history of the establishment of this festival is simply as follows:—In early times it was celebrated as one of the Lord's festivals (ἑορτὴ δεσποτική)—in the fifth century it gradually assumed the character of a Saint's Day—and in the course of the sixth century it was universally observed under that character."‡ For the antiquity of this feast it is further claimed that it is mentioned in the *Sacramentary* of Pope

* *Antiquities of the Christian Church.*
† *De Festis Beatæ Mariæ Virginis.*
‡ Riddle's *Manual of Christian Antiquities.*

Gelasius the First (492-496); and that Sergius the First (687-701) is recorded by Platina to have "appointed Litanies to be chanted yearly through the city on the day of Simeon and the Annunciation of the Virgin Mother."* It may be mentioned that the Spanish Church, scandalized at the occurrence of a festival in Lent, and at the want of uniformity in several of the Spanish provinces, decreed, at the Council of Toledo, A.D. 656, "that the Feast of the Annunciation of the Blessed Virgin should be fixed to the eighteenth of December, eight days before the Nativity of our Lord."

Amongst the ancients the day was variously designated. It was the *Day of Salutation;* the *Day of the Gospel;* the *Day of the Conception of Christ,* and of the *Annunciation of Christ;* the *Annunciation of the Angel to St. Mary;* and the *Festival of the Incarnation.* And it was in Rome, France, and England the first day of the ecclesiastical year; as it is now, under its vernacular name of Lady-Day, one of the quarterly divisions of the year.

We have no very precise or abundant information as to the mode in which the ancient Church celebrated the Feast of the Annunciation, which, perhaps, is the more remarkable from the fact that St. Bernard, speaking therein the mind of St. Chrysostom and other Fathers, entitles it *Radix omnium Festorum,* the *Root of all Festivals;* and Ivo Carnotensis, speaking of the Day, says that it "commemorates *exordium nostræ Reparationis,* the beginning of our Redemption."† There are, however, many Homilies extant which directly take this Day for a subject; and the Christian muse, from the time of John of Damascus and Cosmas of Jerusalem, has been almost continuously busy with its illustration. To the Christian artist its mystery and glory have never lost their attractiveness. In the old Greek pictures, and in the most ancient Western ones, both the Angel and

* *De vitis et gestis Summorum Pontificum.*
† Sermon *De Annuntiatione Beatæ Mariæ.*

the Virgin are depicted as standing; whilst in later representations the Angel genuflects before her, and she is either kneeling in prayer, or reading, with a large book open on a desk before her. From the mouth of Gabriel proceeds the Angelic salutation, *Ave Maria! Gratiâ Plena;* and he bears in his hand a sceptre, a palm, an olive branch, or a lily, as if about to offer, along with the salutation, the emblem of rule, of victory, of peace, or of purity. But it is the lily which is regarded as the peculiar emblem of the Annunciation, as symbolizing *her* innocence who must have been more than spotless before the event of the Day could have exhibited even the faintest approach to credibility. The consciousness in the mind of the Virgin of anything short of the purity of Heaven would have been a most just impediment to her becoming the Bride of Heaven. Without this, her heart dared not have whispered to itself, nor her lips have faltered to others, that she had been selected from all generations of women for so unique and supreme a token of the Divine favour and approbation.

The following, entitled "The Virgin," and forming one of Wordsworth's "Ecclesiastical Sonnets," is devoted to an exposition specially of the purity, with a glance at the honours generally, of the Mother of our Lord.

> Mother! whose virgin bosom was uncrost
> With the least shade of thought to sin allied;
> Woman! above all women glorified,
> Our tainted nature's solitary boast;
> Purer than foam on central ocean tost;
> Brighter than eastern skies at daybreak strewn
> With fancied roses, than the unblemished moon
> Before her wane begins on heaven's blue coast;
> Thy Image falls to earth. Yet some, I ween,
> Not unforgiven, the suppliant knee might bend,
> As to a visible Power, in which did blend
> All that was mixed and reconciled in Thee
> Of mother's love with maiden purity,
> Of high with low, celestial with terrene!

The particulars of the Annunciation are given in the first chapter of St. Luke's Gospel; but the narrative, which mentions Nazareth as the place, and points, at least, according to ecclesiastical inference, to the twenty-fifth of March as the day, leaves the exact moment undecided; on which account, as Pope Benedict XIV. mentions, "the Church desired the faithful, at three different hours of the day, to recall this holy mystery; and ordained that at dawn, at mid-day, and at eventide, the bells should sound to admonish Christians to its due celebration."* Another minor question, which the Evangelist leaves an open one, has respect to the age of the Virgin at the time of the Annunciation. Cardinal Cajetan arrives at the conclusion that she was twenty-seven, or twenty-four, or at least twenty-two years of age; whilst Catharinus contends that she was not more than fourteen or fifteen.

The Doctrine of the Day, so far, at least, as it is conversant about the Infant then announced and conceived, is substantially the same with the doctrine of the Nativity, of which it was the necessary antecedent. The Annunciation was, in fact, the inception, the first stage, of the Incarnation; and its design was "to give a Saviour to the world, a Victim of propitiation to the sinner, a Model to the just, a Son to the Virgin remaining still a Virgin, and a new Nature to the Son of God, the Nature of man, capable of suffering pain and anguish in order to the satisfaction of God's justice for our transgression."† It was the Day on which the prophecy was fulfilled:—"Behold, a Virgin shall conceive" a Son, whose name at his birth should be Immanuel; it was the Day on which "the Word of God was for ever united to humanity;"‡ the Day whereon "the womb of the Virgin became the gate of heaven, by which God descended to men, that He might afford an

* *De Festo Sanctissimæ Annuntiationis Beatæ Mariæ.*
† Alban Butler's *Lives of the Saints.*
‡   Ditto.   Ditto.

access to heaven for them."* It was the Day on which were fulfilled, or made immediately possible of fulfilment, those promises that had been the stay of prophets and kings through a long succession of tearful, prayerful, expectant ages.

To a devout mind like that of the Virgin, well-instructed in the fondest—yet, for each individual, the most shadowy—hopes of her countrywomen, the vision called up by the announcement that it was She, She, who had been chosen as the vehicle of the fulfilment of all the Messianic prophecies, would come upon her, not gradually, as these had been delivered, but suddenly, cumulatively, overwhelmingly. It was not a panorama which stretched before her, at one end of which glimmered the Morning Star, whilst at the other, through a long interval of chequered and fitful yet ever-increasing light, blazed the Sun of Noon; but it was one abrupt and transcendant scene of glory, in which she saw herself girt all at once and on all sides with an Infinite and a Divine Effulgence. Blessed, indeed, was the humility that could dictate even to her ecstasy, the pious response to the Angelic message:—" Behold the handmaid of the Lord!" All the isolated Messianic prophecies which, from Eden downwards, had trickled or meandered along their lonely courses, had been merged as mere affluents in that full rolling tide of Evangelical prediction which had been discovered by Isaiah; much of whose wondrous imagery our own Pope has grouped together in his well-known "Sacred Eclogue," entitled "Messiah," and first published in the *Spectator* for May 4th, 1712. This poem, it may be remarked in passing, was professedly written in imitation of Virgil's "Pollio," which itself was almost certainly an adaptation from the inspired bard whose lips had been touched with a live coal from off the altar of God.

* Ivo Carnotensis: *De Annuntiatione Beatæ Mariæ.*

POPE'S "MESSIAH."

Ye Nymphs of Solyma! begin the song;
To heavenly themes sublimer strains belong.
The mossy fountains and the sylvan shades,
The dreams of Pindus and the Aonian maids,
Delight no more—O Thou my voice inspire,
Who touched Isaiah's hallowed lips with fire!

Rapt into future times, the Bard began:—
A Virgin shall conceive, a Virgin bear a Son!
From Jesse's root behold a Branch arise,
Whose sacred Flower with fragrance fills the skies:
The Æthereal Spirit o'er its leaves shall move,
And on its top descends the mystic Dove.
Ye Heavens! from high the dewy nectar pour,
And in soft silence shed the kindly shower!
The sick and weak the healing Plant shall aid,
From storms a Shelter, and from heat a Shade.
All crimes shall cease, and ancient fraud shall fail;
Returning Justice lift aloft her scale;
Peace o'er the world her olive wand extend;
And white-robed Innocence from Heaven descend.
Swift fly the years, and rise the expected Morn!
Oh, spring to light, auspicious Babe, be born!
See, Nature hastes her earliest wreaths to bring,
With all the incense of the breathing Spring;
See lofty Lebanon his head advance:
See nodding forests on the mountains dance;
See spicy clouds from lowly Sharon rise,
And Carmel's flowery top perfumes the skies!
Hark! a glad voice the lonely desert cheers:
Prepare the way! a God! a God appears!
A God! a God! the vocal hills reply,
The rocks proclaim the approaching Deity.
Lo! earth receives Him from the bending skies!
Sink down, ye mountains; and ye valleys rise!
With heads declined, ye cedars, homage pay;
Be smooth, ye rocks; ye rapid floods, give way!
The SAVIOUR comes! by ancient bards foretold:
Hear Him, ye deaf; and all ye blind, behold!
He from thick films shall purge the visual ray,
And on the sightless eyeball pour the day.

'Tis He the obstructed paths of sound shall clear,
And bid new music charm the unfolding ear;
The dumb shall sing; the lame his crutch forego,
And leap exulting like the bounding roe.
No sigh, no murmur, the wide world shall hear;
From every face He wipes off every tear.
In adamantine chains shall Death be bound;
And Hell's grim Tyrant feel the eternal wound.
As the good Shepherd tends his fleecy care,
Seeks freshest pastures and the purest air;
Explores the lost, the wandering sheep directs,
By day o'ersees them, and by night protects;
The tender lambs he raises in His arms,
Feeds from his hand, and in his bosom warms:
Mankind shall thus His guardian care engage,
The promised Father of the future age.
No more shall nation against nation rise,
Nor ardent warriors meet with hateful eyes,
Nor fields with gleaming steel be covered o'er,
The brazen trumpets kindle rage no more;
But useless lances into scythes shall bend,
And the broad falchion in a ploughshare end.
Then palaces shall rise; the joyful son
Shall finish what his short-lived sire begun;
Their vines a shadow to their race shall yield,
And the same hand that sowed shall reap the field.
The swain in barren deserts with surprise
Sees lilies spring, and sudden verdure rise;
And starts amidst the thirsty wilds to hear
New falls of water murmuring in his ear.
On rifted rocks, the dragon's late abodes,
The green reed trembles, and the bulrush nods.
Waste sandy valleys, once perplexed with thorn,
The spiry fir and shapely box adorn:
To leafless shrubs the flowering palm succeed,
And odourous myrtle to the noisome weed.
The lambs with wolves shall graze the verdant mead,
And boys in flowery bands the tiger lead;
The steer and lion at one crib shall meet,
And harmless serpents lick the pilgrim's feet.
The smiling infant in his hand shall take
The crested basilisk and speckled snake;
Pleased, the green lustre of the scales survey,

And with their forky tongue and pointless sting shall play.
Rise, crowned with light, imperial Salem, rise!
Exalt thy towery head, and lift thy eyes!
See a long race thy spacious courts adorn!
See future sons and daughters yet unborn
In crowding ranks on every side arise,
Demanding life, impatient for the skies!
See barbarous nations at thy gates attend,
Walk in thy light, and in thy temple bend;
See thy bright altars thronged with prostrate kings,
And heaped with products of Sabæan springs!
For thee Idume's spicy forests blow,
And seeds of gold in Ophir's mountains glow.
See Heaven its sparkling portals wide display,
And break upon thee in a flood of day!
No more the rising sun shall gild the morn,
Nor evening Cynthia fill her silver horn;
But lost, dissolved in thy superior rays,
One tide of glory, one unclouded blaze,
O'erflow thy courts: the LIGHT HIMSELF shall shine
Revealed, and God's eternal day be thine;
The seas shall waste, the skies in smoke decay,
Rocks fall to dust, and mountains melt away;
But fixed His word, His saving power remains;
Thy realm for ever lasts, thy own Messiah reigns!

It would be difficult indeed to exhaust the admiring and affectionate epithets and sentiments which poets and others have lavished on the Feast of the Annunciation. The Day is the commemoration of the grandest embassy of the Universe; an embassy sent by the King of kings, not to kings or potentates, but to a poor and simple Virgin. The Ambassador is not an envoy sent at random; but one of the chief princes of the court of Heaven. To-day the Spirit which brooded over chaos, broods over the Virgin; to-day a star prepares to bring forth the Sun. To-day Heaven greets the earth, an Angel salutes a Maid; and to-day Infinity shelters in her womb. To-day the divine praises are celebrated by the angelic choirs; and to-day the whole world rejoices by reason of the exceeding joy at the coming of Christ through the overshadowing of the Spirit.

When we see of what unprecedented and unexampled incentives to pride the blessed Virgin was the object—when we turn our eyes to the giddy pinnacle of her elevation above all other mortals, the half-celestial level on which she comported herself with such quiet grace and dignified propriety—when we regard these things, we at once comprehend how it should be that the humility of the Maid-Mother has always been reckoned, if not her most illustrious, at least as her most exemplary, because her most difficult, virtue. Humility, indeed, was the typical virtue which we saw suggested by her conduct at the Purification, when it was displayed in association with such a reverence for Law as shrank from availing itself of a just and reasonable exemption. To-day, on the Feast of the Annunciation, we see the same humility in alliance with an entire deference and submission to the will of Heaven. Already she is a partaker of the mind of Jesus. The spirit of Christ in the depths of His singular agony is the spirit of Mary at the summit of her singular blessedness. "Not my will, but Thine, be done!" is the analogue of "Behold the handmaid of the Lord; be it unto me according to Thy word!"

The poetry of submission, that is, of a baptized stoicism, which takes for its motto, "Thy will be done!" is, as is natural in a world of crosses and sufferings, of very plentiful occurrence, and of very popular appreciation. There is no one to whose heart and experience such poetry does not appeal; and the sentiments it fosters and enunciates are equally due to God, and expedient in man. Towards the Infinite and infinitely Powerful, the discerning feeble and finite can hold but one attitude. In transcribing a single representative of this kind of poetry it is our wish to present excellence as thorough as possible, without risking the offence of offering verses whose over-popularity,

SUBMISSION OF THE WILL.

as it may have rendered them trite, would render their insertion an impertinence. Upon verses of the desired character we seem to have fallen in the following poem from Miss Winkworth's "Lyra Germanica," in which it has for its title, "The Annunciation;" for its motto, the final speech of St. Mary to the just-departing Gabriel; and for its object to exhibit the "happiness of the soul that has no will but God's." It must be conceded that its picture of resignation and acquiescence is so complete as to be worthy of that symbol with which it concludes, of an ocean of glass spreading out broadly, and without a ripple, under the azure peace of a faithfully reflected heaven. Its author was John Joseph Winkler, a native of Luckau, in Saxony, where he was born, December 23rd, 1670. "Winkler was first pastor in Magdeburg, afterwards chaplain in the army, and accompanied the troops to Holland and Italy. Subsequently he returned to Magdeburg, where he became chief minister at the Cathedral, and member of the Consistory. He died there August 11th, 1722. He was an excellent man, of a deeply cultivated mind, and left ten very good hymns, contained in Freylinghausen's hymnbook." *

> Yes, my spirit fain would sink
> In Thy heart and hands, my God,
> Waiting till Thou shew the end
> Of the ways that Thou hast trod;
> Stripped of self, how calm her rest
> On her loving Father's breast!
>
> And my soul repineth not,
> Well content whate'er befall;
> Murmurs, wishes, of self-will,
> They are slain and vanquished all;
> Restless thoughts, that fret and crave,
> Slumber in her Saviour's grave.

* Rev. Theodore Kübler's *Historical Notes to the Lyra Germanica.*

And my soul is free from care,
　For her thoughts from all things cease
That can pierce like sharpest thorns,
　Wounding sore the inner peace.
He who made her careth well,
She but seeks in peace to dwell.

And my soul despaireth not,
　Loving God amid her woe;
Grief that wrings and breaks the heart,
　Only they who hate Him know;
They who love him still possess
Comfort in their worst distress.

And my soul complaineth not,
　For she knows not pain or fear,
Clinging to her God in faith,
　Trusting though He slay her hero.
'Tis when flesh and blood repine,
Sun of joy, Thou canst not shine.

Thus my soul before her God
　Lieth still, nor speaketh more,
Conqueror thus o'er pain and wrong,
　That once smote her to the core;
Like a silent ocean, bright
With her God's great praise and light.

St. Mark's Day.

April 25.

THREE persons bearing the name of Mark or Marcus are mentioned in Holy Scripture; and this circumstance has given rise to so much confusion, that it is necessary at once to difference the Evangelist from John, who was surnamed Mark, and Mark who was sister's son to Barnabas.

Throughout the New Testament there occurs only a single allusion to the Evangelist (1 St. Peter v. 13.); and that is of such a nature as to invite the inference that he was a convert of the Apostle Peter, of whom also he was probably the nephew, and certainly the companion, interpreter, and amanuensis. St. Mark is believed to have been born of Jewish parents, of the tribe of Levi, and the line of the priesthood. His Hebrew name has not been clearly ascertained; the one by which he is venerated throughout Christendom being one assumed, in accordance with a custom very prevalent amongst the Jews of his time, for the convenience of intercourse with the Latin-speaking Gentiles.

The time of the first institution of a festival in his honour cannot be precisely determined. In a MS. note to Wheatly's Introduction, Dr. Waterland has remarked that "St. Mark's festival is certainly as old as the ninth century. It appears not in the Calendar of Athelstan's *Psalter*; but is found (April 25) in the Calendar of C.C.C., Wanl., p. 107, and in Ado, and in Bede's genuine Martyrology, p. 360. It is, therefore, as old as 730." [*] Earlier than this it cannot be traced; and on the whole, it may be concluded, that there was no observance of the day, in the Western Church, at least, before the end of the seventh century. And its absence from the legislative decrees of the earlier Councils is conspicious; the first enactment for the observance of a day in commemoration of the Evangelist, being that found in the 21st Canon of the Council of Cognac (A.D. 1254), which enjoins its celebration "*cum omni reverentia et honore.*" Brady arbitrarily fixes the institution of the festival to the year 1090. [†]

What the festival of St. Mark seems to lack in the way of antiquity, may be thought to be compensated by the universality of its observance. The Latin, Greek, and Coptic Churches are at one in their reverence for it; and there is little or no divergence from the uniformity as to the day of its celebration; with the exception of a local one, at Alexandria, where it was observed on the 23rd of September.

Alternative reasons are offered for the general celebration of the festival of St. Mark on the 25th of April; one of which is to the effect that on this day the Evangelist attained the crown of martyrdom, at Alexandria, and the other, that on this day the translation of his relics from Alexandria to Venice was completed—the date of the translation itself being doubtfully claimed for the fifth century and the ninth.

The circumstances which led to the composition of the Gospel of St. Mark are collected by Eusebius from Clement of Alexandria and other ancient writers to the effect, that, when Peter was teaching at Rome, his hearers were so

---

[*] Riddle's *Manual of Christian Antiquities.*
[†] *Clavis Calendaria.*

interested in the discourses he delivered, that they begged of Mark, the companion of the Apostle, to reduce to writing the doctrines enunciated by the latter; and Mark, in accordance with their entreaties, compiled his Gospel. The Gospel so written, having been seen by St. Peter, was, with commendations of the hearers to whose devotion it had been indebted for its existence, confirmed by the Apostle, and ordered to be read publicly in their religious assemblies.* It is for this reason that Tertullian calls the Gospel according to St. Mark, the " Gospel of St. Peter;" and that St. Athanasius says of it, that "the Gospel of Mark was dictated by Peter, although published by Mark." To give consistency and completeness to the theory of the Gospel of St. Mark having been compiled under the circumstances just mentioned, it was natural and almost necessary to hold that it first appeared in the vernacular of the people to whom it was primarily addressed. Accordingly some have maintained that the Gospel of St. Mark was originally written in Latin; an opinion to which it may be said, however, that several distinguished authorities are adverse. The dutiful impartiality of Mark, and the fine candour of Peter, appear in this—that the Gospel named after the former, and dictated by the latter, relates with no less particularity and aggravation of detail than any of the others, the facts of Peter's shameful fall and apostasy.

The Epistle for St. Mark's Day is taken from the fourth chapter of St. Paul's Epistle to the Ephesians, which sets forth the unity of the Spirit, and the diversity of the gifts and graces bestowed by Christ upon His Church. The special text of the following hymn by Dr. Doddridge is the eleventh verse of the same chapter:—
"He gave some, apostles; and some, prophets; and some, evangelists; and some, pastors and teachers."

* Eusebius: *Ecclesiastical History;* lib. ii., c. 16; iii., c. 39; &c., and St. Jerome: *De Viris Illustribus.*

Father of mercies, in Thy house,
Smile on our homage and our vows;
While with a grateful heart we share
These pledges of our Saviour's care.

The Saviour, when to heaven He rose,
In splendid triumph o'er His foes,
Scattered His gifts on men below;
And wide His royal bounties flow.

Hence sprang the Apostles' honoured name,
Sacred beyond heroic fame:
Hence dictates the prophetic sage,
And hence the Evangelic page.

In lowlier forms, to bless our eyes,
Pastors from hence, and teachers rise;
Who, though with feebler rays they shine,
Still guide a long extended line.

From Christ their varied gifts derive,
And, fed by Christ, their graces live:
While, guarded by His potent hand,
'Midst all the rage of hell they stand.

So shall the bright succession run,
Through the last courses of the sun;
While unborn churches, by their care,
Shall rise and flourish, large and fair.

Jesus, our Lord, their hearts shall know,
The spring whence all these blessings flow;
Pastors and people shout His praise
Through the long round of endless days.

Touching the later activities of St. Mark, it is related that he became the first Bishop of Aquileia, in the Venetian territory; and that afterwards he proceeded to Alexandria, where—with the intermission of a successful tour of about two years' duration, in the direction of Libya—he mainly fixed his residence, founding a noble church, in the oversight and direction of which he was as discreet as he was unwearied, and where his honourable and useful career was finally terminated by his martyrdom, about A.D. 68. St. Mark suffered at the season of " Easter, at the time the solemnities of Serapis happened to be celebrated. The people being excited to vindication of the honour of their idol, broke in upon St. Mark, while he was employed in divine worship; and binding his feet with cords, dragged him through the streets, and thrust him into prison, where in the night he had the comfort of a divine vision. Next day the enraged people renewed the tragedy, and used him in the same manner, till his flesh being raked off, and his blood run out, his spirits failed, and he expired. Some add, that they burnt his body, and that the Christians decently entombed his bones and ashes, near the place where he used to preach. But all this account is given by authors whose credit we cannot depend upon, and therefore must be received with grains of allowance." * It is a commonly received opinion that the body of St. Mark was removed with great pomp from Alexandria to Venice about A.D. 800, where it is yet reverenced and exhibited in the stately church erected in his memory. His festival is observed by the people of Venice, of which city he is the patron saint, with uncommon solemnity; and to this day, as often as his Gospel is read in St. Mark's Church, the priest points his finger towards the body of the Evangelist with the prefatory words *Evangelium secundum hunc.*

The lines which follow are the translation of a Hymn from the Paris Breviary:—*Vos succensa Deo splendida Lumina.* They are from the pen of Dr. Isaac Williams, and stand, in *Lyra Apostolica*, at the head of a series of poems which have the general title of *Commune Doctorum*. We venture somewhat to narrow their application to the Evangelists, the Doctors of the Doctors, the teachers upon

* Nelson's *Festivals and Fasts.*

whom all succeeding doctrine, if it would stand securely
must be based; and narrowing their application still further, we quote them in connection with that Evangelist
who is so far typical that his festival falls first of them all,
in the secular year, to be observed.

>Hail, glorious Lights, kindled at God's own urn,
>Salt of the nations—whence the soul imbue
>Savours of God-head, virtues pure and true,
>So that all die not—whence serenely burn
>In their bright orbs sure Truth and Virtue bold,
>Putting on virgin honours undefiled:
>Bounteous by you the World's Deliverer mild
>Of treasured wisdom deals His stores untold.
>Hail! channels where the living waters flow,
>Whence the Redeemer's field shows fair, and glow
>The golden harvests: ye from realms above
>Bring meat for manly hearts, and milk for babes in love.
>
>These bear, great God, Thy sword and shield,
>These rear the eternal Palace Hall,
>Skilled with one hand Thine arms to wield,
> With one to build Thy Wall.
>Ye in your bright celestial panoply
> O'ercame dark Heresy;
>And when her brood from Stygian night
> Renew the fight,
>We too may grasp your arrows bright;
>Even till this hour we combat in your mail,
>And with no doubtful end—we combat and prevail.
>
>Hail! heavenly truth, guiding the pen
> Of wise and holy men;
>To thee, though thou be voiceless, doth belong
> A spirit's tongue,
>Which in the heart's deep home uttereth a song.

At the conclusion of a notice of St. Mark, it may not be
out of place to devote a few sentences to an investigation of
the artistic and symbolical history of the Four Evangelists.
This investigation we are able to make by deputy of a
writer in the *Kalendar of the English Church*, in which its

results appear in the following lucid and compendious form:—"The earliest type under which the Four Evangelists are figured is an emblem of the simplest kind: four scrolls placed in the four angles of a Greek cross, or four books (the Holy Gospels), represented allegorically those who wrote or promulgated them. The second type chosen was the four rivers of Paradise, Gihon, Tigris, Euphrates, and Pison; the river that was parted and became into four heads, being explained of Christ, the various acts of whose life on earth are divided between the Four Evangelists. Representations of this kind, in which the Saviour figured as a Lamb holding the Cross, or in His human form with a Lamb near Him, stands on an eminence, from which gush four rivers or fountains, are to be met with in the catacombs, on ancient sarcophagi preserved among the Christian relics in the Vatican, and in several old churches constructed between the second and the fifth century. At what period the four mysterious creatures in the vision of Ezekiel were first adopted as significant symbols of the Four Evangelists, does not seem clear. The Jewish doctors interpreted them as figuring the Four Archangels, SS. Michael, Gabriel, Raphael, and Uriel, and afterwards applied them as emblems of the four great Prophets, Isaiah, Jeremiah, Ezekiel, and Daniel.

"The general application of the Four Creatures to the Four Evangelists is of much earlier date than the separate and individual application of each symbol, which has varied at different times: that propounded by S. Jerome, in his commentary on Ezekiel, has since his time prevailed universally. Thus then (1), to S. Matthew was given the *Angelic*, or *Human* semblance, because he begins his Gospel with the human generation of Christ; or, according to others, because in his Gospel the Human Nature of the Saviour is more insisted on than the Divine. In the most ancient mosaics, the type is *human*, not angelic, for the head is that of a man with a beard. (2) S. Mark has the

Lion because he has set forth the royal dignity of Christ; or, according to others, because he begins with the mission of S. John Baptist, 'the voice of one crying in the wilderness,' which is figured by the Lion; or, according to a third interpretation, the Lion was allotted to S. Mark because there was, in the middle ages, a popular belief that the young of the lion was born dead, and after three days was awakened to vitality by the breath of its sire; some authors, however, represent the lion vivifying his young not by his breath but by his roar. In either case the application is the same; the revival of the young lion was considered as symbolical of the Resurrection, and S. Mark was commonly called the 'Historian of the Resurrection.' Another commentator observes that S. Mark begins his Gospel with 'roaring;' 'the voice of one crying in the Wilderness;' and ends it fearfully with a curse, 'He that believeth not shall be damned;' and that, therefore, his appropriate attribute is the most terrible of beasts, the lion. (3) S. Luke has the *Ox* because he has dwelt on the priesthood of Christ, the ox being the emblem of sacrifice. (4) S. John has the *Eagle*, which is the symbol of the highest inspiration, because he soared upwards to the contemplation of the Divine Nature of the Saviour. The *order*, however, in which, in ecclesiastical art, the symbols are placed, is not the same as the order of the Gospel according to the Canon. Rupertus considers the Four Beasts as typical of the Incarnation, the Passion, the Resurrection, and the Ascension; an idea previously dwelt upon by Durandus, who adds, that the Man and the Lion are placed on the right, because the Incarnation and the Resurrection are the joy of the whole earth; whilst the Ox is on the left, because Christ's Sacrifice was a trouble to the Apostles; and the Eagle is above the Ox, as suggestive of our Lord's upward flight into Heaven. According to others, the proper order in the ascending scale is this:

at the lowest point on the left, the Ox; to the right, the Lion; above the Ox, the Eagle; and above all, the Man.

"In Greek art the four emblems are united in one mysterious cherub-like form called a *Tetramorph*, its wings full of eyes, and its feet on winged wheels full of flame; and with the four heads of a Man, a Lion, an Ox, and an Eagle joined on to one body. This is evidently an attempt to realize the vision of Ezekiel. In early Western Art the heads alone of the Four Beasts are shown joined on to separate winged bodies, of vague form, and having arabesque-like terminations. Sometimes the plain natural animal alone is drawn winged, and holding or standing upon a book or scroll, and this form, varied according to the style of art in vogue, is the one most generally found in mediæval work. Sometimes these symbols have been combined with the human form, so that the Evangelists are themselves represented as men with the heads of a Lion, Ox, and Eagle. In later and modern art the Evangelists appear as men (though occasionally with wings, to show that they, like the holy angels, were the bringers of good tidings), and are attended by their respective symbols; S. Matthew's winged man now becomes an Angel, but the Lion and the Ox are often wingless. The symbols of the Evangelists sometimes applied to the Four Great Doctors of the Latin Church; and to Christ as Man, King, Priest, and God."

St. Philip and St. James's Day.

May 1.

IN the earlier ages of the Church the generality of the Apostles enjoyed only a *mass* commemoration, which was celebrated on the 1st of May, and called the Feast of all the Apostles. A festival in honour of All Martyrs and Saints obtained in the Eastern Church as early as the fourth century, and was celebrated on the octave of Pentecost, our Trinity Sunday. It was not, however, till about the year 731 that the Western Church—in which Boniface III. had already (A.D. 609) instituted a Feast of All Martyrs, whose day was the thirteenth of May—definitely substituted for its commemorations of All Martyrs and All Apostles the more comprehensive one of All Saints; which last feast was transferred (A.D. 834) by Gregory IV. from the month of May to the season of its modern celebration, the first day of November. With the allocation of a special day to each individual of the Apostolic College, the Feast of All Apostles had become unnecessary, and its name irrelevant; and the first of May being left free for the use of a more particular celebration, was, in the long run, adopted as the day on which to do honour to the memory of St. Philip and St. James. Of the reason for associating these two Apostles together in a joint Festival, there is no conclusive information; and "in the absence of more authentic history, we are compelled to adopt a story concerning the mingling of their relics at Rome as the probable foundation of the observance. It is said that when Christians began to collect and treasure up the relics of celebrated martyrs and saints (about the middle of the fourth century), the remains of Philip were conveyed from Hierapolis to Rome, and there placed in the same grave with those of St. James. Afterwards, in the sixth century, Pelagius, bishop of Rome, dedicated a church which he built to the two Apostles; and the combination, thus established, has continued ever since.

"It is impossible to say when the Festival of these Apostles was first instituted. If the foregoing history be true, such a festival may have been established in the sixth or seventh century. When the Feast of All the Apostles grew into disuse, it was ordered that the day on which it had been celebrated should be observed in honour of the two Apostles, St. Philip and St. James.

"We have no means of ascertaining whether this Festival was at first of a local or provincial character, or generally observed." *

The Greek Church provides for St. Philip and St. James a separate commemoration—for the former on the fourteenth of November, and for the latter on the ninth of October.

St. Philip was a native of Bethsaida, in Galilee; and it has been insisted upon as a peculiar privilege "that he had the honour of being first called to be a disciple of our blessed Saviour; because, though our Saviour, after His return from the wilderness, first met with St. Andrew and his brother Peter, and had some conversation with them, yet they immediately returned to their trade; and the next day, as He was passing through Galilee, He found Philip, whom He commanded to follow Him (John i. 43), the constant form He used in choosing His disciples. And it

* Riddle's *Manual of Christian Antiquities.*

was a whole year after that the other two were called to be disciples, when John was cast into prison." *

Philip's response to the call of our Lord was prompt and cordial. " He immediately engaged in His service although he had not seen any miracle. But it is reasonable to believe that he was acquainted with Moses and the prophets, and that he was awakened with the expectation then general among the Jews, that the Messias would immediately appear; besides, we are to suppose the Divine grace did particularly accompany the command of Christ, and dispose those that He called to believe him to be the Messias. The first effect of his faith was a forwardness of mind to direct others in the same way of happiness with himself; for he finds Nathanael, a person of note and eminency, and acquaints him with the welcome news of his discovery, that he had found Him of whom Moses and the prophets did write, the anointed of God, the Saviour of the world, and conducts him to Him. From which we are to learn readily to obey all the suggestions and offers of Divine grace, and to prepare our minds for the reception of supernatural truth. Zealously to propagate that Christian knowledge to others, which the good providence of God hath graciously bestowed upon us; which obligeth pastors in respect of their flock, parents of their children, masters of their servants, and all Christians in some degree in regard of one another, boldly to profess the truth when the providence of God calls us to give testimony to it." †

From such benevolent effort neither personal joy nor personal sorrow ought to bar us; rather it should be regarded as a relief to the one and a safeguard to the other. It is on such grounds that the following poem by Mr. Wilcox, an American poet, incites to " Christian Activity."

* Nelson's *Festivals and Fasts of the English Church.*
† Ditto   Ditto.

Wouldst thou from sorrow find a sweet relief?
Or is thy heart oppressed with woes untold?
Balm would'st thou gather for corroding grief?
Pour blessings round thee like a shower of gold?
'Tis when the rose is wrapt in many a fold
Close to its heart, the worm is wasting there
Its life and beauty; not when, all unrolled,
Leaf after leaf, its bosom rich and fair
Breathes freely its perfumes throughout the ambient air.

Wake, thou that sleepest in enchanted bowers,
Lest these lost years should haunt thee on the night
When death is waiting for thy numbered hours
To take their swift and everlasting flight;
Wake, ere the earth-born charm unnerve thee quite,
And be thy thoughts to work divine addrest;
Do something—do it soon—with all thy might;
An angel's wing would droop if long at rest,
And God Himself, inactive, were no longer blest.

Some high or humble enterprise of good
Contemplate, till it shall possess thy mind,
Become thy study, pastime, rest, and food,
And kindle in thy heart a flame refined.
Pray Heaven for firmness thy whole soul to bind
To this thy purpose—to begin, pursue,
With thoughts all fixed, and feelings purely kind;
Strength to complete, and with delight review,
And grace to give the praise where all is ever due.

Rouse to some work of high and holy love,
And thou an angel's happiness shalt know,
Shalt bless the earth, when in the world above,
The good begun by thee shall onward flow
In many a branching stream, and wider grow;
The seed that in these few and fleeting hours
Thy hands unsparing and unwearied sow,
Shall deck thy grave with amaranthine flowers,
And yield thee fruits divine in Heaven's immortal bowers.

The early part of a remarkable discourse of Christ, recorded by St. John, is interrupted by the dullness of faith and spiritual apprehension of two of the disciples. In answer to a question of Thomas, which the context shows to have been really the question of Philip also, "Jesus saith, I am the way, and the truth, and the life: no man cometh unto the Father, but by me" (John xiv. 6). The question of the disciples has ever been the question of an alienated humanity:— How shall the finite and the sinful approach the Infinite and the Holy? The devout piety of Bishop Hall, successively of Exeter and Norwich, in one of his "Anthems for the Cathedral of Exeter," points first the hopeless longing, and then the efficacy of revelation to turn despair into faith and hope and love.

> Lord, what am I? a worm, dust, vapour, nothing!
> What is my life? a dream, a daily dying!
> What is my flesh? my soul's uneasy clothing!
> What is my time? a minute ever flying:
>   My time, my flesh, my life, and I;
>   What are we, Lord, but vanity?
>
> Where am I, Lord? down in a vale of death:
> What is my trade? Sin, my dear God offending;
> My sport sin too, my stay a puff of breath:
> What end of sin? Hell's horror never ending:
>   My way, my trade, sport, stay, and place,
>   Help to make up my doleful case.
>
> Lord, what art Thou? pure life, power, beauty, bliss:
> Where dwell'st Thou? up above in perfect light:
> What is Thy time? eternity it is:
> What state? attendance of each glorious sprite:
>   Thyself, Thy place, Thy days, Thy state,
>   Pass all the thoughts of powers create.
>
> How shall I reach Thee, Lord? Oh, soar above,
> Ambitious soul: but which way should I fly?
> Thou, Lord, art Way and End: what wings have I?
> Aspiring thoughts of faith, of hope, of love:
>   Oh, let these wings, that way alone,
>   Present me to thy blissful throne!

St. Philip laboured many years in Upper Asia, and so successfully that he effected an almost *national* conversion of the Scythians; taking leave of whom, he at length visited Hierapolis, in Phrygia, a rich and prosperous city, but a stronghold of idolatry, where, amongst many objects of superstitious veneration, there was a huge dragon or serpent, to which extraordinary honours were paid. After St. Philip had caused the death or the demission of this monster, he took occasion to admonish the people on the evils attending so degraded a superstition; and his teaching was followed with so much success that the magistrates moved with envy of his influence, caused him to be thrown into prison and severely scourged. After this preliminary cruelty, he was led to execution, and, having been bound, he is variously said to have been hung up by the neck against a pillar; and to have been crucified, and then stoned whilst suffering the agonies of the cross. The authorities who favour crucifixion as the mode of St. Philip's death, however, are comparatively late ones; so that Hildebrand calls Isidore of Seville (570-636) "the first author of an assertion to the effect that Philip was crucified." The holy Apostle died in the act of exhorting the assembled brethren to hold fast the doctrine of the Lord Jesus, and to confirm the people in the same; and in prayer that the Lord would preserve His Church according to His promise. St. Philip migrated—to use one of those sweet flowers of speech with which the ancient Church wreathed the front of Christian death—in the eighty-seventh year of his age, and was buried at Hierapolis, by his sister Mariamne and St. Bartholomew his fellow-labourer; the latter of whom had endured a like scourging with St. Philip, and had already undergone the preliminary stages of a like execution, when the completion of his murder was stayed by an earthquake in which the people of Hierapolis seemed to hear the threats of Divine vengeance.

St. James the Less, surnamed "the Just," is called in Scripture the brother of our Lord; but upon grounds which the known practice of the Jews in reckoning relationship has left debateable. "But the ancient Fathers, especially of the Greek Church, make St. James and them that were styled brethren of our Lord, children of Joseph by a former wife; and then, as he was reputed and called our Saviour's father, so they might well be accounted and called His brethren."*

We have no particulars of St. James furnished to us during the time that he attended upon our Lord; until, after His Resurrection, a special manifestation of Himself was vouchsafed to him by his risen Master. St. Paul mentions this manifestation as one of the proofs of Christ's Resurrection:—"After that He was seen of James" (1 Cor. xv. 7); which simple assertion is considerably expanded in the *Evangelium Secundum Hebræos*, the Hebrew Gospel of the Nazarenes, which was much used by Origen, and of which St. Jerome made a Greek and a Latin translation. James, it is said, had made a vow, after partaking of the bread distributed by Christ at the Last Supper, "that he would eat no more until he had seen Jesus risen from the dead." Jesus, coming to him, had a table set and bread placed upon it, which bread he blessed and gave to James, with the words, "Eat thy bread now, my brother, since the Son of Man has risen from the dead." †

After the Ascension of our Lord, St James was elected Bishop of Jerusalem, the "Mother of all other Churches," over which he presided for thirty years, with such a character for sanctity and integrity that the Christians would press round him in order to touch the hem of his garment. Eusebius and St. Jerome follow Hegesippus and Epiphanius in describing St. James as a Nazarene, who drank no wine or strong drink, who ate no flesh, who neither shaved his beard, nor anointed himself with oil, nor used a bath. He was so abstemious that his body was pale

---

* Nelson's *Festivals and Fasts of the English Church*.
† St. Jerome: *De Viris Illustribus*.

with fasting; and so constant in prayer that his knees became as hard and brawny as the knees of camels.* George Herbert thus sings of "Prayer":—

> Prayer, the Church's banquet, Angel's age,
> God's breath in man returning to his birth,
> The soul in paraphrase, heart in pilgrimage,
> The Christian plummet sounding heaven and earth;
>
> Engine against the Almighty, sinner's tower,
> Reversed thunder, Christ-side-piercing spear,
> The six days' world transposing in an hour,
> A kind of tune, which all things hear and fear;
>
> Softness, and peace, and joy, and love, and bliss,
> Exalted Manna, gladness of the best,
> Heaven in ordinary, man well drest,
> The milky way, the bird of Paradise;
>
> Church-bells beyond the stars heard, the soul's blood,
> The land of spices, something understood.

But even the common reverence of both Jews and Christians could not suffice to ward off the attacks of malice from the estimable Apostle. The enemies of Christianity, with guileful and flattering words, caused him to be conveyed to a pinnacle of the Temple, in order that from thence, in the sight and hearing of the people then crowding Jerusalem upon the occasion of the Paschal Feast, he might speak in contravention of the claims of Jesus to be regarded as the Messiah. "Tell us," they said, "O Justus! whom we have every reason to believe, seeing that the people are thus generally led away with the doctrine of Jesus who was crucified, tell us what is this institution of the crucified Jesus!" To which the Apostle with a loud voice answered:—"Why do ye enquire concerning Jesus, the Son of Man?. Lo! he is now sitting in Heaven, at the right hand of the Majesty on high, and will come again in

---

* Eusebius: *Ecclesiastical History;* lib ii., c. 23; St. Jerome: *De Viris Illustribus.*

the clouds of Heaven!" At this, the populace responded with loud cries of "Hosanna to the Son of David!" The Scribes and Pharisees, enraged at a result so contrary to their calculations, exclaimed that James himself was seduced; and cast him headlong from the Temple. Falling bruised and mangled, but not slain, the Apostle presently struggled to his knees, and in that attitude prayed fervently for the forgiveness of his enemies, who all the while kept up a shower of stones upon his battered form. A Rechabite who stood by, and who is identified by Epiphanius as Simeon, the Apostle's kinsman and successor in his Episcopate, entreated the Jews to spare him. "The just man," he said, "prays for you; why, therefore, do ye slay him?" But they never the more restrained their cruelty, continuing to stone the Apostle until a fuller with his club mercifully despatched him by beating out his brains. According to Epiphanius, the martyrdom of St. James took place when he was in the ninety-sixth year of his age.*

The General Epistle of St. James is eminently practical, being devoted to an enforcement of all Christian virtues—of constancy, patience, purity, charity, and others. There is no real virtue which is not based upon that peculiar excellence of character which conferred upon St. James the title of "the Just"; and we would conclude our notice of this Apostle with a poetical tribute to the immortal savour of that virtue of virtues. James Shirley, the author of the lines we are about to quote, was known as "the last of a great race" of dramatists (1594-1666). He was a sometime clergyman in Hertfordshire, who, going over to the Church of Rome, became successively a schoolmaster at St. Alban's, and a dramatic author in London. The following short poem from "The Contention of Ajax and Ulysses for Achilles' Armour," published in 1659, carries its own recommendation; whilst the fact that it was a

* Eusebius: *Ecclesiastical History*, *lib* ii., c. 23; Epiphanius: *Adversus Octoginta Hæreses*; *Hæres*. 78.

great favourite with Charles II., may serve to vindicate the character of that somewhat frivolous monarch as not altogether unsusceptible of grave and serious reflection:—

> The glories of our birth and state
>   Are shadows, not substantial things;
> There is no armour against fate;
>   Death lays his icy hands on Kings;
>   Sceptre and crown
>   Must tumble down,
> And in the dust be equal made
> With the poor crookéd scythe and spade.
>
> Some men with swords may reap the field,
>   And plant fresh laurels where they kill;
> But their strong nerves at last must yield,
>   They tame but one another still.
>   Early or late,
>   They stoop to fate,
> And must give up their murmuring breath
> When they, pale captives, creep to death.
>
> The garlands wither on your brow,
>   Then boast no more your mighty deeds;
> Upon death's purple altar, now,
>   See where the victor victim bleeds;
>   All heads must come
>   To the cold tomb,
> Only the actions of the Just
> Smell sweet, and blossom in the dust.

St. Barnabas the Apostle.

June 11.

Hail! Princes of the host of heaven,
To whom by Christ, your chief, 'tis given
On twelve bright thrones to sit on high,
And judge the world with equity.

'Tis yours to cheer with sacred light
Those who lie sunk in sin's dark night;
To guide them in the upward path,
And rescue them from endless wrath.

With no vain arts, no earthly sword,
Ye quell the rebels of the Lord:
The cross, the cross which men despise,
'Tis that achieves your victories.

Through you the wondrous works of God
Are spread through every land abroad;
Thus every clime records your fame,
And distant ages praise your name.

And now to God, the Three in One,
Be highest praise and glory done,
Who calleth us from sin's dark night,
To walk in His eternal light.

Translation, by the Rev. J. Chandler.

THE ancestors of St. Barnabas, who were of the tribe of Levi, had emigrated to the Island of Cyprus, where, in common with other Jewish families, it is probable they had sought refuge from the acts of violence perpetrated in their native country of Judæa by the Syrians, Romans, or other Gentiles. The law which prohibited members of the tribe of Levi from holding landed property at home, was not considered binding upon them abroad; for we know that St. Barnabas was the proprietor of an estate which he magnanimously alienated for the benefit of the poorer Christians when a common fund was proposed by the Apostles to minister to their necessities (Acts iv. 36, 37). As the parents of St. Barnabas—or Joses, as he was then called—were in opulent circumstances, they sent their son for his education to Jerusalem, where he was trained under Gamaliel, a famous doctor of the law, and the teacher of St. Paul, with whom, whilst they were fellow-disciples of their illustrious master, St. Barnabas contracted a friendship which was renewed and continued in after years of co-operation in the cause of Christ.

St. Barnabas is believed to have been one of the seventy disciples (Luke x. 1)*; although the particular circumstances of his first adhesion to Christ have not been ascertained. It has been surmised, on the other hand, that he was one of the converts of the Day of Pentecost; and, in any case, his name appears immediately after that season as a member of the Church of Jerusalem, and he was already a Christian of some standing at the date of the conversion of St. Paul. The name bestowed upon him at his circumcision was Joses, a Hellenized form of the historic name of Joseph, which was changed, after a fashion common amongst the Apostles, to Barnabas, "which is," says St. Luke, "being interpreted, the Son of Consolation" (Acts iv. 36). By some who interpret the name of Barnabas as a Son of Prophecy, or a Son of Exhortation, it is believed that he acquired the designation on account of those prophetic gifts for which he was remarkable; whilst St. Chrysostom, who translates the word as Son of Consolation, as in our authorized version, discovers the reason

* Eusebius: *Ecclesiastical History*; lib. i. c. 12.

for such a designation in the fact of his mild and gentle disposition, which fitted him pre-eminently to minister to minds diseased and troubled, and in the fact of that ready charity which prompted him to take the lead in selling his estate for the comfort and consolaton of his Christian brethren.* The very slight literal difference between the two names has sometimes caused Barnabas to be identified with Barsabas, whose name also was Joseph—or Joses— and whose surname was Justus; and who was the competitor with St. Matthias for the vacant apostleship of Judas Iscariot (Acts i. 23). But against this confusion St. Chrysostom records a very precise and emphatic protest.†

When the disciples at Jerusalem, distrustful of the professions of Paul, "were all afraid of him, and believed not that he was a disciple," it was his friend Barnabas who introduced him to the Apostles, "and declared unto them how he had seen the Lord in the way, and that he had spoken to him, and how he had preached boldly at Damascus in the name of Jesus" (Acts ix. 26, 27).

The first public employment of Barnabas was on a mission of confirmation to the infant Church of Antioch, in which city he and Paul—whom he had fetched from Tarsus when he saw the importance and responsibility of the work—laboured together for a year in the establishment of that Church. "And the disciples were called Christians first at Antioch" (Acts xi. 26).

The particulars of the travels which Barnabas and Paul prosecuted together during a joint labour of fourteen years, are recorded in detail by St. Luke in the Acts of the Apostles, and are glanced at by St. Paul himself in his Epistle to the Galatians. As their co-operation had begun at Antioch, so there it determined. So sharp a dispute arose between them about the retention of Mark—the nephew of Barnabas—in their company on a projected tour

* St. Chrysostom: *In Acta Apostolorum; Hom.* xxi. ¶ 1.
† St. Chrysostom: *In Acta Apostolorum; Hom.* xi. ¶ 1.

of all the Churches they had founded or edified, that St. Paul, taking Silas with him, " went through Syria and Cilicia confirming the Churches;" whilst " Barnabas took Mark, and sailed unto Cyprus" (Acts xv. 39. 41).

What became of St. Barnabas after his separation from St. Paul is uncertain, for St. Luke does not follow him further than to his native island of Cyprus. Some writers affirm that he visited Italy, and preached the Gospel in Liguria, where he founded the ancient church of Milan; whilst others relate that he passed over into Egypt and consecrated his nephew St. Mark the first Bishop of the Christian Church at Alexandria. The second of these alternatives has the drawback of confounding Mark, "sister's son to Barnabas," with Mark the Evangelist; two persons who in all probability ought to be discriminated. The latter years of the life of St. Barnabas would seen to have been passed in Cyprus, where, according to traditions perpetuated by Alexander, a monk of that island, he employed himself in furthering the spread of the Gospel among the Jews. In the process of this good work he was finally called upon to embrace the fate of martyrdom; certain Jews having come over from Syria, who stirred up the people against him. Foreboding his own immediate death, St. Barnabas celebrated the Eucharist with the brethren, and bade them farewell; giving his nephew Mark the instructions necessary for his interment, and charging him with a dying message to the Apostle Paul. Having so done, he went into the synagogue at Salamis, and began, as was his custom, to preach Christ to the people. But the Jews at once laid hands on him, and shut him up in the synagogue till night, when, dragging him cruelly forth, they first stoned him to death, and then endeavoured to burn his mangled body. The corpse, however, is said to have resisted the action of the flames; and Mark secretly conveyed it to a distance of about five stadia from the city of Salamis, where he buried it in a cave; after which pious duty he immediately repaired to St. Paul at Ephesus, and when the Apostle left for Rome, accompanied him thither. The date of the martyrdom of St. Barnabas is uncertain; but it would seem to have occurred not later than A.D. 64. His relics are said to have been discovered in the reign of the Emperor Zeno, A.D. 485; by whom they were removed to Constantinople, and a stately church built over them, which had its dedication in honour of the Apostle. Upon the breast of the latter, as he lay in the cave near Salamis, had been discovered a copy of St. Matthew's Gospel, written in the Hebrew tongue, and, presumably, by the hand of Barnabas himself. A Catholic Epistle referred to St. Barnabas as its author, is full of instruction and edification, although it has never been admitted into the Canon of Scripture, and is classed by St. Jerome amongst the apocryphal writings.*

About the festival of St. Barnabas there is little information to be given. Mr. Riddle remarks that "it is rarely mentioned in old calendars; and many writers on heortology pass it over in silence. Hospinian dates the institution of this festival in the twelfth century; but it has been thought that it ought to be placed as high as the eighth, or higher.

"The eleventh of June has been appropriated to the commemoration of St. Barnabas in both the Latin and Greek Churches; but the reason of this appointment is not known. Perhaps the day may have been connected with some unknown tradition concerning the Apostle, or with some history relating to his relics." †

The comparatively late emergence of this festival may be partly accounted for by the fact that St. Barnabas was not one of the original Twelve; and in illustration of the fortunes of his day in our own Calendar, we would refer

---

* "*Inter Apocryphas Scripturas legitur.*" St. Jerome: *De Viris Illustribus.*

† Riddle's *Manual of Christian Antiquities.*

the reader to a note from Wheatly, which finds a place in the pages devoted in this volume to the Conversion of St. Paul.*

The call of St. Barnabas to the Apostolate—jointly with that of St. Paul—was an extraordinary one (Acts xiii. 2, 3, 4); and it is on this account we have thought it well to place at the head of this notice of St. Barnabas a hymn which is conceived in honour of the Apostles generally, or of the Apostolic office. It is a translation of an ancient hymn, *Cœlestis aulæ Principes*; and is taken from the Rev. J. Chandler's volume of translations of "Hymns of the Primitive Church."

In the "Christian Year" the poem for the festival of St. Barnabas is suggested by the passage in the Acts of the Apostles, wherein he is spoken of as "The Son of Consolation, a Levite" (Acts iv. 36).

> The world's a room of sickness, where each heart
>   Knows its own anguish and unrest;
> The truest wisdom there, and noblest art,
>   Is his, who skills of comfort best;
> Whom by the softest step and gentlest tone
>   Enfeebled spirits own,
>   And love to raise the languid eye,
> When, like an angel's wing, they feel him fleeting by :—
>
> *Feel* only—for in silence gently gliding
>   Fain would he shun both ear and sight,
> 'Twixt Prayer and watchful Love his heart dividing,
>   A nursing-father day and night.
> Such were the tender arms, where cradled lay,
>   In her sweet natal day,
>   The Church of Jesus; such the love
> He to his chosen taught for His dear widow'd Dove.
>
> Warm'd underneath the Comforter's safe wing
>   They spread the endearing warmth around:
> Mourners, speed here your broken hearts to bring,
>   Here healing dews and balms abound:

* See pages 324—326.

Here are soft hands that cannot bless in vain,
  By trial taught your pain:
  Here loving hearts, that daily know
The heavenly consolations they on you bestow.

Sweet thoughts are theirs, that breathe serenest calms,
  Of holy offerings timely paid,*
Of fire from Heaven to bless their votive alms
  And passions on God's altar laid.
The world to them is closed, and now they shine
    With rays of love divine,
  Through darkest nooks of this dull earth
Pouring, in showery times, their glow of " quiet mirth."

New hearts before their Saviour's feet to lay,
  This is their first, their dearest joy:
Their next, from heart to heart to clear the way†
  For mutual love without alloy:
Never so blest, as when in Jesu's roll
    They write some hero-soul,
  More pleased upon his brightening road
To wait, than if their own with all his radiance glow'd.

Oh happy Spirits, mark'd by God and man
  Their messages of love to bear,‡
What though long since in Heaven your brows began
  The genial amarant wreath to wear,
And in th' eternal leisure of calm love
    Ye banquet there above,
  Yet in your sympathetic heart
We and our earthly griefs may ask and hope a part.

Comfort's true sons! amid the thoughts of down
  That strew your pillow of repose,
Sure, 'tis one joy to muse, how ye unknown
  By sweet remembrance soothe our woes,

---

* Having land, sold it, and brought the money, and laid it at the Apostles' feet. Acts iv. 37.

† Barnabas took him, and brought him (Saul) to the Apostles. Acts xi. 27.

‡ Acts xi. 22 : xiii. 2.

And how the spark ye lit, of heavenly cheer,
  Lives in our embers here,
 Where'er the Cross is borne with smiles,
Or lightened secretly by Love's endearing wiles:

 Where'er one Levite in the temple keeps
  The watch-fire of his midnight prayer,
 Or issuing thence, the eyes of mourners steeps
  In heavenly balm, fresh gather'd there;
 Thus saints, that seem to die in earth's rude strife,
  Only win double life:
  They have but left our weary ways
To live in memory here, in Heaven by love and praise.

St. John Baptist's Day.

June 24.

ST. John the Baptist was an embodiment of the highest Jewish hopes of his time, an incarnate epitome of the purest national aspirations; and his ministry constituted the transition period between the Mosaic and Christian dispensations. The last and greatest of the Old Testament order of Prophets, one, indeed, who, as the Forerunner of the Messiah, was "much more than a prophet"; he was yet less than "the least in the kingdom of God" (Luke vii. 26-28). "He was behind Christianity, because he was yet prejudiced by his concep- ception of the Theocracy as external; because he did not clearly know that Messiah was to found His kingdom by *sufferings*, and not by miraculously triumphing over His foes; because he did not conceive that His kingdom was to show itself from the first, not in visible appearing, but as a Divine power, to develop itself spiritually from within outward, and thus gradually to overcome and take possession of the world. The least among those who understood the nature and process of development of the Divine Kingdom, in connection with Christ's redemption, is in this respect greater than the Baptist, who stood upon the dividing line of the two spiritual eras. But John was above the prophets (and Christ so declared) because he conceived of the Messiah and His kingdom in a higher and more spiritual sense than they had done, and because he directly pointed men to Christ, and recognised Him as the manifested Messiah."*

John the Baptist was not alone in his retirement into the desert for contemplative and didactic purposes; for many of his contemporaries, pious and earnest men among the Jews, disgusted with the corruptions of the times, retired, like the monks and hermits of Christianity at a later day, into wilderness places, and there, becoming teachers of Divine wisdom, collected disciples around them. The surpassing distinction of John above these preachers of righteousness was that he alone had been designated in Prophecy, and announced by the Angel Gabriel, as the Messenger to prepare the way before Him for whose deferred arrival the hearts of Israel were faint; and that he alone should have the honour of heralding the "Lamb of God, which taketh away the sin of the world" (John i. 29).

His appearance, training, and manner of life in the desert are sketched in the following lines from the late Rev. Robert Montgomery's " Messiah":—

> The great precursor, whose proclaiming voice,
> "Repent ye!" travelled on the desert wind,
> Was robed in hairy sackcloth; round his loins
> A leathern girdle wound; the mountain spring,
> That bubbled through the vale, his drink supplied;
> His meat was honey, and the locust wild.—
> Alone, but angel-watched, the orphan grew
> To manhood; nursed amid the elements,
> A son of Nature,—where the desert waved
> Her wildest bough, or flung her blackest gloom,
> The caverned eremite with God communed,
> In storm or stillness, when the thunder voiced
> His anger, or the sunshine brought His smile!
> One awful loneliness His life became,
> In thought and prayer mysteriously it passed;

---

* Neander's *Life of Jesus Christ*.

And oft sublime!—as when at sunset hour
A red magnificence of dying hues
Came o'er the desert, and each rocky cres
Of mountains with volcanic lustre blazed,
While slept the sultry air,—the prophet knelt;
And the wild glory of his dreaming eye
To heaven was turned, in meditative awe!
The hush of woods, the hymn of waters faint
  nd a blue prospect of the midland sea
Beyond the desert, glimmering and vast,
And dying cadence of some distant bird,
Whose song was fading like a silver cloud,—
While thus around Creation charmed, and looked,
Earth had no grander scene, than when the hour,
Of Syrian twilight heard the Baptist pray!

As the position of John the Baptist is unique amongst the Saints of the Old Dispensation; so his honours are unique amongst the Saints of the New. Whilst all the rest are commemorated on the day on which they "migrated to their Lord"—St. Paul excepted, the anniversary of whose Conversion, rather than that of his martyrdom, is observed—it is the actual Nativity of the Baptist which is singled out for special veneration, on account not only of his peculiar character, but of the significant events which preceded his birth, and of his consecration to the Divine service from the very womb. There was anciently another day, the 9th of August, set apart as the anniversary of his Beheading; which the Romish Church still celebrates by the title of *Festum Decollationis*, being a corruption, according to Durandus, of *Festum Collectionis Sancti Johannis Baptistæ*, the Feast of the Gathering-up of the Relics of St. John the Baptist.

The Martyrdom of the Baptist would not appear, however, to have been entirely omitted from consideration on the anniversary of his Nativity; and " Augusti conjectures that the *Festum Decollationis*, the feast of the Beheading, which occurs in the *Sacramentary* of Gregory the Great, was originally not distinct from that of the Nativity." * The words of Wheatly are to the same effect:—" Now," he says, " the Church celebrates both his Nativity and death on one and the same day; whereon, though his mysterious birth, is principally solemnized, yet the chief passages of his life and death are severally recorded in the portions of Scripture appointed for the day." †

The Festival of the Nativity of John the Baptist was of comparatively early introduction in the Church; and on the evidence of *Homilies* on the season by Maximus Taurinensis, St. Augustine, and Leo the Great, it may be concluded to have become thoroughly established by the year 400. It would appear to have been of customary celebration by the Egyptians so early as A.D. 424. In the fourth Canon of the Council of Agde (A.D. 506) its claims to a distinguished position amongst the commemorative days of Saints are recognised; and after this date it makes its constant appearance in the Calendars. The eighth Canon of the Council of Oxford (A.D. 1222), decrees the solemn celebration of "each of the feasts of St. John the Baptist." The vigil of St. John the Baptist, which the same Council of Oxford makes one of obligation, was formerly kept with great solemnity and circumstance; and its observance was often associated with various customs of Pagan origin, some of which met with a formal reprobation from Ecclesiastical Councils.

The career of John the Baptist is exclusively of Evangelical narration; for while Josephus paid a handsome tribute to his character and his mission, and even referred the misfortunes of Herod to the circumstance of his murder, he yet fails, owing to his Jewish prejudices and prepossessions, to see for himself, or to help others to discern, the spiritual significance of the Baptist's mission,

* Riddle's *Manual of Christian Antiquities.*
† *Rational Illustration of the Book of Common Prayer.*

and the place he occupies in the Divine order of successive dispensations.

The mission of the Baptist reached its highest fulfilment when he was called upon to administer the sacred rite to the Messiah; and in the following lines, published first in *Lyra Apostolica*, and, more recently, in a volume of *Verses on Various Occasions* (1869), Dr. Newman derives a practical lesson from the presumed feelings of John upon that occasion when he exclaimed, "I have need to be baptized of Thee, and comestThou to me?"

> How didst Thou start, Thou Holy Baptist, bid
>   To pour repentance on the Sinless Brow!
> Then all thy meekness, from thy hearers hid,
>   Beneath the Ascetic's port and preacher's fire,
> Flowed forth, and with a pang thou didst desire
>   He might be chief, not thou.
>
> And so on us at whiles it falls, to claim
>   Powers that we dread, or dare some forward part;
> Nor must we shrink as cravens from the blame
>   Of pride, in common eyes, or purpose deep;
> But with pure thoughts look up to God, and keep
>   Our secret in our heart.

It is related that after the Beheading of John the Baptist, his disciples took his body and buried it at Sebaste, a city of Palestine, anciently called Samaria. Herodias, however, was careful to have the head buried apart at Jerusalem, within the palace of Herod, fearing lest the Prophet should rise again from the dead if his head and his body were buried together. The place of the interment of the head was revealed, about A.D. 392, to two monks of the Macedonian heresy; and it was conducted, after several haltings and difficulties, to a place called Hebdoma, in the suburbs of Constantinople, where the Emperor Theodosius had a spacious and magnificent church erected to do honour to the holy relic.* At the sepulchre

---
* Sozomen: *Ecclesiastical History*; lib. vii., c. 21.

of St. John the Baptist at Sebaste, so many miracles were daily performed, that multitudes of people constantly resorted thither; on which account the Apostate Julian is said to have commanded the heathen to scatter the sacred relics over the fields, in order to shame and to spite the Christians. As the miracles did not cease, it was determined that the bones should be re-collected for the purpose of being burned. A number of Christians, mingling with those employed in gathering them, contrived to preserve a number of the bones from the flames; and these relics, having been sent to Athanasius at Alexandria, were for the most part deposited there, whilst of the remainder a distribution was made amongst the various Churches, to the great advantage of the faithful, on account of their ineradicable power of working miracles. It may perhaps be permitted to hesitate to receive as authentic the accounts of wonders wrought posthumously by the *disjecta membra* of one of whom it is expressly said whilst living, that " John did no miracles " (John x. 41).

The salient points of the Baptist's career and mission are thus presented in a hymn for his Day in the " People's Hymnal:"—

> Hail, O thou of women born,
> Highest station claiming,
> By the holy Angel called
> " John " on day of naming.
> Hallowed from thy mother's womb,
> Herald-beacon lighted
> To enlighten them that sit
> In Death's shade benighted.
>
> Hail thou, to the wilderness
> From the world retreating,
> Who didst camel's hair put on,
> Desert honey eating.
> Free from taint of carnal sin,
> Water was thy potion;
> Thus the world thou puttest off,
> Putting on devotion.

Hail, thou shepherd sent before
 To prepare the pasture ;
With thy finger thou didst point
 To the Lamb thy Master.
At the Jordan thou didst cry,
 With the voice of warning,
Telling that the night is past,
 Near is Heaven's morning.

Hail, alone of human kind
 To whose charge 'twas given
To baptize the Sacred Head
 Of the LORD of Heaven :
Who didst hear the FATHER'S voice
 That blest rite attending,
Who didst see the HOLY GHOST,
 As a dove descending.

Hail, bright rose-bud, blushing red
 With thy passion's flower,
Lily sweet of chastity
 In life's sunset hour;
May thy voice yet cry aloud
 With its warning sentence,
When GOD'S kingdom is at hand,
 Calling to repentance.

St. Peter's Day.

June 29.

IN the ancient Church St. Peter and St. Paul were honoured with a joint commemoration on the twenty-ninth of June, a day on which it was believed they each achieved the crown of martyrdom, although by different methods of execution, and in different parts of the city of Rome. Against this tradition an idle polemical objection—which runs counter to the general voice of antiquity—has sometimes been taken, on the ground that it cannot be proved that St. Peter was ever at Rome at all; as if such an objection were valid against the pretensions of the Popes, who assume to be his successors in the chair of a universal episcopate. The objectors against the precedence and authority of the see of Rome would, perhaps, better serve their purpose if they were to set up a rival claim on behalf of the Church of Jerusalem, which, as the "Mother of all the Churches," and as locally situated in the head-quarters of Judaism— of which Christianity was a spiritualized development— might naturally, and by inheritance, appropriate any authority or sanctity that could attach to one see over another from considerations of time and place. There seems little to be gained by disputing the sometime residence of St. Peter at Rome, except the suspicion of a want of candour on the part of objectors to claims which could be better met on other and larger grounds.

It is stated by Hospinian that the joint festival "was instituted in the place of the feast of Hercules and the Muses, which was celebrated at Rome on the twenty-ninth of June." * Be this as it may, the commemoration of the two Apostles was of early observance in the Church. If the genuineness of a controverted *Homily* of St. Chrysostom could be established, it would follow that the festival was known in the East as early as the middle of the fourth century; whilst its observance in the West, in the latter part of the same century and the beginning of the fifth, is certified by the undisputed *Homilies* of Maximus Taurinensis,† St. Ambrose,‡ Leo the Great,§ and St. Augustine.|| It was about the year 500 that the festival attained its greatest splendour of celebration; at which time Festus, a Roman senator, was sent on a mission to the Emperor Anastasius at Constantinople. The piety of Festus was grieved on discovering the comparatively slight amount of honour which was done to the memory of two such mighty champions for the faith; and he addressed himself by way of petition to the Empress Ariadne, with the intent to ensure her influence for an anniversary of greater pomp and circumstance. The request coincided with the disposition of the Empress; and from the period of the visit of Festus to Constantinople the feast of the two great Apostles was celebrated with a solemnity it had never previously enjoyed.¶ In the course of years it was felt to be something less than seemly that two so illustrious pro-

* *De Origine Festorum Christianorum.*
† *Sermones* lxvi.-lxix; *In Natali Sanctorum Petri et Pauli.*
‡ *Sermones* liii. and liv; *In Natali Sanctorum Apostolorum Petri et Pauli*; and *De Neglecta solemnitate Beatorum Apostolorum Petri et Pauli.*
§ *Sermo*; *In Natali Apostolorum Petri et Pauli.*
|| *Sermones* ccxcv-ccxcix; *In Natali Apostolorum Petri et Pauli.*
¶ Theodorus Lector; *Ecclesiastical History*; lib. ii. c. 16.

pagators of the faith should be partners in a single commemoration; and Gregory the Great (590-604), reserving the twenty-ninth of June for the commemoration of St. Peter alone, appointed the day after for the festival of St. Paul;* the feast of whose Conversion is observed in the English Church on the twenty-fifth of January.

It is known that the place of St. Peter's nativity was the city of Bethsaida, on the Sea of Galilee, but the time of that event has not been ascertained; and it has been debated whether the seniority should be adjudged to him or to his brother Andrew, who first brought him to the Saviour, and whose fellow-disciple in the school of John the Baptist he had probably been. The original name of Peter was Simon or Simeon; and upon his vocation to the Apostolate he received in addition the title of Cephas, which in the Aramaic dialect spoken in Palestine in the days of our Lord is the equivalent of the Greek Πέτρος, the Peter of our vernacular.

Peter was one of our Lord's most intimate companions, and admitted by Him to the peculiar evidences of His Divine glory, as well as to His agony and humiliation for the fulfilment of the prophecies. Peter was so forward in zeal and attachment that he is constantly seen in the forefront of the Twelve; and his promptness of speech, whether to avow or to question, or, after the Ascension of Christ, to preach and to organize, gained for him among the Fathers the *sobriquet* of the "Mouthpiece of the Apostles."

The Evangelists abundantly establish the character of St. Peter for unequivocal piety, and ardent affection for his Master, and jealousy for His honour. His mind, however, was rather quick than accurate in its perceptions, and his feelings were rather hasty in their impulse than determined and tenacious in their exercise. Always ready to give utter-

* Hugo Menard's *Notæ et Observationes in S. Gregorii Magni Librum Sacramentorum.*

ance to his opinions, he was rash in their formation; and his exuberant courage was liable to collapse in the presence of new and appalling forms of danger. Of such a character the narrative of St. Peter's denial and repentance, his fall and recovery, offers a natural exposition.

"Peter stood more firmly after he had lamented his fall than before he fell; insomuch that he found more grace than he lost grace." These words of St. Ambrose are appended, in Quarles's "Emblems," to a poem in paraphrase of the text: "A just man falleth seven times, and riseth up again; but the wicked shall fall into mischief" (Proverbs xxiv. 16).

> 'Tis but a foil at best, and that's the most
>   Your skill can boast:
> My slippery footing failed me; and you tript,
>   Just as I slipt:
> My wanton weakness did herself betray
>   With too much play:
> I was too bold: he never yet stood sure,
>   That stands secure:
> Who ever trusted in his native strength,
>   But fell at length?
> The title's crazed, the tenure is not good,
> That claims by th'evidence of flesh and blood.
>
> Boast not thy skill; the righteous man falls oft
>   Yet falls but soft:
> There may be dirt to mire him, but no stones
>   To crush his bones:
> What if he staggers? Nay, but case he be
>   Foiled on his knee?
> That very knee will bend to Heaven, and woo
>   For mercy too.
> The true-bred gamester ups afresh, and then
>   Falls to 't again;
> Whereas the leaden-hearted coward lies,
> And yields his conquered life, or cravened dies.
>
> Boast not thy conquest; thou that every hour
>   Fall'st ten times lower;

Nay, hast not power to rise, if not, in case,
    To fall more base :
Thou wallow'st where I slip ; and thou dost tumble
    Where I but stumble :
Thou glory'st in thy slavery's dirty badges,
    And fall'st for wages ;
Sour grief and sad repentance scours and clears
    My stains with tears :
Thy falling keeps thy falling still in ure ;
But when I slip, I stand the more secure.

Lord, what a nothing is this little span,
    We call a Man!
What fenny trash maintains the smothering fires
    Of his desires !
How slight and short are his resolves at longest :
    How weak at strongest!
Oh, if a sinner, held by that fast hand,
    Can hardly stand,
Good God! in what a desperate case are they,
    That have no stay !
Man's state implies a necessary curse ;
When not himself, he's mad ; when most himself, he's worse.

The practical piety of George Wither extracts from the circumstances of St. Peter's fall a warning and a prayer. The verses which, in the "Hymns and Songs of the Church," illustrate "St. Peter's Day," are the following :—

    How watchful need we to become,
        And how devoutly pray,
  That Thee, O Lord, we fall not from,
        Upon our trial day !
  For if Thy great Apostle said
        He would not Thee deny,
  Whom he that very night denayed,
        On what shall we rely ?

  For of ourselves we cannot leave
        One pleasure for Thy sake ;
  No, nor one virtuous thought conceive,
        Till us Thou able make :

Nay, we not only Thee deny,
    When persecutions be,
But or forget, or from Thee fly,
    When peace attends on Thee.

O let those prayers us avail,
    Thou didst for Peter deign,
That when our foe shall us assail,
    His labour may be vain!
Yea, cast on us those powerful eyes,
    That moved him to lament;
We may bemoan with bitter cries
    Our follies, and repent.

And grant that such as him succeed
    For pastors of Thy fold,
Thy sheep and lambs may guide and feed,
    As thou appoint'st they should;
By his example speaking what
    They ought in truth to say,
And in their lives confirming that
    They teach them to obey.

It is a very natural and just remark that the fall and recovery of St. Peter operated most beneficially upon the Apostle's mind; being connected, as they were, with the mysterious events of his Master's Crucifixion and Resurrection, and with the new light thrown by them upon His character and mission. From this time forward, Peter is presented in a new aspect. The hasty zeal of the past is lost in the sober dignity and firmness, in the sagacity and prudence, of the present; whilst his love, more rather than less, shows itself no longer in loud or extravagant protestation, but in active labour and much-enduring patience in the service of Christ. In the Acts of the Apostles are recorded many remarkable incidents which befel him in the course of his Apostolate; and which, being so recorded, we may pass over, content with reminding the reader of the memorable encounter between him and Simon Magus, because in the course of a few sentences we shall see him once again in final conflict with that discomfited and vengeful magician.

After having exercised his function with so extraordinary and miraculous success at Jerusalem after the outpouring of the Spirit, St. Peter founded a Church at Antioch, over which he presided for the space of six or seven years. Then he preached the Gospel to the Jews dispersed in Pontus, Galatia, Bithynia, Cappadocia, and Asia;[*] and finally repaired to Rome, where he is said to have exercised the episcopate for a period of twenty-five years.[†] But this is probably an over-statement.

At his first arrival in the imperial city, St. Peter devoted himself chiefly to the Jews, his countrymen; who, ever since the time of Augustus, had dwelt in the region beyond the Tiber. Whilst at Rome he is said to have contracted a friendly and intimate acquaintance with Philo Judæus, who had lately come thither on his second embassy in behalf of the Jews settled at Alexandria. After a stay of several years at Rome, the Apostle was banished by an edict which the Emperor Claudius issued against the Jews on account of the seditious proceedings of some of their nation. Hereupon he returned to Jerusalem, where he took part in the great Apostolic Synod. Subsequent to this, the movements of St. Peter are uncertain; and amongst the theories concerning them is one which makes him the bringer of the glad tidings of salvation to our own Island.

Towards the latter end of Nero's reign, St. Peter repaired again to Rome, where he presently encountered Simon Magus, whom he had formerly confounded in Samaria, when that wretched man sought to purchase the gifts of the Holy Spirit (Acts viii.). Simon was a native of Githeus, a village of Samaria, bred up in the arts of sorcery and divination, and by the help of the powers of darkness performed so many strange feats of wonder and activity that

---

[*] Eusebius: *Ecclesiastical History*; lib. iii., c. 1.
[†] St Jerome: *De Viris Illustribus*; c. 1.

he was generally regarded as "the great power of God" (Acts viii. 10). But being discovered and rebuked by St. Peter in Samaria, he left the East, and fled to Rome; where by witchcraft and sorceries, he insinuated himself to such an extent into the favour of the people, and the confidence of the Emperors, that no degree of veneration seemed too extravagant to be paid to him. It is even related by Justin Martyr and others, that the Romans had erected a statue in his honour, with an inscription—*Simoni Sancto Deo; To Simon the Holy God.* St. Peter was a frequent opponent of the impostor; and upon one critical occasion outdid by a reality the utmost power to which Simon could only pretend. A kinsman of the Emperor Nero died; and was so regretted that it was judged expedient to have him restored, if possible, to life. Simon Magus essayed to effect this, but failed; whilst Peter accomplished it to the great chagrin of Simon, who, calling upon the Apostle to do the same, had staked his own life upon the issue. The enraged populace would forthwith have stoned the impudent magician, but by the influence of St. Peter his life was spared. Simon, however, rendered desperate by the utter shattering of his prestige, caused it to be proclaimed that on a certain day he would fly up to his native Heaven. On the day named he accordingly went up to the Capitoline Mount, and from a tower began his flight, which, indeed, instead of being upwards, was so precipitate as to bring him to the ground fatally bruised and mangled.* As this happened in accordance with the prayers of St. Peter and St. Paul, who wished the befooled people to be undeceived, the former Apostle was held by Nero, the patron of Simon Magus, as answerable for his death. The Emperor was probably already incensed against Peter for being a participator with St. Paul in the conversion of women who had ministered to the imperial pleasures. The two Apostles

---

* Cyril of Jerusalem: *Catecheses* xxiii.; *Cat.* vi. *De Uno Deo.* cc. 14 & 15; Philastrius: *Liber de Hæresibus; Simon Magus.*

were therefore apprehended and cast into the Mamertine prison, where they spent some time, daily engaging in the offices of religion, and especially in preaching to the prisoners, and to those who resorted to them.

Whilst the fatal stroke was momently impending, Peter, who was not chained like St. Paul, was entreated by the faithful at Rome to take counsel for his safety by flight; to which step he was at length reluctantly persuaded. On the night following his arrival at the resolution to escape, he set out for the gate of the city, where he was startled by an apparition of the Lord, who, being asked by Peter " whither He was going ? " replied, " I am going to Rome, that I may be crucified a second time." St. Peter read this answer as a rebuke; and inferred that it was his duty to return to suffer the martyrdom by which Christ would be crucified afresh in the person of His servant. The little Church of " Domine Quo Vadis ? " is believed to stand on the spot sanctified by this reported mysterious meeting.

The place of the execution of St. Peter was the Vatican Mount; and its manner that of crucifixion, which he obtained as a favour should be with the head downwards. It has been variously contended that St. Peter and St. Paul suffered on the same day of the same year, and at the same hour of the day; and, again, that the interval of one year, or two years, elapsed between their respective martyrdoms. But the parts of the city in which they suffered were different, as well as the instruments of their death, —Paul, as a Roman citizen, enjoying the privilege of being beheaded, as a more honourable mode of death than the odious one of crucifixion.*

The body of St. Peter is said to have been embalmed by Marcellinus, the presbyter, and to have been buried in the Vatican, near the Triumphal Way. After one or more removals, it was re-conveyed, about A.D. 250, by Cornelius, the twentieth Bishop of Rome, to the Vatican, where it

* See page 327.

rested somewhat obscurely until the reign of Constantine, who caused a stately church to be erected on the spot, which afterwards increased so much in splendour and magnificence, that the Church of St. Peter has long been held to be one of the wonders of the world.

Touching any personal prerogative which may be claimed for St. Peter as universal pastor and head of the Church, Nelson judiciously remarks, that "though he is first placed among the Apostles (Matt. x. 2.), because, as most think, he was first called; and that his age and gravity qualified him for the primacy of order, without which no society can be managed and maintained: yet it doth not appear that he enjoyed any other particular privilege; because, in confessing Christ, he spake not only his own, but the sense of his fellow Apostles, and which Nathanael professed as well as he (John i. 49): if he is styled the rock (Matt. xvi. 18), all the Apostles are equally styled foundations, upon which the wall of the New Jerusalem is erected (Rev. xxi. 14); and the power of the keys is promised to the rest of the Apostles as well as to St. Peter (John xx. 23)."*

St. Peter had thrice denied his Lord; a sin which he so bitterly bewailed, that he is said to have hollowed his cheeks into furrows through the coursing down of incessant tears, for the purpose of wiping which away, he carried a linen napkin constantly attached to the breast of his garment. It was in allusion to the thrice enacted denial that the Saviour gave him the opportunity, even at the expense of grieving the Apostle, of thrice avowing his love for Him, and of thrice receiving the command to "feed His flock." The question of love to Christ is the testing one of His religion; and is by the late Rev. John Newton thus brought into debate as a matter still personal to every one of Christ's disciples. The following verses, which form one of the *Olney Hymns*, are suggested by the enquiry, "Lovest thou Me?" (John xxi. 16.)

* *Festivals and Fasts of the Church of England.*

"LOVEST THOU ME?"

'Tis a point I long to know,
Oft it causeth anxious thought!
Do I love the Lord, or no?
Am I His, or am I not.

If I love, why am I thus?
Why this dull, this lifeless frame?
Hardly, sure, can they be worse,
Who have never heard His name!

Could my heart so hard remain,
Prayer a task and burden prove,
Every trifle give me pain,
If I knew a Saviour's love?

When I turn my eyes within,
All is dark, and vain, and wild:
Filled with unbelief and sin,
Can I deem myself a child?

If I pray, or hear, or read,
Sin is mixed with all I do;
You that love the Lord indeed,
Tell me, Is it thus with you?

Yet I mourn my stubborn will,
Find my sin a grief and thrall:
Should I grieve for what I feel,
If I did not love at all?

Could I joy His saints to meet,
Choose the ways I once abhorred,
Find, at times, the promise sweet,
If I did not love the Lord?

Lord, decide the doubtful case!
Thou who art Thy people's sun,
Shine upon Thy work of Grace,
It it be indeed begun.

Let me love Thee more and more,
If I love at all, I pray;
If I have not loved before,
Help me to begin to-day.

St. James the Apostle.

July 25.

THIS Apostle owed his peculiar designation to the necessity of discriminating between him and his namesake who was called the Less; although it has been left doubtful whether he received the title of Great on account of his seniority, his superior stature, or the particular favour bestowed upon him by our Lord, of whose kindred he was. His father was Zebedee, a fisherman of some substance; and his mother, Mary, surnamed Salome, was cousin-german—*Hebraicè* sister—to the Blessed Virgin. James was therefore the brother of St. John the Evangelist, with whom and St. Peter he was associated in so close an intimacy with Christ as to be admitted to situations of affection and confidence from which the rest of the Twelve were excluded. The two brothers, James and John, were called by Christ, Boanerges, or Sons of Thunder, possibly from the noble vehemence and the moral power of their teaching, which seemed to reverberate throughout the world.

Salome was ambitious for her sons, and they for themselves: and a prayer was presented to Christ, that they might be His assessors, one on the right hand and one on the left, in His kingdom—a prayer which brought down upon them a rebuke from our Lord, and which stirred the indignation and jealousy of the other disciples.

> Rash was the tongue, and unadvisedly bold,
>   Which sought, Salome, for thy favoured twain
>   Above their fellows in Messiah's reign
> On right, on left, the foremost place to hold.
> More rash, perhaps, and bolder, that which told
>   Of power the Saviour's bitter cup to drain,
>   And, passing stretch of human strength, sustain
> His bath baptismal. Lord, by Thee enrolled
> Thy servant, grant me Thy Almighty grace,
>   My destined portion of Thy griefs to bear,
> Even what Thou wilt! But chiefly grant, Thy face
>   Within Thy glory's realm to see, where'er
> Most meet Thy wisdom deems; whate'er the place,
>   It must be blest, for Thou, my God, art there!

The foregoing Sonnet is taken from the late Bishop Mant's "Happiness of the Blessed," in which volume it has for its title, "The Ambitious Disciples;" and the one which follows, from the same volume, defines the spirituality of the method to be observed in order to attain the objects of "Christian Ambition."

> "Ambition is the vice of noble souls!"
>   If 'tis a vice, then let those souls beware,
>   Thrice noble though they be, and passing fair
> In the world's eye, and high upon the scrolls,
> Her favoured minions where the world inrolls,
>   Lest it conduct to shame! Be thine the care,
>   Soldier of Christ, that nobler strife to dare,
> Which the rash spirit of the world controls,
> And makes ambition virtue! Be it thine
>   To win thy bright unfading diadem
> By works of love!—Around *his* brows shall shine
>   In heaven from glory's source the purest beam,
> Whose aspect here, with beauty most divine,
>   Reflects the image of the GOOD SUPREME.

Ambition is one of the most common phases of discontent; but although its spring be simple and readily intelligible, its streams and currents are many and perplexing. Its phenomena are well-nigh endless. Now it would rule, now it would love, now it would execute justice, now it would bring hope and safety—but always without and beyond the bounds of ordained and legitimate activity. In the series of Sonnets which we are about to present to the reader, the changing desire to stand in different, though always in spectacular and magnificent, relations to the world according to its different phases is exhibited, and, in the last of them, rebuked. The cravings of an indiscriminating benevolence, equally with the impulses of an utterly selfish ambition, must be tamed to acquiescence. Neither the sovereignty of the world, nor the salvation of the world, can be relegated to any hand which is less than divine. The "Sonnets" referred to are transcribed from the "Churchman's Family Magazine" for December, 1866.

> Ten fathoms on the other side of steep,
> The mighty cliff on whose bare top I stood
> O'erhung the ravings of the breaking flood,
> And mocked unmoved the trouble of the deep;
> It seemed nor land nor sky, but more the keep
> Where spirits of a godlike hardihood
> Planned all aloft their own aërial good,
> And left the pitiful earth to smile or weep.
> The eagle fed her brood a mile below,
> The arch of heaven seemed scarce a mile above;
> And from my loftiness, all undismayed,
> In sunshine higher than the line of snow,
> I scorned Olympus and its puny Jove:
> "Lord, let me rule the world!" I proudly prayed.

> O'er seas remote and near, and many a land,
> And many a gossamer cloud that sailed between,
> Taking all colours from the constant sheen,
> I looked before, behind, on either hand;
> Whilst Beauty smote the distance with her wand,
> Till lands and seas wore purple over green,
> And to my thought Earth seemed a sleeping queen.
> I, who, upon my glorious vantage-stand,
> Felt every inch a King, and more than all,
> Yet stooped to tenderness for things so fair;

And, growing larger-hearted in my pride,
Commended Nature in her regal pall;
   And as she dearer grew, and yet more dear,
    "Lord let me love the world!" I fondly sighed.

Then, as my gaze grew ever more intense,
   Keener my eyes became, so that the whole
   Unveiled its parts from pole to distant pole;
And, peering from my aëry eminence,
Cities and men first fixed my wandering sense
   Of sight; then struck my ear; then vexed my soul,
   Till wrath took hold on me without control,
And all things grouped in one supreme offence.
Theft cheated theft; and lie lied back to lie;
   And murder murder slew; and crime shamed crime;
   And oath at oath, and curse at curse was hurled,
Till the charged air shook with the blasphemy.
   Then, in a grand impatience of the time,
   Fiercely I prayed, "Lord, let me smite the world!"

Then up from seething city and from plain,
   And up from battle-field and flowery mead,
   Went forth a mighty cry as if of dread,
And fear, and terror, and of bitter pain;
The giant anguish echoed from the main;
   All life to all things but to woe was dead,
   And suffering sin did for a Saviour plead.
Arose a mist as if of floating rain,
A bank of clouds formed out of countless tears
   And infinite human weeping, and before
   Where all guilt's banners flaunted forth unfurled,
The signals of a myriad deep despairs
Drooped heavily, as if to float no more:
   Fainting I cried, "Lord, let me save the world!"

Then, as my senses rallied from my swoon,
   Upward I lifted either troubled eye,
   And saw a Sceptre in the central sky,
Beyond the cycles of the sun and moon
Borne in a Hand unseen within the noon
   Of Light approachless; and all suddenly
   A streamer graced the spaceless space on high,
Blazoned with Love in letters gold and boon.

> Anon there seemed a flaming two-edged sword
>   Threatening the earth, save that the nail-pierced Hand
>   Of Mercy claimed the world to save and free.
> Rebuke was in the vision; then, "O Lord!"
>   I asked, "give me some nook and Thy command,
>   That I may pray for all and work for Thee!"

Amongst the privileges which his peculiar intimacy with the Lord Jesus conferred upon St. James, was that of being one of the three witnesses of His Transfiguration. Bearing in mind the worldly conception of Christ's Kingdom which we have just seen to have been entertained by James and his brother, it may be proper to introduce here a poem which, whilst devoted to a deprecation of earthly distinctions, owes its suggestion to the proposal of Peter, to make on the Mount of Transfiguration three Tabernacles, one for Christ, one for Moses, and one for Elias (Matt. xvii. 4). Its author, Herbert Knowles, was a youthful poet, whose fame, like that of Wolfe, is almost entirely based upon a single production. Knowles was born at Canterbury in 1798, and died in the year 1817. At the age of eighteen, he produced the following "Lines written in the Churchyard of Richmond, Yorkshire;" which soon obtained general circulation and celebrity. They were once thought to "have much of the steady faith and devotional earnestness of Cowper:"—

> Methinks it is good to be here,
> If Thou wilt, let us build—but for whom?
>   Nor Elias nor Moses appear;
> But the shadows of eve that encompassed with gloom,
> The abode of the dead and the place of the tomb.
>
>   Shall we build to Ambition? Ah, no!
> Affrighted, he shrinketh away;
>   For see, they would pin him below
> In a small narrow cave, and begirt with cold clay,
> To the meanest of reptiles a peer and a prey.
>
>   To Beauty? Ah, no! She forgets
> The charms which she wielded before;
>   Nor knows the foul worm that he frets.

The skin which but yesterday fools could adore,
For the smoothness it held or the tint which it wore.

  Shall we build to the purple of Pride,
The trappings which dizen the proud?
  Alas! they are all laid aside,
And here's neither dress nor adornments allowed,
But the long winding-sheet and the fringe of the shroud.

  To Riches? Alas! 'tis in vain;
Who hid in their turns have been hid;
  The treasures are squandered again;
And here in the grave are all metals forbid,
But the tinsel that shines on the dark coffin-lid.

  To the pleasures which Mirth can afford,
The revel, the laugh, and the jeer?
  Ah! here is a plentiful board!
But the guests are all mute as their pitiful cheer,
And none but the worm is a reveller here.

  Shall we build to Affection and Love?
Ah, no! they have withered and died,
  Or fled with the spirit above.
Friends, brothers, and sisters are laid side by side,
Yet none have saluted, and none have replied.

  Unto Sorrow?—The Dead cannot grieve;
Not a sob, not a sigh meets mine ear,
  Which Compassion itself could relieve.
Ah, sweetly they slumber, nor love, hope, or fear;
Peace! peace is the watchword, the only one here.

  Unto Death, to whom monarchs must bow?
Ah, no! for his empire is known,
  And here there are trophies enow!
Beneath—the cold dead; and around—the dark stone,
Are the signs of a sceptre that none may disown.

  The first tabernacle to Hope we will build,
And look for the sleepers around us to rise!
  The second to Faith, which ensures it fulfilled;
And the third to the Lamb of the great sacrifice,
Who bequeathed us them both when He rose to the skies.

Neither from the inspired writings nor from the ecclesiastical historians do we derive much information concerning St. James after our Lord's Ascension. He would seem to have confined his ministrations to his native country of Judæa or its immediate neighbourhood; and to have been especially active in Jerusalem, where his zeal and energy at length made him so obnoxious to King Herod Agrippa, that when he "stretched forth his hands to vex certain of the Church, he killed James, the brother of John, with the sword" (Acts xii. 1, 2). This event took place before the days of unleavened bread, about A.D. 45.

Amongst the adversaries whom St. James confronted in the interests of Christianity, it is said there was a certain *Magus*, by name Hermogenes, who sent one of his disciples to refute the arguments of the Apostle. When the scholar found this task to be beyond his powers, Hermogenes in a rage ordered the demons to bring St. James to him by force. This command of the master fell as powerless upon the Apostle as the reasoning of the scholar had done; and when the discomfited Hermogenes was obliged to recognise its futility, he professed himself a convert to the faith of Christ, destroyed his household images, burned his books of magic, and distributed amongst the poor the wealth he had amassed in the exercise of his profession.

Notwithstanding the credit acquired by so remarkable a conversion, St. James was accused by the Jews to Herod, who ordered his apprehension, and sentenced him to death. On the way to execution, St. James performed a miracle of healing upon a paralytic, by which the principal witness against him, Josias, a Scribe, was so affected that he threw himself at the feet of the Apostle, and begged his forgiveness. St. James, after recovering from his surprise at the sudden change, raised him up, and embraced him with a kiss, saying, "Peace be to thee, my brother." Hereupon Josias boldly professed himself to be a Christian, and was on that account condemned to be beheaded with the sword at the same time and place as the Apostle whose words, and the remarkable spirit which they evidenced, had been instrumental in his conversion.*

The peace which was the salutation and the legacy of the dying Apostle to Josias, was the peace of another world; for in this the rest of his life was short and troublous. The true and abiding Peace is a native of a far country—far, yet only the journey of an instant to the departing faithful. The following lines, from the pen of Henry Vaughan, the "Silurist," (1621-1695), are original and picturesque, and very lively and stirring in their movement, and deserving of a wider popularity than they have lately enjoyed:—

> My soul, there is a country
>   Far beyond the stars,
> Where stands a winged Sentry,
>   All skilful in the wars.
> There, above all noise and danger,
>   Sweet Peace, sits crowned with smiles,
> And One born in a manger
>   Commands the beauteous files.
>
> He is thy gracious Friend,
>   And (O my soul awake!)
> Did in pure love descend
>   To die here for thy sake.
> If thou canst get but thither
>   There grows the flower of Peace,
> The rose that cannot wither,
>   Thy fortress and thy ease;
>
> Leave, then, thy foolish ranges,
>   For none can that secure;
> But One who never changes—
>   Thy God, thy Life, thy Cure.

St. James the Great has the honour of being the "Protomartyr of the Apostles," as Stephen has that of being the Protomartyr of the Church in general; and thus he had a

* Clement of Alexandria, quoted by Eusebius; lib. ii., c. 9.

pre-eminence in drinking of that cup of which he had long before hastily and ignorantly professed to his Lord his willingness and ability to partake (Mark x., 38, 39). As for Herod, he was marked for the Divine vengeance, which overtook him in a horrible form of death, of which St. Luke gives a brief account (Acts xii. 20-23), and the details of which are narrated at greater length by Josephus the historian.*

There is little or no reason to believe otherwise than that St. James was buried by the faithful at Jerusalem. He has long been regarded as the Patron Saint of Spain, where he is held in especial veneration, as having been the first to introduce Christianity into that country, to which, indeed, a tradition avers that his remains were translated, and where they are now deposited in his church at Compostella. The tradition, however, is a comparatively late one; and Hospinian, who devotes some space to its investigation, sums up against its historic credibility with an expression of opinion that it was invented and developed by the bold cupidity of the priests.†

The commemoration of St. James's day has with much probability been assumed to have had an earlier local origin in Spain; but it does not appear to have become universal before the eleventh century. In the Greek Church it is observed on the 30th of April, the anniversary of the Apostle's martyrdom; as the 25th of July, the day on which he is commemorated in the Western Church—and this may be taken as an argument that Spain is the country in which it had its local (Western) institution—is the anniversary of the presumed translation of his remains.

* *Wars of the Jews;* lib. i., c. 33.
† *De Origine Festorum Christianorum.*

St. Bartholomew the Apostle.

August 24.

THE date of the first institution of the festival in honour of this Apostle is uncertain. By some authorities it has been referred to the eleventh century; whilst others appeal to ancient calendars for evidence that it was known as early as the eighth. The Greeks, whose days for commemorating the Apostles and Evangelists coincide with our own in two or three cases only, celebrate the martyrdom of St. Bartholomew on the 11th of June, reserving the 24th of August, the day on which it is observed in the Western Church, for the anniversary of the translation of his relics. In Rome, however, St. Bartholomew is honoured one day later, that is, on the 25th of August.

The name of Bartholomew is a patronymic, implying that he was the "son of Tholmai;" or, according to some learned writers, that he was a *Tholmæan*, a scholar or disciple of the school of Tholmai, the leader and eponymous of a sect amongst the Jewish students of the Law. A more popular tradition—popular, that is, in the sense of being capricious and uninstructed—maintains that Bartholomew was a son of Ptolemy, King of Syria—a tradition which manifests an utter ignorance of the true seat of the rule of the Ptolemaic family. It is more safe to regard the Apostle as a native of Cana in Galilee (John xxi. 2); and to relegate him to that occupation of a fisherman which was dignified by some of the most illustrious of the Apostles.

There is little reason to doubt that the name of Bartholomew was conferred upon him by way of distinction, in addition to, or in substitution for, that of Nathanael, which was probably the name he received at his circumcision. The proof of this, or the probability which scarcely stops short of proof, is found in the circumstance that, whilst the other Evangelists never speak of Nathanael, but of Bartholomew, and place the latter in juxtaposition with Philip, St. John speaks exclusively of Nathanael, whom he places in the relative position to St. Philip, which Bartholomew occupies in the other Gospels (Matthew x. 3; Mark iii. 18; Luke vi. 14; John i. 43-51).

The only scene in the Evangelic drama in which Nathanael alone, with his Master, fills the stage, is that which exhibits his call to the Apostolate; and the character of the person called, and the circumstances under which he responded to the call, are so singular and instructive as to justify a moment's pause for their consideration. "In the case of a JOHN," says Neander, writing of the calling of Nathanael—"in the case of a JOHN, the full impression of Christ's personality, first received, prepared the depths of his youthful soul for sudden and separate impressions of the Divinity of Jesus, which soon brought him to a complete decision. But the narrow prejudices of a NATHANAEL had to be overcome by a separate supernatural sign before he could receive the impression of Christ's manifestation and nature as a whole. When Philip first announced to him that Jesus of *Nazareth* was the Messiah, he expressed both surprise and incredulity that anything so high should come forth from a corner like Galilee. Instead of discussing the point, Philip appeals to his own experience, and tells him to 'come and see.' Nathanael's prejudice was not strong enough to prevent his compliance, or to hinder him from being convinced by facts. Christ sees and esteems his love of truth, and receives him with the words, '*Behold an Israelite, indeed, in whom there is no guile*' (a true and honest-hearted member of the Theocratic nation). The candid youth is surprised to find himself known by a stranger. He expresses his astonishment, and Christ increases the impression made upon his feelings, by a more striking proof still of His supernatural knowledge, telling him that His glance, piercing the barriers of space, had rested on him before Philip called him as he stood 'under the fig-tree' (this probably had some reference to the thoughts which occupied his mind under the fig-tree). His prejudices are readily removed [he acknowledged Christ as '*Son of God and King of Israel*'] Christ admits that he is in the first stage of faith, but tells him that his faith must develop itself from this beginning, and advance to a higher aim (John i. 50, 51). A faith thus resting on a single manifestation might easily be perplexed by some other single one, that might not meet its expectations. That is a genuine faith (according to Christ) which carries itself to the very central-point of revelation, seizes the intuition of Divinity in its immediate nature and manifestation as a whole, and obtains, through immediate contact with the Divine in the Spirit, a stand-point which doubt can never reach. Nathanael was to see 'greater things' than this isolated ray of the supernatural. He was to see the '*heavens opened upon the Son of Man*,' into whose intimacy he was about to enter, and '*Angels of God ascending and descending*' upon Him. He was to learn Christ in His true relation to the development of humanity, as Him through whom human nature was to be glorified; through whom the locked-up heavens were again to be opened; the communion with heaven and earth restored; to whom and from whom all the powers of heaven were to flow. Such was to be His Divine glory in its *full* manifestation; all other signs were but individual tokens of it."*

* Neander: *Life of Jesus Christ.*

The Gospel for St. Bartholomew's Day (Luke xii. 24, 30) narrates the rebuke which Christ administered to the Disciples upon the occasion of a strife arising among them, "which of them should be accounted the greatest." It is necessary to remember on the one hand, that in heaven or earth there is nothing great but God; and on the other, that, regard being had to the destinies of man, there are in human duties and affairs, no such thing as trifles. Motive may illustrate the meanest of offices. In the sight of God, all actions which are done, and all functions which are discharged, in His fear and love have their own peculiar dignity and sanctity. George Herbert sets this forth in his poem entitled "The Elixir."

> Teach me, my God and King,
> In all things Thee to see,
> And what I do in anything,
> To do it as for Thee:
>
> Not rudely, as a beast,
> To run into an action;
> But still to make Thee prepossest,
> And give it his perfection.
>
> A man that looks on glass,
> On it may stay his eye;
> Or if he pleaseth, through it pass,
> And then the heaven espy.
>
> All may of Thee partake:
> Nothing can be so mean,
> Which with his tincture (for Thy sake)
> Will not grow bright and clean.
>
> A servant with this clause
> Makes drudgery divine;
> Who sweeps a room, as for Thy laws
> Makes that and the action fine.
>
> This is the famous stone
> That turneth all to gold:
> For that which God doth touch and own,
> Cannot for less be told.

When the Apostles entered upon the provinces which had been severally assigned to them after the Ascension of Christ and the Day of Pentecost, St. Bartholomew travelled as far as Northern India, where his advent was signalised by a miraculous and *restrictive* power over the gods of the country, and where he made many converts to the faith of Christ. The fruits of his labours were seen in the second century, when Pantænus, a convert from Stoicism to Christianity, who visited India under a commission from the Bishop and Church of Alexandria, found a Hebrew copy of St. Matthew's Gospel, which the tradition of the Christians in whose hands it was, affirmed to have been left with their ancestors by St. Bartholomew.*

From Hither India, the Apostle returned to the more Western and Northern parts of Asia. At Hierapolis, in Phrygia, he was in company with St. Philip, and engaged with him in instructing the people in the doctrines of Christianity, and convincing them of the folly of their blind idolatries. The magistrates of the city, enraged at the success which attended their labours, destined them for a common martyrdom. But this purpose took effect only in the case of St. Philip; for after St. Bartholomew had been fastened to a cross, with a view to his execution, a panic apprehension of the Divine vengeance seems to have dismayed his persecutors, who took him down from the cross and set him at liberty.

Afterwards St. Bartholomew prosecuted his Apostolic labours in Lycaonia, the people of which, according to a *Homily* ascribed to St. Chrysostom, he instructed and trained up in the Christian discipline.† Finally he journeyed into Armenia, where, as a tradition reproduced by Hospinian avers, he converted Polemon the king, with his wife and subjects, to the Christian faith. But his

---

* Eusebius: *Ecclesiastical History*; lib. v., c. 10.
† *In Sanctos Duodecim Apostolos.*

success was fatal to him; for it caused so much envy on the part of the priests of the country, that they used their influence with Astyages, the brother of King Polemon, to have the Apostle brought to execution. They were successful in their application; and St. Bartholomew, in accordance with a custom formerly in use among many Oriental nations, was sentenced to be flayed alive, and then beheaded.

An alternative tradition as to the mode of his martyrdom, is to the effect that he was crucified, like St. Peter, with his head downwards. But he may, living or dead, have been the object of each of these three most cruel operations; as it is possible, with perfect consistency of the two accounts, to suppose crucifixion to have supervened upon his excoriation, and to have anticipated his beheading. He was interred at Albanopolis, a city of the Greater Armenia, which was the scene of his passion; and from thence his remains were afterwards translated successively to Daras, a city on the confines of Persia; to the island of Lipari; to Beneventum; and finally to Rome.

The sentiments of devotion and self-sacrifice, the real tortures—the two martyrdoms, one in will, and the other in both will and deed—of this much-suffering Apostle encourage us to append to our remarks upon his festival a poem which seems to breathe the identical spirit by which he was actuated. It is entitled "Cupio dissolvi;" and is the last poem in the third part of William Habington's "Castara," which he opens with a delineation in prose of the character of "A Holy Man." Habington was "a gentleman," to use the words of Langbaine, "that lived in the times of the late civil wars; and, slighting Bellona, gave himself up entirely to the Muses." He was a quiet and retiring member of a family remarkable for its political restlessness; and his greatest poetical effort was the chivalrous and noble celebration of "Castara"— Lucia, daughter of the first Lord Powis—whom he afterwards married. Habington both entered and quitted life at Hendlip, in Worcestershire; the dates of his birth and death being respectively 1605 and 1654.

> The soul which doth with God unite,
> Those gaieties how doth she slight
>   Which o'er opinion sway!
> Like sacred virgin wax, which shines
> On altars or on martyrs' shrines
>   How doth she burn away!
>
> How violent are her throes till she
> From envious earth delivered be,
>   Which doth her flight restrain!
> How doth she doat on whips and racks,
> On fires and the so dreaded axe,
>   And every murdering pain!
>
> How soon she leaves the pride of wealth,
> The flatteries of youth and health
>   And fame's more precious breath;
> And every gaudy circumstance
> That doth the pomp of life advance,
>   At the approach of death!
>
> The cunning of astrologers
> Observes each motion of the stars,
>   Placing all knowledge there:
> And lovers in their mistress' eyes
> Contract those wonders of the skies,
>   And seek no higher sphere.
>
> The wandering pilot sweats to find
> The causes that produce the wind,
>   Still gazing on the pole.
> The politician scorns all art
> But what doth pride and power impart,
>   And swells the ambitious soul.
>
> But he whom heavenly fire doth warm,
> And 'gainst these powerful follies arm,
>   Doth soberly disdain
> All these fond human mysteries
> As the deceitful and unwise
>   Distempers of our brain.

ST. BARTHOLOMEW THE APOSTLE.

He as a burden bears his clay,
Yet vainly throws it not away
    On every idle cause;
But with the same untroubled eye
Can or resolve to live or die,
    Regardless of th' applause.

My God! If 'tis Thy great decree
That this must the last moment be
    Wherein I breathe this air;
My heart jobeys, joyed to retreat
From the false favours of the great,
    And treachery of the fair.

When Thou shalt please this soul to enthrone
Above impure corruption;
    What should I grieve or fear,
To think this breathless body must
Become a loathsome heap of dust
    And ne'er again appear?

For in the fire when ore is tried
And by that torment purified:
    Do we deplore the loss?
And when Thou shalt my soul refine,
That it thereby may purer shine,
    Shall I grieve for the dross?

St. Matthew the Apostle.

September 21.

ANCIENTLY there was a tradition which discriminated Matthew and Levi, and named the latter, in addition, among the prominent heralds of the Gospel. It is not impossible that this tradition may have been founded on the truth; but the more generally received opinion is that Matthew and Levi were the two names of the same individual. If we take the identity for granted, we find that St. Matthew was the son of Alpheus (Mark ii. 14); and are therefrom led to the safe inference that he was a Hebrew, and probably a Galilæan. Matthew, or Levi, was a publican, a collector of the Roman taxes, whose peculiar office it appears to have been to collect the customs paid upon exports and imports at the Sea of Tiberias. The office and person of a publican were obnoxious to the Jews for several reasons; the principal of which was that the publicans were native representatives of a foreign supremacy, men who—having farmed the taxes from a Roman superior, who had before farmed the entire revenues of a province from the Senate—were constantly tempted to injustice, cruelty, and extortion. To this temptation they appear to have so habitually yielded, that both by Jew and Gentile they were cited as monsters of insidious theft, oppression, and violence. But just in proportion as the business of a publican involved fraud and dishonesty, did it also involve wealth and profit; so that it attaches to the call of St. Matthew as a singular characteristic, that at the summons of the Saviour—for which, from the fact of his residence at Capernaum, he had probably been to some extent prepared—he cast off at once as well his professional and his personal covetousness, and forsook all to follow Him. Thus for poverty, he gave up plenty; for rich and powerful masters, he adopted a despised One; in short, he repudiated the world, and submitted to Christ.

> What is the gold of all this world but dross?
> The joy but sorrow, and the pleasure pain;
> The wealth but beggary, and the gain but loss;
> The wit but folly, and the virtue vain;
> The power but weakness, and but death the life;
> The hope but fear, and the assurance doubt;
> The trust deceit, the concord but a strife,
> Where one conceit doth put another out;
> Time but an instant, and the use a toil;
> The knowledge blindness, and the care a madness,
> The silver lead, the diamond but a foil,
> The rest but trouble, and the mirth but sadness?
> Thus, since to heaven compared, the earth is such
> What thing is man to love the world so much?

We have transcribed the foregoing Sonnet from the "Soul's Harmony" of Nicholas Breton, a worthy man and a prolific writer (1555-1624), because the duty which a consideration of St. Matthew's example is calculated to enforce, is the repudiation of covetousness, and the postponement of all the advantages and amenities of earth for the joys of Christ's conversation and devotion to His love. It was not that Matthew the publican did not understand the advantages of a plentiful subsistence; but that he knew there were other considerations to which those of mere worldly ease and prosperity were not even to be reckoned as *real* antagonists. The final use to which he put those

gifts of fortune which he was about to forego and to abandon
—the very feast at which he entertained the Saviour and
His disciples—seems to have been an expression in symbol
of the heartiness with which, loving all, he yet abandoned
all, and the gladness with which he adopted the unsettled
poverty of his just-recognised Master. It is possible that
from the date of this feast, St. Matthew may have commenced
the course of abstinence from luxuries which
ancient authorities tell us afterwards attained to the dimensions
of a negative asceticism—an asceticism, we mean,
which stopped at self-denial, and short of the self-infliction
of positive suffering. The austerity of the later life of
St. Matthew may be suggestively connected with his
former career as a publican; the abstinence of his age may
have been a continued expression of penitence for the fact
that he had spent so much of his youth in the exercise of
a voracious profession. To him there was no pleasure in
unblessed indulgence; and, as compared with other objects
of even proper and lawful affection, he may be said to
have had his "delight in God only," and to have been
ready to ask, in the words of the Psalmist—which form the
motto of the following poem from Quarles's "Emblems"—
"Whom have I in heaven but Thee? and there is none
upon earth that I desire beside Thee " (Psalm lxiii. 25).

> I love (and have some cause to love) the earth;
> She is my Maker's creature, therefore good:
> She is my mother, for she gave me birth;
> She is my tender nurse; she gives me food:
>   But what's a creature, Lord, compared with Thee?
>   Or what's my mother, or my nurse, to me?
>
> I love the air; her dainty sweets refresh
> My drooping soul, and to new sweets invite me;
> Her shrill-mouthed choir sustain me with their flesh,
> And with their polyphonian notes delight me;
>   But what's the air, or all the sweets, that she
>   Can bless my soul withal, compared to Thee?

I love the sea; she is my fellow creature,
My careful purveyor; she provides me store;
She walls me round; she makes my diet greater;
She wafts my treasure from a foreign shore:
 But, Lord of oceans, when compared with Thee,
 What is the ocean, or her wealth, to me?

To heaven's high city I direct my journey,
Whose spangled suburbs entertain mine eye;
Mine eye, by contemplation's great attorney,
Transcends the crystal pavement of the sky:
 But what is heaven, great God, compared to Thee?
 Without Thy presence, heaven's no heaven to me.

Without Thy presence, earth gives no refection;
Without Thy presence, sea affords no treasure;
Without Thy presence, air's a rank infection;
Without Thy presence, heaven itself's no pleasure;
 If not possessed, if not enjoyed, in Thee,
 What's earth, or sea, or air, or heaven, to me?

The highest honours that the world can boast
Are subjects far too low for my desire;
The brightest beams of glory are (at most)
But dying sparkles of Thy living fire:
 The proudest flames that earth can kindle be
 But mighty glow-worms, if compared to Thee.

Without Thy presence wealth are bags of cares;
Wisdom, but folly; joy, disquiet sadness;
Friendship is treason, and delights are snares;
Pleasure's but pain, and mirth but pleasing madness;
 Without Thee, Lord, things be not what they be,
 Nor have their being, when compared with Thee.

In having all things, and not Thee, what have I?
Not having Thee, what have my labours got?
Let me enjoy but Thee, what farther crave I?
And having Thee alone, what have I not?
 I wish nor sea, nor land; nor would I be
 Possessed of heaven, heaven unpossessed of Thee!

After the vocation of St. Matthew to the Apostolate, he continued with the rest of the Sacred College until the

Ascension of our Lord; and then, for the first eight years, at least, preached throughout his native country of Judæa. On his preparing at length to betake himself to the conversion of the Gentile world, he was entreated by the Jewish converts, and even enjoined by the Apostles, to commit to writing the history of our Saviour's life and actions. Complying with a request thus authoritatively fortified, the Evangelist produced his Gospel, which, as having been written in Judæa, for the use of Jews, was by the ancients unanimously held to have been written in Hebrew.

"Matthæus Christi Miracula scripsit Ebræis."

The Gospel of St. Matthew was very soon translated into Greek; but by whose hand, whether of St. John, or St. James, or of some other, does not sufficiently appear. The Apostles approved the version, and it was received as of the same authority with the original text, which, after the production of the Greek, fell almost exclusively into the hands of the Nazarites and Ebionites, to favour whose heresies it soon came to be interpolated and generally corrupted.

After the completion of his Gospel, St. Matthew "withdrew into Egypt, and thence proceeded as far as Æthiopia, on which account St. Chrysostom says of St. Matthew, that 'he washed the Æthiopians white;' that is, he is stated to have converted them to the faith, because he was the Apostle of the Æthiopians, and to this day the Abyssinians profess that they received the faith from St. Matthew."*

As against this last pretension it has been held that the Æthiopia to which St. Matthew travelled was not that in Africa, but what was called the Asian Æthiopia, and conterminous, if not the same, with Chaldæa.

The labours of the Apostle were blessed with an abundant success, and over his many converts in divers places,

* Joachim Hildebrand: *Diebus De Festis.*

he took care to ordain men of piety and judgment for their edification and direction; especially during his own absence on a tour in Parthia. Returning from the country last mentioned, St. Matthew is said to have encountered martyrdom, but in what manner, or in what circumstances, has not been settled. Indeed, his claim to the honours of martyrdom at all has been challenged on the ground that he appears enrolled amongst the "noble army" for the first time in the records of the second century. This objection may be thought sufficiently critical; but, assuming his martyrdom, we have more than one account of that event. By Nicephorus it is stated that St. Matthew, whilst engaged in instructing the Anthropophagi in the city of Myrmena, was transfixed to the earth by a huge nail. He is said otherwise to have been slain at Nadabar, a city of Æthiopia, by command of King Hirtacus, who sent an assassin to transfix St. Matthew with a sword, as he stood praying with outstretched hands before the altar.[*]

In the Greek Church St. Matthew is commemorated on the 16th of April; and not, as in our Calendar, on the 21st of September. Concerning the origin or first institution of the festival little is known; and it is most likely that it did not achieve a universal observance till towards the end of the eleventh century.

But no uncertainty on points of minor importance can detract from the value of the lessons to be inculcated from the example of the unselfish and uncalculating Saint whom the day commemorates; a day with which, in conclusion, we wish to connect the verses entitled "The Quip," by George Herbert.

> The merry world did on a day
> With his train-bands and mates agree,
> To meet together, where I lay,
> And all in sport to jeer at me.

---

[*] Hildebrand: *De Diebus Festis Libellus.*

First, Beauty crept into a rose;
Which when I pluckt not, Sir, said she,
Tell me, I pray, whose hands are those?
But Thou shalt answer, Lord, for me.

Then Money came, and chinking still,
What tune is this, poor man? said he;
I heard in Music you had skill:
But Thou shalt answer, Lord, for me.

Then came brave Glory puffing by,
In silks that whistled, who but he!
He scarce allowed me half an eye:
But Thou shalt answer, Lord, for me.

Then came quick Wit and Conversation,
And he would needs a comfort be,
And, to be short, made an oration:
But Thou shalt answer, Lord, for me.

Yet when the hour of Thy design
To answer these fine things shall come;
Speak not at large, say, I am Thine,
And then they have their answer home.

St. Michael and all Angels.

September 29.

LTHOUGH there is a tradition that the Feast of St. Michael and all Angels was instituted so early as the fourth century by Alexander, Bishop of Alexandria, its celebration took a long time to work its way into uniform and general acceptance. About the year 366 a sect called Angelites seem to have numbered many adherents in Phrygia, where they dedicated oratories and chapels to St. Michael, to whom they offered prayers as to the Chief Captain of the Host of God. The heresy became of sufficient importance and dimensions to attract the reprobation of the Council of Laodicea, which, in the fourth century, decreed that "we ought not to leave the Church of God, and invocate angels." Superstitious and heretical excesses would naturally have the effect of retarding the general acceptance and consolidation of a festival to which attached the discredit of having once been tainted with them. Yet, after all, it did so happen that the celebration of the day was based upon a piety so fond as to carry it very near to, if not over, the marches of superstition. For the festival was not instituted in commemoration of the appearances of St. Michael and other Angels, attested in the Scriptures, but rather in remembrance of several Apparitions of St. Michael in divers places, which were treasured in ecclesiastical tradition as having occurred from the fifth to the eighth century.

Of these Apparitions, three principal ones have become famous. The one most celebrated amongst the members of the Greek Church is that which is said to have occurred at Chonæ, in Phrygia, the Colossæ of St. Paul. Constantine the Great had already built a famous church about four miles from Constantinople, which he called Michaelion, in honour of the Archangel; to whom there were at one time as many as fifteen churches in Constantinople itself, which had been dedicated by several Emperors. But the Greeks had at least three different feasts of St. Michael, with as many different days of celebration, the chief of these being referred to the 8th of November.

Amongst the Latins, the most celebrated Apparition of St. Michael is that which is said to have taken place on Mount Garganus, May 8th, 490. At this time Apulia was infested by northern invaders; and the Christians, after a three days' fast, obtained a signal victory, for which they were fain to believe themselves indebted to the presence and prestige of the warlike Archangel. A church was at once erected on Mount Garganus, where he was said to have appeared; and the consecration of this building took place September 29, 793, which day, as well as the day of his apparition, became a stated festival in his honour.

The third principal Apparition which gave its own date to another celebration of St. Michael's day, was one reported to have occurred on Mount Tumba or its neighbourhood, October 16th, in or about the year 707. On this occasion the Archangel thrice counselled Autbert, Bishop of Abrincatæ (Avranches, in Lower Normandy), that he should found a memorial church in his honour on a sea-side eminence called Tumba, and *In Periculo Maris*, wishing that a reverence should be paid to him in the sea equal to that he enjoyed on Mount Garganus. This legend frequently localised itself during the Middle Ages, and churches to St.

Michael became frequent wherever eminences, crags, or the crests of isolated hills, looking down upon the sea, invited such a dedication. The most noted example of this tendency in our own country is to be found in the romantic St. Michael's Mount that "wards the western coast" of Cornwall; which, no less than Mont St. Michel, the Peril of the Sea, in Normandy, was looked upon as a scene of past conflict between the Archangel and the arch-fiend.

We have thus various churches inscribed to St. Michael in ancient times, whose dedication is mentioned as having been celebrated by a special office. These several dedications would appear to have gradually coalesced into one festival, observed on the 29th September, and called the "Dedication of St. Michael the Archangel." Baronius observes that "although called a Dedication, it does not follow that the Dedication was like that of other churches; but rather in honour and remembrance of St. Michael and the Angels; and that it only seemed to be called a Dedication because the first observance of the feast coincided with the day of Dedication."

But, as we have already intimated, it was a long time before uniformity obtained as to the day to which the Festival of St. Michael should be referred. In some particular Martyrologies the victory of the Archangel over the Dragon is found conjoined with the anniversary of the Death of Christ, and commemorated on the 25th March. The Copts celebrated the day of St. Michael on the 6th September; and the Æthiopians observed more than one anniversary: whilst in some part or other of Spain it was being constantly honoured on nearly every day of every month between March and October, both inclusive. Finally, however, the divergent traditions were reduced to something like harmony; and an almost universal practice settled on one particular day. But it does not appear that this day was kept by the Church collectively until the eighth century; and it was first formally recognised in the 36th Canon of the Council of Mentz, A.D. 813. "After this authorization the custom prevailed more and more; and its observance was at length secured in the Greek Church in the twelfth century, when it was established in that communion by order of the Emperor Michael Comnenus.

How it is that St. Michael alone stands nominally in the forefront of his fellow angels in the designation of their Festival, to the prejudice of St. Gabriel, the Angel of the Annunciation, who "stands in the presence of God," may be understood from the fact that St. Michael was always regarded as the Angel of the Resurrection and the vanquisher of Satan. It was he who repeated his historic conflicts with the Devil, in the mind and person of every believer. It was his special province to strike for and to animate the faithful in their contests with Antichrist; to expose the frauds and fallacies and lying wonders of the great Deceiver; and to defend at the Last Judgment the souls of the saints against the charges of the great Accuser. It has, moreover, been inferred from the offices he sustains, that St. Michael was the chief and prince of the good, as Lucifer was of the fallen, angels; and on this account he was formerly accepted as the tutelary Angel of the Jewish Synagogue, as afterwards as the Guardian of the Christian Church.

Drummond of Hawthornden signalizes the victorious valour and prowess of the champion of light against darkness, in a short poem, "On the Feast of St. Michael the Archangel."

> To Thee, O Christ! Thy Father's light,
> Life, virtue, which our heart inspires,
> In presence of Thine angels bright,
> We sing with voice and with desires:
> Ourselves we mutually invite,
> To melody with answering choirs.
>
> With reverence we these soldiers praise,
> Who near the heavenly throne abide;

> And chiefly him whom God doth raise,
> His strong celestial host to guide—
> Michael, who by his power dismays
> And beateth down the Devil's pride.

Michael was revealed to the prophet Daniel as "one of the chief princes" who fought against their enemies on the side of the children of the Captivity; and, again, as "the great prince who stood for the children of the people" of the prophet. It was Michael who, contending with the devil, disputed about the body of Moses; and it is he, with his angels, who is depicted as fighting against the great Dragon and *his* angels—a combat issuing in the casting out from heaven of the "great Dragon that old serpent, called the Devil and Satan, together with his angels." And with this casting out of the "accuser of our brethren," come "salvation, and strength, and the kingdom of our God, and the power of His Christ."

Such proofs and details of the victorious intrepidity of Michael give an air of naturalness to the opinion, otherwise fanciful and unsupported, that it was he who, in his capacity of *præses* of the Jewish Church and people, stirred up the valour of Gideon to the salvation of Israel; and that it was he who smote to death the myriads of Sennacherib as they lay before Jerusalem.

The angel Gabriel is represented as standing in the presence of God; and to him was committed the Annunciation of the Birth of Jesus to the Virgin Mary.

The *nominal* intervention of Raphael—who is sometimes put forward as the representative "Power" in the hierarchy of heaven—in human affairs is limited to the apocryphal Book of Tobit, where his principal mission is to cure Tobit of his blindness; to heal Sara, and give her as a wife to Tobias; to bind Asmodeus, the evil spirit; and to concern himself generally in the welfare of Tobit and his family.

In order to complete the quaternion of the Heavenly Host whose names are known to us by means of the Scriptures, Canonical or Apocryphal, it may be mentioned that Uriel is described in the Second Book of Esdras as the angel commissioned to interpret unto Esdras the will and ways of God.

Whilst in this connection, and before saying a few words about the nature of angels, and their relations to God, it may be proper to glance at the various methods of their beneficent activity in favour of mankind. The magnificent stanzas which open one of the cantos of Spenser's "Faerie Queene" here infallibly suggest themselves:—

> And is there care in Heaven? and is there love
> In Heavenly spirits to these creatures base
> That may compassion of their evils move?
> There is: else much more wretched were the case
> Of men than beasts: but oh! the exceeding grace
> Of highest God, that loves His creatures so;
> And all His works with mercy doth embrace,
> That blessed angels He sends to and fro,
> To serve to wicked man—to serve His wicked foe!
>
> How oft do they their silver bowers leave
> To come to succour us that succour want!
> How oft do they with golden pinions cleave
> The flitting skies, like flying pursuivant,
> Against foul fiends to aid us militant!
> They for us fight, they watch and duly ward,
> And their bright squadrons round about us plant;
> And all for love, and nothing for reward:
> Oh, why should Heavenly God to men have such regard?

Of old, angels were sent visibly to favoured men to give them the benefit of their high communion; to explain or to reveal to them difficult or future circumstances; and to fortify their faith in the truths which their souls had previously accepted. It was by the disposition of angels that the children of Israel received the Law; and it was by a multitude of the heavenly host that the Nativity of the Incarnate Gospel was celebrated over the sheepfolds of Bethlehem. Whilst for the most part, the errands on which angels visited our world were errands of love and mercy, their exceptional mission was to stand as adversaries in the path of the wicked; and to destroy cities and to smite nations which had impiously withheld from God the glory due unto His name. At the end of the world, as we gather from the New Testament, when the Son of Man shall come in the clouds, with great power and glory, then shall He send His angels, and shall gather together His elect; and the Angels shall come forth, and they shall gather out of His Kingdom all things that offend, and them which do iniquity; and they shall sever the wicked from among the just; and shall cast them into the furnace of fire, where shall be wailing and gnashing of teeth.

Angelic manifestations sometimes occurred in dreams, " in a vision of the night, when deep sleep falleth upon man." Again, angels talked with men face to face, having the appearance and speaking with the voices of men. The angel of the Lord encampeth round about them that fear Him, and delivereth them; and over such persons God gives His angels charge to keep them in all their ways, to accompany them and to prosper them, and to redeem them from all evil. It was by them that God comforted Israel, delivered Lot out of Sodom, Daniel from the devouring lions, and St. Peter from his imprisonment and the wrath of Herod; and filled the mountain, unseen, with horses and chariots of fire for the protection of Elisha. Especially they ministered in the desert, and comforted in the garden of agony the Son of Man; and announced His resurrection. And now, by command of their Master and ours, the angels watch over the feeblest of His brethren; rejoice over the tears of a penitent sinner; bring before God the remembrance of alms and prayers; and carry up the souls of the faithful departed into Paradise.

All these offices are set forth in his usual exhaustive manner, and, it must be said, with his usual pedestrian muse, by Bishop Ken, in his poem, entitled "Angels," one of a group of poems on "God's Attributes, or Perfections." Ken, indeed, so well loved, and so strongly held and inculcated the doctrine of the ministry of angels, as to have written an epic poem, "Hymnotheo; or, the Penitent," the primary object of which seems to be the demonstration, or, at least the illustration, of their society and guardianship. Not only is each individual shown to have his guardian angel; but almost every virtue, quality, or phenomenon of the human mind is elevated to an angelic personality. The unconscious activity of the intellect during sleep, for example, is attributed to Phylonar, the Angel of Dreams. In accordance with the views to which it was Ken's delight to give such remarkable prominence, it was held by him that in every church, country, and nation, as in every soul of man, the lists are set as for a conflict between angelic squadrons, good and bad. In the breast of each individual is repeated that war between Michael and Satan, about which we have so mysterious and unique an intimation in the Epistle of St. Jude. But, to go back for a moment to a period hundreds of years anterior to the time of Ken, we may remark that St. Ambrose held very definitely that all things—the air, the heavens, the earth, the seas—were full of angels.

We have just mentioned two several poems of Bishop Ken's; but it is not from either of these we propose to offer an extract. The following is transcribed from another poem of the Bishop's, "On St. Michael;" of which we present so many stanzas as have reference to the charitable offices of the angels unto faithful men. Ken says, addressing the angels :—

> You on the Heirs of Heaven attend,
> To comfort, counsel, warn, defend,
> You in their Infant-age,
> To tender them engage,
> You quicken Saints who grow remiss,
> And you at Death transport their souls to Bliss.

You Abram of a Son assured,
   You Lot from Sodom's flames secured,
      You bless'd Elijah fed,
      You circle a Saint's bed,
   To work our bliss, to guard from woe,
You the Expanse pass hourly to and fro.

You in the Furnace cool'd the Saints,
   You kept fierce Lions in restraints;
      You Peter freed when chained,
      You Paul in storm sustained;
   You God's high Will in Dreams detect,
You pious Souls to faithful Guides direct.

You in God's House Trisagions sing,
   You veil your rays with awful wing,
      Our temples you frequent,
      Devotion to foment,
   God's boundless Wisdom there to hear,
Mysterious Truths to learn and to revere.

Your piercing eyes inspect our ways,
   You sing for our conversion praise,
      You, all the Saints you meet,
      Like Fellow-Servants treat,
   At the great Day of all the Just,
You shall collect their dissipated Dust.

The company of angels in heaven is said to be innumerable; and they are described as more excellent in strength, power, wisdom, and goodness than man, who, even at his best in Paradise, was a "little lower" than they. Yet even their excellence has its limitations. The wisdom of these bright and glorious beings is folly in the sight of God; and to none of them did He ever say, "Thou art my Son, this day have I begotten thee;" or, "Sit on my right hand, until I make thine enemies thy footstool." Their moral qualities may be summarized in the statement that they are everywhere in the Scriptures represented as models of perfect obedience, purity, affection, and self-abnegation. They are "holy," "elect," "ministers of God that do His pleasure;" yet are they creatures of

His hand, who, casting their crowns before Him, confess Him alone to be Holy, Holy, Holy! As sings Herrick, in his "Noble Numbers:"—

> Angells are called Gods; yet of them, none
> Are Gods, but by participation;
> As just men are entitled Gods, yet none
> Are Gods, of them, but by adoption.

As to the essential nature of angels, there has been more speculation than positive information. They are ministering *spirits;* and, themselves incorporeal, they have adopted human forms and characteristics in order to fulfil particular functions and ministrations. As pure spirits and uncompounded, they are exempt from the weaknesses of our frail, earthly frame; and their gifts of grace and glory are proportioned to the superiority of their nature. Mankind, however, has the set-off and compensation of the Incarnation, in which the Son of God, not stooping to take on Him the nature of angels, stooped lower to assume that of man; and, as Man, is constituted by His Father lord of all creatures.

Dr. Townsend, in his "Ecclesiastical and Civil History," puts forth an ingenious and plausible theory that the correlative superiority and inferiority of men and angels may in the course of blissful ages be reversed by the progress and growth of the former, whilst the latter are presumably to remain stationary and undeveloping. "I *believe*," he says, "and I will, therefore, express my conviction, that it will be found in our immortality, that man is the being next to God; that neither angel nor archangel is superior to him; that as the dog or the elephant are stationary in creation, and the new-born infant is inferior to them in sagacity and instinct, but very soon surpasses them in knowledge, judgment and faith in an invisible Redeemer—so also it is, that the angel and the archangel are stationary in their higher places in the universe, while the souls of the believers in revelation, who are admitted to that state to which the Son of God invites them, will, at the period of their admission be inferior to the hierarchy of heaven; but they will pass them—they will pass the angel and archangel in their places before their common Creator. As the infant of a King is higher in rank than the highest statesman before the throne of his father, because he is a son, while they are but the most honourable of his servants; so are the Christian believers: they are sons, not servants. Angels are but the ministering spirits to the heirs of salvation; the heirs of salvation are the children of God, and joint-heirs in the inheritance with Christ!"

It may certainly be very legitimately questioned, whether a goodness of necessity and without an alternative, is so real as a goodness which, after disentangling the right from the wrong, elects to abide by the former. On this ground, whilst we as men confess ourselves a little lower than our fellow-servants the angels, the "high courtiers of Heaven," it is a proud thing, amidst our hazards, to think that we, although in a less magnificent service, are probably in a more picturesque position, than they, and one which gives an opportunity of demonstrating, under fierce and chronic temptations, rectitude of character and conduct of a kind morally more grand than theirs.

Leaving the question of the relative dignity of men and angels, whether in the present or the future, a few words are due to the somewhat curious efforts which have been made to settle the question of angelic precedence amongst themselves. Dionysius the Areopagite, or the author of the works attributed to him, in a book on the *Celestial Hierarchy*, divides the nine choirs of angels into three ranks. In the first and highest rank, the Seraphim stand first, and after them the Cherubim and Thrones. In the second rank stand the Virtues, Dominations, and Powers; and in the third, the Principalities, Archangels, and Angels. St. Gregory ranges them in an inverted order, as follows:—Angels, Archangels, Principalities, Powers, Dominations, Virtues, Thrones, Cherubim and Seraphim. Thomas Heywood—little known in this age, in spite of his wonderful fecundity as a dramatist, and scarcely known at all as the author of a quaint, pious, and learned folio on the "Hierarchie of the Blessed Angells; their names, orders, and offices," (1635)*—adopts the order we have just given as that of the *pseudo*-Dionysius, except that he allows the Dominations precedence over the Virtues. The names of the representative angels of his several orders are as follow:—(1) Uriel; (2) Jophiel; (3) Zaphkiel; (4) Zadchiel; (5) Hamiel; (6) Raphael; (7) Camael; (8) Michael; and (9) Gabriel.

Such an attempt, however, at marshalling the host of heaven according to their precise precedence, is an abortive one, and likely to continue to be so ; for St. Paul himself seems to have doomed to confusion the effort to blazon their respective or relative dignities. In his recital of some of the angelic orders in his Epistle to the Ephesians, the Apostle uses a different sequence to that which he observes in his Epistle to the Colossians ; and, in addition to this the *Thrones* of the latter escape in the former into the haze of a general allusion to " every name that is named in the world to come." It would be well if patristic speculation, and, more especially, if scholastic subtlety had never sought to go into any investigations with reference to angels, less refined or prurient than those about the celestial hierarchy.

After such comparative trivialities, we would seek to recover tone for our subject in the majestic words of Richard Hooker, who seems to speak them magisterially and from the ermine. "Angels," he says, in the fourth chapter of the first Book of his "Ecclesiastical Polity"— "Angels are spirits immaterial and intellectual, the glorious inhabitants of those sacred palaces where nothing but

* See pages 287 and 288.

light and blessed immortality, no shadow of matter for tears, discontentments, griefs, and uncomfortable passions to work upon; but all joy, tranquillity, and peace, even for ever and ever doth dwell. As in number and order they are huge, mighty, and royal armies, so likewise in perfection of obedience unto that law which the Highest, whom they adore, love, and imitate, hath imposed upon them, such observants they are thereof, that our Saviour Himself, being to set down the perfect idea of that which we are to pray and wish for on earth, did not teach to pray or wish for more than only that here it might be with us as with them it is in heaven. God, which moveth mere natural agents as an efficient only, doth otherwise move intellectual creatures, and especially His holy angels; for, beholding the peace of God, in admiration of so great excellency they all adore Him, and being rapt with the love of His beauty, they cleave inseparably for ever unto Him. Desire to resemble Him in goodness maketh them unweariable and even unsatiable in their longing to do, by all means, all manner of good unto all the creatures of God, but especially unto the children of men, in the countenance of whose nature, looking downward, they behold themselves beneath themselves, even as upward in God, beneath whom themselves are, they see that character which is nowhere but in themselves and us resembled."

The right celebration of a festival instituted in honour of the angels demands a particular gratitude to God for the bliss which they enjoy, and a large sympathy with their felicity; and the recollection of that clause in the Lord's Prayer which refers to their love for God on account of His holiness, beauty, and truth, and to the worship and imitation of Him. It requires also a recognition of the goodness which has constituted such glorious beings to minister to our comfort and final victory; and it includes, further, an effort after communion with them, and a feeling of sacred emulation of being counted worthy to carry on the work of God on earth with the same fidelity, fervour, and purity, as they carry it on with in heaven.

A festival commemorative of such lessons of communion and affection has always offered a picturesque and attractive theme for the Christian lyre. It has not opened subjects so infinitely awful, and sublime, and unapproachable as some other celebrations; as, for example, that of Trinity Sunday, where the pious and baffled muse would fain sink into silent and mysterious adoration. Yet it has an ascertained grandeur of its own; as how, indeed, could it be otherwise, when it declares the abysses and the splendours of the world of spirits; the experiences, the aids and hindrances, of mortal warfare and pilgrimage; the chequered glory and catastrophe of the final Judgment; the eternal defeat of the Adversary; and the eternal and peaceful communion of the Saints in light.

The next contribution to our angelic anthology is a cento from the Canon of the "Bodiless Ones," which is transcribed from the late Dr. Neale's "Hymns of the Eastern Church." We preface it by a few particulars which Dr. Neale gives of its author, St. Joseph of the Studium, whom he calls the most voluminous writer of the *third period* of Greek Hymnology.

"A Sicilian by birth, Joseph left his native country on its occupation by the Mahometans in 830, and went to Thessalonica, where he embraced the monastic life. Thence he removed to Constantinople, but, in the second Iconoclastic persecution, he seems to have felt no vocation for confessorship, and went to Rome. Taken by pirates, he was for some years a slave in Crete, where he converted many to the faith; and having obtained his liberty, and returned to the Imperial City, he stood high in the favour, first of St. Ignatius, then of Photius, whom he accompanied into exile. On the death of that great man he was recalled, and gave himself up entirely to hymnology. A legend, connected with his death, is related of him. A citizen of Constantinople betook himself to the church of St. Theodore in the hope of obtaining some benefit from the intercessions of that martyr. He waited three days in vain; then, just as he was about to leave the church in despair, St. Theodore appeared. 'I,' said the vision, 'and the other Saints, whom the poet Joseph has celebrated in his Canons, have been attending his soul to Paradise: hence my absence from my church.'"

The poem we have selected as proper for our purpose is entitled "Stars of the Morning."

> Stars of the morning, so gloriously bright,
> Filled with celestial resplendence and light;
> These that, where night never followeth day,
> Raise the Trishagion ever and aye:
>
> These are Thy counsellors: these dost Thou own,
> God of Sabaoth! the nearest Thy Throne;
> These are Thy ministers; these dost Thou send,
> Help of the helpless ones! man to defend.
>
> These keep the guard, amidst Salem's dear bowers:
> Thrones, Principalities, Virtues, and Powers:
> Where with the Living Ones, mystical Four,
> Cherubin, Seraphin, bow and adore.
>
> "Who like the Lord?"—thunders Michael the Chief:
> Raphael, "the Cure of God," comforteth grief:
> And, as at Nazareth, prophet of peace,
> Gabriel, "the Light of God," bringeth release.
>
> Then, when the earth was first poised in mid-space,—
> Then, when the planets first sped on their race,—
> Then, when were ended the six days' employ,—
> Then all the Sons of God shouted for joy.
>
> Still let them succour us; still let them fight,
> Lord of angelic hosts, battling for right!
> Till, where their anthems they ceaselessly pour,
> We with the Angels may bow and adore!

This poem of St. Joseph of the Studium, points almost exclusively to the duties and occupations of the angels, as watching and praising, in their celestial abodes, the magnificent operations of their Creator. Our next specimen of Michaelmas poetry exhibits the angels in their activity towards men; and is a song of praise to God, founded directly upon the text, which describes the angels as "ministering spirits, sent forth to minister for them that shall be heirs of salvation." It is the expression and recognition of benefits conferred, or possibly to be conferred, upon mankind through angelic agency. Its author is Johann Rist, a German poet, born March 8th, 1607, at Pinneberg, near Hamburg. After having studied theology in Germany and Holland, Rist became pastor of Wedel, on the Elbe, and received later the dignities of Count Palatine and Ecclesiastical Councillor. From his youth he had been a devotee of the Muses; and was one of the most fecund and most popular poets of his time. He seems to have taken Opitz as a standard of imitation, but without sharing in the predilection which Opitz manifests for the ancient models. Rist, who is the author of a great number of poems, written in a pure and elegant style, has been reputed a correct rather than an enthusiastic poet. Yet he had suffered much in his youth from mental struggles, as he did in after years from plunder, pestilence, and all the horrors of war; so that he could refer the production of his poems to the chequered and deep experiences of his own heart. "The dear Cross," he used to say, "hath pressed many songs out of me." He died August 31st, 1667.

The title of his poem coincides exactly with the designation of the festival, being inscribed to "St. Michael and All Angels." We are indebted to the version we now place before the reader to Miss Winkworth's "Lyra Germanica."

> Praise and thanks to Thee be sung,
> Mighty God, in sweetest tone!
> Lo! from every land and tongue,
> Nations gather round Thy Throne,

ST. MICHAEL AND ALL ANGELS.

Praising Thee, that Thou dost send,
   Daily from Thy Heaven above,
   Angel-messengers of love,
Who Thy threaten'd Church defend.
Who can offer worthily,
   Lord of angels, praise to Thee!

'Tis your office, Spirits bright,
   Still to guard us night and day,
And before your heavenly might,
   Powers of darkness flee away;
Ever doth your unseen host,
   Camp around us, and avert
All that seeks to do us hurt,
Curbing Satan's malice most.
Lord, who then can worthily,
   For such goodness honour Thee!

And ye come on ready wing,
   When we drift toward sheer despair,
Seeing nought where we might cling,
   Suddenly, lo, ye are there!
And the wearied heart grows strong,
   As an angel strengthened Him,
   Fainting in the garden dim,
'Neath the world's vast woe and wrong.
Lord, who then can worthily,
   For such mercy honour Thee!

Right and seemly were it then
   We should glory, that our God
Hath such honour put on men,
   That He sends o'er earth abroad
Princes of the realm above,
   Champions, who by day and night,
   Shield us with His holy might;
Come, behold how great His love!
Lord, who then can worthily,
   For such favour honour Thee!

Praise and thanks to Thee be sung,
   Mighty God, in sweetest tone.
Lo! from every land and tongue,
   Nations gather round Thy Throne,

"ANGELIC GUIDANCE."

> . Praising Thee that Thou dost send,
>   Hourly from Thy glorious sphere,
>   Angels down to help us here,
>   And Thy threatened Church defend.
>   Let us henceforth worthily,
>   Lord of angels, honour Thee!

Our next contribution is a poem which belongs to that department of our subject in which the angels are regarded as lovingly taking part in the affairs and the well-being of "Christ's own." The subject is essentially the same as Rist's; but the manner is nearly as different as possible. There is little movement; and the sense seems somewhat involved in the mazes of the sonnet, and the contemplative treatment of the author. It is taken from "Verses on various Occasions," a recent volume by Dr. Newman, which incorporates his contributions to "Lyra Apostolica," and in which it is entitled "Angelic Guidance."

> Are these the tracks of some unearthly Friend,
>   His foot-prints, and his vesture-skirts of light,
>   Who, as I talk with men, conforms aright
> Their sympathetic words, or deeds that blend
> With my hid thought;—or stoops him to attend
>   My doubtful-pleading grief;—or blunts the might
>   Of ill I see not;—or in dreams of night
> Figures the scope in which what is will end?
> Were I Christ's own, then fitly might I call
> That vision real; for, to the thoughtful mind
> That walks with Him, He half unveils His face;
> But when on earth-stained souls such shadows fall,
> These dare not claim as theirs what there they find,
> Yet, not all hopeless, eye His boundless grace.

Wherever the balance of excellence will allow us, we wish to offer to our readers the angelical poems of less known or less easily accessible authors. We are fain, notwithstanding this desire to lay before them what is comparatively fresh or else recondite, to fall back upon the late Mr. Keble for an illustration of that very interesting department of Michaelmas contemplation which is found radiating from the words of our Lord:—" Take heed that ye despise not one of these little ones; for I say unto you, that in heaven their angels do always behold the face of my Father." It is some comfort to think that it is not the " Christian Year," but the less marvellously popular " Lyra Innocentium," that we lay under contribution. But our best apology will be, that it would be hard indeed to find a poet with a better claim to sing of Christ's little ones than John Keble; of whom it has been said that he never found himself in the presence of children without forming, if he did not utter, in their behalf the words of spontaneous supplication.

The quaint but suggestive title of Keble's poem is " Carved Angels."

> Greatest art Thou in least, O Lord,
>   And even Thy least are great in Thee:
> A mote in air, a random word,
>   Shall save a soul if Thou decree:—
>   Much more their presence sweet,
> Whom with an oath Thou didst into Thy kingdom greet.
>
> A little child's soft sleeping face
>   The murderer's knife ere now hath staid:
> The adulterous eye, so foul and base
>   Is of a little child afraid.
>   They cannot choose but fear,
> Since in that sign they feel God and good angels near.
>
> For by the Truth's sure oath we know,
>   There is no christened babe but owns
> A Watcher mightier than his foe,
>   One of the everlasting Thrones,
>   Who in high Heaven His face
> Beholding ever, best His likeness here may trace.
>
> As in each tiny drop of dew,
>   Glistening at prime of morn, they mark
> Of Heaven's great Sun an image true,
>   Hear their own chantings in the Lark,
>   So, sleeping or awake,
> They love to tend their babes for holy Bethlehem's sake.

And so this whole fallen world of ours,
    To us all care, and sin, and spite,
    Is even as Eden's stainless bowers
      To the pure spirit out of sight,—
        To Angels from above,
And souls of infants, sealed by new-creating Love.

Heaven in the depth and height is seen;
    On high among the stars, and low
    In deep clear waters: all between
      Is earth, and tastes of earth: even so
        The Almighty One draws near
To strongest seraphs there, to weakest infants here.

And both are robed in white, and both
    On evil look unharmed, and wear
    A ray so pure, ill Powers are loth
      To linger in the keen bright air.
        As Angels wait in joy
On Saints, so on the old the duteous-hearted boy.

God's Angels keep the eternal round
    Of praise on high, and never tire.
    His lambs are in His Temple found
      Early, with all their hearts' desire.
        They boast not to be free,
They grudge not to their Lord meek ear and bended knee.

Oh well and wisely wrought of old,
    Nor without guide be sure, who first
    Did cherub forms as infants mould,
      And lift them where the full deep burst
        Of awful harmony
Might need them most, to waft it onward to the sky:

Where best they may in watch and ward
    Around the enthroned Saviour stand,
    May quell, with sad and stern regard,
      Unruly eye and wayward hand,
        May deal the blessed dole
Of saving knowledge round from many a holy scroll.

What if in other lines than ours
   They write, in other accents speak?
There are whom watchful Love empowers
   To read such riddles; duteous seek,
      And thou shalt quickly find.
The Mother best may tell the eager babe's deep mind.

Haply some shield their arms embrace,
   Rich with the Lord's own blazonry.
The Cross of His redeeming grace,
   Or His dread Wounds we then descry.
      His standard-bearers they:
Learn we to face them on the dread Procession Day.

And O! if aught of pride or lust
   Have soiled thee in the world, take heed:
Entering, shake off the mire and dust.
   Angelic eyes are keen, to read
      By the least, lightest sign,
When we foul, idle thoughts breathe in the air divine.

And how, but by their whisperings soft,
   Feel virgin hearts when sin is near,
Sin even in dreams unknown? Full oft
   Such instinct we may mark in fear,
      Nor our own ill endure
In presence of Christ's babes, and of their Guardians pure.

One other poem will enable us to complete the cycle of Angelical meditation. The scene of the goal is the same as that of the starting-point; we are to leave off, as we began, in Heaven. We have contemplated, so to say, the relation in which God stood to the angels; and, with St. Joseph, have seen the relation in which they stood to God. With Ken, Rist, and Newman, we have pondered on their affectionate and vigilant ministrations in their capacity of guardians of the faithful; whilst with Keble, we have been half recalled to the highest spheres of thought for the contemplation of the celestial types and representatives of terrestrial Innocents.

There are, so far as we can at present understand, three grand eras in the economy of Heaven. The first was that unbeginning one during which God dwelt alone, an Infinite end and centre unto Himself; the second was that in which the universe became a government and a polity by the creation first of angelic and then of human existences; and the third and unending one is to be that in which—defection and treason, whether done in heaven or on earth, by incorporeal or by incarnate spirits, being visited with eternal chastisement and exile—the family of the saved of Mankind shall join the family of the elect Angels in the immediate presence and bliss of God for ever and ever. There is, we think, a fitness in taking from Thomas à Kempis—the putative author of the "Imitation of Christ,"—a hymn "On the Joys of Heaven," which illustrates the glorious era to which all faithful souls in all worlds are tending; and in which the "Tersanctus'" of the very earliest Liturgies, and of our own Communion Service, shall be realized by sight, as now it is believed on the evidence of faith and love:—" Therefore with Angels and Archangels, and with all the Company of Heaven, we laud and magnify Thy glorious Name; evermore praising Thee, and saying, Holy, Holy, Holy, Lord God of hosts, heaven and earth are full of Thy glory: Glory be to Thee, O Lord most High. Amen."

The following translation of the Hymn of Thomas à Kempis is by the author of the "Voice of Christian Life in Song."

> High the angel choirs are raising
>   Heart and voice in harmony:
> The Creator King still praising,
>   Whom in beauty there they see.
>
> Sweetest strains, from soft harps stealing;
> Trumpets, notes of triumph pealing;
> Radiant wings and white stoles gleaming,
> Up the steps of glory streaming;

ST. MICHAEL AND ALL ANGELS.

Where the heavenly bells are ringing,
Holy, holy, holy! singing
   To the mighty Trinity!
Holy, holy, holy! crying;
For all earthly care and sighing
   In that City cease to be!

Every voice is there harmonious,
Praising God in hymns symphonious;
Love each heart with light enfolding,
As they stand in peace beholding
   There the Triune Deity!
Whom adore the seraphim,
   Aye with love eternal burning;
Venerate the cherubim,
   To their fount of honour turning;
   Whilst angelic thrones adoring
     Gaze upon His Majesty.

Oh how beautiful that region,
And how fair that heavenly legion,
   Where thus men and angels blend!
Glorious will that City be,
Full of deep tranquility,
   Light and peace from end to end!
All the happy dwellers there
   Shine in robes of purity,
   Keep the law of charity,
   Bound in firmest unity;
Labour finds them not, nor care.
   Ignorance can ne'er perplex,
   Nothing tempt them, nothing vex;
Joy and health their fadeless blessing,
   Always all things good possessing.

St. Luke the Evangelist.

October 18.

"NO historical account," says Mr. Riddle, "concerning the origin of this festival is extant. It was probably contemporary with the other festivals of the Apostles; which may, for the most part, be assigned to about the eleventh or twelfth centuries—at least so far as regards their general adoption. But Dr. Waterland, in a MS. note to Wheatly, observes that this feast is to be referred to the fifth century, 'as appears from the Carthage calendar.' "* Brady fixes upon the year 1130 as that of its first institution.†

But little is known of the personal history of St. Luke; who, in addition to his honours as an Evangelist, bears also the distinction of having been the earliest of ecclesiastical historians. By some authors, who evidently do not consider his claims barred by the somewhat ambiguous inscription of his Gospel to Theophilus, he is reckoned to have been one of the Seventy Disciples, of whose commission he is the only one of the Evangelists to take notice. Others, considering that he *does* bar his claims to be regarded as an eye-witness and minister of the Word from the beginning (Luke i. 1-4), speak of him as one of St. Paul's converts at Antioch, of which city, according to Eusebius,

---
* *Manual of Christian Antiquities.* † *Clavis Calendaria.*

he was a native.* A third party find something like a middle path between these two theories, and, holding that Luke was one of the disciples who "walked no more with Jesus" after the unwelcome discourse detailed in the sixth chapter of St. John's Gospel, believe him to have been reclaimed merely, and not converted *ab initio*, by the Apostle Paul. Doubt even attaches to his profession; and there is a tradition that he was a skilful painter who executed the pictures of Christ and the Blessed Virgin which are yet exhibited at Rome. Hospinian meets this tradition with an *à priori* denial, saying that St. Luke "painted Christ and His Mother in the vivid colours of his eloquence, in which he appears to have had an excellent faculty; but that he certainly had no leisure to paint them in any other manner."† It may be that such a tradition took its rise from confounding the Evangelist with another Luke, an early Greek painter, some of whose works are still preserved. Some authors, again, lovers of doubt and uncertainty, see nothing in the plain description of St. Luke as the "beloved physician" (Coloss. iv. 14), but a figure which is intended to apply to him as a healer of souls only. But the natural and professional meaning of the word physician is not destroyed merely because a fuller and more spiritual significance is induced upon it. The Collect for St. Luke's Day assumes this beautiful duplicity of meaning; which is also the key-note to the following Hymn for St. Luke's Day, for which we are indebted to the Rev. Gerard Moultrie's "Hymns and Lyrics for the Seasons of the Church."

> O Jesu, O Redeemer,
>   Physician of the soul,
> Receive, receive Thy people,
>   And cleanse and make them whole.

* *Ecclesiastical History*; lib. iii., c. 4.
† *De Origine Festoram Christianorum.*

For health, for strength, for healing,
   The stream is never dry,
Whose fountain-head flows ceaseless
   From holy Calvary.

O Lamb of GOD, O JESU,
   Upon the altar slain,
The blood of Thine atonement
   Shall purge our guilty stain:

Not now in type and figure
   Of bull or heifer seen,
The blood of the Redeemer
   Shall sprinkle the unclean.

The guests await the summons,
   Their robes are white and fair,
Washed in the Blood of JESUS
   From sin and from despair:

And He, the great All-healer,
   His wine and oil shall pour
Upon their wounds, and bear them
   From trouble evermore.

The banquet-hall is ready,
   The banquet-hall of CHRIST,
He calls the loved physician,
   The blest Evangelist;

The marriage feast awaits him,
   The joy of his reward;
Receive, then, faithful servant,
   The wages of thy LORD.

By those who think of St. Luke as one of the Seventy, it has been held that he was the fellow-traveller with Cleophas when the Lord joined Himself to their society on the way to Emmaus. The least probability that such may have been the case is sufficient to plead in justification of the insertion of a few lines, which, if they cannot be shown to have any right to appear in this place, have at least no special claim to any other throughout our volume. They are extracted from Cowper's "Conversation;" and the author appends to the narrative a recommendation of it as affording a model of lofty and familiar discourse.

> It happened on a solemn eventide,
> Soon after He that was our Surety died,
> Two bosom friends, each pensively inclined,
> The scene of all those sorrows left behind,
> Sought their own village, busied as they went
> In musings worthy of the great event:
> They spake of Him they loved, of Him whose life,
> Though blameless, had incurred perpetual strife;
> Whose deeds had left, in spite of hostile arts,
> A deep memorial graven on their hearts.
> The recollection, like a vein of ore,
> The farther traced, enriched them still the more;
> They thought Him, and they justly thought Him, one
> Sent to do more than He appeared to have done;
> To exalt a people, and to place them high
> Above all else, and wondered He should die.
> Ere yet they brought their journey to an end,
> A stranger joined them, courteous as a friend,
> And asked them with a kind engaging air
> What their affliction was, and begged a share.
> Informed, he gathered up the broken thread,
> And, truth and wisdom gracing all he said,
> Explained, illustrated, and searched so well
> The tender theme on which they chose to dwell,
> That reaching home, "The night," they said, "is near,
> We must not now be parted, sojourn here."
> The new acquaintance soon became a guest,
> And, made so welcome at their simple feast,
> He blessed the bread, and vanished at the word,
> And left them both exclaiming, "'Twas the Lord!
> Did not our hearts feel all He deigned to say,
> Did they not burn within us by the way?"
> Now theirs was converse, such as it behoves
> Man to maintain, and such as God approves:
> Their views, indeed, were indistinct and dim,
> But yet successful, being aimed at Him.
> Christ and His character their only scope,
> Their object, and their subject, and their hope;

They felt what it became them much to feel,
And, wanting Him to loose the sacred seal,
Found Him as prompt as their desire was true,
To spread the new-born glories in their view.

As St. Luke was a convert and disciple, so he seems to have become the almost inseparable companion and fellow-labourer, of St. Paul. To the great Apostle of the Gentiles, indeed, he seems to have stood in the same relation that Mark occupied to St. Peter; and, as Mark compiled his Gospel from the discourses of Peter, so Luke is represented to have compiled *his* chiefly from the narrative of St. Paul. "But as in the prologue of his Gospel, it is said that he took many things from those who had companied together with the Lord, and as St. Paul had not done so, the inference is that he did not derive his information exclusively, but only principally, from that Apostle. For many circumstances he must have been dependent upon others beside St. Paul; and it is believed that he had recourse to the Blessed Virgin, as to the Ark of the Testament, and was by her certified of many things, especially such as were known to her only—as, for instance, the Angelic Annunciation, the Nativity of Christ, and others of this kind."* The Gospel of St. Luke is said to have given so much satisfaction to the Apostle Paul that he esteemed it the Gospel *par excellence;* to which he is to be understood as referring whenever he has occasion to allude to an Evangelist (Rom. ii. 16). The Gospel of St. Luke is supposed to have been written during the travels of the author with St. Paul in Achaia; and to have had in view the refutation of various "false and fabulous relations, which even then began to be obtruded upon the world," to supply anything that seemed wanting in the works of the two preceding Evangelists, and also especially to insist upon what belongs to Christ's priestly office and character.

* Durandus: *Rationale Divinorum Officiorum.*

Dr. Watts devotes a few lines to showing that "Christ is the Substance of the Levitical Priesthood:"—

> The true Messiah now appears,
>   The types are all withdrawn;
> So fly the shadows and the stars
>   Before the rising dawn.
>
> No smoking sweets, nor bleeding lambs,
>   No kid, nor bullock slain;
> Incense and spice of costly names
>   Would all be burnt in vain.
>
> Aaron must lay his robes away,
>   His mitre and his vest,
> When God Himself comes down to be
>   The offering and the Priest.
>
> He took our mortal flesh, to show
>   The wonders of His love:
> For us He paid His life below,
>   And prays for us above.
>
> "Father," He cries, "forgive their sins,
>   For I Myself have died;"
> And then He shows His opened veins,
>   And pleads His wounded side.

St. Luke particularly endeared himself to St. Paul "by attending him in all his dangers; by being present with him in his several arraignments at Jerusalem; by accompanying him in his hazardous voyage to Rome; where he served his necessities, and supplied those ministerial offices which the Apostle's confinement would not suffer him to discharge, especially in carrying messages to those Churches where he had planted Christianity; and in sticking to him when others forsook him (2 Tim. iv. 11)."* It is in relation to this text, which, indeed, he takes as a motto, that Dr. Kynaston has written the following poem for St. Luke's Day, which, in his "Occasional Hymns," has for its title, "Only Luke is with me."

* Nelson's *Festivals and Fasts*.

What, only Luke!—and Demas gone—
As by the Cross stood only John—
And all have turned, who wept so sore
That they should see thy face no more,
Fell on thy neck—O woe the day—
As Orpah kissed, and went away! *

Go, gentle healer of the soul,
The sick, they need thee, not the whole;
They need thee not whose course is done,
Whose fight is fought, whose crown is won:
He needs thee most to ease his chain
Who turns him to the world again.

O twice Evangelist of love,
Begun below, fulfilled above, †
Thy gentle scrolls in pardon meet,
Like angels at the Mercy-seat;
Still brooding o'er the sinner's loss,
Upon the Throne, athwart the Cross!

O Brother still, when all decline
Who linked their loving words with thine,
Alone, unheeded by the three,
Was Christ, or Paul bereft of thee?
There is Whose love, when all depart,
Clings closer than a brother's heart. ‡

The Book called the Acts of the Apostles was written by St. Luke, in continuation of his Gospel; and is supposed to have been produced at the end of the two years' imprisonment which St. Paul suffered at Rome. Upon the enlargement of the latter, St. Luke is said to have left St. Paul at Rome, and to have betaken himself into Egypt and Libya, where he preached the Gospel, wrought miracles, converted multitudes, constituted guides and ministers of religion, and took upon himself the episcopal charge of the city of Thebais. Another account, however, favoured by Epiphanius, relates that St. Luke preached first in Dalmatia and Galatia, and afterwards in Italy and Macedonia.

* Ruth ii. 14; Acts xx. 37, 38; 1 Tim. i. 15.   † Acts i. 1.
‡ Prov. xviii. 24: 2 Tim. iv. 16, 17; St. John xvi. 32.

The place, the time, and the manner of St. Luke's death have none of them been satisfactorily or unanimously determined. He is variously reported to have died in Egypt, in Bithynia, at Ephesus, and at Patræ, a city of Achaia, where he is said to have been seized by a party of infidels, who, for want of a cross, suspended him from the branch of an olive-tree, A.D. 74.

Whether from Bithynia, as Hermannus Contractus says; or from Achaia, as say Theodorus, Eusebius, and Platina, it is by common consent allowed that the remains of St. Luke were, about A.D. 358, translated to Constantinople, by order of the Emperor Constantius, and deposited, along with those of St. Andrew and St. Timothy, in the church which Constantine the Great had built in honour of the twelve Apostles.*

There are still two doubts to be expressed in connexion with St. Luke. Some authorities hesitate to affirm that he died the death of a martyr at all; and it is not ascertained whether the 18th of October is commemorated because it is the anniversary of his decease, or of the translation of his relics to Constantinople.

---

* St. Jerome: *De Viris Illustribus*; Baronius: *Annales Ecclesiastici.* A.D 358.

St. Simon and St. Jude, Apostles.

October 28.

THE joint commemoration of these two Apostles was usual from the time of their first allotment of a festival; the date of which, in the absence of any precise historical information, may be referred to the eleventh or twelfth century. Their association in one day derives its fitness not only from their fellowship and community in the same act of martyrdom, but also from their presumed fraternal relationship; which, if it could be established, would make them also severally identical with two of the four reputed brothers of our Lord (Matthew xiii. 55).

In the catalogues of the Apostles, Simon is styled the Canaanite, a designation which has given rise to a diversity of opinion; some writers supposing that he is so called from having been a native of Cana in Galilee, whilst others say that the expression contains no reference to his country, but denotes either his former membership with the sect of the *Zealots*, or else his ardent and enthusiastic temperament, which prompted him to the most impassioned exertions for the propagation of the Gospel, and for the defence of the purity of its doctrines. In any case the fact remains that St. Luke, rendering the Hebrew word by its Greek equivalent, calls *him* Simon Zelotes, whom

St. Matthew and St. Mark call Simon the Canaanite (Matthew x. 4; Mark iii. 18; Luke vi. 15).

The sect of the Zealots, to which it is fair to assume that St. Simon belonged, "began in Mattathias, the root of the Maccabean family, and was continued among the Jews till our Saviour's time. They looked upon Phineas as their patron, who, in a mighty zeal for the honour of God, did immediate execution upon Zimri and Cosbi. (Numbers xxv.) They took upon them a power of executing the law upon offenders, without any formal trial and accusation, and that not only by connivance, but with the leave both of the rulers and the people. Under this pretence, their zeal afterwards degenerated into licentiousness and extravagance, and they became the occasion of great miseries to their own nation; as is largely related by Josephus (*De Bel. Jud.*, lib. 4)."*

The only account we have of St. Simon in the Holy Gospels is that of his call to the Apostolate; although there is a tradition—to support which, however, the exploded territorial significance of his designation as a Canaanite is all but necessary—that it was at his nuptials that the Lord condescended to perform His first miracle of turning water into wine.

On the dispersion of the Apostles after the great day of Pentecost, St. Simon is said to have laboured successively in Egypt, Cyrene, Africa, Libya, and Mauritania. Some of the Greek Menologies expressly assert that he subsequently visited Britain, and that he was crucified by the unbelieving inhabitants, after he had made numerous converts to the faith. Others, again, affirm that he was put to death at Suanir, a city of Persia, at the same time as St. Jude, who, meeting him in Mesopotamia, had accompanied him to Persia. This double martyrdom is generally supposed to have taken place A.D. 74.

The following poem from the "School of the Heart,"

* Nelson: *Festivals and Fasts of the Church of England.*

and entitled "The Inflaming of the Heart," is an enlightened aspiration after an impartation of that quality, rightly directed, for which St. Simon was famous, and from which he obtained his name of Zelotes.

> Welcome, holy, heavenly fire,
>   Kindled by immortal love:
>   Which, descending from above,
> Makes all earthly thoughts retire,
>   And give place
>   To that grace,
> Which, with gentle violence,
>   Conquers all corrupt affections,
>   Rebel nature's insurrections,
> Bidding them be packing hence.
>
> Lord, Thy fire doth heat within,
>   Warmeth not without alone;
>   Though it be an heart of stone,
> Of itself congealed in sin,
>   Hard as steel,
>   If it feel
> Thy dissolving power, it groweth
>   Soft as wax, and quickly takes
>   Any print Thy Spirit makes,
> Paying what Thou say'st it oweth.
>
> Of itself mine heart is dark;
>   But Thy fire, by shining bright,
>   Fills it full of saving light.
> Though 't be but a little spark
>   Lent by Thee,
>   I shall see
> More by it than all the light,
>   Which in fullest measure streams
>   From corrupted nature's beams,
> Can discover to my sight.
>
> Though mine heart be ice and snow
>   To the things which Thou hast chosen,
>   All benumbed with cold, and frozen,
> Yet Thy fire will make it glow.

> Though it burns,
> When it turns
> Towards the things which Thou dost hate;
> Yet Thy blessed warmth, no doubt,
> Will that wild-fire soon draw out,
> And the heat thereof abate.
>
> Lord, Thy fire is active, using
> Always either to ascend
> To its native Heaven, or lend
> Heat to others: and diffusing
> Of its store,
> Gathers more,
> Never ceasing till it make
> All things like itself, and longing
> To see others come with thronging,
> Of Thy goodness to partake.
>
> Lord, then let Thy fire inflame
> My cold heart so thoroughly,
> That the heat may never die,
> But continue still the same:
> That I may
> Ev'ry day
> More and more, consuming sin,
> Kindling others, and attending
> All occasions of ascending,
> Heaven upon earth begin.

St. Jude was of our Lord's kindred, being brother to St. James the Less, and probably also to St. Simon. The Gospels give no account of his vocation to the Apostolate. In addition to the name by which he is commonly known, he was distinguished amongst the Apostles by the names of Lebbæus and Thaddæus, which served the twofold purpose of witnessing to his piety and wisdom, and of discriminating between him and the traitor Judas.

After the Ascension of Christ, St. Jude laboured at first in Judæa and Galilee, from whence he extended his travels to Samaria and Idumæa. In the opinion of St. Jerome, St. Jude is to be identified with that Thaddæus whose name is so honourably distinguished in the conversion of Abgarus, the king or toparch of Edessa, and his people, to the Christian faith.* But a more critical opinion differences them, and makes the Thaddæus who converted Abgarus to have been one of the Seventy.

Having travelled as far as Mesopotamia, St. Jude there encountered St. Simon; and both together proceeded into Persia. In the latter country they were engaged in several contests with the Magi, and especially with two of extraordinary celebrity, who were named respectively Zoroe and Arphax. "But the Apostles," says Joachim Hildebrand, "so discomfited their opponents, that the conversion of the king followed, and they themselves were recognised as little less than divinities. To their nod the demons who held possession of the idols were so perfectly subservient as to speak or to remain silent at command. * * * * At length, after having preached for a long time in Persia, the two Apostles were conducted to an image of the Sun, in order that they might sacrifice to it as to a god. But the demons of the idol, under the form of Æthiopians, submitted to the Apostles, and themselves broke the image of the Sun to pieces. The priests, enraged at such a portent, fell upon the Apostles and put them to death upon the spot, so that the *Nativity* of each of these martyrs—brothers in faith, in wonder-working, and in fortitude, if not in blood—which also is most probable—falls upon the same day, and is so commemorated by the Church. The circumstances of their passion have been transmitted in Hebrew by Abdias, Bishop of Babylon; by Eutropius in Greek; and in Latin by Julius Africanus."†

It is narrated by Eusebius that two of the posterity of St. Jude were summoned to appear before the Emperor Domitian, who, in his anxiety to secure stability to his own dominion, had conceived an inordinate jealousy of the de-

* Eusebius: *Ecclesiastical History*; lib. i., c. 13.
† Hildebrand: *De Diebus Festis Libellus*.

scendants of the royal line of David. The grandsons of the Apostle, after a strict interrogation on the part of Domitian as to the Kingdom of Christ, and after having satisfied him that the royal pretensions of the Saviour were of a spiritual kind only, and not concerned about earthly rule, were dismissed as unworthy of the tyrant's apprehensions. He could see no danger to his Empire from the lowly proprietors of a petty patrimony, the tillage of which, as the hardness of their hands and their stooping figures testified, they carried on themselves.*

The purport of the Catholic Epistle for which we are indebted to St. Jude is to exhort and encourage Christians "earnestly to contend for the faith which was once delivered unto the saints"; and to warn them against the heresies of false teachers—chiefly, the Gnostics, as it is fair to infer from the general tenor of the Epistle. It may add somewhat to the significance of the Epistle of St. Jude, if we devote a few concluding sentences to an exposition of the doctrines, and the results of these in manners and morals, against which it was conceived.

Gnosticism was doubtless the *Antichrist* of St. John (1 John iv. 1, 2, 3; 2 John, 7), the spirit of which, so soon as the Apostolic times, had begun to work in many, and the brand of which was the denial that Jesus Christ had come ἐν σαρκί, *in the flesh*. In Gnosticism the intellect lorded it over the soul, and scorned the body to the extent of utter indifference. It was transcendental to all preceding or contemporaneous systems; superior to all rites and symbols, whether of Heathenism or of the Mosaic dispensation; and to the common notions and beliefs of Christianity. It is not necessary to concern ourselves about the minute differences of its sections, or even with its grander divisions as determined and characterized by Pantheism or Dualism. We have rather to do with the

---

* Eusebius: *Ecclesiastical History*; lib. iii., c. 20.

idea, and the doctrines therefrom deducible, common to most of the Gnostics, of the irreclaimable evil of matter, and especially of the human body as *hylic* or material. The vileness of the body was a corollary from the oriental doctrines which Gnosticism assimilated; and it followed that Christ, the Son of God, could not have come *in the flesh*—could not have allied His Nature to what was inherently and irredeemably depraved. The Divine "Emanation" which was manifested under the form of Christ, was not clothed in a real, but only in an illusive phantom body.

The effect of such a notion on ethical principles and on moral practices is not to seek. Sensuality was encouraged; the endeavour after Christian perfection in both kinds, of soul and body, was repudiated; guards and restraints were fitted only for the spiritual and *soulical* parts of humanity, and all checks were removed from the flesh, unrecognised as this last was as a possible vehicle of morality or immorality. The presentation of the body, upon which St. Paul insisted as a "holy, acceptable sacrifice, and reasonable service," was to the illuminated inadmissible and irrational. The letter of the law, whether positive or prohibitive, was only for the weak and the imperfect, who were unable to take in the prospect from the summit of the mount of vision. But the true Gnostic, who was in possession of the spiritual sense, rose to a virtue so sublime, that all distinction of good and evil, in external actions, disappeared to his eye. This distinction was as the phantom of virtue, a spectre without reality, which appeared in the night of the human mind, and which vanished when from the heights of science (gnosis) the soul saw the light of the Pleroma—prime source and ultimate receptacle—dawn, and the divine day begin.

Finally, with the introduction of a phantasmal body of Christ, vital or important doctrines of Christianity receded altogether. For there could, on this hypothesis, have been no true atonement or redemption; no *bond fide* death;

and no resurrection or ascension of our nature, glorified in the person of the Saviour, to the right hand of the Father. Thus it was the overthrow of all the hopes, the basis of which St. Paul had so exultingly and elaborately laid in his first Epistle to the Corinthians. It was the merciless upfolding of that glorious transfiguration pageant, in which the corruptible was seen putting on incorruption, and the mortal clothing itself with immortality.

The verses which appear in the "Christian Year" for St. Jude's Day, owe their suggestion to the third verse of his Epistle:—"That ye should earnestly contend for the faith which was once delivered unto the saints":—

> Seest thou, how tearful and alone,
>   And drooping like a wounded dove,
> The Cross in sight, but Jesus gone,
>   The widowed Church is fain to rove?
>
> Who is at hand that loves the Lord?
>   Make haste, and take her home, and bring
> Thine household choir, in true accord
>   Their soothing hymns for her to sing.
>
> Soft on her fluttering heart shall breathe
>   The fragrance of that genial isle,
> There she may weave her funeral wreath,
>   And to her own sad music smile.
>
> The Spirit of the dying Son
>   Is there, and fills the holy place
> With records sweet of duties done,
>   Of pardoned foes, and cherished grace.
>
> And as of old by two and two
>   His herald saints the Saviour sent
> To soften hearts like morning dew,
>   Where He to shine in mercy meant;
>
> So evermore He deems His name
>   Best honoured and His way prepared,
> When watching by His altar-flame
>   He sees His servants duly paired.

He loves when age and youth are met,
  Fervent old age and youth serene,
The high and low in concord set
  For sacred song, Joy's golden mean.

He loves when some clear soaring mind
  Is drawn by mutual piety
To simple souls and unrefined,
  Who in life's shadiest covert lie.

Or if perchance a saddened heart
  That once was gay and felt the Spring,
Cons slowly o'er its altered part,
  In sorrow and remorse to sing,

Thy gracious care will send that way
  Some spirit full of glee, yet taught
To bear the light of dull decay,
  And nurse it with all pitying thought;

Cheerful as soaring lark, and mild
  As evening blackbird's full-toned lay,
When the relenting sun has smiled
  Bright through a whole December day.

These are the tones to brace and cheer
  The lonely watcher of the fold,
When nights are dark, and foemen near,
  When visions fade and hearts grow cold.

How timely then a comrade's song
  Comes floating on the mountain air,
And bids thee yet be bold and strong—
  Fancy may die, but Faith is there.

All Saints' Day.

November 1.

F all the magnificence of imperial Rome, the best preserved monument is that sublime and wonderful structure known of old as the Pantheon, and in Christian times as Santa Maria della Rotonda. The beauty of this building has been the amazement and delight of nearly nineteen centuries; and its name has long been reckoned synonymous with architectural perfection. It is unanimously conceded to be beyond criticism; and has been described, so far as we know, without cavil, as "more than faultless." The characteristics of the Pantheon have been summed up in a line of Lord Byron's Childe Harold:—

"Simple, erect, severe, austere, sublime."

It is one of the edifices, "*complura et egregia,*" mentioned in the mass by Suetonius as having been conferred on Rome by the taste and magnificence of M. Agrippa, a distinguished friend and partisan of the Emperor Augustus, whose nephew and son-in-law he successively became by the last two of the three marriages, which, in the course of his life, he contracted. On the frieze of the Pantheon, the portico if not the whole of which is thereby still authentically referred to Agrippa, appears the inscription M. Agrippa L. F. Cos. Tertium Fecit. The third consulship of Agrippa, which is thus fixed as the era of the completion of the Pantheon, coincided with the year 27 before Christ.

With the name of its founder, however, and the date of its dedication, the precise history of the very earliest objects of the Pantheon determines. The popular belief —which, to confine ourselves to home-bred authors, the venerable Bede adopted, which Bishop Andrewes approved, and which Lord Byron poetically endorsed—that the Pantheon was dedicated to *all the gods* of antiquity, celestial, terrestial, and infernal, is *à priori* shaken by the fact that the religious practice of the Romans demanded the devotion of a separate temple to a separate divinity. An argument of this kind, however, is not conclusive; for it would be absurd to deny the possibility of innovations: and there are some trusted historians who do not hesitate to say that the Pantheon " was dedicated to the gods connected with the Julian gens, Jupiter, Mars, Venus, J. Cæsar, and others." An alternative *rationale* of its ancient designation is given by Dion, who prefers to settle its name on a mingled base of etymology and symbolism—its dome represented the heavens, and the heavens were the residence of *all the gods.* But other accounts present us with a plentiful variety. One of these sets forth that the Pantheon was dedicated to Jupiter the Avenger, in compliment to Augustus upon his victory at Actium over Antony and Cleopatra; and a second, given by an anonymous writer in *Montfaucon*, is to the effect that "the Pantheon was vowed by Agrippa to Cybele and Neptune." If we may invest the last-named deity with the Homeric attributes of Oceanus, it will be seen that, according to this account, the popular belief is all but amply justified; for all the gods might be said to be worshipped, in effect, where their ancestors and representatives were enshrined. The asserted dedication to Cybele and Neptune is thus understood as an almost absolutely comprehensive one. But after all, our conclusion must be inconclusive: and we must consent to add the dedication of the Pantheon to those countless subjects, so feelingly known to the seeker after historical accuracy, about which investigation vindicates itself as a process by which we successfully arrive at indecision.

When Christianity first became the dominant religion of the Roman empire, the superstitious forces of Paganism were still vivacious and widely spread. It seemed, therefore, too hazardous that its temples should be consecrated to the rites of Christianity, lest the taint of heathen abominations should still linger about them. Destruction, rather than conversion, approved itself as the generally safer course. A series of emperors, beginning with Constantine, carried on, with less or more of vigour, the process of demolition both in the East and West. In the East, the destruction of the temples was well nigh completed by the Emperor Theodosius the younger, in the early part of the fifth century—a particular Rescript occurring in the Code called by his name, that the Pagan temples should be plucked down, as fit to be the dens of devils or unclean spirits. Honorius, the uncle of Theodosius, contented himself with closing the temples of the West, out of a feeling of respect for the former architectural magnificence of the empire. "As we forbid," ran a rescript of Honorius, " the sacrifices of the Gentiles so we will that the ornament of their public works be preserved." It was this æsthetic patriotism which saved, amongst others, the Pantheon, to undergo a subsequent conversion into a Christian church—an event which took place at a time when the purer religion was fondly supposed to have triumphed over the danger of idolatrous observances. In his ecclesiastical direction of the affairs of the Anglo-Saxons, Gregory the Great rather puzzlingly exemplified the practice at once of Theodosius and Honorius. In a letter, dated June 22nd, 601, to the recent convert, Ethelbert, King of Kent, he exhorts that prince to "suppress the worship of idols, and to overthrow the structures of the temples";* although in a letter, addressed *five days before* to the Abbat Mellitus—then on the eve of proceeding to England, and afterwards successively Bishop of London and Archbishop of Canterbury—he had instructed him " to tell the most reverend Bishop Augustine, that he had upon mature deliberation on the affairs of the English, determined that the temples of the idols in that nation ought not to be destroyed. But let the idols that are in them be destroyed; let holy water be made and sprinkled in the said temples, let altars be erected and relics placed. For if those temples are well built, it is requisite that they be converted from the worship of devils to the service of the true God; that the nation, seeing that their temples are not destroyed, may remove error from their hearts, and, knowing and adoring the true God, may the more familiarly resort to the places to which they have been accustomed."†

About the year 609, Boniface IV., the successor of Gregory, at two or three removes, in the bishopric of Rome, obtained from the Emperor Phocas a grant of the Pantheon for the purpose of consecrating it to the Christian rite. Bede's simple account of this conversion is to the effect that Boniface, "having purified the Pantheon from contamination, dedicated a church to the holy mother of God, and to all Christ's martyrs, to the end that, the devils being excluded, the blessed company of the saints might have therein a perpetual memorial." ‡ The sometime heathen temple—the structure of which was preserved unchanged—received at its consecration the designation of Santa Maria ad Martyres; and is now, as we have said already, popularly known as Our Lady of the Rotonda, or, more simply, as the Rotonda. Thus it was that, to the

* Bede's *Ecclesiastical History*; lib. i. c. 32.
† Ditto Ditto lib. i. c. 30.
‡ Ditto Ditto lib. xi. c. 5.

piety of that age, Christ seemed to be receiving "the heathen for His inheritance."

It is to the circumstance of the conversion of the Pantheon,'that the celebration of the Feast of All Saints in the Western Church is to be traced. The festival of the dedication of Santa Maria ad Martyres was observed on the thirteenth of May; a feast in honour of All Apostles having formerly been kept on the first of the same month. "A festival in honour of All Martyrs and Saints," Mr. Riddle tells us, quoting St. Chrysostom as his authority, "obtained in the Eastern Church as early as the fourth century; where it was celebrated on the Octave of Pentecost, our Trinity Sunday." But it was not till about the year 731 that the Western Church definitely substituted for its commemorations of All Apostles and All Martyrs, the more large and inclusive one of All Saints. In the year just mentioned, Gregory III. consecrated, as Anastasius informs us, a chapel in St. Peter's church, to the memory of All Saints; from which date the Feast derives its titular or nominal existence. Henceforth its celebration was constant at Rome; and it gradually spread to the dimensions of an observance of the Church catholic. In the year 834, Gregory IV. removed the Feast from the month of May to the season of its present celebration, the first day of November. A year or two afterwards, the same Pope solicited from Lothario an ordinance for the keeping of All Saints' Day throughout Germany and Gaul. The prince agreed to the ordinance, and his bishops assented to co-operate in promoting it.

The tendency to pay egregious and even unwarrantable respect to the departed whose lives or deaths had presented an aspect of uncommon sanctity, was, as in the order of things was natural, more early to manifest itself than the consolidation of such respect into a festival. It happened very early in Christian history that the intercession of Saints and Martyrs, and especially of the Virgin

Mary, was invoked in a profane conjunction with the intercessions of the "one Mediator between God and Men." Further on, in the time of Gregory the Great, when it was represented to that Pope that the images of Christ, of the Virgin Mary, and of the Saints, were placed in many churches to be worshipped, he declared that though they were certainly not to be regarded as objects of worship, they might very properly be used to instruct the ignorant, and to stimulate devotion. The disposition to accommodation which arises from a zeal for the conversion of unbelievers, is one which is calculated worthily to excite our interest and, indeed, our admiration. Yet such a disposition is to be very closely questioned, and very jealously indulged. Subsequent history has all too well shown us that it wanted only time to develope Gregory's allowance of reverence to the effigies of the Saints into a degrading worship of their relics, and into a disgraceful and fraudful commerce in the same. We transcribe from the late Dean Milman's *History of Latin Christianity* a paragraph, as temperate as it is eloquent, which concisely and philosophically traces the rise and progress of popular Saint-worship. The Dean has just been discussing that phase of the "Belief of Latin Christianity" which was exhibited in the doctrine of Angels; and he proceeds to the consideration of another class of supposed mediators, whose experience of a past incarnation seemed to promise a greater degree of nearness to their votaries, and a more intimate kind of sympathy, than could be expected from mere spirits who had never groaned beneath the weight of clay.

"The angels were not the only guardians and protectors of the faithful against the swarming, busy, indefatigable malignant spirits, which claimed the world of man as their own. It might seem as if human weakness required something less impalpable, more sensibly real, more akin to itself, than beings of light and air, which encircled the throne of God. Those Beings, in their essence immaterial, or of a finer and more ethereal matter, might stoop to earth, or might be constantly hovering between earth and heaven; but besides them, as it were of more distinct cognisance by man, were those who, having worn the human form, retained it, or re-assumed it, as it were clothing over their spiritualised being. The Saints, having been human, were more easily, more naturally conceived as still endowed with human sympathies; intermediate between God and man, but with an imperishable, ineffaceable manhood more closely bound up with man. The doctrine of the Church, the Communion of Saints, implied the Church militant and the Church triumphant. The Christians yet on earth, the Christians already in heaven, formed but one polity; and if there was this kindred, if it may be so said, religious consanguinity, it might seem disparagement to their glory and to their union with Christ to banish the Saints to a cold unconscious indifference, and abase them to ignorance of the concerns of their brethren still in the flesh. Each Saint partook, therefore, of the instinctive omniscience of Christ. While unabsorbed in the general beatified community, he kept up his special interest and attachment to the places, the companions, the fraternities of his earthly sojourn; he exercised, according to his will, at least by intercession, a beneficent influence; he was tutelar within his sphere, and therefore within that sphere an object of devout adoration. And so, as ages went on, saints were multiplied and deified. I am almost unwilling to write it; yet, assuredly, hardly less, if less than Divine power and Divine will was assigned by the popular sentiment to the Virgin and the Saints. They intercepted the worship of the Almighty Father, the worship of the Divine Son. To them, rather than through them, prayer was addressed; their shrines received the more costly oblations: they were the rulers, the actual disposing Providence on earth: God might seem to have abandoned the Sovereignty of the world to those subordinate yet all-powerful agencies." *

The foregoing affords an exhibition, we may observe, under Christian or *quasi*-Christian conditions, of that human yearning which Dion Chrysostom not unpathetically describes in his twelfth *Oration* :—" The wise may, indeed, adore the gods as being far from us ; but there exists in all men an eager longing to adore and worship the gods as nigh. For as children, torn from father and mother, feel a powerful and affectionate longing, often stretch out their hands after their absent parents, and often dream of them—so the man who heartily loves the gods for their benevolence towards us and their relationship with us, desires to be continually near them, and to have intercourse with them ; so that many barbarians, ignorant of the arts, have called the very mountains and trees gods, that they might recognise them as nearer to themselves."

Dean Milman proceeds to remark upon the frequency of canonization; and the plentifulness of candidates for that honour supplied by both the Eastern and Western Churches, each of which was to a great extent ignorant of the Hagiology of the other. Many things conspired to crowd the calendar of either communion—the imagination of the faithful, and their generous admiration of transcendent goodness, transcendent learning, or transcendent austerity; the rivalry of city with city, of kingdom with kingdom, of Church with Church, and of one religious Order with another. Grosser interests were also evoked. The multiplication of shrines made for the benefit of the priesthood and of the traders who alike shared in the profit which resulted from the fame of the miracles of local Saints, whose worship was stimulated on the one hand by gratitude for imputed blessings, and on the other by the fear of deprecated evils. Against all these motives it was possible to oppose the single voice, still, small, and little regarded, of reason alone.

* Milman's *History of Latin Christianity*: b. xiv., ch. 2.

At length Saints became so numerous that they jostled and incommoded each other on the calendar; and to stay their extravagant increase, "the Pope assumed the prerogative of advancing to the successive ranks of Beatitude and Sanctity. If this checked the deification of such perplexing multitudes, it gave still higher authority to those who had been recognised by more general consent, or who were thus more sparingly admitted to the honours of Beatification and Sanctification (those steps, as it were, of spiritual promotion were gradually introduced). The Saints ceased to be local divinities; they were proclaimed to Christendom, in the irrefragable Bull, as worthy of general worship."*
It was Pope Alexander III., whose arrogance had been fortified by imperial opposition, who reserved for the Sovereign Pontiff alone the prerogative of canonization, which had formerly vested in him jointly with the metropolitans. With the latter had rested the right of initiation, whilst it was necessary to procure the sanction of the Pope for the consummation of the candidature. This associate prerogative marked the second or intermediate period of the three into which canonization has been distributed; whilst in the first of these periods, which came to a close in the tenth century, "the Saint had been exalted by the popular voice, the suffrage of the people with the Bishop."

Although, perhaps, most of the Saints enjoyed a local *cultus* only, there were others to whom recognition was accorded by the votes of universal Christendom; as, for instance, the Apostles and the earliest Martyrs. Of all local Saints, of all Saints whose claims were less than universal, those were of greatest fame under whose patronage a kingdom or an empire reposed. Every Christian realm was referred to its tutelary Saint, just as amongst the Jews every kingdom was referred to its guardian Angel. France adopted the patron Saints of the various countries which she absorbed or incorporated—St. Martin, St. Remi, and

* *History of Latin Christianity.*

St. Denys—whilst her royal race elected St. Louis as their special and family patron. Spain claimed the guardianship of St. Jago de Compostella; Scotland, the protection of St. Andrew; Ireland, of St. Patrick; whilst England, unaccountably overlooking her home-bred or naturalised Saints, as Alban and Augustine, chose from beyond the sea a patron in the person of St. George of Cappadocia, a man of doubtful, or scarcely doubtful, reputation.

"As the Church grew in wealth"—we recur once more directly to Milman—"Kings or Nobles, magnificent donors, were the Saints; as it grew in power, rose hierarchical Saints, like Becket. St. Louis was the Saint of the Crusades and Chivalry: St. Thomas Aquinas and Bonaventura, of Scholasticism. Female prophets might seem chosen to vie with those of the Fraticelli and of the Heretics; St. Catherine of Sienna, St. Bridget,* those Brides of Christ, who had constant personal intercourse with the Saints, with the Virgin, with our Lord Himself. In later days, Christian charity, as well as Mysticism, had its Saints, St. Vincent de Paul, with St. Teresa, and St. Francis de Sales."

The history of the fortunes of canonization offers an example of the recognized tendency of popular superstition to work upwards; for no superstition has ever been tolerated or encouraged amongst the vulgar by their teachers, without in time bringing the teachers themselves under its influence. Infection in this kind is caught from below. "The master of superstition," observes Lord Bacon, "is the people, and in all superstition wise men follow fools, and arguments are fitted to practice in a reversed order." Councils of the Church early learned to reduce to dogma the sentimental extravagance which the ignorant had originated. The Council, for instance, which assembled at Nice in 787, and which was convened by the Empress Irene, the

* "St. Bridget was beatified by Boniface IX., canonized by John XXIII., at the Council of Constance, confirmed by St. Martin."

image-loving widow of Leo the Iconoclast, especially decreed that images of Christ, of the Virgin Mary, of the Angels, and of the Saints, should be held as sacred; and if any should teach otherwise, or dare to throw away books or pictures bearing the painted cross or the effigies of these holy personages, or treat with contempt the relics of Martyrs, they should fall under the censures and punishments of the Church. Offenders in holy orders, it was added, should be deposed, and all others excommunicated from the rites of religion. Nearly eight centuries afterwards, kindred questions were discussed and legislated for at a still more famous Council—that of Trent—which, at its 25th session, December 3 and 4, 1563, passed the following Decree, "On the Invocation, Veneration, and Relics of Saints and of Sacred Images :—

"The holy Synod enjoins on all bishops, and others who sustain the office and charge of teaching, that, agreeably to the usage of the Catholic and Apostolic Church, received from the primitive times of the Christian religion, and agreeably to the consent of the holy Fathers, and to the decrees of sacred Councils, they especially instruct the faithful diligently concerning the intercession and invocation of Saints; the honour (paid) to relics; and the legitimate use of images: teaching them, that the Saints, who reign together with Christ, offer up their own prayers to God for men; that it is good and useful suppliantly to invoke them, and to have recourse to their prayers, aid, and help, for obtaining benefits from God, through His Son, Jesus Christ, our Lord, who is our alone Redeemer and Saviour; but that they think impiously, who deny that the Saints, who enjoy eternal happiness in heaven, are to be invocated; or who assert either that they do not pray for men; or, that the invocation of them to pray for each of us even in particular, is idolatry; or, that it is repugnant to the word of God; and is opposed to the honour of the *one Mediator of God and men, Christ Jesus;* or, that it is foolish to supplicate, vocally, or mentally, those who reign in heaven. Also, that the holy bodies of holy Martyrs, and of others now living with Christ,— which bodies were the living members of Christ, and *the temple of the Holy Ghost*, and which are by Him to be raised unto eternal life, and to be glorified,—are to be venerated by the faithful; through which (bodies) many benefits are bestowed by God on men; so that they who affirm that veneration and honour are not due to the relics of Saints; or, that these and other sacred monuments, are uselessly honoured by the faithful; and that the places dedicated to the memories of the Saints are in vain visited with a view of obtaining their aid; are wholly to be condemned, as the Church has already long since condemned, and now also condemns them."

The same Council had, at its twenty-second Session, held on the 17th September, 1562, already given a deliverance " On Masses in honour of the Saints ":—

"Although the Church has been accustomed at times to celebrate certain masses in honour and memory of the Saints; not therefore, however, doth she teach that sacrifice is offered unto them, but unto God alone, who crowned them; whence neither is the priest wont to say, 'I offer sacrifice to thee, Peter, or Paul'; but, giving thanks to God for their victories, he implores their patronage, that they may vouchsafe to intercede for us in heaven, whose memory we celebrate upon earth."

And again, the fifth of the Tridentine " Canons on the Sacrifice of the Mass," is to the effect that:—

"If any one saith, that it is an imposture to celebrate masses in honour of the Saints, and for obtaining their intercession with God, as the Church intends; let him be anathema."

This Canon, including its anathema, was probably not only directly, but personally, levelled at Luther and his memory; and the Doctors of Trent would seem to have been on their mettle to affirm with penalties the doctrines and traditions which the German Reformer had impugned. "The papists," Luther was accustomed to say, as he said in his *Colloquia Mensalia*, or *Table Talk*—"The papists took the invocation of Saints from the heathen, who divided God into numberless images and idols, and ordained to each its particular office and work. * * * The invocation of Saints is a most abominable blindness and heresy; yet the papists will not give it up. The Pope's greatest profit arises from the dead; for the calling on dead Saints brings him infinite sums of money and riches, far more than he gets from the living. But thus goes the world; superstition, unbelief, false doctrine, idolatry, obtain more credit and profit than the upright, true, and pure religion."

One of Wordsworth's *Ecclesiastical Sonnets*, entitled "Saints," is applied by its author to the era of reform and reaction in England against the extravagances of the worship of Saints and Angels, who had had forced upon them for so long a time an honour they would have repudiated.

> Ye, too, must fly before a chasing hand,
> Angels and Saints, in every hamlet mourned!
> Ah! if the old idolatry be spurned,
> Let not your radiant shapes desert the Land:
> Her adoration was not your demand,
> The fond heart proffered it—the servile heart;
> And therefore are ye summoned to depart,
> Michael, and thou, St. George, whose flaming brand
> The Dragon quelled; and valiant Margaret
> Whose rival sword a like opponent slew:
> And rapt Cecilia, seraph-haunted Queen
> Of harmony; and weeping Magdalene,
> Who in the penitential desert met
> Gales sweet as those that over Eden blew!

Is it, then, impossible that "the memory of the Just should be blessed," without superstition? May not "the Righteous be in everlasting remembrance," without impiety? Is there no legitimate and edifying commemoration of departed Saints possible to their brethren and their posterity who are yet fighting in mortal combat with their foes of earth and hell, and of their own hearts? Or, if the possibility and the lawfulness of such a commemoration be established, what are the limits of the reverence to be paid to their bright examples and their glorified persons? The reply to these questions is easy; but we shall answer them by deputy of two great names. The following passage from St. Augustine's *De Vera Religione* finds a counterpart in a paragraph of his *De Civitate Dei*. The extract may be regarded as at once a faithful protest against contemporary and budding error, and as the result of a rare prescience of future and full-blown abuses. " Let not our religion," he says, "be the worship of dead men, because if they lived piously they are not so disposed as to seek such honours; but they wish Him to be worshipped by us, by whom being enlightened they rejoice that we are deemed worthy of being partakers with them. They are to be honoured, then, on the ground of imitation, not to be adored on the ground of religion; and if they lived ill, wherever they be, they must not be worshipped. This also we may believe, that the most perfect angels themselves, and the most excellent servants of God, wish that we, with themselves, should worship God, in the contemplation of whom they are blessed. * * * Therefore, we honour them with love, not with service. Nor do we build temples to them; for they are unwilling to be so honoured by us, because they know that, when we are good, we are as temples to the most high God. Well, therefore, is it written, that a man was forbidden by an angel to adore him."

We can rightly pay no tribute of honour to departed saints which does not penetrate beyond them; and all worship is idolatry which stays short of their Master and ours. That calm, clear light of the Church, Richard Hooker, has shown how it is because Christ is glorified in saints and angels that it is allowable to reverence them generally, or to commemorate them at appointed seasons:—" Forasmuch as we know that Christ hath not only been manifested great in Himself, but great in other His Saints also, the days of whose departure out of the world are to the Church of Christ as the birth and coronation days of Kings or Emperors, therefore especial choice being made of the very flower of all occasions in this kind, there are annual selected times to meditate of Christ glorified in them which had the honour to suffer for His sake, before they had age and ability to know Him; glorified in them which knowing Him, as Stephen, had the sight of that before death whereinto so acceptable death did lead; glorified in those Sages of the East that came from afar to adore Him, and were conducted by strange light; glorified in the second Elias of the world sent before Him to prepare His way; glorified in every of those Apostles whom it pleased Him to use as founders of His Kingdom here; glorified in the Angels as in Michael; glorified in all those happy souls that are already possessed of heaven." *

We offer a poetical illustration of that limitation of the respect to be paid to saints which we have just seen enunciated by St. Augustine. It is from the pen of George Herbert; and is remarkable for its touching expression of that *religious instinct* of adoration of the Virgin which, we venture to say, is incidental to the Christian in his cognate character of gentleman, and which is to be checked and regulated only by the master voice of the *religious reason*. Herbert's poem is addressed "To All Angels and Saints."

> Oh! glorious spirits, who after all your bands
> See the smooth face of God, without a frown,
>   Or strict commands;
> Where every one is king, and hath his crown,
> If not upon his head, yet in his hands:

* *Ecclesiastical Polity:* Book v. ch. lxx. 8.

> Not out of envy or maliciousness
> Do I forbear to crave your special aid.
>   I would address
> My vows to thee most gladly, blessed Maid,
> And Mother of my God, in my distress:
>
> Thou art the holy mine, whence came the gold,
> The great restorative for all decay
>   In young and old;
> Thou art the cabinet where the jewel lay:
> Chiefly to thee would I my soul unfold.
>
> But now, alas! I dare not; for our King,
> Whom we do all jointly adore and praise,
>   Bids no such thing:
> And where His pleasure no injunction lays,
> ('Tis your own case) ye never move a wing.
>
> All worship is prerogative, and a flower
> Of His rich crown from whom lies no appeal
>   At the last hour:
> Therefore we dare not from His garland steal,
> To make a posy for inferior power.
>
> Although then others court you, if ye know
> What's done on earth, we shall not fare the worse,
>   Who do not so;
> Since we are ever ready to disburse,
> If any one our Master's hand can show.

Up to this point we have dealt almost exclusively with the word Saints as it is applied to persons whose claims to canonization, whether well or ill-founded otherwise, have received at the hands of the Church—from people, bishop, or pontiff—a formal ratification. But the significance of the word may very properly and profitably be widened. The commemoration of All Saints, as celebrated by the Reformed Churches, is a commemoration of all those who by the favour of God have passed from a condition of earthly trial into a state of heavenly assurance and beatitude. The *personnel* of our roll of saints, if we could have authentic knowledge of the names that illustrate it, would thus scarcely be found to coincide with the calendar of the Romish Church. It must differ from the latter either by excess or defect; indeed, by both—by excess, for obvious reasons; by defect, so long as it cannot be shown that canonization is an absolute voucher for salvation. Charitably hoping all things, we shrink from the arrogance of dictating to our Maker; and awfully and reverently leave the occurrence or the non-occurrence of names in the "Book of Life" to be determined by His love and justice.

But in order adequately to commemorate the bliss of the ransomed in heaven, it is necessary to look to their antecedents of character and circumstances in this world; and of these we may form a generally correct idea from observing the character and circumstances of their successors and representatives yet living on the earth. The Church Militant and the Church Triumphant—those grand and palpable divisions of Sainthood which must obtain till all warfare, even that with death, is swallowed up in victory —if taken separately, are only partly intelligible; each is to be fully understood only in the light of the other. The past of the one is the present of the other; but before both, though not yet with the same clearness, spreads out the same eternal future. Even yet, however, the subject is not satisfied. Its infinite suggestiveness leads us at large beyond the *flammantia mœnia mundi*, until at last we recognise, amazed and dazzled but not confounded, the completed company of the Saints in that "great multitude which no man can number," who from east and west, from north and south, from far as the infinite poles asunder, have been gathered into the immediate fold and presence of God, for which they have been prepared under the various *regimes* of probation, as men; of perfect service and duty, as angels; or, as may be imagined, of spiritual growth and development throughout the various nurseries and colonies

INDIFFERENCE OF CIRCUMSTANCES.

of heaven which we call the universe. Need we say, then, that the subjects of the All Saints' muse are, in one sense —as infallibly presenting one or another phenomenon of interest to the saintly life—well nigh co-extensive with the subjects that engage the muse of Christianity herself; or that to place before the reader the Biblical passages which refer individually, departmentally, or collectively, to the estate of Sainthood, would be to incorporate a large proportion of the Holy Scriptures? In these is set forth every various phase of sanctification, which marks its course from the first tears of penitence to the splendours and comforts of the Apocalyptic vision.

The aspects under which the saints may be considered, are, as we have just indicated, almost infinitely varied. The most ordinary are those in which they are regarded as belonging to or comprising the Church Militant and the Church Triumphant. The whole Church on earth may be considered as a unity; or it may be looked upon as an aggregate of particular Churches; and these again may be disintegrated into groups, territorial or otherwise, into families, and finally into individuals.

The saints on earth are of all conditions, for holiness is independent of fortune or accidents; through their common relationship to Christ, the monarch is brother unto Lazarus. Whatever the magnificence or the squalor of their outward circumstances, theirs is the common tribulation; the common sorrow; the common strife with common foes; the common weariness of a common pilgrimage. Theirs are the common joys of a common love; the common interest in a common Lord, faith, and baptism; the common hopes of a common glory. For them, for their spiritual fathers and posterity, the world was created; for them, in a special sense, it was redeemed; for their sakes, and by their prayers, it is for a time preserved; and by them, as assessors with Christ, it is finally to be judged. All are looking, though not with equal intentness, to the prize of their high calling; all are on the way, though not with equal steps, to the perfection of holiness, the perfect realisation of rest and victory and the sonship of God. In their march to the land of promise, they encounter many impediments; in their warfare they sustain many reverses. They are too strong and too weak for themselves. "The flesh lusteth against the spirit, and the spirit against the flesh:" "the good that they would, they do not; but the evil that they would not, that they do." Happy for them that their Judge "knoweth their frame, and remembereth that they are dust;" that He, as only an omniscient Being can, sees the motive apart from the deed, the effort apart from the performance, and is gracious to consider the integrity of thought, and will, and desire, in the confusions of an unlaurelled struggle!

It would be hard, we think, to find the inequalities and reverses of a conflict, the issue of which if not doubtful, is yet undeclared, more compendiously set forth than in one of the *Olney Hymns*, which Newton, its author, entitles "Inward Warfare." The singular felicity with which this hymn presents the antitheses of the baptized soul, may well be allowed as a sufficient apology for its poetical pedestrianism.

> Strange and mysterious is my life,
> What opposites I feel within!
> A stable peace, a constant strife;
> The rule of grace, the power of sin;
>   Too often I am captive led,
>   Yet daily triumph in my Head.
>
> I prize the privilege of prayer,
> But oh! what backwardness to pray!
> Though on the Lord I cast my care,
> I feel its burden every day;
>   I seek *His* will in all I do,
>   Yet find my own is working too.

> I call the promises my own,
> And prize them more than mines of gold;
> Yet though their sweetness I have known,
> They leave me unimpressed and cold:
>   One hour upon the truth I feed,
>   The next I know not what I read.
>
> I love the holy day of rest,
> When Jesus meets His gathered saints;
> Sweet day, of all the week the best!
> For its return my spirit pants;
>   Yet often, through my unbelief,
>   It proves a day of guilt and grief.
>
> While on my Saviour I rely,
> I know my foes shall lose their aim:
> And therefore dare their power defy,
> Assured of conquest through His name:
>   But soon my confidence is slain,
>   And all my fears return again.
>
> Thus different powers within me strive,
> And grace and sin by turns prevail;
> I grieve, rejoice, decline, revive,
> And victory hangs in doubtful scale:
>   But Jesus has His promise past,
>   That grace shall overcome at last.

All the sheep of the Great Shepherd are not of one fold. A child may love the parent whom it has never seen; or may present an attitude apt and akin to love for one of whom it has never heard. The charity of to-day believes that the spirit of Christ is not confined to the sphere of formal Christianity. In his admiration for Socrates, Erasmus was accustomed to refer to him the honours of canonization; and the large-hearted piety of all ages has trusted that the souls of such as Socrates are "with the Saints." Dr. Newman, in a little poem called "Heathenism," the second of a series bearing the general title of "Religious States," touches very delicately upon a subject which, after all speculation, we are fain hopefully to dismiss with the question:—" Shall not the Judge of all the earth do right?" The poem we are about to quote is to be found in the author's recent volume of " Verses on Various Occasions;" and was first published in *Lyra Apostolica*, in which occur many poems illustrative of different phases of Christian life and character. " Hidden saints" is the title of a small group of these, and it is sufficient to suggest to the reader an interesting *angle* of our subject, which we content ourselves with mentioning as an inviting one for charitable and comfortable meditation. The verses on "Heathenism" run thus:—

> Mid Balak's magic fires
> The Spirit spake, clear as in Israel;
> With prayers untrue, and covetous desires
> Did God vouchsafe to dwell;
> Who summoned dreams, His earlier word to bring
> To patient Job's vexed friends and Gerar's guileless king.
>
> If such o'erflowing grace
> From Aaron's vest e'en on the Sibyl ran,
> Why should we fear the Son now lacks His place,
> Where roams unchristened man?
> As tho', when faith is keen, He cannot make
> Bread of the very stones, or thirst with ashes slake.

There is a sanctity of trial, and a sanctity of ignorance. The one is holy because it "holds the good," the other because it knows not evil. The one is a sanctity of a distinctively human order, bearing the burden and heat of the day of earthly temptation, and sin, and sorrow, and darkness, and affliction. This is, we say, the ideal sanctity of humanity. The other is a sanctity of innocence, more immaculate, it may be, than the former—which ever bears, at least, the smell of the fire through which it has passed —but, as we said in our remarks upon St. Michael and All Angels, less picturesque, and less interesting. This is the typical sanctity of angels, and of infants or children without actual sin, whose "angels do always behold the face of the Father which is in heaven." The Bishop of

PROCESSION OF THE SAINTS.

Winchester has personified these two schools, so to say, of sanctity. The man and woman of the following poem on "All Saints" represent the ideal purity of humanity, that is, of tried and adult humanity; whilst the little child represents the purity common to angels and sinless infancy. The poem is transcribed from a volume of *English Lyrics*, edited by the Rev. Robert H. Baynes, and dedicated to the Bishop, then of Oxford.

    It was upon the morning of All Saints—
A glorious autumn morn:—The crimson sun
With rays aslant lit up a silver mist
Which had crept on all night—as some great host—
Through every lowland valley, but was now
Melting in softest light, like childhood's dream.
Above me the clear sky shewed almost dark,
To deep its blue beside the gorgeous east.
No cloud had stained it yet, but here and there
A snowy vapour, severed from the rest,
Hung high above, as though the visible breath
Of passing Angels. I had sat me down
Upon a high hill-side, to see day break,
And think upon All Saints. I know not now
Whether I slept—but so it seemed to me,
My tranced senses sunk o'erpowered before
The glorious presence of an Holy One,
A watcher from on high, who thus to me,
Reading my thoughts spake graciously:—"Thou would'st
Behold this goodly army of All Saints,
And scan their noble bearing: watch awhile
With eye intent, and I will pass before thee
The sight for which thou cravest."
                             Fixed I sat
With earnest gaze upon the glowing sky,
Where, as I deemed, with all its glory wreathed,
The pageant I should see of passing hosts
Bright with celestial radiance.—Nought I saw;
Only with tottering steps before mine eyes
A meek old man moved by, who feebly helped
The utter weariness of aged feet
With a poor staff. And then on that hill-side

A woman passed, belike a new-made widow,
With her deep weeds—and on her sunken cheek
Sat the pale hue of nights unrestful, spent
In heart-sick watching by some bed of pain :—
Yet on her brow, which the sun's rays now lighted,
Methought there dwelt a glow, brighter than his,
Of peace and holy calm. And so she passed.
Nor saw I more—save that a little child,
Of brightest childlike gentleness, passed by,
Lisping his morning song of infant praise
With a half-inward melody; as though
He were too happy for this creeping earth.—
Yet I sat watching : till upon my ear
Broke that same heavenly voice—"What would'st thou more,
Or why this empty gaze? Already thou
In those that passed thee by hast seen All Saints."

We owe to Sir Archibald Edmonstone a couple of Sonnets on "The Church, Militant and Triumphant;" the first of which sketches in bold outline the life and troubles of the saints on earth in their collective or corporate character. To insert the second in this place, is, by a very little, to anticipate our progress; but the unity of authorship, and the fact that the two Sonnets are companion word-pictures, protest against the idea of their separation. The Sonnets appeared in a volume entitled, after its most considerable poem, "The Progress of Religion."

THE CHURCH MILITANT.

How strong are her foundations! the opening
How glorious of her portals! Yet, within,
What Babel-sounds of strife! Without, what din
Of malice and of wrath! Those choirs which sing
Eternal Alleluias to their King,
How must they wondering view the power of sin,
Which, round her sacred boundary who must win
And fold God's Flock, such direful spell could fling,
Marring her holy work—our Sion's height
O'ershadowing with gloom, where once shown clear
Heaven's purest radiance! O for a light,
Glimmering albeit afar! "Dispel thy fear,"
A Voice exclaims, "My Church's mourning night
Is well nigh spent; her Dayspring draweth near!"

The Church Triumphant.

Who is it clad in garments radiant white,
Love on her breastplate graven, on her brow
Salvation diademed ? Above, below,
Ten thousand thousand Spirits wing their flight,
A shining company. With glory bright
The army of Martyrs circle, which through woe
And peril, pain and death, dared face the foe,
Bearing their palms, with victor-chaplets dight.
In mild but awful majesty, to meet
The Bride comes forth the Bridegroom, in the skies
Enthroning on her everlasting seat.
From myriad voices shouts of triumph rise,
"Her warfare is accomplished ; at her feet
Fallen is the captive's chain—the conqueror prostrate lies!"

About the present state of all God's " servants who have departed this life in His faith and fear," we have so little definite knowledge, that speculation and imagination have a very wide field in which to exercise themselves. In the first Lesson for the morning of All Saints' Day—the day on which we especially express our gratitude to God for their happiness, and on which we are called upon to brace ourselves by their example—we read that "the souls of the righteous are in the hand of God, and there shall no torment touch them. In the sight of the unwise they seemed to die; and their departure is taken for misery, and their going from us for utter destruction: but they are in peace" (Book of Wisdom iii. 1—3). Still the happiness of departed saints, however perfect of its kind, is not, so far, of a perfect nature; for there are capacities for bliss that are yet held in abeyance. A part of each yet remains to be re-assumed; the body of each yet reposes on the bosom of their native planet. Not so is it to be for ever. One day, the corruptible is to put on incorruption; the mortal is to put on immortality. That which was sown in dishonour is to be raised in glory; that which was sown in weakness is to be raised in power. The trumpet shall sound, and the dead shall be raised; and the first to answer to the summons shall be the dead in Christ. From every quarter shall be seen the mustering troops of the holy, and the world itself shall appear as one great pageant of transfiguration. This is one of the grandest and most spectacular of the associations of All Saints' Day.

One aspect after another of our exhaustless subject opens before us. The " Communion of Saints," for instance, is a theme for a volume; and many volumes have, in fact, been devoted to its consideration. Of this communion there are several phases—the communion of saint with saint, and with the whole body of the saints, on earth; the communion of saint with saint, and with the whole body of the saints, in heaven; the inter-communion between saints on earth and saints in heaven; the inter-communion of the Church militant, as a whole, with the Church triumphant, as a whole; and finally the eternal communion of the united family of heaven, recruited, an infinite longing would tell us, from all the worlds that throw their radiance across the immeasurable wilds of space. We do not stay to illustrate the Communion of Saints by any poem devoted expressly to it; but we may offer a few words from Hooker which, on the authority of the New Testament, define as dogma what might otherwise be dissipated in the more formless domains of poetry. "They which belong," he says, "to the mystical body of our Saviour Christ, and be in number as the stars of heaven, divided successively by reason of their mortal condition into many generations, are notwithstanding coupled every one to Christ their Head (Ephes. iv. 15); and all unto every particular person amongst themselves (Rom. xii. 5; 1 Cor. xii. 27; Ephes. iv. 25), inasmuch as the same Spirit which animated the blessed soul of our Saviour Christ doth so formalise, unite, and actuate His whole race, as if both He and they were so many limbs compacted into one body, by being quickened all with one and the same soul."

* *Ecclesiastical Polity:* Book v., ch. lvi., 11.

We have already said that the Church militant and the Church triumphant, to be fully intelligible, must be considered not separately and apart, but each in the light of the other. What the former is, the latter has been; what the latter is, the former shall be. Thus it happens that no poem which celebrates the saintly life on earth can avoid some expression anticipative of the saintly life in heaven; and, on the other hand, no poem which celebrates the glory of the palm and the harp and the crown of the golden city, can avoid a reference to the staff and the sword and the helmet of the armed pilgrimage. Poetry and philosophy are equally imperative in insisting upon this forward or backward glance—poetry, because it delights in the chiaroscuro; and philosophy, because it desiderates some answer to its questions of, whence? whither? to what end?

The Pro-Epistle for All Saints' Day (Rev. vii. 2), contains the vision of the sealing of the elect of the Twelve Tribes, and of the "great multitude which no man could number." We adopt from Miss Winkworth's "Lyra Germanica" an English version of a paraphrase of the latter part of the Pro-Epistle, which will be found to bear out our remarks upon the almost necessarily reminiscent attitude of the earthly Muse when she places her finger upon a lyre of heaven. Various renderings of this hymn are within reach of the English reader, as in "A. T. Russell's *Psalms and Hymns*, No. 145; F. E. Cox's *Sacred Hymns*, p. 89; the latter version having been introduced into *Hymns Ancient and Modern*, No 255."

Its author was Henry Theobald Schenck, who "was head master at the school, and subsequently chief pastor in Giessen, where he died in 1727. Nothing further is known of him. The original of this beautiful hymn has twenty verses."[*] It bears the title of "All Saints' Day."

[*] Kübler's *Historical Notes to the Lyra Germanica.*

ALL SAINTS' DAY.

Who are those before God's throne,
   What the crownèd host I see?
As the sky with stars thick-strown
   Is their shining company:
Hallelujahs, hark, they sing,
Solemn praise to God they bring.

Who are those that in their hands
   Bear aloft the conqueror's palm,
As one o'er his foeman stands,
   Fallen beneath his mighty arm?
What the war and what the strife,
Whence came such victorious life?

Who are those arrayed in light,
   Clothed in righteousness divine,
Wearing robes most pure and white,
   That unstained shall ever shine,
That can nevermore decay;
Whence came all this bright array?

They are those who, strong in faith,
   Battled for the mighty God;
Conquerors o'er the world and death,
   Following not sin's crowded road;
Through the Lamb who once was slain,
Did they such high victory gain.

They are those who much have borne,
   Trial, sorrow, pain, and care,
Who have wrestled night and morn
   With the mighty God in prayer;
Now their strife hath found its close,
God hath turned away their woes.

They are branches of that Stem,
   Who hath our Salvation been,
In the blood He shed for them,
   Have they made their raiment clean;
Hence they wear such radiant dress,
Clad in spotless holiness.

They are those who hourly here
  Served as priests before their Lord,
Offering up with gladsome cheer
  Soul and body at His word.
Now, within the Holy Place,
They behold Him face to face.

As the harts at noonday pant
  For the river fresh and clear,
Did they ofttimes long and faint,
  For the Living Fountain here.
Now their thirst is quenched, they dwell
With the Lord they loved so well.

Thitherwards I stretch my hands;
  O Lord Jesus, day by day,
In Thy house in these strange lands,
  Compassed round with foes, I pray,
Let me sink not in the war,
Drive for me my foes afar.

Cast my lot in earth and heaven
  With Thy saints made like to Thee,
Let my bonds be also riven,
  Make Thy child who loves Thee free;
Near the throne where Thou dost shine,
May a place at last be mine!

Ah! that bliss can ne'er be told,
  When with all that army bright,
Thee, my Sun, I shall behold,
  Shining star-like, with Thy light,
Amen! Thanks be brought to Thee,
Praise through all eternity.

The moral of a contemplation of the faith and the virtues, the patience and the achievements, of the Saints, is an injunction: "Go thou and do likewise." The Collect for All Saints' Day, opening with an ascription of praise to "Almighty God, who has knit together His elect in one communion and fellowship, in the mystical body of His Son Christ our Lord," proceeds to petition for grace to follow the "blessed Saints in all virtues and godly living," that so we may at length be partakers of their "unspeakable joys." We can scarcely make a better end of our consideration of All Saints, or, indeed, of our volume, than by turning this prayer into words of exhortation. Such are the words, winged and burning, and stirring the heart like the sound of a trumpet, of the "Idiomela for All Saints," written by John Damascenus, who "has the double honour," says the late Dr. Neale, "of being the last of the Fathers of the Eastern Church, and the greatest of her poets." The following spirited version (̄ ̄ ̄ ̄ ̄for All Saints—τὰς ἰδρὰς τὰς αἰωνίας—is from Dr. Neale's *Hymns of the Eastern Church*.

<blockquote>
Those eternal bowers
  Man hath never trod,
Those unfading flowers
  Round the throne of God :
Who may hope to gain them
  After weary fight ?
Who at length attain them
  Clad in robes of white ?

He who gladly barters
  All on earthly ground ;
He who, like the Martyrs,
  Says, "*I will* be crown'd :"
He, whose one oblation
  Is a life of love ;
Clinging to the nation
  Of the Blest above.

Shame upon you. legions
  Of the Heavenly King,
Denizens of regions
  Past imagining !
What ! with pipe and tabor
  Fool away the light,
When He bids you labour,—
  When He tells you " Fight ! "
</blockquote>

THE GLORY TO FOLLOW.

While I do my duty,
  Struggling through the tide,
Whisper Thou of beauty
  On the other side!
Tell who will the story
  Of our *now* distress:
Oh the future glory!
  Oh the loveliness!

www.ingramcontent.com/pod-product-compliance
Lightning Source LLC
Chambersburg PA
CBHW031945290426
44108CB00011B/687